General editors: Andrew S. Thompson and Alan Lester

Founding editor: John M. MacKenzie

When the 'Studies in Imperialism' series was founded by Professor John M. MacKenzie more than thirty years ago, emphasis was laid upon the conviction that 'imperialism as a cultural phenomenon had as significant an effect on the dominant as on the subordinate societies'. With well over a hundred titles now published, this remains the prime concern of the series. Cross-disciplinary work has indeed appeared covering the full spectrum of cultural phenomena, as well as examining aspects of gender and sex, frontiers and law, science and the environment, language and literature, migration and patriotic societies, and much else. Moreover, the series has always wished to present comparative work on European and American imperialism, and particularly welcomes the submission of books in these areas. The fascination with imperialism, in all its aspects, shows no sign of abating, and this series will continue to lead the way in encouraging the widest possible range of studies in the field. 'Studies in Imperialism' is fully organic in its development, always seeking to be at the cutting edge, responding to the latest interests of scholars and the needs of this ever-expanding area of scholarship.

The bonds of family

Manchester University Press

SELECTED TITLES AVAILABLE IN THE SERIES

WRITING IMPERIAL HISTORIES
ed. Andrew S. Thompson

GENDERED TRANSACTIONS
Indrani Sen

EXHIBITING THE EMPIRE
ed. John M. MacKenzie and John McAleer

BANISHED POTENTATES
Robert Aldrich

MISTRESS OF EVERYTHING
ed. Sarah Carter and Maria Nugent

BRITAIN AND THE FORMATION OF THE GULF STATES
Shohei Sato

CULTURES OF DECOLONISATION
ed. Ruth Craggs and Claire Wintle

HONG KONG AND BRITISH CULTURE, 1945–97
Mark Hampton

The bonds of family

SLAVERY, COMMERCE AND CULTURE IN THE BRITISH ATLANTIC WORLD

Katie Donington

MANCHESTER UNIVERSITY PRESS

Copyright © Katie Donington 2020

The right of Katie Donington to be identified as the author of this work has been asserted by her in accordance with the Copyright, Designs and Patents Act 1988.

Published by Manchester University Press
Altrincham Street, Manchester M1 7JA, UK
www.manchesteruniversitypress.co.uk

British Library Cataloguing-in-Publication Data is available

ISBN 978 1 5261 2948 2 hardback
ISBN 978 1 5261 5751 5 paperback

First published by Manchester University Press in hardback 2020

This edition published 2021

The publisher has no responsibility for the persistence or accuracy of URLs for any external or third-party internet websites referred to in this book, and does not guarantee that any content on such websites is, or will remain, accurate or appropriate.

Typeset by Newgen Publishing UK

To my grandmother Joyce Maxwell

CONTENTS

List of figures—viii
List of family trees—ix
Acknowledgements—x
List of abbreviations—xiii

Introduction: Family matters: slavery, commerce and culture   1

Part I Family business: commerce, commodities and credit   25
1   Manchester   27
2   Jamaica   50
3   London   78

Part II Family politics: defending the slave trade and slavery   105
4   Defending the slave trade   107
5   Defending slavery   133

Part III Family culture: domesticating slavery   157
6   Part I: Intimate relations: the colony   159
     Part II: Intimate relations: the metropole   183
7   Consuming passions: collecting and connoisseurship   217
8   The culture of refinement: country houses and philanthropy   253

Epilogue: Family legacies: after abolition   282

Select bibliography—293
Index—309

FIGURES

1 Cross Street Chapel, Manchester, 1835, in W. H. Shercliff, *Manchester: A short history of its development* (Manchester: Municipal Information Bureau, 1960) — page 33
2 Diagram of the *'Brookes* Slave Ship', 1789 (© Museum of London) — 56
3 Hibbert House, James Hakewill, c. 1820 (© Nicholas Hibbert Steele, Hibbert Family Archives and Collection, Australia) — 60
4 Thomas senior, unknown artist (© Katie Donington) — 62
5 'Monument of the late Thomas Hibbert, Esq. at Agualta Vale Penn', James Hakewill, *A picturesque tour of the island of Jamaica from drawings made in the years 1820 and 1821* (© The British Library Board, 1486.gg.11) — 65
6 *An elevated view of the new docks & warehouses now constructing on the Isle of Dogs near Limehouse for the reception & accommodation of shipping in the West India Trade ...*, William Daniell, 1802 (© PLA Collection/Museum of London) — 96
7 'Hibbert Ship Gate' (© Katie Donington) — 99
8 Perambulation of Clapham Common, 1800, in C. Smith, *The chronicles of Clapham Common, being a selection from the reminiscences of Thomas Parsons, sometime member of the Clapham Antiquarian Society* (© Lambeth Archives) — 201
9 *The Marriage Feast at Cana*, Bartolomé Esteban Murillo (© The Henry Barber Trust, The Barber Institute of Fine Arts, University of Birmingham / Bridgeman Images) — 229
10 George Hibbert, James Ward after John Hoppner (© National Portrait Gallery) — 230
11 Elizabeth Hibbert, James Ward after John Hoppner (© National Portrait Gallery) — 231
12 *George Hibbert*, Thomas Lawrence, 1811 (© PLA Collection/ Museum of London) — 233
13 *Hibbertia dentata* (© Biodiversity Heritage Library) — 243
14 *Reconstructed Portrait with Lloyd Gordon as Robert Wedderburn*, Paul Howard, 2007 (© Paul Howard) — 245
15 View of Portland Place, Anon., c. 1814 (© Museum of London) — 257
16 *Chalfont House from the South-West*, J. M. W. Turner, c. 1799 (© Tate) — 259
17 *Portrait of Mrs Thomas Hibbert*, Thomas Gainsborough, 1786 (© Bayerische Staatsgemäldesammlungen) — 260
18 The London Institution, Thomas Hosmer Shepherd, 1827 (© Museum of London) — 272

FAMILY TREES

The family trees constructed are not exhaustive. Instead they highlight the key relationships relevant to each chapter they precede.

1	The Hibbert family tree	*page* xiv
2	The Hibberts in Manchester	26
3	The Hibberts in the Jamaica operation	49
4	The Hibberts in the London operation	77
5	The Hibbert family in Jamaica	158
6	The Hibbert family in Clapham	182
7	Country house owning Hibberts	252

ACKNOWLEDGEMENTS

I first encountered George Hibbert at the Museum of London, Docklands in 2009 when I was putting together a proposal for a PhD studentship. His portrait sits at the centre of the 'London, Sugar, Slavery' exhibition. As a Londoner the exhibition posed a challenge to what I knew about the local history of the city. It invited me to reimagine familiar spaces and rethink how the local and the global interconnected to create a tangled set of legacies that continue to inform the present. In some very real ways it brought the issue of slavery home and has formed the basis of what has now become a decade-long engagement with the Hibberts and the complicated histories that their family story intersects with. I was incredibly fortunate to work with the ESRC-funded 'Legacies of British slave-ownership' project at University College London for my PhD thesis. The support and generosity of Catherine Hall, Nick Draper, Keith McClelland and Rachel Lang have made this project possible. Their commitment to the work and to making sure that it finds a voice outside of academia continues to inform my own practice. In particular I would like to thank Catherine: as my mentor and supervisor her belief and encouragement have sustained me over the years and her work is threaded through this book. My research was developed further during my time as a post-doctoral researcher with phase two of the project – the ESRC/AHRC-funded 'Structure and significance of British Caribbean slave-ownership 1763–1833'. This time allowed me to better understand and integrate the family story in Jamaica. My thinking has been sharpened and expanded by working with Kristy Warren. Her friendship and critical thinking have been invaluable. My thanks also to Chris Jeppesen, Hannah Young and James Dawkins for sharing their scholarship on gender and family history.

The research for this book has been aided enormously by staff of the Jamaica Archives, National Library of Jamaica, Institute of Jamaica, Jamaica National Heritage Trust, University of the West Indies, Institute of Commonwealth Studies Library, Senate House Library Special Collections, The National Archives (UK), Gloucestershire Archives, Derbyshire Record Office, Lambeth Archives, the Wilberforce Institute and the London Metropolitan Archives. I owe a particular debt of gratitude in terms of research material to Nicholas Hibbert Steele, who allowed me access to Robert Hibbert junior's diaries. My thanks to both him and to Bev Steele – our conversations about the Hibberts have never

ACKNOWLEDGEMENTS

failed to challenge and stimulate. My time in Jamaica was enriched enormously by Gemma Romain, Emma Ranston-Young, Annie Paul, Patricia Jackson, Carole Narcisse, Ann Hodges and Enith Williams. My conceptualisation of the use and meaning of local history was sharpened by my Arts Council-funded work with Hackney Archives and Museum, in particular with Emma Winch, Cheryl Bowen, Toyin Agbetu and Lucy Capes. My thanks also to the inspirational students of Hackney BSix College. Over the years I have received support and advice from Margot Finn, John Oldfield, Christer Petley, Gad Heuman, Corinne Fowler, Richard Huzzey, Sadiah Qureshi, Clare Midgley, Alan Rice, Julian Hoppit, James Robertson, Matt Smith, Anita Rupprecht and Nick Hewitt. My work has been critiqued and improved by friends who have offered new perspectives, in particular Ryan Hanley, Jessica Moody, Charlotte Lydia Riley, Emily Manktelow, Onni Gust, Laura Ishiguro, Mary Wills, John Siblon, Michael Morris, Stephen Mullen, Robin Whitburn and Abdul Mohamud. Colleagues at London South Bank University have provided support and enthusiasm in the final stages of finishing the book. In particular my thanks to Charlotte Clements, Lisa Pine and Caitriona Beaumont. The image licensing for the book was paid for by a generous award from the Law and Social Sciences Research Fund at London South Bank University. In 2018 I approached the Museum of London about creating an exhibition based on the cultural legacies which the Hibberts left behind. I would like to thank Danielle Thom, Glyn Davies, Emily Durant and Melissa Bennett for their commitment to making my research publicly accessible and for bringing the project full circle to where it began with the 'Slavery, Culture and Collecting' exhibition. At Manchester University Press I would like to thank both the reviewers for their insightful commentary, which has made this a significantly better book. A big thank you also to Paul Clarke, Christopher Feeney, Rebecca Willford and especially to Emma Brennan for her patience and support throughout the process.

This book is centrally concerned with family and this work would not have been possible without the unswerving support of my own. A debt that I will find hard to ever repay is owed to my mother and father, Jean and Charles, and my sister Sophie. They have never failed to provide the love and belief which has kept me grounded and given me the confidence to persevere. Some family members are of your own making and my friendship with Becci Connolly has been a constant source of strength. For the gentle words, the endless waiting, the respite of laughter and the years of love – thank you to my partner Kevin Fisher. This book could not have been written without him. From my grandmother, Joyce Maxwell, I inherited a love of history. She wanted

ACKNOWLEDGEMENTS

to go to university to study the subject but the onset of deafness in her teens prevented her from doing so. After my grandfather died leaving her pregnant with my mother, she typed theses and book manuscripts to support her young family. She died in 2007, but I would like to think she would be proud that I have written a book and I dedicate this work to her.

ABBREVIATIONS

Archival source abbreviations are used when the archive is cited five or more times.

BL/GHCB	British Library, London, George Hibbert's Commonplace Book
CARICOM	Caribbean Community and Common Market
DRO/WHOCP	Derbyshire Record Office, Matlock, Wilmot-Horton of Osmaston and Catton Papers
GA/BFDP	Gloucestershire Archives, Gloucester, Blathwayt Family of Dyrham Papers
HFAC	Hibbert Family Archives and Collection, Melbourne, Australia
ICS/SHL/TVAP	Institute of Commonwealth Studies, Senate House Library, London, Taylor and Vaneck-Arcedekne Papers
ICS/SHL/WICP	Institute of Commonwealth Studies, Senate House Library, London, West India Committee Papers
JFSGRL	Jamaican Family Search Genealogy Research Library
LMA/LI	London Metropolitan Archives, London, Letters, printed notices and papers relating to the founding of the London Institution
LMA/RHT	London Metropolitan Archives, London, Records of Holy Trinity, Clapham Common
NLW/SPD	National Library of Wales, Aberystwyth, Slebech Papers and Documents
SEAST	Society for Effecting the Abolition of the Slave Trade
SWIPM	Society of West India Planters and Merchants
TNA/COP	The National Archives, Kew, Colonial Office and Predecessors
NLW/SPD	National Library of Wales, Slebech Papers and Documents

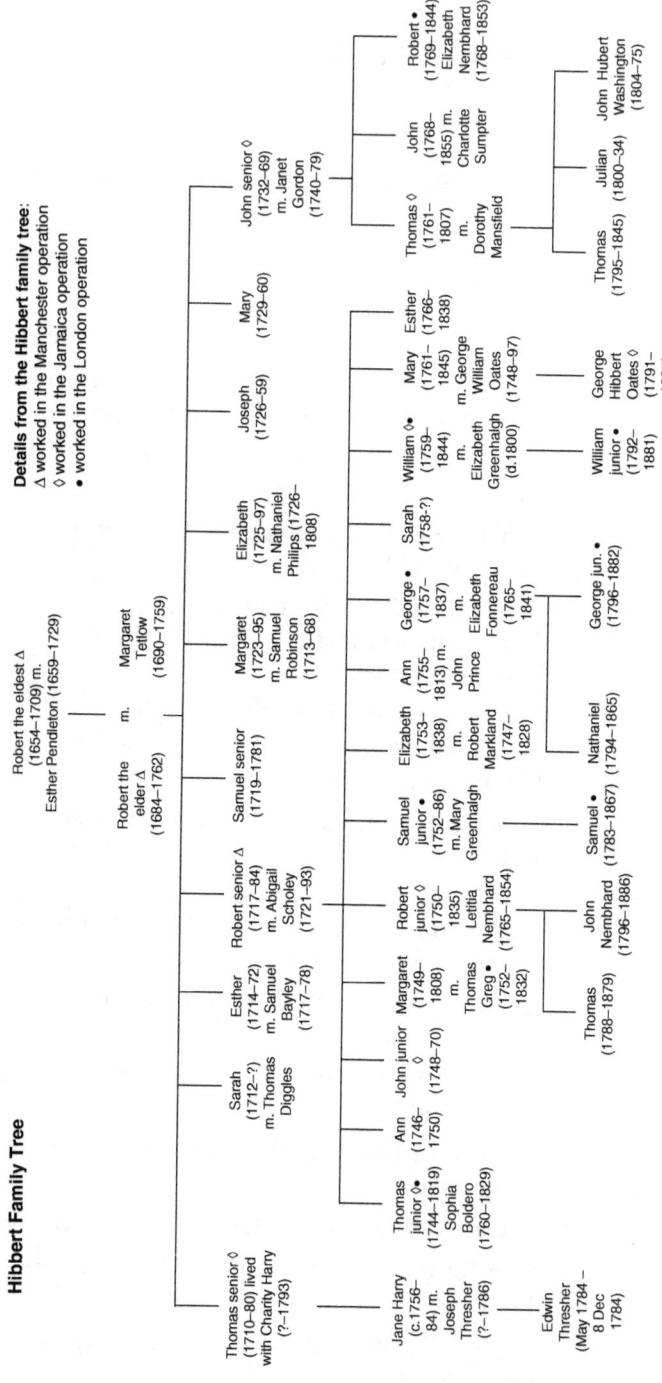

Family tree 1 The Hibbert family tree

Introduction: Family matters: slavery, commerce and culture

'The partnership is entirely <u>within the Family</u> where I believe it will ever remain, so long as that Family exists', opined Thomas Hibbert junior in 1772.[1] Writing at a moment in which the Hibbert family's commercial star was ascending, Thomas junior's emphatic underlining of those three words reflected his absolute confidence in the future of the family firm and the system that underpinned it – slavery. For four generations the Hibbert family story was entwined with the world of transatlantic commerce; slave trading, plantation ownership, colonial commodities, shipping, insurance and credit were the lifeblood of their family economy. Slavery transformed the Hibberts from their unremarkable mercantile beginnings in Manchester to the 'first house in the Jamaica trade'.[2] It gave them access to the kinds of social, political and cultural power that allowed them to position themselves within the metropolitan and colonial elites. Thomas junior's unshakeable belief in both the harmonious continuation of the counting house and the exploitative labour practices that supported it, is indicative of the widespread acceptance of the institution of slavery in Britain. The system reaped great rewards for both the Hibbert family and the nation; it created a new transatlantic world of commerce, consumption and cultivation, forging new societies structured by, and reliant on, the coercive violence of race-based slavery.

The Hibbert family's involvement with the slave economy began in the late seventeenth century in Manchester. Starting out in trade as linen merchants they realised the enormous potential for expanding their interests into the emerging colonial market. Having set up their business supplying cloth to Liverpool for use in the slave trade, the family eventually sent their eldest son, Thomas senior, to Jamaica in 1734. As the colonial founder, Thomas senior enjoyed spectacular success; in evidence given to Parliament in 1791 he was remembered as 'the late Mr. Thomas Hibbert, who had for forty or fifty years before been the most eminent Guinea factor in Kingston'.[3] Thomas senior was eventually joined by his brothers, nephews and great-nephews. Together they built an empire that encompassed a variety of different aspects of the profitable business of slavery. Capitalising on their commercial dominance, the family sought out civic and political position in the colony, before returning to repeat this pattern in the metropole. Thomas senior's nephew, Thomas junior, eventually opened a branch house of the Jamaica business in London. Tired of the world of commerce, he retired to the country estate he had purchased in 1791, allowing his younger brother George to take command of the family interest. Over the course of his lifetime George became the most powerful Jamaica merchant in Britain. Serving as the Chairman of the Society of West India Merchants, a Member of Parliament and the Agent for Jamaica, he was acknowledged as *the* leading spokesman for those with mercantile interests in Caribbean slavery. His influence extended beyond the commercial sphere as he embedded himself within London's political and cultural elite. Adopting the mantle of philanthropist, connoisseur and collector, George was every inch the fashionable metropolitan gentleman. He was eventually joined in the business by his cousin, younger brothers, sons and nephews, and the future prospects of the family seemed assured.

For families like the Hibberts success in the world of colonial commerce, whilst never guaranteed, could bring with it the kind of wealth that transformed social status and maintained multigenerational dynasties. For over 150 years involvement in the slave economy was considered to be 'a public benefit rather than a public issue'.[4] Supported by the Government as a legitimate form of trade, participation in the business of slavery was no barrier to respectability, indeed for some it was the route to it. Involvement filtered through a broad cross-section of British society, from the aristocracy, to the merchant classes, to the ordinary men and women who bought and consumed slave-produced commodities. The incredulity with which abolition was met was clear from a statement made to Parliament by George in 1790. 'I confess', he stated, 'that the abolition of the Slave Trade was a measure not in my contemplation as not believing it probable.'[5] To the West India planters and merchants slavery was an integral facet of British colonial trade and an essential part of empire building – it was simply too important to be allowed to fail.

In 1807, some seventeen years after George expressed his disbelief to Parliament, his brother Robert junior anxiously contemplated the fate of 'the Senior or Junior Branches of our Family, who have before them Prospects not quite so bright as they had some years ago'.[6] The abolition of the slave trade was the source of Robert junior's disquiet, representing in the minds of many with slaving interests the slow disintegration of the economic and social structures upon which their fortune and position was built. Confidence turned to self-doubt as the Hibberts grappled with the shifting political climate. Conscious of the family interest, George had been a vocal proslavery advocate since the advent of an organised abolitionist movement in 1787. As a key member of the London West India lobby he used his connections, influence and political acumen to delay the progress of abolition and help secure a generous remuneration package for those individuals who claimed property in people. His efforts were eventually rewarded when the Hibbert family collectively received over £103,000 of compensation money in the wake of the Slavery Abolition Act in 1833.[7] Today this vast amount is the equivalent (at a conservative estimate) of £8.9 million. In accepting the arguments made by George and his fellow West Indians regarding the legitimacy of property in people, the Government enabled the Hibberts, and many others like them, to maintain their respectable status and augment their already considerable wealth.

Despite Robert junior's nervous predictions for the future prosperity of the family, the Hibberts' West India merchant house continued on into the 1860s. In the wake of abolition, the family also diversified into a number of emerging financial markets both at home and in the wider empire. Success in business was matched by other members of the family who variously entered the army, navy and the landed aristocracy. From tentative beginnings in the late seventeenth century, the longevity of the family business marked it as an unusually successful colonial venture. It also provides the historian with a transgenerational lens through which to explore the complicated history and legacies of slavery. This book is concerned with the ways in which the family figured in the networks of religion, commerce, culture and politics that made the system work across both time and place. More intimately it focuses on the family as a site for the interplay between race, gender, sexuality and class. In examining the inner world of the family, the book demonstrates how the Hibberts' story imbricates the personal and the political, the private and the public, the local and the global. It is both the particular narrative of an extended family and a frame through which to negotiate Britain's multifaceted engagement with the business of slavery.

Commerce

Family capitalism was the backbone of British business during the eighteenth and nineteenth centuries[8] and was central to the complicated operations of transatlantic trade.[9] For the middle classes, kinship 'constituted one of the inner structures which joined individuals and different forms of capital together in communities of interest'.[10] Men, women and children all played their part in strengthening and enlarging these networks. The organisation of the counting house and plantation management were heavily filtered through relations of family and friendship. 'Capital was not anonymous', Catherine Hall has stated, 'it had "blood" coursing through its veins and this had implications for how it functioned on both sides of the Atlantic.'[11] Ties forged through marriage and mutual purpose nurtured the bonds of duty, trust and loyalty – all essential characteristics for working within the high-risk world of the slave economy. Close-knit commercial networks based on personal relationships were crucial to longevity and success. Formal and informal methods of vouching and recommendation existed to protect the business from the threat of the unknown. In a period in which trust played a fundamental role in building the credit relations necessary for investment in long-distance colonial commerce, family and kin provided a sense of security based on shared endeavour and collective responsibility.[12] Transactions within the slave economy were long-term affairs; cyclical indebtedness was endemic, making reputation and personal connections a central part of mercantile culture. Character was a fiercely guarded commodity, as Thomas junior indicated: 'the Opinion of the World, so far as it might affect the Credit of the House, was an Object of very serious Consideration'.[13] The Hibberts enjoyed a reputation for solidity and probity precisely because their business was managed by a single extended family operating on both sides of the Atlantic.

The reproductive labour of women was vital for the continuation of the family business. This was true of both the middle-class Hibbert women and in very different ways the enslaved women whose bodies were harnessed to plantation productivity as both workers and mothers.[14] The British Atlantic merchant house relied on the children of immediate and extended family members, as well as close friends, to provide the personnel necessary for their commercial operations to function smoothly across both time and space. The system of mercantile apprenticeship commonly utilised these kinds of intimate connections to place young sons in commercially strategic positions. The careful expansion of the family structure represented new opportunities for the family enterprise; the marrying of interests, often constituted through matrimonial alliances, enabled the consolidation and diversification of commercial networks, whilst allowing wealth to circulate within defined boundaries. Though Thomas senior had no

INTRODUCTION: FAMILY MATTERS

legitimate male children, his brother Robert senior had ten children. Six of his sons were involved in the Jamaica and London branches of the family business. Three of his daughters made useful marriages to men involved in commerce, land ownership and insurance. As the Hibberts transformed from merchants to country gentlemen, their children occupied positions that gradually grew more distant from the family's commercial roots. In this way they represented a pathway for future social elevation.

Of course, the bonds of family could never guarantee the smooth running and success of a business venture. Personal relationships could sour, death and the vexed issue of inheritance might impact on the balance of power within a partnership, family could not always be trusted. The collapse of the West India partnership Boddington & Co. in 1797 served as a cautionary example of what might happen when family relationships broke down. The lucrative firm was dissolved after Benjamin Boddington eloped with his partner (and cousin) Samuel's wife.[15] When the Hibberts' own mercantile partnership experienced a brief period of financial instability in 1796, Robert junior refused to countenance any discussion of putting his country house up as collateral to support the family business. In later years his elder brother Thomas junior offered his estate, Chalfont, and his younger brother George sold off part of his art collection to shore up the counting house. Family businesses like any other were a risky undertaking, as the roll call of bankruptcies highlighted by Julian Hoppit has made clear.[16] Despite their problems, the family remained a stable foundation for negotiating the choppy waters of transatlantic trade and as such is a key unit of analysis when considering the financial operations of the slave economy.

Property

For planter-merchant families like the Hibberts the counting house represented just one aspect of the business. As land owners with large sugar works, enslaved populations, and cattle pens in Jamaica, as well as town and country houses, ships, wharfs and warehouses in England, the issue of property management and inheritance revolved around the family structure. Property, including human property, was bound up in the practices of family life and death. The transference of ownership, or the legal claim to profits generated through another's ownership, was one of the ways in which family relationships were articulated within the system of slavery. An examination of the wills of various slave owners across the Caribbean reveals the intimate connections between and within families sometimes expressed through the allocation of property. Large-scale inheritance of estates could, and often did, follow the tradition of primogeniture, though there usually followed a detailed breakdown of the distribution of other forms of property. The designation of an enslaved individual, or group of people, as a token of remembrance, or perhaps as a way to secure against future financial instability, was common. It is through these kinds of practices that many women came into property in people, whether as direct owners, or as the recipients of annuities settled on them by relatives keen to ensure their future living.[17] The slavery compensation records reflect these kinds of associations, revealing that approximately 43 per cent of claimants were women. Enslaved people could be gifted as a wedding present, or included as part of a marriage settlement; a daughter might receive her enslaved childhood companion when setting up a new household, or a son his man servant. Wills might also set out the terms for the loss of property through the manumission of enslaved people. This could represent an expression of gratitude for a lifetime's service, and in some instances constituted the freeing of a slave owner's illegitimate mixed-heritage family. Whether gestures of affection, remembrance or financial acumen the connections of property reveal glimpses into the ways in which the slave owners interpreted particular relationships. How these bonds were imagined by either the recipient or the enslaved is another matter. For close family members, friends and associates inclusion in the will as beneficiaries, trustees, guardians or executors represented an affirmation of their position in relation to the household.

Sometimes embedded in the legalese of these document was the muted admission of different kinds of familial ties. Employing the discreet language of 'housekeepers' and 'reputed children', some slave owners also recognised and provided for their illegitimate families. Banished from the official recounting of the family Bible, and absent from the published genealogical records, these 'outside' families emerged in the legal fine print. In Jamaica mixed-heritage individuals were barred from inheriting large sums of money and property following the introduction of a law in 1761 to limit the inheritance of people of African descent.[18] The Jamaica Assembly did allow a series of individual exceptions, usually for the offspring of the wealthy elite. The documented exemptions, in the form of a series of private acts, provide much telling information in regard to the relationships between the individuals involved. Tracing property – both ownership of and legal access to – can help the historian to reconstruct family relationships and the ways in which slavery reconfigured them.

INTRODUCTION: FAMILY MATTERS

Family life

While understanding the family as an economic unit is vital for understanding how the system of slavery functioned, the importance of the family cannot simply be interpreted through an analysis of the Hibberts as property owners or commercial agents. For too long there has existed an 'unfortunate division ... between family history and economic or business history'.[19] This artificial separation has led to unproductive disciplinary silos that have in some instances masked the interconnectedness of the social, cultural, political and economic spheres. Empire families have been the subject of a number of recent historical works that have provided the impetus for thinking through and with the 'imperial relations' that gave meaning to a wide variety of colonial experiences.[20] Family, it has been argued, 'constituted key sinews of empire. But empire, too, could operate as a key sinew of family. It was not simply that one "needed" relations – that family connections underpinned the operation of empire in political, economic, social and emotional ways – but also that imperial processes remade relations and created new ones.'[21] Family structured empire, but conversely empire altered the structure of the family. Like many men in the colonies, the Hibberts engaged in sexual relations with both free and enslaved women of colour. The degree to which these relationships can be considered consensual within the context of a highly racialised and gendered power system is difficult to judge.[22] Charity Harry was named in Thomas senior's will as his 'housekeeper' and, along with her surviving daughter, Jane, she received a significant bequest following a private act to remove restrictions on their inheritance. As will be explored in Chapter 6 (part 1), Jane's life story is revealing of the ways in which family structures could be made and subsequently unmade through the system of slavery. Her casting-off by the metropolitan Hibberts in the wake of her father's death and her absence from the official family record were part of a process of forgetting – her illegitimacy and her race a reminder of colonial transgressions best left in the past.

The Hibberts' encounter with empire profoundly altered family life in Britain as generations of Hibbert men repeatedly traversed the Atlantic, bound by a sense of family duty to make the business work. On his twenty-first birthday in 1771, following the death of his brother John junior, Robert junior recalled a toast he made with his family before his departure for Jamaica:

> We all remember the last time we gathered together when my brother John was in receipt of his package and the hopes for the future that he aspired to ... alas it was not to be ... and I ask you to drink to his memory

and remember his fellowship and good humour ... I have decided to take the position of my brother in Jamaica and will be accompanying my uncle to Kingston to take the place of my brother John and join brother Thomas.[23]

The decision to leave for Jamaica was not to be taken lightly, for death was a constant in the Caribbean and many Hibbert family members were laid to rest in colonial graves. John junior had only arrived in Jamaica in 1769, a year prior to his death, having been summoned from England to replace his uncle, John senior, who had died aged thirty-seven the same year. The experience of living in a slave society was not necessarily one that was relished by all, and both Robert junior and his brother Thomas junior expressed feelings of acute homesickness. On the departure of his deceased uncle's wife for England, Robert junior wrote: 'My spirits depressed beyond what I never before experienced ... After the company leave, my spirits which had hitherto kept up reasonably well, droop to a degree of absolute despondency – this world seems a desert.'[24] For the two brothers Jamaica was a place to be endured before their eventual triumphant return to England. Unlike his older brother, Robert junior returned frequently to the island, having married a white Creole woman. He was certainly the most transatlantic figure within the Hibbert family, as he commented to his sister Mary: 'The Life I have led has kept me so constantly on the move.'[25] Whilst his nephews pined for home and return, Thomas senior laid down roots in Jamaica, creating a new identity and sense of belonging.[26] Having arrived in 1734, he lived on the island for forty-six years, dying aged eighty at his estate, Agualta Vale. Despite his enormous wealth, the life of an absentee in England held no pull for him (bar the occasional visit for the sake of his business and his health) and he was buried on his land atop a hill and memorialised with a vast funerary urn proclaiming his virtues.[27] Thomas senior was unique among the Hibberts in his commitment to making Jamaica a permanent home; by the 1840s the family had no physical presence on the island, reducing their connection to an entirely mercantile interest.

Family history

Family history – complicated, messy and affective – has sometimes been cast as the poor relation of academic history. Frequently caricatured as an amateurish pastime and once reviled as 'the history of darning socks', it is a subject that has been re-energised in particular by feminist scholarship, but also by an incredible upsurge of interest among the public.[28] In a period in which family was *the* central organising structure the diligence of genealogical labour is

INTRODUCTION: FAMILY MATTERS

vital for unpicking the tangled web of human relations that threaded through the multiple layers that made up British society. This task is made all the more complex when we consider that shared ancestry, as Naomi Tadmoor has reminded us, was not the only way in which family was constituted during the period.[29] The household, which could be made up of unrelated individuals, apprentices, servants or kin, was also described as a family. Based on relations of authority rather than biology, these families conformed to Samuel Johnson's definition of family as 'those who live in the same house'.[30] The meaning of family changed over the course of time and within different cultural settings. Within the context of slavery this poses interesting questions: did – as some slave owners argued – the master–slave relationship uncomplicatedly reprise that of the master–servant? To what degree did the plantation recreate or deconstruct notions of the household family?[31] Could property be admitted into that most quintessential of human relationships – the family? 'Family and kin', Leonore Davidoff suggested, 'are understood as ongoing processes, flexible and variable, filled with contradictions and tensions.'[32] People could move in and out of the family under different circumstances, as the Hibberts' expulsion of Jane Harry indicated – the ties that bound could be broken as well.

The study of the family is the study of human relations, it offers a route into the past that begins with the familiar. For those who practise this discipline in relation to their own family it is often a means to self-knowledge, an attempt to understand who we think we are. The popularity of family history reflects our continued attachment to family as a way of coming to know the past. Andrea Stuart's *Sugar in the blood: A family's story of slavery and empire* demonstrates the enduring appeal of the family not only as a narrative device but also as an anchor to a personal connection. Her book opens with the quotation 'In every conceivable manner, the family is link to our past, bridge to our future.'[33] Transatlantic slavery is an institution with a global reach that came to shape the world we know today, and the scale of this history and the magnitude of its legacies have tended to erase the individual. Descended from both slave owners and the enslaved, Stuart wrote of her family history that this was 'a story of migration, settlement, survival, slavery and the making of the Atlantic world ... My family's story is at once very particular, but also wholly typical and representative. It is a story that belongs not just to me but to many, many others.'[34] This sentiment is echoed in the inclusion of a family history display in the 'Legacies' section of the International Slavery Museum in Liverpool. Volunteer tour guide Barbara Tasker has used her own family narrative to navigate her way temporally and geographically from Caribbean slavery through to present-day Britain. Shifting between Bermuda, New York, Liberia and Liverpool, her talk is rooted in both family and local history. Using the global interconnections that shaped her ancestors' lives is an incredibly effective way of linking people and place for her audience. Family history creates a past that becomes, to a degree, more knowable through these recognisable patterns of human connections.

Given that family history is bound up with a sense of both memory and identity, links to the system of slavery can represent a challenge. Saved for posterity and often circulated solely within private hands, family archives are deeply personal. What is kept, what is lost and what is made accessible may be dependent on a variety of factors: damage, loss, destruction and how a family perceives and values its own history. The controversy over American actor Ben Affleck's attempt to suppress the publicising of his family's role as slave owners is demonstrative of the emotional connection that binds the past and present. Forced to acknowledge his attempt to influence the narrative arc of his family story on the PBS show *Finding your roots*, Affleck responded by stating that 'I didn't want any television show about my family to include a guy who owned slaves. I was embarrassed.'[35] Affleck added that 'We deserve neither credit nor blame for our ancestors and the degree of interest in this story suggests that we are, as a nation, still grappling with the terrible legacy of slavery.' The research for this book and the project from which it emerged – 'Legacies of British slave-ownership' – has been aided immensely by family historians who provided documents and information about their ancestors. Their efforts represent a willingness, at least in some quarters, to come to terms with the shame that Affleck invoked, although one is left wondering what continues to remain hidden by family gatekeepers who are less accepting of their familial links. When interviewed about the Hibbert family for the BBC2 documentary *Britain's forgotten slave-owners*, Nicholas Hibbert Steele commented on the necessity of a public reckoning with the slaving past. He stated that:

> The subject is too important, it's important to millions of people on all sorts of different levels whether they were involved in slavery or were a product of slavery ... There were some harrowing stories here, there is absolutely no point in trying to bury them, it is truth and reconciliation time, the story has to be outed.

When asked by presenter David Olusoga if some of what he had been working through as an individual was applicable to British society more broadly, Hibbert Steele responded, 'I think that there is a sort of collective shame here and that needs to be acknowledged. I think that what is known should be known by all.'[36]

INTRODUCTION: FAMILY MATTERS

History and national identity

The most recent attempt to grapple publicly with Britain's role in transatlantic slavery was during the bicentenary commemorations of the abolition of the slave trade in 2007.[37] Criticised for a disproportionate focus on William Wilberforce, the official narrative reinforced Britain's self-fashioned reputation as *the* global champion of freedom. The irony of Britain's transformation has been pointed out by Linda Colley, who stated, 'From being the world's greediest and most successful traders of slaves in the eighteenth century the British had shifted to being able to preen themselves on being the world's foremost opponents of slavery.'[38] This, she has argued, 'revealed as much if not more about how the British thought about themselves'. In order for abolition to take centre stage, participation in the business of slavery had to be forgotten. Emerging from the cleansing waters of the 1833 Slavery Abolition Act, the newly converted 'anti-slavery nation' adopted the mantle of emancipator with vigorous energy, using this identification to make further incursions into Africa under the auspices of suppressing slavery and spreading civilisation.[39] The end of slavery did not signal an end to Britain's imperial ambitions, indeed it ushered in a new era of colonial expansion based on ideas of cultural and racial superiority and justified by notions of benevolence and improvement. This tangled history of empire and humanitarian interventionism has left a lasting imprint on Britain's understanding of both itself and its place within the world.

That abolition is still imagined as a defining moment in the formation of British national identity has been demonstrated time and again by politicians on both side of the traditional divide. In 2004 Gordon Brown, then chancellor of the exchequer, delivered a speech on Britishness at the Commonwealth Club. In defining the national character he evoked Britain's 'unique' history in order to assert that 'Britain can lay claim to the idea of liberty.'[40] He opined that 'it was in the name of liberty that in the 1800s Britain led the world in abolishing the slave trade'. The omission that slavery continued on for many decades only to be replaced by the inequities of colonial rule is precisely the kind of active forgetting that is required in order to make the history of abolitionism fit with a framing of freedom as central to Britishness. In 2014, Prime Minister David Cameron similarly centred the antislavery past in a newspaper article on 'British values' in the *Daily Mail*. The text included a reminder that 'this is the country that helped ... abolish slavery'.[41] The following year the names of Wilberforce and his abolitionist allies were invoked repeatedly during parliamentary discussions in the lead-up to the passing of the Modern Slavery Act in 2015. Antislavery was cast as part of the national DNA, a heritage to be drawn upon in the fight against the continued scourge of the old foe. This undue focus on abolition, without proper regard for what came before and after, has impeded a serious national reckoning with both the legacies of slavery and the failures of freedom that continue to shape the present.

In 2014 the Caribbean Community and Common Market (CARICOM) set out a ten-point plan for reparatory justice. The publicity surrounding the move reminded the nation, and indeed the world, that any easy affinity with antislavery must always be tempered by the knowledge that for many hundreds of years prior to that Britain, and other European nations, participated enthusiastically in the slavery business. Historical amnesia around Britain's slaving past has served to obscure the ways in which it created and sustained ideas about culture and identity. Prior to the advent of organised abolition, proslavery patriotism rooted in ideas of commercial greatness, maritime power and racial superiority, had much purchase in Britain. 'Rule Britannia', first performed in 1740, trumpeted the nation's special claim to freedom whilst declaring that 'Britons never will be slaves'.[42] Written during a period of great expansion for the British slave trade, the author James Thomson saw no contradiction in Britain championing liberty whilst simultaneously subjecting African people to enslavement. Instead his words delineated the limits of full citizenship and national belonging, for if Britons could never be 'slaves' then conversely enslaved people would never be British. The struggle over abolition was about more than just the right to trade in and possess people – it was a debate over the nature of both British national and imperial identity.[43] As has been seen in the debates over Brexit, discussions about trade and commerce can, and do, act as a cipher for much more deep-rooted conflicts about culture and identity. The figure of both the slave owner and the enslaved were sites of bitter political contestation in which difference played a crucial role in defining Britishness. Ideas about Africa and Africans were informed by troubling hierarchical assumptions about race which were common to both pro and antislavery supporters. In the abolitionist imaginary the slave owner was cast as a cruel despot whose tyranny made him ultimately un-English. Whilst there can be absolutely no denial of the violence and exploitation of slavery, it is unhelpful to think about slave owners and their supporters as monstrous aberrations, particularly in the context of Britain's wider imperial history. There is an ordinariness rather than an exceptionalism to the everyday accommodation with racial violence that underpinned slavery and imperialism. Probing the lives of one of the many 'respectable' families who were implicated in, and acclimatised to, the brutality of the system offers a window into understanding the mentality of perpetration. It is this history of the perpetrator which unsettles the narrative of British history as being woven through with the 'golden thread of liberty ... of the individual standing firm for freedom and liberty against tyranny'.[44] Whilst the history of antislavery has served, and continues to serve, as a useful proxy for politicians keen to present a particular vision of the nation, this myopic view of the past requires a silencing of the less palatable aspects of Britain's role in transatlantic slavery.

The culture of proslavery

Culture has played a central role in the analysis of the formation of antislavery in Britain.[45] Sentimentality, benevolence, philanthropy, improvement and religion have all been interrogated in relation to the development of concepts of humanitarianism and reform. Proslavery existed in the same cultural moment; it intersected with these discourses, harnessing their language in order to appeal to an emerging public political sphere. Culture is key to understanding ideas about race that were crucial to both pro and antislavery arguments. Whilst they might have differed in their views on slavery, both sides of the debate shared a belief in European cultural superiority. As David Bindman has pointed out, 'The ability to make aesthetic judgements could in itself be a way of dividing the "civilised" from the "savage".'[46] Taste as a form of imperial power became a means of discerning between the ruler and the ruled. The relationship between slavery and culture at a more practical level stemmed from the relationship between colonial labour, transatlantic wealth generation and metropolitan habits of consumption. The cultural world of the slave owners in the Caribbean has received increasing scholarly attention.[47] There has been less work done on the cultural lives of the absentee planters and merchants in Britain.[48] The histories that have been written of these groups have not been 'particularly interested in the identity and social tensions of a slave-owning family in private and public life'.[49] Paula Dumas's recent work has shed light on some of the ways in which arts and culture were used to convey an anti-abolition message. Her focus, however, is on explicit political productions rather than the ways in which a personal connection to collecting, patronage, charity and religion might have impacted on the organisation and representation of proslavery.[50] Cultural networks constituted through membership of clubs and societies, philanthropic activities, the culture of connoisseurship, even attendance at church, reinforced a sense of shared identity, as well as offering opportunities for lobbying through personal relationships. The Hibberts were part of a social and cultural milieu that provided them with access to power outside of, but nonetheless intimately linked to, the world of formal politics. A serious interest in collecting elevated George into London's cultural elite, introducing him to individuals who could, and did, further his family's interests when pressed to do so. Cultural participation and acceptance also allowed the Hibberts to fashion a sense of self that was a direct repudiation of the abolitionists' public representation of the slave owner as debased and un-English.

In fascinating and largely unexplored ways the cultural arena acted as a site for interplay between pro and antislavery campaigners. Culture provided the social lubrication necessary to smooth any political frictions that might otherwise have impeded the enjoyment of polite gentlemanly pursuits. George was a founder of the London Institution. He was joined in this endeavour by a large number of his West India commercial associates. Perhaps more surprisingly the abolitionists Zachary Macaulay and brothers Henry and John Thornton were also involved. George, his brother William and their nephew Samuel, all lived in Clapham Common with their respective families. George was a trustee for Holy Trinity Church – the spiritual centre of abolitionist activities. The family owned prestigious pews in the church, they contributed to its maintenance and a number of them were buried in the graveyard – sharing the same space in death with their political rivals in life. In adopting the social mores of their abolitionist detractors, the Hibberts could present slave ownership as a respectable occupation which sustained useful members of the community and by extension the nation. Exploring the social and cultural dimension of the lives of metropolitan slave owners and merchants complicates our understanding by challenging the two-dimensional caricature offered by the abolitionists. This is not done as a means of redeeming tarnished reputations, but in order to demonstrate that a brutal system does not necessarily require its supporters to conform to any one particular form of identity or pattern of behaviour. Without ever once visiting Jamaica or wielding the whip, George was one of the most powerful proslavery lobbyists, and was all the more effective because of his perceived urbanity and cultivation.

Archival power

Documentary traces of the Hibberts' story can be found in private, commercial, institutional, political, colonial, literary and art historical papers. The geographic span of their public archival presence takes in regional record offices in Gloucester, Derby, Devon, Surrey and Cambridge. Material can be found in the National Library of Wales and The National Archives in England. Internationally records relating to the family are housed in the Jamaica National Archives and the Island Record Office, as well as in a series of repositories in America. Part of the family's private archive is located in Melbourne, Australia, where it has been carefully complied by family descendant

INTRODUCTION: FAMILY MATTERS

Nicholas Hibbert Steele. The distance travelled in the production of this research is indicative of the ways in which histories of both slavery and the family connect the local, national and global. As the geographic spread of the slavery compensation records have confirmed, Britain's links to the slave economy cannot be contained within a port city narrative. If we follow the money, the archives and the families, there are concentrations in expected places (London, Bristol, Liverpool and Glasgow) but also dispersals as patterns of habitation and interest changed over time. Over the course of several generations the Hibberts shifted from the mercantile classes to the landed gentry. Their commercial properties in cities like London disappeared and were gradually replaced by country houses. As these changes occurred their histories, and that of the system of slavery that underpinned them, became interwoven with rural narratives.[51] These transatlantic connections pose a challenge to little-Englander provincialism and exclusionary forms of local history and identity.

There is no single repository for the Hibbert archive – like the family itself it inhabits both public and private spaces. Political and commercial material is far easier to come by as the records have been preserved for posterity. Archival practice has privileged the affairs of political men, assuming that they will occupy the historian and are therefore worthy of conservation and digitisation. Business archives are more patchy; some of the Hibberts' commercial letters can be found in the collections of their wealthy correspondents, but their own mercantile records have not survived. The continued existence of the West India Committee (formerly the Society of West India Planters and Merchants) has ensured that their papers have been collected and archived. The documents are a vital record of the activities of proslavery campaigners, offering a window into the tactics of one of the most powerful lobbying groups of the period. Taken together these document caches record and reflect the important work of men. As Adele Perry has noted, 'the official archive is gendered from the start, associated with male authority and textual records, and disassociated from women, speech, and fiction'.[52] This 'gendered schism of record-keeping' inevitably privileges the Hibbert men over the Hibbert women. Like Perry's history of the Douglas-Connolly family this book will not be able to 'adequately restore' the Hibbert women to the historical record.

Some of the correspondence that survives documents a female-centred network of knowledge exchange. Family matriarch Abigail wrote regularly to all her children, as well as her sons' wives, sharing gossip and advice. Anxious letters between members stand as testament to the ways in which empire penetrated the family's inner life. From fretting about the noxious climate's ill effects on the health of cherished sons, to the 'apprehension of a second Domingo affair', the family letters are a fascinating mixture of domestic, imperial, commercial and political concerns.[53] The correspondence, alongside both Robert junior's diaries and George's commonplace book, offers a more intimate perspective on family life. Robert junior, for example, noted down each of his wife's births and miscarriages in his diary. He recorded the heights of his surviving children as they grew. Incidences of first love and loss, family squabbles and even sexually transmitted diseases were detailed. Disturbingly mingled amongst the social commentary were regular entries referring to the sale of various 'Cargoes' – Robert junior's euphemistic description of the enslaved Africans. The interweaving of business, pleasure and the day-to-day musings of a regular diarist reflect the ways in which slavery was unremarkable for those who made their living from it. These connections can be read materially in the physical object of the diary, as Robert junior noted on the opening page: 'The following memoirs were originally written in a temporary manner in an unbound stitched paper book which had contained the Sales of the *Bonaventura* cargo sold so long ago as January 1779.' Recognising that 'The book is of course perishing, and to save the events from perishing also, I think it best to publish them in this bound Book, during exceptional rain.'[54] Similarly, George's commonplace book also contained writings that allow us to enter into his private realm. Including both self-authored works and carefully copied texts, his commonplace book offers a window into his thoughts on a variety of subjects. In it can be found plays he had written for his children to perform, with each role allocated via annotations in the margins. Passages on marriage and gender roles, instructive verses on good behaviour for his daughters, patriotic speeches for his sons and his own poems dedicated to his sick, dying and dead children articulated the emotional depth of the family bonds. Combined together these documents enable us to see empire not only as a function of state policy or the expansion of trade, but also as an embodied and affective lived experience.

Because they were an eminent family active within public life there is a wealth of records detailing the Hibberts, yet it is far harder to find evidence that supports an examination of the lives of the enslaved people whose labour propelled the family into archival visibility. The official archive, an entity that both reflected and circumscribed the lived experiences of colonial subjects, was never designed to animate the subjectivity of the enslaved. Documents relating to enslaved people offer moments in which the individual emerges, but very rarely on their own terms. In the Slave Registers

INTRODUCTION: FAMILY MATTERS

for Jamaica the first triennial count in 1817 referred to enslaved people by name, but subsequent counts noted only 'increase' or 'decrease' in relation to the population of the estate. Couched in the language of a commercial inventory, this form of accounting for the enslaved can only ever be a fleeting record of a life lived. Claims to individual subjecthood are further compromised when we consider the naming practices of plantation society – it was the owner's prerogative to bestow a given name. This is evident in the records of the Hibbert plantations, where a number of enslaved people were named for various family members. Indeed within the naming practices on the Hibbert plantations it is easier to trace their own family connections. An entry in the 1817 register for the family's plantation Agualta Vale records two enslaved people named George Hibbert and Samuel Markland.[55] The former was named for the senior partner in the Hibberts' London counting house and the latter bore the surname of his nephew, Robert Markland junior, a Jamaica slave trader. Mirroring some of the gaps and silences within the Hibbert family story, Andrea Stuart has lamented the historical imbalance in terms of the presence of the slave owners and the enslaved within the historical record. She has written that 'Ghosts haunt this tale, small men whose lives leave only very faint footprints and slaves whose sufferings leave no mark at all.'[56] This book is written with a recognition that the records privilege the slave owner and in some ways this volume will amplify the racialised power dynamics of historical representation. In reconstructing a history of an elite planter-merchant family this book reconnects metropolitan power with colonial exploitation. It is an attempt to put both slave ownership and the enslaved back into a narrative of British history by exploring the ways in which it impacted on a broad cross-section of society over the course of over a hundred years of family history. The book cannot, and does not, do the work of recovery for the many thousands of enslaved people who were bought and sold by the Hibberts.

Part I of the book details the foundation of the Hibberts' transatlantic business. Beginning in Manchester in the early years of the eighteenth century, Chapter 1 explores the relationship between slavery, cotton and capitalism by documenting the family's initial interest in Atlantic commerce as cotton manufacturers trading to Liverpool. It places the family within a network that was constituted through religious identity and marriage. Complicating the relationship between non-conformity and abolition, Chapter 1 sheds light on the Unitarian network engaged in the slavery business and linked through the Cross Street Chapel in Manchester. Shifting the narrative from Britain to Jamaica, Chapter 2 considers how the

Hibberts established themselves within the merchant-planter elite during the mid-eighteenth century. It charts the family's adoption of civic and political power, their merchant houses, slave trading activities, commercial correspondents and plantation interests. It reflects on ideas of colonial masculine sociability through an analysis of daily life in their townhouse in Kingston. Chapter 2 also includes details of the experiences of enslaved people on some of the Hibberts' estates, both during the period of slavery and in the immediate post-emancipation era. Traversing the Atlantic once again, Chapter 3 examines the London commercial world and its ties to slavery through an account of the structure and operations of the Hibberts' counting house. It documents the multi-layered interests the Hibberts had within the slave economy, including the significance of their involvement in the funding and management of the West India Docks. It outlines how the personnel reconfigured over the course of three generations of Hibberts, until the winding-up of the firm in the 1860s.

Part II considers the Hibbert family's involvement in the politics of proslavery. Chapter 4 documents the formal and informal political sphere of the London West India interest during the campaign to abolish the slave trade. It considers how both George and his brother Robert junior articulated anti-abolition arguments in evidence given to Parliament. It charts George's rise to prominence and his impact on strategy and rhetoric, in particular following his election as a Member of Parliament in 1806. Chapter 4 explores the divisions within the West India interest, arguing for the existence of a distinctive form of metropolitan proslavery discourse. Chapter 5 considers the period of amelioration leading up to the renewed campaign to end slavery. It was during this crucial period that George became Agent for Jamaica, making him the colony's most powerful spokesman in Britain. His position as a leading proslavery advocate made the family a target for the abolitionists, who looked to undermine George's construction of slavery as a benevolent institution by focusing on the treatment of the Hibberts' own enslaved workers. Chapter 5 gives details of the scandal that erupted over conditions on George's cousin Robert's plantation and the pamphlet war which ensued. It also recounts the part that George played in negotiating the final process of abolition including details of his role in securing compensation.

Part III of the book moves from the public realm to the private. Chapter 6 (part I) focuses on family life in Jamaica through an examination of the different forms of intimate relationships that the Hibbert men experienced. It gives an account of their marriages to

INTRODUCTION: FAMILY MATTERS

Creole women and how these relative outsiders were perceived by the metropolitan family. It details sexual relations, diseases, miscarriage and infant death experienced as part of everyday life on the island. Where possible it records the Hibbert men's relationships with enslaved and free women of colour and their children. In particular it examines the story of Thomas senior's daughter Jane Harry in relation to ideas about class, race and gender in the period leading up to the onset of abolition. Chapter 6 (part II) considers family life in England, documenting a close-knit network whose lives were deeply intertwined. In choosing to settle in Clapham, the Hibberts mirrored the Christian respectability of their antislavery neighbours. Through an analysis of George's commonplace book Chapter 6 (part II) explores ideas of domestic masculinity during a time in which concepts of manliness were changing in response to the development of the notion of separate spheres. It analyses George's attitude towards marriage and parenthood, and how these ideas shaped the expectations of gender in relation to both his wife and children.

Chapter 7 explores the cultural lives of absentee planters and merchants through an examination of George's collecting practices, patronage and participation in elite clubs and societies. It considers the role of culture and taste in the formation of racialised ideas of civilisation. In documenting the family's collection Chapter 7 considers the financial and cultural capital accumulated through the investment of slave-based wealth in the arts. Engaging with recent scholarship on slavery and the country house, Chapter 8 discusses the Hibberts' transition into the country house owning gentry. It documents their purchasing, building, renovation and landscaping of country estates, arguing that this left behind a distinctive legacy in terms of the built environment and heritage. In relation to both their country houses and also more broadly their individual cultural and political interests, Chapter 8 discusses the philanthropic activities of different family members. Benevolent bequests and charitable giving formed an important part of gentlemanly culture, and also offered an opportunity to create an identity and memory separate to that of the slave owner. Chapter 8 ends with a discussion of the relationship between slavery and philanthropy, and the complicated legacies that this has left behind.

Collectively this book argues for the centrality of the family in our understanding of the commercial, political and cultural world sustained by transatlantic slavery. It is also suggestive of the different ways in which the family was profoundly altered by its encounter with it. Slavery transformed the Hibberts, propelling them into positions of power both at home and in the empire. During the years of turmoil brought about by the abolition campaign it was their involvement with slavery which threatened to dislodge them from their respectable position. In the end the family prevailed and were able to use the compensation money they received to reorient themselves away from the plantation economy. Whilst over time their commercial connections to the Caribbean were severed, their story remains enmeshed with the history and legacies of slavery both in Britain and Jamaica. If empire sought to create a (distinctly unequal) family of nations, it was the family itself that was at the centre of making that empire. This book reconnects metropole and colony, the slave owner with the enslaved – it argues that Britain's history is both local and global in its reach and impact. The narrative speaks to what is remembered and what is forgotten, what is represented and the gaps and silences that both define and deny visibility. It is the story of trade, colonisation, enrichment and the tangled web of relations that gave meaning to the transatlantic world. It is the Hibberts' story and it is Britain's 'island story'.

Notes

1 National Library of Wales, Aberystwyth, Slebech Papers and Documents (NLW/SPD), 9212, Letter from Thomas Hibbert junior to Nathaniel Phillips, 20 August 1772.
2 R. G. Thorne, *The history of Parliament: The House of Commons, 1790–1820* (London: Secker and Warburg, 1986), p. 193.
3 Hercules Ross, quoted in Richard B. Sheridan, 'The commercial and financial organisation of the British slave trade, 1750–1807', *Economic History Review*, 11:2 (1958), p. 255.
4 Srividhya Swaminathan, 'Developing the proslavery position after the Somerset decision', *Slavery & Abolition*, 24:3 (2003), p. 43.
5 *Select Committee appointed to take the examination of witnesses respecting the African slave trade. Minutes of the evidence taken before a committee of the House of Commons appointed for the purpose of the examination of such witnesses who have petitioned against the abolition of the slave trade* (London: House of Commons, 1790), p. 390.
6 Gloucestershire Archives, Gloucester, Blathwayt Family of Dyrham Papers (GA/BFDP), D1799/C153, Letter from Robert Hibbert junior to Mary Oates, 5 May 1807.
7 For an account of the compensation process see Nicholas Draper, *The price of emancipation: Slave-ownership, compensation and British society at the end of slavery* (Cambridge: Cambridge University Press, 2010).
8 Geoffrey Jones and Mary B. Rose, 'Family capitalism', *Business History*, 35:4 (1993), pp. 1–16; Mary B. Rose, 'The family firm in British business, 1780–1914', in M. W. Kirby and M. B. Rose, *Business enterprise in modern Britain from the eighteenth to the twentieth century* (London: Routledge, 1994), pp. 61–87; Margaret Hunt, *The middling sort: Commerce, gender and the family in England, 1680–1780* (Berkley: University of California Press, 1996); Leonore Davidoff and Catherine Hall, *Family fortunes: Men and women of the English middle class, 1780–1850* (London: Routledge, 2002).
9 Richard Pares, *A West India fortune* (London: Longmans, 1950); Richard Pares, 'A London West-India merchant house, 1740–1769', in Richard Pares and A. J. P. Taylor (eds) *Essays presented to Sir Lewis Namier* (London: Macmillan, 1956),

INTRODUCTION: FAMILY MATTERS

pp. 75–107; S. G. Checkland, *The Gladstones: A family biography 1764–1851* (Cambridge: Cambridge University Press, 1971); Simon D. Smith, *Slavery, family and gentry capitalism in the British Atlantic* (Cambridge: Cambridge University Press, 2006); Albane Forestier, 'Risk, kinship and personal relationships in late eighteenth-century West Indian trade: The commercial network of Tobin & Pinney', *Business History*, 52:6 (2010), pp. 912–31

10 Davidoff and Hall, *Family fortunes*, p. xxxix
11 Catherine Hall, 'Gendering property, racing capital', *History Workshop Journal*, 78:1 (2014), p. 30.
12 For a discussion on the relationship between trust and credit see Margot Finn, *The character of credit: Personal debt in English culture, 1740–1914* (Cambridge: Cambridge University Press, 2003).
13 NLW/SPD, 9212, Letter from Thomas Hibbert junior to Nathaniel Phillips, 20 August 1772.
14 For a discussion of different aspects of the maternal experience under slavery see Camillia Cowling, Maria Helena Pereira Toledo Machado, Diana Paton and Emily West (eds), 'Mothering slaves: Comparative perspectives on motherhood, childlessness, and the care of children in Atlantic slave societies', *Slavery & Abolition*, Special Issue, 38:2 (2017).
15 'Samuel Boddington: Profile and legacies summary', Legacies of British Slave-ownership database. www.ucl.ac.uk/lbs/person/view/772 [accessed 6 May 2016].
16 Julian Hoppit, *Risk and failure in English business 1700–1800* (Cambridge: Cambridge University Press, 2002).
17 Hannah Young, 'Forgotten women: Anna Eliza Elletson and absentee slave-ownership', in Katie Donington, Ryan Hanley and Jessica Moody (eds), *Britain's history and memory of slavery: The local nuances of a 'national sin'* (Liverpool: Liverpool University Press, 2016), pp. 60–82.
18 For a discussion of the laws affecting mixed-heritage Jamaicans see Daniel Livesay, *Children of uncertain fortune: Mixed-race Jamaicans in Britain and the Atlantic family, 1733–1833* (Chapel Hill: University of North Carolina Press, 2018), pp. 32–52.
19 Davidoff and Hall, *Family fortunes*, p. xxxv.
20 Elizabeth Buettner, *Empire families: Britain and late imperial India* (Oxford: Oxford University Press, 2004); Barbara Caine, *Bombay to Bloomsbury: A biography of the Strachey family* (Oxford: Oxford University Press, 2005); Sarah Pearsall, *Atlantic families: Lives and letters in the later eighteenth century* (Oxford: Oxford University Press, 2008); Emma Rothschild, *Inner lives of empire: An eighteenth-century history* (Princeton, NJ: Princeton University Press, 2011); Catherine Hall, *Macaulay and son: Architects of imperial Britain* (New Haven, CT: Yale University Press, 2012); Emily Manktelow, *Missionary families: Race, gender and generation on the spiritual frontier* (Manchester: Manchester University Press, 2013); Adele Perry, *Colonial relations: The Douglas-Connolly family and the nineteenth-century imperial world* (Cambridge: Cambridge University Press, 2015); Jennifer L. Palmer, *Intimate bonds: Family and slavery in the French Atlantic* (Philadelphia: University of Pennsylvania Press, 2016).
21 Esme Cleall, Laura Ishiguro and Emily Manktelow (eds), 'Imperial relations: Histories of family in the British Empire', *Journal of Colonialism and Colonial History*, Special Issue, 14:1 (Spring 2013), p. 1.
22 For a discussion of the complicated relationships between slave owners and enslaved women see Trevor Burnard, *Mastery, tyranny and desire: Thomas Thistlewood and his slaves in the Anglo-Jamaican world* (Chapel Hill: University of North Carolina Press, 2004); Meleisa Ono-George, '"Washing the Blackamoor white": Interracial intimacy and coloured women's agency in Jamaica', in Will Jackson and Emily J. Manktelow (eds) *Subverting empire: Deviance and disorder in the British colonial world* (Basingstoke: Palgrave Macmillan, 2015), pp. 42–60; Meleisa Ono-George, '"By her unnatural and despicable conduct": Motherhood and concubinage in the *Watchman and Jamaica Free Press*, 1830–1833', *Slavery & Abolition*, 38:2 (2017), pp. 356–72.

23 Hibbert Family Archives and Collection (HFAC), Melbourne, Australia, Diary of Robert Hibbert junior, 12 October 1771. With thanks to Nicholas Hibbert Steele.
24 *Ibid.*, 26 May 1772.
25 GA/BFDP, D1799/C153, Letter from Robert Hibbert junior to Mary Oates, 6 January 1803.
26 The difficulty of negotiating life as an absentee is discussed in Michael Craton, 'Reluctant Creoles: The planters' world in the British West Indies', in Bernard Bailyn and Phillip D. Morgan (eds), *Strangers within the realm: Cultural margins of the first British empire* (Chapel Hill: University of North Carolina Press, 1991), pp. 347–9.
27 For a discussion of the funerary urn see Vincent Brown, *The reaper's garden: Death and power in the world of Atlantic slavery* (Cambridge, MA: Harvard University Press, 2010), pp. 239–41.
28 David Noakes, 'The importance of darning socks', *The Spectator*, 10 July 1987. http://archive.spectator.co.uk/article/11th-july-1987/35/the-importance-of-darning-socks [accessed 17 January 2017].
29 Naomi Tadmor, 'The concept of the household-family in eighteenth-century England', *Past & Present*, 151 (1996), pp. 111–40.
30 Samuel Johnson, quoted *ibid.*, p. 112.
31 Thavolia Glymph, *Out of the house of bondage: The transformation of the plantation household* (Cambridge: Cambridge University Press, 2008).
32 Leonore Davidoff, *Thicker than water: Siblings and their relations, 1780–1920* (Oxford: Oxford University Press, 2012), p. 5.
33 Alex Haley, quoted in Andrea Stuart, *Sugar in the blood: A family's story of slavery and empire* (London: Portobello Books, 2012), p. 1.
34 *Ibid.*, p. 3.
35 Rob Crilly and Philip Sherwell, 'Ben Affleck reveals name of slave-owning ancestor after apology in "censoring" row', *The Telegraph*, 23 April 2015. www.telegraph.co.uk/news/worldnews/northamerica/usa/11553967/Ben-Affleck-says-he-regrets-covering-up-slave-owner-in-the-family.html [accessed 19 January 2017].
36 Nicholas Hibbert Steele interviewed by David Olusoga, in Episode 2, 'The price of freedom', *Britain's forgotten slave-owners*, BBC2, aired 22 July 2015, 47:00–48:00.
37 For a discussion of the public politics of 2007 see Laurajane Smith, Geoffrey Cubitt, Ross Wilson and Kalliopi Fouseki (eds), *Representing enslavement and abolition in museums: Ambiguous engagements* (Abingdon: Routledge, 2011).
38 Linda Colley, *Britons: Forging the nation, 1707–1837* (London: Pimlico, 1994), p. 351.
39 Richard Huzzey, *Freedom burning: Anti-slavery and empire in Victorian Britain* (Ithaca, NY: Cornell University Press, 2012), pp. 5–20.
40 Gordon Brown, 'The golden thread that runs through our history', *The Guardian*, 8 July 2004. www.theguardian.com/politics/2004/jul/08/britishidentity.economy [accessed 3 May 2018].
41 David Cameron, 'British values', *Daily Mail*, 15 June 2014. www.gov.uk/government/news/british-values-article-by-david-cameron [accessed 23 July 2015].
42 James Thomson, 'Rule, Britannia!', in J. Logie Robertson (ed.), *The complete poetical works of James Thompson* (Oxford: Oxford University Press, 1908), p. 422.
43 Srividhya Swaminathan, *Debating the slave trade: Rhetoric of British national identity, 1759–1815* (Farnham: Ashgate, 2009).
44 Brown, 'The golden thread'.
45 David Turley, *The culture of English antislavery, 1760–1860* (London: Routledge, 1991). For a feminist reading of the development of antislavery culture see Clare Midgley, *Women against slavery: The British campaigns, 1780–1870* (London: Routledge, 1992).
46 David Bindman, *Ape to Apollo: Aesthetics and race in the eighteenth century* (London: Reaktion, 2002), p. 12.
47 David Lambert, *White Creole culture, politics and identity during the age of abolition* (Cambridge: Cambridge University Press, 2005); Kay Dian Kriz, *Slavery, sugar and refinement: Picturing the British West Indies, 1700–1840* (London: Yale University Press, 2008); Christer Petley, *Slaveholders in Jamaica: Colonial society*

and culture during the era of abolition (London: Pickering & Chatto, 2009); Christer Petley and Stephen Lenik (eds), 'Material cultures of slavery and abolition in the British Caribbean', *Slavery & Abolition*, Special Issue, 35:3 (2014).

48 Alexandra Franklin, 'Enterprise and advantage: The West India interest in Britain, 1774–1849' (PhD thesis, University of Pennsylvania, 1992); Simon Gikandi, *Slavery and the culture of taste* (Princeton, NJ: Princeton University Press, 2011); David Hancock, *Citizens of the world: London merchants and the integration of the British Atlantic community, 1735–1785* (Cambridge: Cambridge University Press, 1995), in particular 'Part III: Becoming a gentleman', pp. 279–383.
49 Draper, *The price of emancipation*, p. 9.
50 Paula Dumas, *Proslavery Britain: Fighting for slavery in an era of abolition* (London: Palgrave Macmillan, 2016), ch. 3, 'Proslavery arts and culture', pp. 89–115.
51 See the AHRC-funded project 'Reconnecting diverse rural communities: black presences and the legacies of slavery and colonialism in rural Britain, c. 1600–1939'. www.nottingham.ac.uk/isos/research/rural-legacies.aspx [accessed 14 February 2017].
52 Perry, *Colonial relations*, pp. 7–8.
53 GA/BFDP, D1799/C153, Letter from Abigail Hibbert, 16 April (year unknown).
54 HFAC, Diary of Robert Hibbert junior, front page.
55 The National Archives, Kew, Office of Registry of Colonial Slaves and Slave Compensation Commission, T71/33, Jamaica Slave Registers, St Mary's (1817), p. 1106.
56 Stuart, *Sugar in the blood*, p. xviii.

PART I

Family business: commerce, commodities and credit

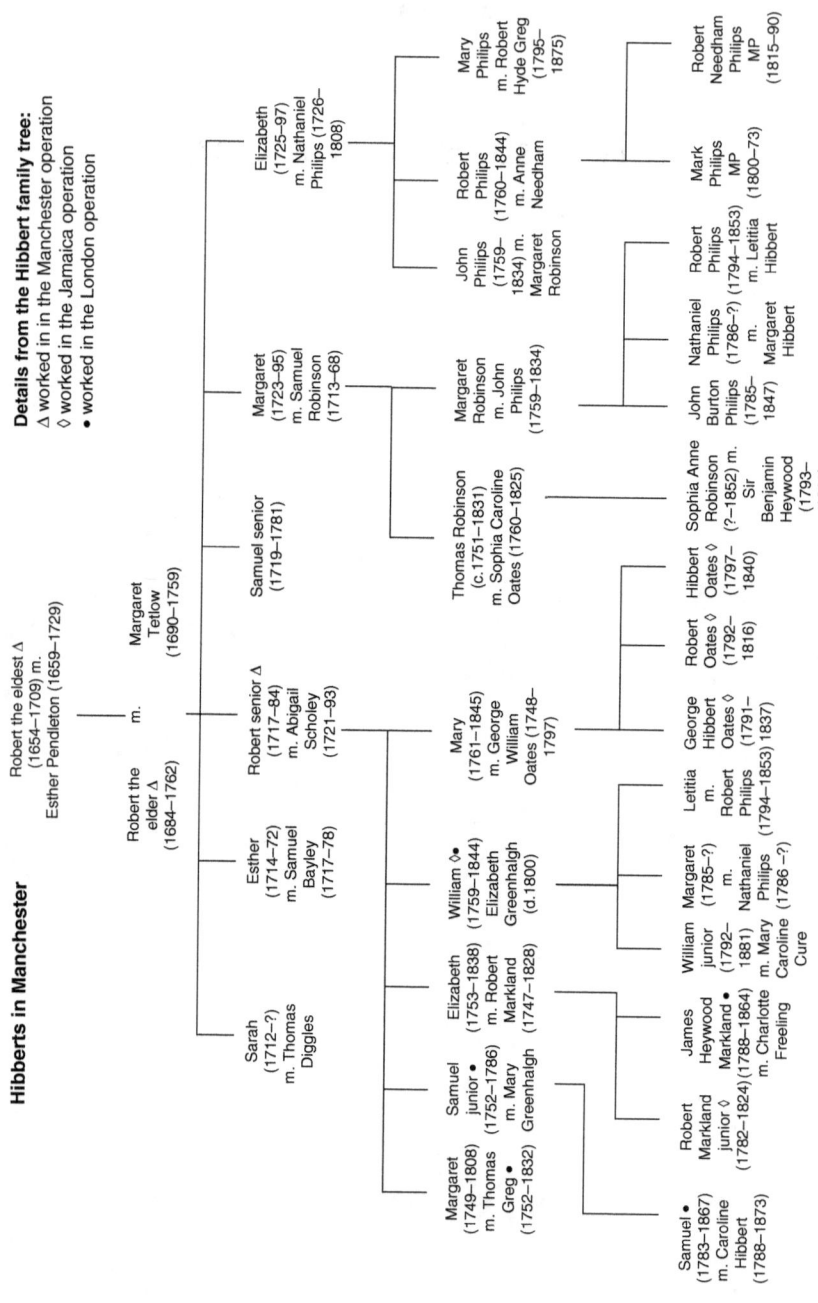

Family tree 2 The Hibberts in Manchester

CHAPTER ONE

Manchester

> In the course of the present reign, the manufacture of cotton occupied an attention in Britain very far superior to what it had ever employed before in any country ... The means which have brought this grand department of national industry to its present zenith, are no doubt the same as have conducted our manufacturers and merchants to such success in every other department – sound and comprehensive ability, invention, sagacity, enterprise, skill, and the capitals which were fostered under free and equitable laws ... But all the genius of an Arkwright, and all the liberality and talents of Manchester, with the highest degree of industry and skill, can make no cotton manufacture without cotton wool. Whence comes cotton wool to Britain? It comes chiefly from the labour of Negroes.
> Robert Bissett, *The history of the negro slave trade, in its connection with the commerce and prosperity of the West Indies, and the wealth and power of the British empire*, vol. II (London: W. McDowall, 1805), pp. 339–42

According to Jerom Murch, the Hibberts' story began in Marple, Cheshire during the reign of Edward IV in the fifteenth century. Laying claim to a most respectable historical stock, Murch noted that Nicholas Hibbert of Marple was recorded in Burke's *Landed gentry* and that his descendants 'branched off in various directions, settling chiefly in Lancashire and Cheshire, and devoting themselves much to commerce and manufactures'.[1] The Hibberts were not of aristocratic birth, but were part of the dissenting merchant classes of northern England. Their ascent into the commercial elite came through their initial involvement in the cloth industry. The growing importance of Manchester in the eighteenth century stemmed from the expansion of empire and the rise of slavery, which in turn secured the area's role in the cotton economy. Sven Beckert has described Manchester as the 'centre of a world spinning empire – the empire of cotton'.[2] The cloth trade and its associated businesses provided jobs and prosperity for the local population. Finished cotton pieces were in demand in Liverpool for use in the Guinea trade as one of a number of desirable commodities used to barter for enslaved people on the coast of West Africa. Raw cotton produced by enslaved workers in both the Americas and the Caribbean was then shipped back to the port at Liverpool for processing in Lancashire. The centrality of Manchester to the slavery business was outlined by Eric Williams, who argued that 'Manchester received a double stimulus from the colonial trade. If it supplied goods needed on the slave coast and on the plantations, its manufacturers depended in turn on the supply of raw material.'[3] Williams went on to identify some of the key local figures, including the 'leading Manchester firm' of the Hibbert family. Starting out as linen drapers in the seventeenth century, by the early eighteenth century the Hibberts were manufacturing cloth and supplying finished pieces for use in the slave trade. The story of their increasing entanglement with transatlantic commerce is instructive in understanding Manchester's regional role as slavery's hinterland in the north.

Describing the city around 1700 Celia Fiennes wrote that 'Manchester looks exceedingly well ... Very substantial buildings; the houses are not very lofty, but mostly of brick and stone ... The Market place is large; it takes up two streets' length when the market is kept for their linen cloth [and] cotton tickings which is the manufacture of the town ... This is a thriving place.'[4] As Fiennes observed, the cloth trade dominated both the physical space and the economy of the town. By the 1730s it boasted civic institutions including a college, hospital, free school and a library. The merchants of Manchester had played no small part in the expansion of the area's fortunes. Among those successful merchants was a distinct network of dissenting religious families working in the cloth and cotton trade. Non-conformists were still suffering under discriminatory legislation; barred from political and educational institutions which might have fostered ambitions towards power, individuals from the dissenting community found different ways of securing prestige. Commerce represented an alternative path to wealth, status and influence. Utilising networks of shared religious identity meant that wealth circulated within the confines of the community. The dissenting merchants of Manchester fostered these links using the twin virtues of respectability and trust to ensure the integrity of their social and economic relationships. The Hibberts were members of the Cross Street Chapel congregation. Noted by John Seed as an 'unusually large and opulent' non-conformist place of worship, the chapel attracted the elite of Manchester's merchants and manufacturers.[5] Their business interests intertwined, creating a network bound together by shared commercial, religious and familial relationships.

Women and children played a vital role in expanding the mercantile enterprise. Central to the circulation of wealth, the preservation of reputation and the extension of commercial networks was the role of marriage. Endogamous marriage offered a way in which urban mercantile families could unite their interests with those of similar standing, creating 'a city patriciate, bound by interlocking ties of kinship'.[6] Within the confines of this tight-knit world the Hibberts forged links with the key Manchester families identified by Williams as having significant connections to slavery. Understanding the interconnections between and within these families can only be done through a meticulous unpicking of their marriages, particularly those of the women. These relationships lasted over the course of several generations, with the practice of cousin marriage ensuring that the bonds were further tightened. The production of children strengthened the family enterprise by providing the next generation of personnel, as well as future marital opportunities. Boys were prepared for commercial life through specific forms of schooling and apprenticeships designed to cultivate both the practical skills and genteel masculine attributes necessary to operate in the upper echelons of the mercantile classes.

The extended Hibbert family stretched across Manchester, Liverpool, Leeds and the surrounding rural areas. Cotton, commerce and kinship were the interlocking ties that connected the networks of people and commodities that flowed back and forth. In unravelling these tangled multi-generational relationships it is possible to trace the impact of the wealth generated by an early and lasting engagement with transatlantic slavery. The nature of the relationship between slavery and industrialisation has been long disputed. However, as Robert Bissett stated emphatically in 1805, the cotton economy relied 'chiefly' on 'the labour of Negroes'.[7] From early beginnings in the rural cottage industry, to the large-scale factories and mills, the industrialisation of cotton relied on the production of raw materials by enslaved workers across the New World. Cotton's global threads interwove the histories and peoples of Manchester, Africa, the Americas and the Caribbean, creating a legacy that stretches to the present day.

Family origins

The Hibberts' story has been described as 'literally one of rags to riches via the slave trade'.[8] Whilst it might be true that the family's origins were considerably less illustrious prior to their engagement with slavery, during the late seventeenth century the family was able to make a modest living and gradually improve their lot. Whether deliberate or a simple act of misremembering, the family annals contained a number of discrepancies that were suggestive of a more genteel ancestry. According to a manuscript in the possession of Letitia Hibbert (née Nembhard), the wife of Robert junior, her husband's great-grandfather was 'Robert Hibbert of Booth Hall near Blackley' who had 'married a Middleton Lady of the name of Ashton, great Aunt to the late Sir Ralph Ashton'.[9] Claiming the Ashtons of Middleton, a northern family who traced their roots back to the Norman conquerors, as a line of descent might have allowed the Hibberts to bolster their status through a connection to one of the oldest of the great northern families. It seems far more likely that Robert the eldest was married to Esther Pendleton of Blackley in 1679.[10] The addition 'of Booth Hall' to Robert the eldest's name similarly conferred a degree of respectability on this early forebear. The Hibberts were indeed connected to Booth Hall, but only through a marriage that occurred after Robert the eldest's death.[11]

A commercial correspondent of the Hibberts, the Jamaica planter Simon Taylor, noted in 1800 that prior to the expansion of their interests into Jamaica in the 1730s 'the Family were all weavers'.[12] This early connection to the cloth trade might well have provided them with some of the connections and knowledge necessary to work their way up through the mercantile ranks. There are very few details to provide a window into Robert the eldest and Esther's lives, an indication that their status was considerably lower than that of their family in the years to come. A description of the shifting patterns of life and labour in the linen trade in Manchester during the period is suggestive of the experiences of these early Hibberts. Prior to the 1690s, 'The manufacturers worked hard merely for a livelihood, without having accumulated any capital.'[13] After that period, 'they had begun to acquire little fortunes but worked as hard, lived as plain a manner as before, increasing their fortunes as well by economy as by moderate gains'. Confirming Fiennes's impression of Manchester in the early 1700s, the author went on to add that 'the traders had certainly got money beforehand, and began to build modern brick houses in place of those of wood and plaster'.

In 1684 Robert the eldest and Esther had a son named Robert the elder. Very little is known of his earlier life, though his profession was described as a 'linen draper'.[14] Within this trade he would have been engaged in 'buying and selling, putting out linen yarn [and] cotton wool to the spinning, winding, warping and weaving' as well as 'the calendaring of linen goods, the perching, dyeing and cutting of fustians'.[15] He might have 'employed direct wage labour, or, more often had the work done by independent finishers the fustian cutters, dyers, whittsters and calendermen, who were to be found in large numbers in Manchester and Salford'. The range of jobs associated with the sale and processing of cloth is an indication of the central importance of the industry to the local economy. The cloth trade in Manchester received a significant boost during Robert the elder's career, when the Government capitulated to the northern cotton merchants and successively implemented laws to increase the duties on foreign imports of linen and calico. The legislation effectively excluded Indian-produced cotton from the market, thus securing Manchester's share in the colonial trade. This culminated in the prohibition of all printed or dyed foreign calicos with the Calico Act of 1721, an Act that was not repealed until 1831 when free trade pressure finally began to break down the rule of monopoly.[16]

To consolidate the family enterprise and continue the family name, Robert the elder needed a solid match with a family of similar social standing. On 3 March 1708 he married Margaret Tetlow at St Mary's in Prestwich. There is some confusion surrounding Margaret's parentage; Burke's *Dictionary of the landed gentry* (1846) claimed that Margaret was the daughter of William Mills, Esq. of Ashby Hall in York.[17] The handwritten family history manuscript noted that Margaret's maiden name was 'Mills Tetlow', though the couple's marriage entry does not include this additional name.[18] It is more likely that Margaret was the daughter of Thomas Tetlow of Oldham.[19] Thomas was mentioned in a lawsuit involving Manchester linen draper Joshua Browne that took place in the mid-1680s. The document noted that he was 'of Chadderton, fustian maker'.[20] This would have placed him within a similar social and economic circle to the Hibberts, providing a fair union for both parties. In 1789 Robert junior's diary noted that 'I ride with William [his brother] round by the Old House, Chadderton' indicating he was familiar with the area.[21] As Catherine Hall and Leonore Davidoff have argued, family enterprise required the labour of both genders; amongst other responsibilities the production of children was a necessary part of the continuation of business and the expansion of social circles.[22] Robert the elder and Margaret had five boys and five girls. Their first child, Thomas senior, was born in 1710 and the last, a girl named Margaret, was born in 1736. Altogether Margaret was pregnant, nursing or caring for their young family for over twenty-six years. All of the Hibbert children survived to adulthood, providing their parents with both a significant financial burden, but also the promise of a trusted work force and potential marriage connections. The children did not fail to live up to expectations. Each of the sons, with the exception of Joseph, who died young, contributed to the development of what would become a transatlantic commercial empire. Meanwhile their daughters' marriages brought with them connections, land and increasing influence within the local community.

Becoming respectable

Robert the elder and Margaret lived at Stockfield House near Oldham, a residence which John Seed described as one of the 'fine houses and small estates within the orbit of Manchester'.[23] The move to Stockfield House placed the Hibberts within the burgeoning 'merchant gentry with links to both town and country, land and business, church and Dissent'. The linen drapers enjoyed social standing as 'heads of the trading community and the leaders of the court leet and the vestry'.[24] By the 1740s Robert the elder had achieved respectability and embraced the civic duties of a man of position. In 1744 he became a Constable of Manchester and by 1757 he sat on the jury for the Lancaster Spring Assize. These responsibilities indicated a level of trust from within the local community, particularly amongst the powerful vestry who appointed the Constable. In 1746 Robert the elder was invited to join the trustees of the Cross Street Chapel. The chapel had increasingly moved towards a Unitarian position under the Reverends Joseph Mottershead and John Seddon. Its 'founders and worthies' were dominated by professional men involved in commerce and manufacturing. Reflecting on the ways in which dissenters exerted influence, John Seed has argued that:

> Even where congregations of Rational Dissenters had not captured the corporation or parliamentary representation they were often capable of wielding considerable local power. In many larger urban centres, especially in northern and midland England, the chapels affiliated to Rational Dissent were centres of considerable wealth and influence.[25]

The Cross Street Chapel was one such centre. Dissenters received no state support to fund their chapels, so the trustees were an essential source of finance for the establishment and maintenance of places of worship. Seed explained that a chapel's elite 'generally constituted a self-selecting oligarchy of trustees, appointing the minister and, with their families, sitting in judgement on their preaching'.[26] The Hibberts, Touchets, Diggles, Bayleys, Philips, Jolleys, Heywoods and Robinsons were all dissenting merchant families for whom the chapel formed a social and religious hub. All of these families engaged in local manufactures and colonial trade, and all of them were intermarried. By forging marital alliances that capitalised effectively on their commercial success, the Hibberts became a central part of this network.

Much like the city of Manchester itself, the Cross Street Chapel was a space in which those with slaving interests and their abolitionist opponents coexisted. The interconnected group of congregants who participated in the business of slavery was distinctive and powerful. In later years they were also joined by members of the community involved

Figure 1 Cross Street Chapel, Manchester, 1835, in W. H. Shercliff, *Manchester: A short history of its development*

with the antislavery movement. This intermingling of positions complicates a traditional understanding of the relationship between abolitionism and non-conformity.[27] In the closing decades of the eighteenth century the chapel was closely associated with reformist and radical politics, including the campaign to end slavery. Links between the chapel and the history of abolition have been documented by Clare Midgley, who noted that 'The Bayley, Rigby, Grimshaw, Hardman and Mather families were all member of the influential Unitarian congregation of Cross Street Chapel' and that their wives and daughters were subscribers to the Manchester Abolition Society.[28] At the same time the trustees included men whose families profited both directly and indirectly from the system of slavery.

Commerce, religion and marriage

Robert the elder and Margaret's ascent into the merchant gentry in the 1740s coincided with a number of their children's marriages. This period saw a significant rise in the family's commercial prospects following the departure of the couple's eldest son, Thomas senior, to Jamaica in 1734. By the 1750s he had become firmly entrenched in the colonial elite, with his slave trading partnership considered to be amongst the most powerful on the island. Success in the colonies no doubt boosted the marriageability of his siblings at home. The first child to marry was Thomas senior's younger brother, Robert senior, who wed Abigail Scholey in 1743. Abigail was the daughter of William Scholey and his wife Mary Wilson of Wakefield, a thriving market town with a strong dissenting community. In later years Abigail was described by her son Robert junior as a 'Yorkshire heiress' in reference to an inheritance from her sister Ann Scholey, who died in 1787.[29] The couple started a family immediately, and their first son Thomas junior was born within a year of their marriage. Altogether they had six boys and seven girls, with one daughter, Ann, dying in infancy. Abigail, like her mother-in-law before her, spent well over twenty-two years either in confinement or dealing with very young children. The family shared a 'dwelling house' with warehouses attached to the property on Mount Street, a short distance from the family counting house at 49 King Street and from Cross Street, the site of their chapel.[30] The separation between home and work was still partial during this period and as the children grew up they would have witnessed the operations of the merchant house at first hand.

With his eldest brother away in Jamaica, Robert senior continued on the family firm in Manchester, with the help of his younger brother, Samuel senior. Unlike his father, who was described as a 'linen draper', Robert senior's profession was documented as 'West India merchant'.[31] The direction of trade was clear – the Hibberts were now firmly implicated in the web of commercial activities that made up the Caribbean slave economy. The merchant house thrived and by the 1760s they were supplying both checks and 'imitations of Indian goods' to the African Company for trade in Liverpool.[32] Expertise and knowledge of the cloth trade had deepened over time, so that in a letter of 1765 the Company advised the Hibberts to avoid green and yellows when producing material for the African market.[33] Business was doing well enough for Robert senior to be appointed to the Manchester Committee of Trade in 1774. For three decades the Manchester, Jamaica and London branches of the Hibberts' counting houses worked closely together. It was only in the early nineteenth century that the Manchester branch decided to break away, as Robert senior's son George noted in 1802, 'the Manchester business by their abruptly becoming merchant importers of their own account is greatly changed from what it was in my Father's day and cannot be followed up without great energies'.[34] Alongside commercial success, Robert senior adopted positions of civic power; he acted as the Constable of Manchester in 1759 and was listed among the Grand Jury of the Lancaster Assize in

1771. He was twice appointed as a trustee of the Cross Street Chapel, initially in 1778 and again in 1782. In this way Robert senior, like his father before him, was able to cultivate the forms of power available to dissenters during the period.

On 29 May 1751, Robert the elder and Margaret's third daughter, Margaret, wed Samuel Robinson. Samuel was listed as a 'chapman' on the marriage register.[35] The couple lived together in Ardwick, a small village just outside Manchester which was popular with the mercantile community, who commuted to the city. The couple had a son, Thomas, and a daughter, Margaret. Whilst very few details of Margaret's life have been recorded, her brother Thomas is well documented. He was sent to be educated aged fourteen at Warrington Academy, a dissenting educational institution. He went on to become 'A respectable merchant and most estimable man' and acted as a trustee of the Cross Street Chapel continuously between 1782 and 1831.[36] He purchased a magnificent pile at Crumpsall called Woodlands, 'set in 27 acres of estate, with drawing rooms, a large ball room, a library, seven bedrooms, substantial cellars, and servants' quarters, coach houses, stable'.[37] He lived there with his wife, Sophia Caroline Oates, the daughter of George Oates of Low Hall in Leeds and Sarah Jolley. The Jolleys were another mercantile dissenting family with close connections to the Cross Street Chapel. Sophia's brother, George William Oates, reinforced the ties with the Hibbert family by marrying Robert senior's daughter Mary in 1788. Three of their sons were involved in the slavery business: George Hibbert Oates and Hibbert Oates were both plantations owners and attorneys, their brother Robert Oates was captain of the West India ship *Wellington*.[38] In 1816 Thomas and Sophia's daughter Sophia Anne married Sir Benjamin Heywood, a powerful banker, Member of Parliament for Lancashire and trustee of the Cross Street Chapel.[39] Although Heywood's family had made significant investments in the slave trade in the eighteenth century, despite both his own and his wife's familial links to the slavery business, he spoke out against the practice in the 1830s.[40]

In 1757 Robert the elder and Margaret's fourth daughter, Elizabeth, married Nathaniel Philips of Heath House. The two families shared a number of overlapping interests and remained close, with a series of marriages over several generations. In 1747 Nathaniel and his brother John founded the partnership of J. and N. Philips & Company. As Alfred P. Wadsworth and Julia de Lacy Mann have noted:

> Few families have touched the life of Manchester at so many points during the last hundred and seventy years as that represented by the firm of J. and N. Philips and Company, the great merchanting and manufacturing house ... To write its history would be to epitomise the intense and

varied activity of the years of the Industrial Revolution, when members of the family were engaged simultaneously in every branch of Manchester trade – silk, smallwares, fustians, checks, cotton dealing, hatting; later in West India merchanting, cotton spinning, power-loom weaving; and, still later, as general Manchester and London warehousemen.[41]

It is not clear if there was any business connection between Thomas senior in Jamaica and his brother-in-law Nathaniel Philips. Thomas senior departed for Jamaica over twenty years prior to his sister's marriage, though the two men were close enough for Thomas senior to leave Philips a mourning ring in his will.[42] The families certainly enjoyed socialising together, as a diary entry by Thomas senior's nephew George demonstrated:

> My Brother Toms Birth Day My Aunt and Uncle. P. [Philips] My Aunt R. [Robinson] and Mrs. Taylor, Miss Shore and My Uncle Sam and My Cousin Peg [Robinson] All met here and we Celebrated the Day by a Dance after Supper which Lasted till 12 o'Clock and then Parted, My Father Perform'd Wonders in a Minuet with Miss Shore.[43]

The Philips were influential members of both the Cross Street Chapel in Manchester and the Stand Chapel in Prestwich. They were politically active before and after the restrictions were lifted on dissenters. The vocal support for political reform expressed by the powerful merchants of the Cross Street Chapel led to an attack in 1792 by a 'church and king' mob.[44] Nathaniel and Elizabeth's grandson Mark Philips, a free trader and an abolitionist, went on to become the first Member of Parliament for Manchester following the 1832 Reform Act. The couple had both urban and rural residences; a country house called The Dales at Stand and a town house in Manchester at 10 St. James's Square. The Philips's ancestral home, Heath House, was a grand residence in Tean, Staffordshire. Tean was also the site of their loomhouse, bleach and dye-works and tape manufacturing businesses. Heath House was inherited by Elizabeth and Nathaniel's first son, John, after the death of his uncle in 1813. Cousin marriage was a common practice among wealthy merchants and the landed classes as it allowed property to circulate within the family.[45] In 1783 John married his cousin Margaret Robinson of Crumpsall. To seal the bonds of family two of their sons eventually went on to marry their Hibbert cousins Margaret and Letitia, the daughters of Elizabeth's nephew William.

The last of Robert the elder and Margaret's children to marry were Esther and Sarah. Both women married much later in life and neither were first wives to their husbands. In 1761 Esther, aged forty-seven, married Samuel Bayley, a linen draper, check manufacturer and notable worthy of the Cross Street Chapel. The Bayleys were a landed family and owned an estate at Hope Hall, Eccles. Through Samuel Bayley the Hibberts were connected to the Touchets, Samuel's sister Sarah having married John Touchet in 1734. John and his brother Samuel were heavily involved with cotton, West India commerce and the slave trade. Samuel represented Liverpool as a member of the governing body of the Company of Merchants trading to Africa between 1753 and 1756. The brothers were partners in around twenty West India ships.[46] His success in the cotton trade was such that 'he was suspected by the Manchester manufacturers of seeking a monopoly'.[47] The Bayleys were also related to the Diggles – the family that Esther's sister Sarah married into in 1761 aged forty-five. She was the third wife of Thomas Diggles of Booth Hall in Blackley. The Diggles, like the Hibberts, were involved in various aspects of the slave economy and were also trustees of the Cross Street Chapel.[48]

Mercantile sons

Robert senior and Abigail's thirteen children were instrumental for the future of the Hibberts' burgeoning transatlantic business. Four of their sons – Thomas junior, John junior, Robert junior and William – were sent out to Jamaica to work for their uncle, Thomas senior. The remaining sons – Samuel junior and George – were employed in the London counting house established by their brother Thomas junior on his return. Eventually Thomas junior, Robert junior, Samuel junior, George and William would form a variety of partnerships among themselves in both Manchester and London. Robert senior and Abigail schooled their boys in readiness to take their place in the family business. Education within the dissenting community was taken seriously and some of the academies which developed gained a reputation for academic excellence. In 1759, aged fifteen, Thomas junior left Manchester to be schooled at Newington Green in London.[49] It is likely that he attended the academy set up and run by the radical reformer the Reverend James Burgh. Newington Green was one of *the* great centres of dissent during the period; Richard Price had moved to the area just a year prior to Thomas junior's arrival to minister at the Newington Green Unitarian church. Price served a distinctly mercantile congregation which included West India families like the Vaughans and the Boddingtons, both of whom became known to the Hibberts through their commercial dealings in London in later years.[50]

After leaving London in 1762, Thomas junior went to Liverpool to serve an apprenticeship. By this time Liverpool had overtaken London and Bristol to become the country's premier slaving port. Close to his family in Manchester, this was a natural location for Thomas junior to learn his trade. For a young man in his position 'the ideal apprenticeship in the eighteenth century provided instruction in trade, accounts and languages'.[51] Trainee merchants might be found 'keeping accounts for their principles, attending to customers' or 'busy at the quayside keeping tally of incoming and outgoing cargoes'.[52] Apprenticeships were normally paid for by the apprentice's family, with prices varying from £40 to £450 depending on the location and the reputation of the merchant.[53] Discussing the prospect of finding an apprenticeship for his nephew George Hibbert Oates in 1807, Robert junior gave a fascinating description of how the practice worked:

> The preference he gives Liverpool over Manchester, deserves more attention, because, at the latter Place, a very considerable premium is required with a Boy: which I understand from his Letter, is not the case at Liverpool. As to wages, I never knew any thing of the kind given or expected, during the continuance of Apprenticeship; nor is it usual now to board them, as was the case when my Bro Tom served Mr. Rumbold. Tom Markland gave (I believe) £500, and served Joseph Booth five years ... Our Friend Mrs Jackson ... has a Son in a Compting House there with whom she paid a very considerable Fee and he pays his own Board Lodging etc. Notwithstanding which she told us he was called out of the Compting House the other Day by his Master to hold his Horse for some minutes at the Door, a circumstance which raised his Creole Blood and was nearly occasioning a Rupture with his Master.[54]

Treatment of apprentices varied, however, and those of a higher social standing could expect better conditions, even if on occasion their pride was bruised with requests to undertake menial tasks. Thomas junior was apprenticed to Thomas Rumbold of Hanover Street, a merchant who was among the top fifty slave traders in Liverpool.[55] Between 1754 and 1783 Rumbold was documented as having an interest in seventy-nine transatlantic slave voyages either on his own account or in partnership with other merchants.[56] The enslaved people were sold in America and the British, French and Spanish Caribbean. Henry Laurens, a powerful South Carolina slave trader, was one of Rumbold's correspondents. Rumbold's business focused heavily on Jamaica, with between 40 and 50 per cent of his slave sales concentrated on the island.[57] This connection was beneficial for both Rumbold and the Hibberts, given that Thomas junior's uncle was one of the leading slave factors in Kingston. Rumbold vouched on several occasions for John Boyd, a sea captain whom the Hibberts employed regularly.[58] Details from Rumbold's slaving enterprise reveal the connections between other industrial areas in Britain. In 1761 he was the managing partner of the Liverpool ship *Rumbold*, a slaving vessel destined for Angola. Rumbold arranged for 'heavy Angola muskets' to be purchased from gunsmith Thomas Jordan of Birmingham to trade for enslaved people.[59] The ship eventually disembarked 287 enslaved Africans at Basse Terre in Guadeloupe.[60] Following his apprenticeship Thomas junior left for Jamaica in 1766 to join his uncle Thomas senior's merchant house. In time he was joined by his younger brothers John junior, Robert junior and William.

The younger Hibbert sons Samuel junior and George never visited Jamaica. In 1765 George, then aged eight, was sent to be educated by the Reverend Bartholomew Booth at his newly opened school in the Old Church Yard near the quayside in Liverpool.[61] Given the school's proximity to the docks George would have seen all the comings and goings of a thriving port. Perhaps he might have visited his brother Thomas junior at Rumbold's merchant house, a short walk away on Hanover Street. Liverpool's connection to the slave trade was embedded in the physical landscape; many of its buildings and street names made reference to the trade which had transformed the city. Sailors, merchants and bankers crowded the coffee houses, exchanging shipping news. Advertisements in the local newspapers documented the occasional sale of enslaved people, shackles and chains in these coffee houses, one of which – the Merchants' Coffee House – was adjacent to the Old Church Yard where George went to school.[62]

The school differed from the dissenting academy his brother attended in that Booth was both an Anglican clergyman and had received an Oxford education, although he did not graduate. Booth tailored his curriculum to appeal specifically to the merchant classes. An advertisement in *Williamson's Advertiser* on 7 January 1765 described the educational fare on offer:

> [A]n Academy for the Instruction of Youth in the following useful and polite branches of learning viz. The English Grammar, the Latin, Greek, French & German Languages, Writing in all the different hands, Geometry, Perspective, Arithmetic, the Use of the Globes, Geography, Navigation, the Italian Method of Bookkeeping, Drawing & Music in the Spring, Summer & Autumn Quarters. The Art of Fencing between the hours of twelve and one (during which time Gentlemen will not be permitted to stay in the Rooms). Ladies may be taught Drawing, Writing, Arithmetic, & Geography.[63]

A grasp of languages was essential for business; Europe was still the dominant trading partner for Britain and colonial trade was a cosmopolitan affair. Competency in both European and classical languages was also a marker of refinement. The inclusion of music in the curriculum is demonstrative of the role of culture in defining mercantile gentility. For aspiring parents these attributes would be a necessary acquisition if their child was to be taken seriously within elite social, commercial and political circles. Booth offered subjects like mathematics, navigation and bookkeeping, all of which were vital for the training of prospective merchants. The combination of 'useful and polite branches of learning' is indicative of an educational institution designed to facilitate a middle-class desire for both practical training and polished accomplishment.

In the summer of 1766 Booth's academy removed to the illustrious surroundings of Woolton Hall. The new location was less than an hour's ride to Liverpool, making it an ideal setting for a school dominated by the children of the commercial classes. The move made Booth a neighbour of Bamber Gascoyne, a Member of Parliament and the Board of Trade who owned nearby Childwall Hall. He sent his children to be educated with Booth; two of his sons – Bamber and Isaac – went on to become Members of Parliament, joining their school alumnus George in the parliamentary defence of the slave trade in 1807.[64] Booth realised the potential for attracting the children of colonists to his school, many of whom regarded an English education as vastly superior to what was on offer in the empire. To this end he took out advertisements in the *Virginia Gazette* in 1766.[65] He evidently succeeded and one 'Otway Bird, West Indian' was listed as attending the academy in 1774.

It was within this atmosphere of mercantile refinement, with its grand country house setting and well-connected young pupils, that George took his first steps towards mercantile manhood. His diary indicated some hostility towards his schoolmaster and the women who helped to fund and run the academy, Mary Valens and Anna Bardsley. Writing on 26 May 1773 he recalled that:

> In my walks this day met Joseph Cheetham (a school fellow towards the end of my time at Woolton and who attended Booth up to London). I enquired very particularly after Booth's affairs and found that he either did or should have set out for America the 1st of this month with his two whores.[66]

Despite George's adolescent venom, his nephew James Heywood Markland believed that in his boyhood 'A love of letters had, however, been implanted in him.'[67] George went on to become one of the most powerful Jamaica merchants in London, as well as an avid collector of art, books and botanical specimens. Booth's institution has been described as 'a place of enlightened liberal learning' which delivered a 'stimulating curriculum for an elite.'[68] George's education provided him with the foundation necessary to take his place as the most important figure within his generation of Hibberts.

Marriageable daughters

Abigail and Robert senior's daughters also played a role in furthering the commercial affairs of the counting house. Their marriages and subsequent children ensured that the Hibbert family enterprise was supplied with future personnel. The first to marry was Elizabeth, who wed Robert Markland in 1776. Markland was a check and fustian manufacturer and heir to an estate at Pemberton, near Wigan.[69] He was well connected; his brother Edward was part of the partnership Markland, Cookson & Fawcett, the owners of the largest cotton mill in Leeds.[70] The couple resided at Mabfield, just outside of Manchester, raising four sons, two of whom became involved in the West India trade in different capacities. Their second son, Robert Markland junior, was described as 'formerly of the island of Jamaica' in his obituary of 1825.[71] During his time there he had entered into a slave trading partnership with his uncle Robert junior and the planter Simon Taylor. Robert Markland junior's uncle George made reference to his nephew's activities in a letter to Taylor which stated that 'Tom Hibbert would buy the Negroes if they would voluntarily submit to be renamed and he has given some instructions to Robert Markland'.[72] Robert Markland junior also acted as the Hibberts' attorney until his departure from Jamaica in 1808 as a result of ill health.[73] Robert Markland junior's younger brother, James Heywood Markland, trained as a solicitor in Manchester before he moved to London and joined the legal partnership of Markland & Wright. The firm acted as solicitors for the Society of West India Planters and Merchants. James Heywood became an important member of the London West India interest. He took a leading role in the Literary Committee set up to distribute proslavery propaganda during the abolition campaigns. As a committed bibliophile Markland was 'ideally placed to procure for the West Indians the services of booksellers and publishers. He was, for example, the West Indians' point of contact with both John Murray and William Blackwood.'[74] As the treasurer of the Society for the Propagation of the Gospel in Foreign Parts he was awarded slavery compensation for the Codrington estate in Barbados.[75] He acted as a trustee and executor for his uncle Robert junior and also received compensation for his plantations.

In 1780 Robert senior and Abigail's eldest daughter Margaret married Thomas Greg. The Gregs and the Hibberts moved in similar circles in both Manchester and London. Margaret's family had a property on King Street, the same street as Thomas's brother Samuel's residence, though it is not clear which set of connections brought the two young people together. Thomas was one of fourteen children born to Thomas Greg senior and his wife Elizabeth Hyde. The Gregs were a Presbyterian Scottish family who had emigrated to Ulster in 1715. They were involved in the transatlantic trade, exporting Irish salted provisions, butter and linen to the West Indies and America from Belfast. Thomas's uncle John also owned plantations in Dominica. The Hydes were a dissenting Manchester family with ties to the Cross Street Chapel. Elizabeth's father Samuel Hyde had left England for Ireland and operated within the linen and provisions trade. In 1768 Thomas and his younger brother Samuel went to England; the former set off for London to make his living and the latter departed for Manchester to reside with their uncle Robert Hyde, who had adopted Samuel and made him his heir. As a second son and without his uncle's financial backing Thomas could not expect a significant inheritance. According to Thomas's nephew, Robert Hyde Greg, his uncle was fond of saying that 'he owed nothing to his family but an indifferent education'.[76] Thomas made his way as a marine insurance broker. The expansion of colonial trade brought with it a boom for the nascent insurance industry. Both the slave trade and the trade in slave-produced commodities were high-risk ventures in which the ship owners and investors shouldered most of the financial burden of the voyage. As a result the insurance industry developed to provide some form of protection. By 1772 Thomas was recorded as a member of Lloyd's. With family and kin involved in various aspects of transatlantic shipping and trade Thomas benefited from a ready-made portfolio of clients. Robert Hyde Greg detailed his uncle's early years, writing that:

> [B]y sundry letters he appears to have started on his own account as Insurance Broker, & Underwriter in 1772. He commenced with many good connections, his Father's House of Thos & John Greg of Belfast, Robt & Nath'l Hyde of Manchester, & Philips, Hibberts & others ... The Business was first carried out in Lloyds Coffee House, then Old Bethlehem Broad St, & finally Warnford Court, Threadneedle Street.[77]

As he grew his business Thomas branched out from brokering to underwriting and 'also general London money business, shares, loans'. Robert noted that 'when my uncle retired' his partnership 'was making £10,000/£12,000, a year'. Thomas's chosen profession undoubtedly added to the attraction of a marital alliance between the Gregs and the Hibberts.

Over the years the Gregs strengthened their financial, social and marital ties to the Hibberts. Thomas provided insurance for a number of their clients and in 1801 he was formally invited to join a new co-partnership with them; however, he turned them down.[78] Not only did Thomas work with the Hibberts, he also acquired a property at

25 Broad Street, the same street that his wife's brother George was living on in 1785. Thomas went on to purchase the Coles estate in Hertfordshire in the mid-1780s. The property was in the same county as Munden, the estate which formed part of the inheritance of George's wife Elizabeth. Thomas's younger brother Samuel was also well acquainted with the Hibberts, investing in land speculation with his sister-in-law's brother William.[79] Samuel was the founder of Quarry Bank mill.[80] The mill represented a different but intimately linked facet of the slavery business. Using slave-produced cotton, Samuel revolutionised the manufacturing of cotton through the use of water power. Sven Beckert has written that 'Greg's factory was embedded within globe-spanning networks – and would eventually spark around the world far greater changes than Greg could comprehend'.[81] Sending finished cotton pieces across the empire and beyond, Quarry Bank mill combined the systems of slavery, capitalism and industrialisation altering the way people worked and lived for centuries to come. To seal the bonds within the next generations, Samuel's son, the manufacturer and economist Robert Hyde Greg, married the granddaughter of Nathaniel and Elizabeth Philips (née Hibbert) in 1824.

Conclusion

The network of Manchester families integrated into the system of Atlantic commerce during the eighteenth century is crucial for understanding the development of the city into the 'Cottonopolis' of the nineteenth century. The building of business connections and markets allowed these families to operate at a local and international level. Their intimate stories form part of the history of the empire of cotton. Manchester was central to the system of slavery, not just within the British context, but globally in the wake of the abolition of slavery in the Caribbean. As Marika Sherwood has pointed out, the proportion of slave-grown raw cotton from the USA unloaded in Liverpool 'rose from c. 48 per cent in 1811 to 78 per cent in 1851'.[82] This raw material was destined for the mills and factories of Manchester and the surrounding areas. In the 1860s, despite the severe deprivation caused to themselves and their families, some Lancashire cotton workers agreed to support the Union blockade of slave-produced cotton from the Southern States during the American Civil War.[83] On 19 January 1863 President Abraham Lincoln wrote to the 'working men of Manchester' to thank them for their sacrifice. He lauded their principled position as 'an instance of sublime Christian heroism which has not been surpassed in any age or in any country'.[84] This formed part of a process by which the city's role as a beneficiary of slavery was displaced by its reputation as an abolitionist stronghold. In 1919 a statue of Lincoln was unveiled at Platt Fields in Manchester, before being moved in 1986 to its current location in Lincoln Square. The plinth was engraved with extracts from Lincoln's letter. Alan Rice has written that the statue 'narrates a key tale of transatlantic radicalism ... industrial workers in support of the overthrow of slavery'.[85] The story of struggle against the oppression of class and race presents a version of local history and identity that sits more comfortably than the tale of exploitation and profit which the Hibberts represent.

In 2007 Manchester reappraised its historic connection to the slavery business.[86] The public history project 'Revealing Histories' offered a critical re-evaluation of the accepted narrative of abolitionism. Drawing on the collections of eight different museums and galleries in the region, the project told a much more nuanced story of Manchester's relationship with the system of slavery. Central to that story was the history of cotton. The website stated that 'Some of the wealth from the region's links to slavery has benefited the public as philanthropists, such as the Greg and the Lees families, donated money and artworks to local cultural institutions such as Manchester Art Gallery, Gallery Oldham and the Whitworth Art Gallery.'[87] To these names might be added the Hibberts, who were also involved in projects of improvement. From paying for the upgrade of the roads,[88] to their support of the Manchester Literary and Philosophical Society, the family were fully immersed in the civic spiritedness expected of the mercantile elite.[89] As the 'Revealing Histories' project demonstrated, profiteering from, and resistance to, slavery coexisted in Manchester. Indeed, it also coexisted within some families; if we examine the extended Hibbert network, it is possible to find abolitionist advocates like Hannah Lightbody and Mark Philips within their ranks. Manchester's Atlantic merchants were bound together by ties of business and kinship, their endeavours representing the 'local spark' from which 'industrial capitalism would emerge and spread its wings'.[90] The story of Britain's 'Cottonopolis' is a global history of exploitation and coercion which reshaped society along the fault lines of both race and class. The great cotton merchants of Manchester have been venerated as the embodiment of Britain's entrepreneurial genius. At the vanguard of the Industrial Revolution, their 'invention, sagacity, enterprise, skill', as Bissett wrote, transformed Manchester's fortunes.[91] The systemic violence and suffering that underpinned that transformation was felt by both the enslaved Africans who laboured in the fields to produce the raw materials, and also by the urban poor in Britain who worked in the factories to manufacture the cloth. It was within this transatlantic circuit of exploitation that the Hibbert family's business empire was forged and flourished.

Notes

1 Jerom Murch, *Memoir of Robert Hibbert, founder of the Hibbert Trust: With a sketch of its history* (Bath: William Lewis, 1874), p. 5.
2 Sven Beckert, *Empire of cotton: A new history of global capitalism* (London: Allen Lane, 2014), p. x.
3 Eric Williams, *Capitalism and slavery* (London: Andre Deutsch, 1944), p. 71.
4 'The city and parish of Manchester: Introduction', in William Farrer and J. Brownbill (eds), *A history of the county of Lancaster*, vol. IV (London: Constable, 1911), pp. 174–87. www.british-history.ac.uk/vch/lancs/vol4/pp174-187 [accessed 14 July 2017].
5 John Seed, 'The role of Unitarianism in the formation of liberal culture, 1775–1851: A social history' (PhD thesis, University of Hull, 1981), p. 70.
6 Nicholas Rogers, 'Money, land and lineage: The big bourgeoisie of Hanoverian London', *Social History*, 4:3 (1979), p. 443.
7 Robert Bissett, *The history of the negro slave trade, in its connection with the commerce and prosperity of the West Indies, and the wealth and power of the British empire*, vol. II (London: W. McDowall, 1805), p. 342. For historiographical discussions of the issue see Joseph Inikori, *Africans and the industrial revolution in England: A study in international trade and economic development* (Cambridge: Cambridge University Press, 2002). See also Stephen D. Behrendt, Maxine Berg, William G. Clarence Smith, Henk den Heijer, Pat Hudson, John Singleton, Nuala Zahadieh, 'Reviews of Joseph Inikori, *Africans and the Industrial Revolution in England: A Study in International Trade and Economic Development*', *International Journal of Maritime History*, 15:2 (2003), pp. 279–329. The relationship between cotton, slavery, industry and capitalism has seen an upsurge in scholarly interest in the American context: Edward Baptist, *The half has never been told: Slavery and making of American capitalism* (New York: Basic Books, 2014); Beckert, *Empire of cotton*; Walter Johnson, *River of dark dreams: Slavery and empire in the cotton kingdom* (Cambridge MA: Harvard University Press, 2013). These links have been highlighted through the project 'Global Cotton Connections', which explored slavery's links to industrial cotton heritage sites in England. www.nottingham.ac.uk/isos/news/global-cotton-connections.aspx [accessed 18 July 2017].
8 Nicholas Radburn, 'Guinea factors, slave sales, and the profits of the transatlantic slave trade in late eighteenth-century Jamaica: The case of John Tailyour', *William and Mary Quarterly*, 72:2 (2015), p. 283.
9 'Memorandums respecting the families of the Hibberts of Booth Hall, Lancashire, and of Malpas in Cheshire', Jamaican Family Search Genealogy Research Library (JFSGRL). www.jamaicanfamilysearch.com/Members/bcarib28.htm [accessed 18 July 2017].
10 Sir Thomas Baker, *Memorials of a dissenting chapel, its foundation and worthies; being a sketch of the rise of non-conformity in Manchester and the erection of the chapel in Cross Street, with notices of its ministers and trustees* (Manchester: Johnson and Rawson, 1884), p. 85.
11 John Booker, *A history of the ancient chapel of Blackley* (Manchester: John Simms, 1854), pp. 28–59.
12 Radburn, 'Guinea factors', p. 283.
13 John Aiken, *A description of the country from thirty to forty miles around Manchester* (London: J. Stockdale, 1795), pp. 181–2.
14 Baker, *Memorials*, p. 85.
15 Alfred P. Wadsworth and Julia De Lacy Mann, *The cotton trade and industrial Lancashire, 1600–1780* (Manchester: Manchester University Press, 1965), p. 78.
16 Michael James, *From smuggling to cotton kings: The Greg story* (Cirencester: Memoirs, 2010), p. 16.
17 John Burke, *A genealogical and heraldic dictionary of the landed gentry of Great Britain & Ireland: A to L* (London: Henry Colburn, 1846), p. 569.
18 Manchester Libraries, Information and Archives, L160/1/1/4, no. 589, Manchester, England, Baptisms, Marriages and Burials, 1541–1812, p. 69.

19 Baker, *Memorials*, p. 85
20 Wadsworth and Mann, *The cotton trade*, p. 80.
21 HFAC, Diary of Robert Hibbert junior, 20 November 1789.
22 Leonore Davidoff and Catherine Hall, *Family fortunes: Men and women of the English middle class, 1780–1850* (London: Routledge, 2002), pp. xxxv–xxxix.
23 John Seed, 'Gentlemen dissenters: The social and political meanings of rational dissent in the 1770s and 1780s', *Historical Journal*, 28:2 (1985), p. 303.
24 Wadsworth and Mann, *The cotton trade*, p. 73.
25 John Seed, '"A set of men powerful enough in many things": Rational dissent and political opposition in England, 1770–1790', in Knud Haakonssen (ed.), *Enlightenment and religion: Rational dissent in eighteenth-century Britain* (Cambridge: Cambridge University Press, 2006), p. 147.
26 *Ibid.*, p. 149.
27 David Turley, *The culture of English antislavery, 1780–1860* (London: Routledge, 1991), pp. 113–21.
28 Clare Midgley, *Women against slavery: The British campaigns, 1780–1870* (London: Routledge, 1992), p. 19.
29 JFSGRL, Transcription of the Hibbert family Bible made by Mabel Nembhard. http://jamaicanfamilysearch.com/ [accessed 20 July 2017].
30 Will of Robert Hibbert, quoted in Vere Langford Oliver, *Caribbeana: Being miscellaneous papers relating to the history, genealogy, topography, and antiquities of the British West Indies*, vol. IV (London: Mitchell Hughes and Clarke, 1919), p. 195.
31 Baker, *Memorials*, p. 89.
32 Williams, *Capitalism and slavery*, p. 71.
33 Letter from the African Company to the Messrs. Hibbert of Manchester, 15 August 1765, quoted in Wadsworth and Mann, *The cotton trade*, p. 231.
34 Institute of Commonwealth Studies, Senate House Library, London, Taylor and Vaneck-Arcedekne Papers (ICS/SHL/TVAP), M965/17/52, Letter from George Hibbert to Simon Taylor, 3 March 1802.
35 www.lan-opc.org.uk/Manchester/Ardwick/stthomas/marriages_1742-1753.html [accessed 20 July 2017].
36 'Thomas Robinson c.1757–c.1831', Dissenting Academies Online. https://dissacad.english.qmul.ac.uk/sample1.php?detail=people&personid=2111 [accessed 20 July 2017].
37 Seed, 'Gentlemen dissenters', p. 303.
38 Joseph Foster, *Pedigree of the county families of Yorkshire*, vol. II (London: W. Wilfred Head, 1874).
39 'Benjamin Heywood (1793–1865)', History of Parliament. www.historyofparliamentonline.org/volume/1820-1832/member/heywood-benjamin-1793-1865 [accessed 20 July 2017].
40 http://revealinghistories.org.uk/how-did-money-from-slavery-help-develop-greater-manchester/people/the-heywood-family-of-manchester.html [accessed 17 January 2019].
41 Wadsworth and Mann, *The cotton trade*, p. 288. Another reference to the partnership's West India interests can be found in Williams, *Capitalism and slavery*, p. 156.
42 Will of Thomas Hibbert senior, quoted in Oliver, *Caribbeana*, p. 193.
43 JFSGRL, Diary of George Hibbert, 11 January 1773. www.jamaicanfamilysearch.com/Members/bcarib28.htm [accessed 21 July 2017].
44 John Seed, 'A set of men', p. 148.
45 Nancy Fix Anderson, 'Cousin marriage in Victorian England', *Journal of Family History*, 11:3 (1986), pp. 285–6.
46 Williams, *Capitalism and slavery*, p. 70.
47 Alan J. Kidd, 'Touchet, Samuel (c. 1705–1773)', *Oxford dictionary of national biography* (Oxford: Oxford University Press, 2004). www.oxforddnb.com/view/article/57578 [accessed 8 December 2011].
48 Williams, *Capitalism and slavery*, p. 71.

49 JFSGRL, Manuscript book kept by Letitia Hibbert (*née* Nembhard). Entries recorded as the 'Annals of T. H.' in the hand of Thomas junior. www.jamaicanfamilysearch.com/Members/bcarib28.htm [accessed 25 July 2017].
50 For an excellent discussion of the intersections between proslavery, abolition and dissent see Anthony Page, '"A species of slavery": Richard Price's rational dissent and antislavery', *Slavery & Abolition*, 32:1 (2011), pp. 53–73; Anthony Page, 'Rational dissent, Enlightenment and abolition of the British slave trade', *Historical Journal*, 54:3 (2011), pp. 741–72.
51 Richard George Wilson, *Gentleman merchants: The merchant community in Leeds, 1700–1830* (Manchester: Manchester University Press, 1971), p. 63.
52 Robert M. Andrews, *Lay activism and the high church movement of the late eighteenth century: The life and thought of William Stevens, 1732–1807* (Leiden: Brill, 2015), p. 78.
53 *Ibid.*, p. 79.
54 GA/BFDP, D1799/C153, Letter from Robert Hibbert junior to Mary Oates, 5 May 1807.
55 Kenneth Morgan, 'Liverpool's dominance in the British slave trade, 1740–1807', in David Richardson, Anthony Tibbles and Suzanne Schwartz (eds), *Liverpool and transatlantic slavery* (Liverpool: Liverpool University Press, 2007), p. 29.
56 Transatlantic Slave Trade Voyages. www.slavevoyages.org/voyage/database [accessed 26 July 2017].
57 Morgan, 'Liverpool's dominance in the British slave trade', p. 29.
58 Phillip M. Hamer, George C. Rogers Jr. and Peggy J. Wehage (eds), *The papers of Henry Laurens*, vol. II (Columbia: University of South Carolina Press, 1970), p. 338.
59 Peter Earle, *The Earles of Liverpool: A Georgian merchant dynasty* (Liverpool: Liverpool University Press), p. 110.
60 Transatlantic Slave Trade Voyages. www.slavevoyages.org/voyage/90831/variables [accessed 26 July 2017].
61 Maurice Whitehead, '"Not Inferior to any in this part of our Kingdom": Woolton Academy and the English career of the Reverend Bartholomew Booth, schoolmaster', *Transactions of the Historic Society of Lancashire and Cheshire*, 142 (1992), p. 27.
62 Peter Fryer, *Staying power: The history of black people in Britain* (London: Pluto Press, 1984), p. 59.
63 Whitehead, 'Woolton Academy', pp. 26–7.
64 List of pupils by John Hill *c.* 1774, quoted *ibid.*, pp. 42–3.
65 *Ibid.*, p. 29.
66 George Hibbert's diary for 1773, quoted *ibid.*, p. 43.
67 J. H. Markland, *A sketch of the life and character of George Hibbert Esq., F.R.S., S.A., and L.S.* (London, 1837), p. 3.
68 Whitehead, 'Woolton Academy', p. 46.
69 W. P. Courtney, 'Markland, James Heywood (1788–1864)', rev. Bernard Nurse, *Oxford dictionary of national biography* (Oxford: Oxford University Press, 2004). www.oxforddnb.com/view/article/18073 [accessed 14 January 2012].
70 Stanley D. Chapman, 'Fixed capital formation in the British cotton industry, 1770–1815', *Economic History Review*, 23:2 (1970), p. 239.
71 *The Gentleman's Magazine*, 137 (London: John Nichols and Son, 1825), p. 185.
72 ICS/SHL/TVAP, M965/17/71, Letter from George Hibbert to Simon Taylor, London, 3 December 1806.
73 ICS/SHL/TVAP, M965/17/81, Letter from George Hibbert to Simon Taylor, London, 7 July 1808.
74 Michael Taylor, 'Conservative political economy and the problem of colonial slavery, 1823–33' (PhD thesis, University of Cambridge, 2015), p. 40, quoted in Legacies of British Slave-ownership database. www.ucl.ac.uk/lbs/person/view/45822 [accessed 4 July 2018].
75 'James Heywood Markland', Legacies of British Slave-ownership database. www.ucl.ac.uk/lbs/person/view/45822 [accessed 19 January 2019].

76 Robert Hyde Greg, quoted in James, *From smuggling to cotton kings*, p. 32.
77 Robert Hyde Greg, quoted *ibid.*, p. 33.
78 HFAC, Diary of Robert Hibbert junior, 10 October–27 December 1801.
79 James, *From smuggling to cotton kings*, p. 30.
80 For a detailed history see Mary B. Rose, *The Gregs of Quarry Bank mill: The rise and decline of a family firm, 1750–1914* (Cambridge: Cambridge University Press, 1986).
81 Beckert, *Empire of cotton*, p. 57.
82 Marika Sherwood, *After abolition: Britain and the slave trade since 1807* (London: I. B. Tauris, 2007), p. 46.
83 For historiographical debates on cotton workers' attitudes towards slavery see Mary Ellison, *Support for secession, Lancashire and the American Civil War* (Chicago: University of Chicago Press, 1972); Philip Foner, *British labour and the American Civil War* (New York: Holmes & Meier, 1981).
84 http://revealinghistories.org.uk/the-american-civil-war-and-the-lancashire-cotton-famine/places/statue-of-abraham-lincoln-lincoln-square-manchester.html [accessed 27 July 2017].
85 Alan Rice, *Creating memorials, building identities: The politics of memory in the Black Atlantic* (Liverpool: Liverpool University Press, 2012), pp. 94–5.
86 For a discussion of some of the different museological interventions that took place in Manchester during 2007, see *ibid.*, pp. 55–80.
87 http://revealinghistories.org.uk/how-did-money-from-slavery-help-develop-greater-manchester.html [accessed 27 July 2017].
88 Mary Clementia Hibbert-Ware, *The life and correspondence of Samuel Hibbert Ware* (Manchester: J. E. Cornish, 1882), p. 51.
89 *Memoirs of the Literary and Philosophical Society of Manchester*, vol. I (London: R. Bickerstaff, 1805), pp. xii, ix.
90 Beckert, *Empire of cotton*, p. 60.
91 Bissett, *The history of the negro slave trade*, vol. II, p. 342.

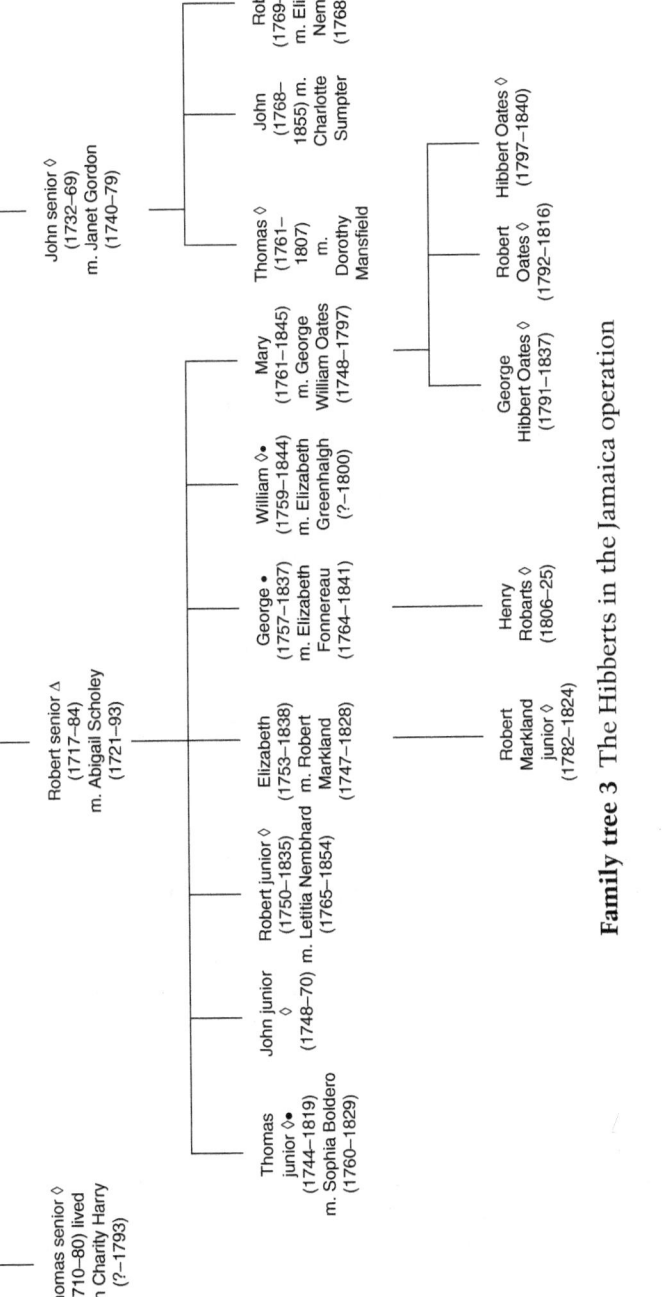

Family tree 3 The Hibberts in the Jamaica operation

CHAPTER TWO

Jamaica

Instead of the Morning London Cries, of Old Clothes, Sweep, &c. my Ears were saluted with Maha-a, Maha-a, the Cries of Goats, kept in Most Houses for their Milk. And presently I heard called the Names of Pompey, Scipio, Casar &c. and again those of Yabba, Juba, Quasheba (Negro Boys and Girls, Slaves in the Family) which first raised an Idea of being in old Rome; & then again of my being transported suddenly to Africa ... But how different did everything appear to me. People of almost all colours! – White, black, yellow, in abundance. Many pale white, and great Variety in the Shades of Black and Yellow. Very few, not one in a Thousand, of a ruddy Complexion.

Diary of Curtis Brett (1748)[1]

In 1734 Thomas senior departed Manchester to journey across the sea to Jamaica. He arrived in Kingston – a bustling mercantile centre of the British Atlantic world and the place that he would make his home for the next forty-six years. During the eighteenth century Kingston was 'the leading metropolis of the British West Indies' and 'was inferior in population only to Havana in the Spanish Caribbean and to Philadelphia and New York in British North America'.[2] Kingston was dominated by its vast natural harbour, making it an ideal centre for the thriving ocean-borne trade in people and goods. Thomas senior arrived at a key point in Kingston's urban development; after the destruction of the earthquake that partially sank the old buccaneering centre of Port Royal in 1692, Kingston began to rapidly develop in the second quarter of the eighteenth century.[3] In 1730 the inhabitants were made up of white colonists (11 per cent), free people of colour (38 per cent) and an enslaved population that accounted for just over half of all people living in the city.[4] The 1740s and 1750s were a commercial highpoint and Thomas senior arrived just in time to reap the rewards. The number of households in Kingston 'increased by 30 per cent between 1745 and 1770', with the population more than tripling in the same period.[5] Having known only the commercial and rural environs of Liverpool, Manchester and Lancashire, what might Thomas senior have made of this new colonial society? The excerpt from Dubliner Curtis Brett's diary at the head of this chapter offers a window into just how alien this new multi-racial world must have appeared. The customs, noises, names and faces of Kingston were entirely unfamiliar to those who had recently departed the metropole. Conjuring up fantasies of ancient Rome and Africa, Kingston was imagined as a new imperial city – the heart of a British Atlantic empire in which slavery might once again provide the means to wealth, power and the expansion of a particular vision of civilisation.

Kingston's flourishing economy relied on its importance as a port; its wharfs and warehouses teemed with sailors, merchants, colonial commodities and those that laboured to produce them – enslaved Africans. Kingston was both a commercial hub with stores and shops, as well as Jamaica's premier slave port. Burnard and Morgan have estimated that of the Guinea ships 'whose disembarkation point is known, 87 per cent landed at Kingston'.[6] Slave pens have been identified in the Poll Tax list for 1745; Port Royal Street had 1,167 enslaved people documented as inhabiting it and close by Orange Street had 1,011.[7] The Caribbean was a dangerous place to be owing to the prevalence of tropical diseases and the level of coercion required to subordinate an unwilling and rebellious workforce. Enslaved Africans purchased from the ships were often kept in pens for a period of seasoning. This was intended to acclimatise them to the physical ravages of disease and the psychological trauma of their removal from Africa into permanent slavery in the West Indies. In reference to his arrival and sale in Barbados, Olaudah Equiano wrote that 'We were conducted immediately to the merchant's yard, where we were all pent up together like so many sheep in a fold, without regard to sex or age.'[8] Alongside the misery of the slave yards, new properties were springing up as Kingston enjoyed a real-estate explosion with newly moneyed merchants building fine houses for themselves and properties to rent to newcomers to the island. African suffering and British enrichment existed side by side in the very materiality of the city's design and architecture.

Slavery and its attendant industries were the lifeblood of the city and during the mid-eighteenth century business was booming. The promise of Kingston's prosperity enticed British colonists of all classes to make the Atlantic crossing and to stay, despite the appalling mortality rate, estimated as 'one in five whites per annum'.[9] Of the ten Hibbert men who went out to Jamaica, four died young as a result of disease, two of them just a couple of months after arrival. As one Bristolian slave factor resident in Kingston proclaimed, the Guinea trade was the 'chief motive of people venturing their fortunes abroad'.[10] Success in the colonies was by no means easy – attaining the staggering wealth of families like the Beckfords was highly unlikely. Yet the promise of riches continued to lure white immigrants determined to improve on their circumstances back in Britain by exploiting the opportunities available to Europeans in the colonies.

The making of a merchant dynasty

Though the early years of Thomas senior's career in Jamaica are unclear, there is a reference in the papers of one of the family's planter clients, Simon Taylor. Thomas senior, wrote Taylor in 1800, 'was sent to this country to collect some debts and got acquainted with a Guinea factor who took him into partnership and by the sale of negroes alone made his fortune'.[11] By the early 1740s Thomas senior had established himself as a slave factor and had entered into partnership with Jonathan Tongue. During the mid-eighteenth century 'Jamaica had the largest demand for slaves of any British colony ... It received one-third of retained slave imports shipped by Britain.'[12] Disease, brutal treatment and a declining birth rate within the enslaved population meant the slave trade flourished. Slave factors purchased enslaved people from the ships on their arrival in dock; if they were large-scale merchants they would buy in large lots, meaning that the 'economies of scale ensured that much of the slave trade was concentrated in relatively few hands'.[13] Investors gave instructions to their ship's captain, who then agreed a bonding contract for the local factor to sell enslaved Africans for no less than a premium price agreed beforehand. As Richard Pares has explained:

> In these cases the factor insensibly became the real purchaser of the slaves: he paid the limit demanded by the owners, resold the slaves to the planters for payment in six, nine or twelve months, and compensated himself – indeed, made his fortune – out of the difference between the cash price and the credit price.[14]

In this way slave factors reaped the benefits of the lucrative mark-up on sale without taking on any of the associated risks of securing and transporting enslaved people from Africa.

Parish tax records indicated that by 1745 Thomas senior jointly owned dockside warehousing space on Water Lane – a necessity for merchants seeking to house or re-export their goods.[15] By the 1750s Thomas senior had embarked on a new partnership with Nathaniel Sprigg. In 1752 they acquired property close to the waterfront on Orange Street, an area identified as housing British America's most densely populated slave yards.[16] Burnard has described Thomas senior's merchant house as 'not only the largest in Kingston but ... legendary for its solidity and commercial probity'.[17] An indication of the level that Hibbert & Sprigg were trading at is indicated by Burnard and Morgan: 'Thirty-one slave ships arriving in Jamaica between September 28, 1751, and May 27, 1752, delivered 7,123 slaves to nine firms ... Hibbert & Sprigg received 3,358' or 47 per cent.[18] Both the market share and the availability of capital required to make such a purchase reveal the scale of the operation. By the early 1750s Thomas senior's reputation was such that when slave ship investors left instructions for their captains on how to conduct business in the West Indies, they recommended the house of Hibbert as a safe bet for the disposal of their valuable human cargo. Writing in 1751 to Captain Earle of the *Chesterfield*, the investors urged him to seek out slave factors who

> will make the most in Sales give the Earliest despatch and Best remittances where you set down we recommend your agreeing for and fixing the Exchange on Bills and time they shall be remitted for the balance and if Possible all of the ships, this not being done give room for advancing the Exchange when such remittances are to be made which lessens our interest greatly.[19]

The issue of assured payment was one of fundamental importance for merchants, planters and investors. Thomas senior's standing in this area was demonstrated by the investors' instruction to Captain Earle to 'proceed to Jamaica, there apply to Messrs Hibbert Woodcock & Sprigg and Mr Peter Furnail either of which will take you on the Best Terms and load your ship with the islands produce'. Entering into the 1760s Thomas senior embarked on a new partnership with Samuel Jackson. The scale of Hibbert & Jackson's trading was vast; between 1764 and 1774 they acted as factor for sixty-one ships, selling 16,254 enslaved people, of whom 10,149 were men and 6,105 were women.[20] Amongst the many transactions which took place, one tells the story of family connections from home. In 1765 Hibbert & Jackson purchased 408 enslaved people from the slave ship *Rumbold*. The vessel was named for and managed by Thomas Rumbold, the merchant to whom Thomas junior had been apprenticed in Liverpool in 1762. Thomas senior's partnership was successful enough to open 'a branch house (Barnard & Montague) at Montego Bay', thus enabling them to capture the market on both the established east and rapidly developing west side of the island.[21] Over the years advertisements in the newspapers in Kingston for slave sales recorded a number of different partnerships involving the Hibberts. These included Robert Hibbert (1781), Robert & Thomas Hibbert (1783), Hibbert, Hall &

Fuhr (1790–93), Robert Hibbert & Co. (1793), and Hibbert & Taylor (1800).[22]

In 1754 Thomas senior's younger brother John senior arrived from Manchester to join the business. John senior was twenty when he arrived, and had been just two years old when his brother left for Jamaica. News of Thomas senior's colonial success undoubtedly travelled home, conveyed by the stream of correspondence and family acquaintances who journeyed across the Atlantic. With a thriving business perhaps Thomas senior sent for his brother to help, or maybe their parents envisaged the same future for their younger son as their eldest child had realised for himself. Eventually the Hibberts' Jamaica firm became a distinctly family affair, with John senior joined by a long line of brothers, nephews and cousins. In 1766 Thomas senior and John senior welcomed their twenty-two-year-old nephew Thomas junior, the son of their younger brother Robert senior. John senior died in 1769 and subsequently Robert senior's second-eldest – John junior – was sent for. Aged twenty-two, he followed his namesake to the grave within a year of his arrival. In 1771 Robert senior's third eldest Robert junior made the journey across the sea to replace his dead brother.

The structure of the partnership between Thomas senior and his two nephews mirrored that of the family. Thomas senior was the patriarch. He wielded ultimate control over the business and some of their clients preferred to make deals with the more experienced partner. Robert junior's diary recorded an instance where '[Peter] Barral calls and talks secrets with my Uncle'.[23] Nicholas Hibbert Steele has speculated that some of Thomas senior's clandestine ventures were related to the lucrative illegal trade with foreign colonies. Barral had contacts in Cuba and there was a steady trade between Kingston and Havana.[24] Thomas junior enjoyed seniority over his younger brother Robert junior, who complained bitterly of his boredom and loneliness during the period in which he was learning the ropes and was forced to spend long days at the stores whilst his brother and uncle went out to tout for business. As the 1770s progressed, old age and infirmity sank in and Thomas senior was forced to relinquish the reins to his nephews. This did not stop him from issuing edicts and moralising about the younger men's deficiencies. As Robert junior noted in 1774, 'my Uncle gives my Bro. a very serious lecture about his headlong mode of managing [John] Nixon's affairs'.[25] The brothers were eventually joined in the business by their Jamaica-born cousin Thomas, the eldest son of their deceased uncle John senior.

Robert junior is key to understanding the Hibberts' mercantile world in Kingston. Throughout his life he kept a diary in which he noted down both social and familial events, as well as his business dealings. The diaries provide a unique insight into the daily routine of a slave factor, giving details of the endless waiting for ships to come in, visits to inspect and purchase the human cargo, the names of the ships, their captains, the number of enslaved people purchased and occasionally the name of the buyer. The fierce commercial competition between slave factors was evident in the rivalry between the Hibberts and the partnership of Richard Watt and Alexander Allardyce. 'My Bro. returns', wrote Robert junior,

> and we go on board the *Penny*. Find Watt has been there already and had mentioned the necessity he was under of taking up the *James* from motives of compassion. We, having Letters of Admin. that she was destined to us, I conceive Watt's interference very impertinent, and write to the Captain making use of that expression. This brings on a visit from Watt who, in my Uncle's presence, threatens that I shall hear from him. The next day Henry delivers me a challenge from Watt which I accept. Sundry letter pass between us ... Benson goes with me to Watt; agree to meet next morning at B.'s store ... The next day we meet; settle the business without concessions on either side.[26]

Robert junior sometimes recorded the condition of the enslaved people on arrival. This encompassed anything from 'a very fine cargo'[27] to 'refuse Negroes' – the old, infirm or undesirable who could be sold at a reduced price.[28] The diary contained numerous references to the 'stores' – the place where the enslaved were kept after they had been removed from the ships. Robert junior wrote, 'Very busy at the Store with the remains of our three cargoes'.[29] This was in reference to three slave ships, the *Jenny*, the *Robert* and the *Marquis of Rockingham*. The Hibberts employed a woman there, 'I go up to Mrs Keill to see the Negroes. Enquire their ages preparatory to advertising them', remarked Robert junior.[30] If the enslaved Africans survived the seasoning process they could be sold at the highest possible price, giving the factor a return of between 4 and 7 per cent of the gross sales.[31] Nicholas Radburn has noted that on 17 March 1783 Robert junior and his brother 'sold 497 captives from the ship *Harlequin* for 29,287 Jamaican pounds and collected 1,426 pounds as their 5 per cent commission'.[32]

Robert junior's diary revealed that in 1787 the Hibberts bought and sold enslaved people from the Liverpool *Brookes* under Captain Molyneux.[33] This was the same vessel which the abolitionists would use to such iconic effect in their campaign a year later. The 609 enslaved people on board had been purchased from Fort William in Anomabu, Cape Coast Castle and Fort Metal Cross at Dixcove. Over the course of the 51 day Middle Passage 19 Africans died. The horrors continued until journey's end, and even then enslaved Africans were still vulnerable to the perils of the sea. In 1787 Robert junior gave an account of an incident in which the *Enterprize*, a Guineaman whose enslaved cargo the Hibberts expected to sell, was wrecked off the coast at Annotto Bay

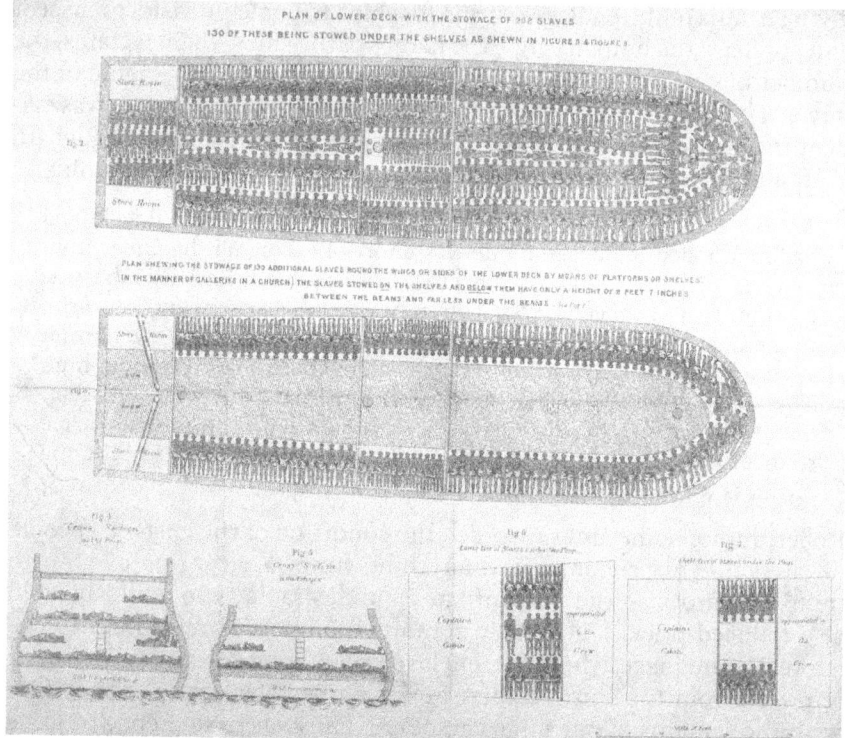

Figure 2 Diagram of the *Brookes* Slave Ship', 1789

in the north of the island. Robert junior wrote that 'we determine to sell her there' and duly departed to make the necessary arrangements. Following the sale he was met at his plantation, Whitehall, by his wife and daughter. On the road back to Kingston the family encountered 'the remainder of the Negroes ex the *Enterprize* coming from AV [Agualta Vale] to Town to be sold there'. Having suffered the terror of a shipwreck the survivors endured the indignity of the slave market as the Hibberts attempted to claw back some of their losses.[34] Incidents such as this were not uncommon – Robert noted both a fire on board the *Cator* and another shipwreck off Portland Point involving the *Mermaid* in which only 6 out of 240 enslaved people survived. Four days after the wreck the traumatised survivors were sold.[35]

The Hibberts sold enslaved people to some of the most powerful men on the island, including John Tharp, Simon Taylor, Edward Long and Nathaniel Phillips.[36] They also traded with those who were operating on a more modest level. Robert junior noted that 'I go to Sally Barrows; sell one to her.'[37] The prevalence of small-scale female slave ownership, particularly in urban areas, has been revealed by the slavery compensation records. Sales could be a long-drawn-out process, with the average time taken running at approximately fifty days.[38] If the market was flooded after the arrival of a number of slave ships prices fell and the slave factor's profit margins with them. If very few ships came into port, as was common during periods of war, then the prices rose. In 1772 Thomas junior wrote to Nathaniel Phillips with the news that only four or five Guinea ships had made it to harbour. Two of these ships dealt exclusively with the Hibberts. The scarcity of enslaved people meant that the on-board sale turned into a 'scramble', with buyers trampling over each other to secure their purchases. As Thomas junior described it, '[I] really expected one half of the white people on board would have been trod to Death by the other half.'[39] These conditions meant that 'we were so circumstanced in the Case of these two Cargoes, that we could not possibly allow what is called a first Choice'. This meant that the enslaved Africans were sold without the Hibberts consulting their most prized customers. This left Phillips down on his 'annual Number', which then impacted on the size of his sugar harvest. The competition during times of scarcity saw the Hibberts command the exceptional price of £65 per head for so-called 'privilege' slaves. Nicholas Radburn has noted that the term 'privilege slave' was used in reference to 'prime' Africans who were offered for sale privately to the factor's elite clients.[40] Thomas junior admonished Phillips, reminding him that he had already advised him to purchase 'proper supplies of Negroe Stock' from the estate's 'Produce of Rum'.[41] This was the linguistic economy of the slave trade; unflinching in its commercialisation of the enslaved, they became objects for barter, a necessary cog in the machine of production and profitability.

One of the key areas of expertise for an experienced slave factor was the ability to judge his client's financial standing. The role of trust cannot be overestimated – the maintenance of a good reputation was an investment for the future. When an unknown buyer wished to make a purchase the Hibberts consulted with their closest correspondents. As Robert junior recorded: 'One McGillon applies for ten [slaves] ex *Corsican Hero*. I go to S. Taylor to enquire his character.'[42] With the system of slave factorage dominated by a few merchant houses, personal connections played an important role in securing business. Credit was a fundamental part of the system of slavery; the network that supported it was both internal to the island, as well as extending to Britain. The inhabitants of the West Indies became renowned for their levels of indebtedness. Successful slave factors like Thomas senior increased their wealth by extending their business to money lending. Using the inventories of wealthy merchants to measure credit and debt,

Burnard has argued that the level of lending within Jamaica itself has been underestimated by historians. The most common large debt was in the form of mortgages, whose importance is borne out in the slavery compensation claims, large numbers of which were contested by and awarded to mortgage holders in lieu of the repayment of debt. Smaller loans were made for the purchase of enslaved people, livestock, plantation equipment and luxury items. Thomas senior was described as 'the wealthiest and most important figure in Kingston's commercial community', and Burnard has speculated that on his death in 1780 he was worth somewhere in the region of '£350,000 with £250,000 in the form of debts owed to him'.[43] The issue of debt owed is confirmed by Marguerite Curtin, who quoted from Thomas senior's will, stating that his 'personal Estate chiefly consists of Securities and outstanding Debts in this Island'.[44] There is a reference to Thomas senior's wealth in the papers of his planter associate Nathaniel Phillips, who puts the figure at £215,000 sterling.[45] If correct, this level of wealth placed him on a par with the Beckfords and the Clarkes – some of the wealthiest families in both Britain and its empire.[46]

Evidence as to the Hibbert men's feelings about the nature of their trade is scarce. Robert junior's diary gave one account during the two-week period in which he was selling enslaved Africans from the slave ship *Will*. He wrote nervously that he was alternately 'vexed and disappointed', 'very anxious', 'unhappy', 'I feel much abo. the slaves'.[47] The tension he experienced stemmed not from any feelings of moral unease, but rather as a result of slow sales. After two weeks of fretting he finally sold the last of the 'cargo' and was able to enjoy a 'Romp with Jenny Boswell'.[48] Thomas junior expressed something closer to what we might interpret as unhappiness with his situation, although the sentiment is frustratingly opaque. Robert junior documented 'a walk in the evening with my Bro. In the back garden when he explains to me how little his present way of life agrees with his feelings and wishes.'[49] Whatever the reason for Thomas junior's discontent, it did not lead to an abandonment of the family business, although following the death of his uncle in 1780 he left Jamaica and never returned. In later life Thomas junior was happy to hand the business over to his younger brother George and retire from commerce altogether. Thomas senior's feelings are likewise unknown; the few mercantile letters that remain in his hand betrayed no trace of emotion, but by their nature would hardly be the place for doubt and shame. In evidence given to the Select Committee in 1791 Hercules Ross recalled that seventeen years earlier Thomas senior had proposed a question to the Attic Society – a gentlemanly club made up of 'the first characters of the place'.[50] The men considered 'whether the trade to Africa for slaves was consistent with sound policy, the laws of nature, and morality'. The discussion occupied several meetings and at last it was determined by a majority, 'That the trade to Africa for slaves, was neither consistent with sound policy, the laws of nature, nor morality.' Vincent Brown has cautioned that this was an 'academic debate', an exercise in reason and argument rather than a serious discussion about dismantling the trade.[51] The outcome of these polite musings failed to move Thomas senior and he remained a key figure in Kingston's slave economy. Despite Ross's support of abolition and his experience of slavery's degradations, he remembered Thomas senior in his evidence as not only 'the most eminent Guinea factor in Kingston' but also 'a most respectable character'.[52]

Hibbert House: politics and masculine sociability

As a prodigious merchant Thomas senior required a house which reflected his newfound status. At some point around 1750 he purchased prime real estate on the south-western corner of Beeston and Stanton Streets, on what is now Duke Street.[53] There he built an impressive neo-classical Palladian town house, the architectural style of the building reminiscent of the ancient slave-owning empires of Greece and Rome. The adoption of Georgian architectural modes transplanted something of European taste into the colony, inscribing the landscape with ambitions towards imperial greatness and acting as a reminder of the home the colonists had left behind. The origins of the house have achieved a folkloric status in Kingston's history. The story goes that a bet was placed between Thomas senior, Eliphalet Fitch and Jasper Hall to see who could build the finest house in Kingston.[54] The prize was the hand of Theresa Constantia Philips, a notorious courtesan who worked in both Kingston and London.[55] Goodman, Seebom and Stewart refer to a piece of doggerel, reputedly spoken by the planter Simon Taylor, that read, 'Hibbert, Hall and Fitch / Built three Houses to please a B-tch.'[56] There is no record of who won the bet but of the houses that were built – Hibbert House, Jasper Hall's Constantine House and Eliphalet Fitch's Harmony Hall – only Thomas senior's still stands. The house passed out of the family's hands in 1814 when it was sold to the War Office of the West India Regiment.

By the early 1750s Thomas senior was involved with island politics. Embarking on this new venture from a strong commercial base enabled the aspiring merchant to establish a network of allies through his business dealings with some of the island's most powerful planters. In 1751 Thomas senior was acting as an Assistant Judge of the Grand Court and a Justice of the Peace. His stature among the island elite was reflected in the fact his house became a regular meeting place for

Figure 3 Hibbert House, James Hakewill, c. 1820

the Jamaica Assembly following the temporary move of the capital from Spanish Town to Kingston in 1754. The Assembly was dominated by Jamaica's plantocracy, who favoured Spanish Town as the seat of power. Moving the capital to Kingston was seen by the merchants as a marker for their growing influence. Thomas senior represented the parishes of St George and Portland before becoming Speaker of the House of Assembly in 1756, thus strengthening his economic influence with the acquisition of significant political power.[57] His position as Speaker allowed him to shape and control the Assembly's discussions. He could secure a place for his own concerns and temper those planters who wished to legislate to the detriment of the merchants. The colonial assembly was ever vigilant towards the overarching powers of the imperial Parliament. As Catherine Hall has noted, the assemblies insisted that their rights 'did not derive from grants from the crown but from the basic English right to representative government, now secured by customary practice and ensuring that men of property had a say in making laws and levying taxes'.[58] The members argued 'that it followed that in the absence of colonial representation in an imperial parliament, they owed allegiance to the monarch through his governor, but had the right to legislate for themselves'.[59] The right to decide internally on issues affecting the colony was grudgingly bestowed on the Assembly in 1738, largely because the island elite paid for the running of the colonial administration and the militia. The merchants and planters were often in agreement, especially as some of the most powerful merchants were themselves also planters, but there remained a distinct difference in their priorities. It was vital for the minority merchants to gain representation if they were to influence legislation directly affecting their business, such as the Act of 1752 which placed a limit on the interest which creditors could charge.

It was this internal dynamic which caused tensions within the white elite, as planter and merchant vied for the dominant position. In a letter to Chaloner Arcedekne in 1765, Simon Taylor noted that both Thomas senior and his fellow wagerer Jasper Hall were involved in an election campaign which saw the two men competing for a position in the Assembly. Despite being elected, Thomas senior's chagrin at gaining fewer votes than his rivals led Taylor to write 'Old Hibbert is so angry to find himself the lowest of the list that out of pique he talks of resigning as soon as the Assembly meets.'[60] Political power was tied to social prestige and economic influence. As a former Speaker of the House, it no doubt irked Thomas senior that he had been displaced by newcomers and old rivals. Over time Thomas senior's example was followed by his nephews. Thomas junior served as both a magistrate and judge, a member of the House of Assembly for St George between 1770 and 1775 and as President of the Chamber of Commerce in 1778. Gratifyingly for the Hibberts their rival in the slave factorage business – Alexander Allardyce – was relegated to Vice-President. Robert junior was a Justice of the Peace at different times for the parishes of Kingston, St George and St Mary. He also served as an Assembly member for Kingston between 1787 and 1790. Robert junior's diary demonstrated the importance for the merchants of having representation in the Assembly, although it also pointed towards their limits. In 1788 he described a 'Violent debate about taxes – Shirley and his party wishing to ease the Planter at the expense of the Merchant. He carries, of course, in an Assembly composed of Planters, every point, and I am at last so disgusted that on Friday I leave them to themselves.'[61] Despite his failure to stop the measure it remained a badge of status to be appointed to the Assembly. Through their adoption of civic and political positions the Hibberts entrenched themselves within the power structures that governed the island.

Thomas senior's house was not just a political meeting place, it also served an important social and economic function. From its widow's walk the Hibberts used a 'glass' to scan the sea for their ships, as Robert

Figure 4 Thomas senior, unknown artist

junior recalled: 'Captain Hanly dines, and my Uncle sits with him on the balcony to see his Ship go down.'[62] Much business was carried on through mercantile sociability, Robert junior noting in his diary: 'On Friday Captn. Burkett & Blundell dine with us, and after dinner we take a sail on board his Ship to see his slaves which are very fine.'[63] The Hibberts' home was always open to slave-ship captains, allowing them an advantage in securing sales. The family also played host to naval officers and seamen, including the celebrated saviour of Jamaica, Admiral Rodney. In 1771 Horatio Nelson embarked on his first voyage to the West Indies on board the Hibberts' ship the *Mary Ann*. The ship sailed to Jamaica and Tobago and it is possible a young Nelson might also have been a guest of the Hibberts in Kingston. Alongside these venerable seamen, the island's plantocratic and mercantile elite were regular visitors. The ambience of the house was distinctly masculine; inhabited by three unmarried men (four from 1778, when John senior's son Thomas joined them), the only regular female presence, apart from the enslaved women who worked there, was Thomas senior's mixed-heritage mistress Charity Harry and their young daughters.[64] Robert junior's diary documented numerous occasions in which dining and heavy drinking facilitated discussion which alternated between 'business or bawdy'.[65] The family patriarch Thomas senior was not himself averse to this kind of raucous masculine sociability, although Robert junior commented in 1776 that 'My Uncle promises to talk no more bawdy.'[66] Robert junior's references to his overindulgence and its effects were manifold; on one occasion he noted that he was 'so drunk as to be carried home. One Belcher carries me upstairs and puts me to bed. The next day sick, and lie ill in bed all day.'[67] Robert junior also used laudanum. Nicholas Hibbert Steele has speculated that this was a habit that began in Jamaica in 1777, when Robert junior noted in his diary that 'I find what I took for relaxation to be a very serious complaint.'[68] Robert junior mentioned a further three occasions in his diary when he used the drug.[69]

In his later years Thomas senior grew increasingly irritable and resented his two nephews' behaviour. He criticised them on this score, as Robert junior wryly noted: 'we dine trio and he reads us an affecting lecture on the subject of our transgressions'.[70] As Thomas senior's health deteriorated he became increasingly ill-tempered; his moods swung from high-spiritedness to despondent gloom, 'damning the Pen, us, himself and all the world'.[71] In 1777 tensions within the household escalated to the point where Robert junior and his brother 'determine to dine as seldom as possible at home. He [Thomas senior] approves the resolutions and himself determines to avoid all company for the future.'[72] Despite the frustration felt by Robert junior and his brother, the family business went on as usual. Robert junior's feelings towards his uncle do not seem to have improved. When Thomas senior was dying, Thomas junior postponed his visit to England and went with his cousin Thomas to their uncle's side. Robert junior, on the other hand, sent a representative – an enslaved man named Simon – but wrote that for his own part he 'decline[d] going over'.[73] On the death of his uncle, Robert junior's diary made no mention of his grief, instead he noted that the day after he had been informed, 'I go down to the Store as usual'.[74]

The gentleman planter

Success as a merchant in Kingston brought Thomas senior exceptional wealth. It was, however, the combination of commercial dominance, political power and land ownership that elevated the Hibberts into the planter-merchant elite. In 1760 Thomas senior purchased a 3,000-acre estate at Agualta Vale in what is today the parish of St Mary but was then St George in the north of the island. The land was in large part wood and pasture with a limited coffee-growing capacity. Thomas senior undertook a series of large-scale improvements, including the introduction of a cattle pen. In 1771 the estate was turned over for sugar cultivation.[75] Whether Thomas senior built the great plantation house has been the subject of speculation. Goodman, Seebom and Stewart have pointed to an advertisement of 1779 that stated, 'Thomas Hibbert and nephew require to work at an estate in St. Mary's, for any time not exceeding Six Months, six or more Negro Carpenters.' They have suggested that the number of craftsmen required and the length of time they were needed for is suggestive of major building work.[76] The purchase of a plantation allowed Thomas senior to enjoy 'the gentlemanly pursuit of horse-breeding'.[77] As noted in the novel *Marly* (1828), owning a horse was a marker for both class and race, 'no disgrace being considered so great in the island, as that of a white man being seen walking on foot'.[78] The Hibberts imported their horses from England, in one instance Robert junior remarked, 'After dinner we go on board *Boyd*; see the horses hoisted out.'[79] The race track at Kingston was a popular space for socialising for the urban elite and the Hibbert men were regular attendees. Agualta Vale was augmented over the years through the purchase of adjacent land. In May 1777 Robert junior spent £14,501 acquiring Orange Hill, a neighbouring small-scale sugar estate. The property was formerly owned by William Beckford Ellis but it was put up for sale on the order of the Court of Chancery.[80]

The 1817 slave register gave the combined population of enslaved people across Agualta Vale, Agualta Vale Pen and Orange Vale (presumably what was once Orange Hill) as 817 people – 418 women and 399 men. There are very few records which shed light on the experiences of the enslaved. Occasionally Robert junior mentioned individuals by name; his manservant London was referenced the most frequently, although over the course of several decades his name appeared only a handful of times. In 1772 Robert junior noted a few days before Christmas, 'London flogged for stealing Collard's wine.'[81] He recorded when Little Monday was bitten by a mad dog and subsequently died.[82] He also wrote in a discontented tone when Pope, described as a 'new Negro', lost his eye after being sent to the workhouse.[83] Evidence from the slave court records indicated that harsh discipline was maintained on the plantation even after general conditions were supposed to have been ameliorated following the reanimation of the antislavery campaigns in the mid-1820s. In 1830 an enslaved man named Patrick was accused of stealing and killing a calf (valued at £2) and a goat (valued at 10 shillings). He was found guilty and sentenced to hard labour for life in the workhouse. The Hibberts were awarded £10 for their loss of property.[84]

Figure 5 'Monument of the late Thomas Hibbert, Esq. at Agualta Vale Penn', James Hakewill, *A picturesque tour of the island of Jamaica from drawings made in the years 1820 and 1821*

Agualta Vale was depicted by James Hakewill in 1825.[85] By this time the institution of slavery was under attack by the abolitionists and Hakewill's print formed part of the proslavery propaganda campaign. Vincent Brown has noted that Hakewill was famed for his depiction of the Roman ruins of Italy and the country estates of England; his rendering of the 'planter picturesque' combined the imperial grandeur of Rome with the ordered management of nature that characterised the landscaped gardens of the gentry and aristocracy.[86] The Agualta Vale vista was dominated by Thomas senior's imposing funerary urn, inscribed with words celebrating his 'persevering industry / Undeviating integrity and liberality of spirit' alongside his 'Enlarged benevolence' and 'ingenious manner'.[87] Hakewill included an African figure receiving instruction from a European gentleman – a symbol of the civilising mastery of both nature and the 'savage' African. For Brown, 'It would be hard to make a stronger claim to permanent tenure on land' and presumably the system that supported it.[88] In Hakewill's description of the property he imagined how Thomas senior 'On this spot' was 'yielded ... many a happy moment, in the reflection of an amiable mind surveying his own creation of wealth and independence.'[89] The textual and pictorial erasure of the African labour upon which Thomas senior's wealth and independence depended was what sustained the myth carved in stone on the memorial. As Elizabeth Bohls has noted, 'intensively cultivated land and coerced labour' was effectively 'transformed into this marble artefact of extracted wealth'.[90] Now both a merchant and a planter, Thomas senior had cemented his position, providing a lasting legacy for his nephews Thomas junior, Robert junior and Thomas, each of whom inherited a third share in the property. In 1785 Robert junior bought out his brother Thomas junior's third share.[91] In 1796 their cousin Thomas became the sole owner of Agualta Vale, having paid off Robert junior. The plantation remained in the family until after slavery had ended.

Over the years the Hibberts acquired a number of plantations, some by purchase and others through the foreclosure of debts. In 1791 Robert junior spent £40,000 purchasing Albion – an estate located 15 miles east of Kingston in what was the parish of St David but is now modern-day St Thomas.[92] Archibald Edgar surveyed Albion in 1794 and noted that it was 1,492 acres with 294 in cane.[93] The size of the enslaved population fluctuated over the course of the period in which the family owned the property, but in 1832 there were 442 people registered on the estate.[94] The Hibberts acted as consignees to the previous owner, John Nixon – the man whom Thomas junior had been scolded about by his uncle in relation to the management of his affairs. In the 1820s, the Reverend Richard Bickell, an abolitionist, visited the property and wrote of his dismay that both the Irish overseer and the enslaved Africans were unable to attend church on a Sunday because of the demands on their labour.[95] Giving evidence to the Select Committee on the Extinction of Slavery in 1832, Robert junior's former attorney James Simpson admitted that despite being 'anxious' to abandon the whip on Albion, 'he was forced to resume it, and made so effectual a use of it for a time he restored order and re-animated industry'.[96] Describing the enslaved as 'naturally indolent', he justified his wielding of the whip as a necessary 'stimulus' for work.

In the early nineteenth century the Hibberts began to buy up land in the western parishes of Jamaica. In 1815 Robert junior acquired Great Valley with its population of 486 enslaved people in Hanover from the heirs of Richard Brissett. As with Agualta Vale, enslaved people from Great Valley can also be found in the slave court records. In this instance a man named Raynes Waite was convicted as an 'incorrigible runaway' who had continued 'absent from the said estate and services of his owner for a term exceeding six months in breach of the 63rd clause of the Consolidated Slave law'.[97] His sentence was to be transported from the island for life. The Hibberts were paid £40 for their loss. The self-emancipatory struggles of the Baptist War of 1831–32 came to the door of Great Valley when the sugar works were burned down during the unrest. The slave court records showed that sixteen enslaved people from Great Valley were tried for their part in the uprising, with fifteen of them convicted and one, John Bell, acquitted. The transcriptions of the trial were incredibly brief, consisting of just a few short uncontested witness statements upon which judgement was based. The longest document recorded the trial of Great Valley's driver, a man named Joseph Brown, who was charged with failing to stop the destruction of property and raiding the stores. His sentence was death. Punishments included hanging, lashings (including an instance of 300 lashes followed by a further 200 on discharge) and imprisonment with hard labour in the workhouse.[98]

In 1819, a few years after his acquisition of Great Valley, Robert junior purchased Coventry plantation in Hanover along with its enslaved workforce of ninety-seven people from the estate of Duncan Mackenzie. Like Great Valley, Coventry was also swept up in the events of 1831–32. Nine of Coventry's enslaved workers were tried for their involvement, including two women, Eliza and Susan James.[99] Eliza and Susan received 200 and 250 lashes respectively, along with two months' imprisonment. Alongside the two women from Coventry who shared her surname, a third women – Ann James – who was described as 'free' was sentenced to death. When the abolitionists Joseph Sturge and Thomas Harvey visited Jamaica in 1837 they went to Coventry and spoke with a formerly enslaved apprentice named Susan Mackenzie. Given the plantation's previous ownership by Duncan Mackenzie it is possible that this was the same woman who was punished under the name Susan James. Her testimony to Sturge and Harvey recalled her treatment:

> During the rebellion she was sent for because she was a 'great Baptist woman'. They tried to make some men swear against her to hang her, but did not succeed; and because she would not say anything against Mr Burchell, three men, with three new cats, were ordered to flog her. They gave her about three hundred lashes, and she remained in the workhouse for three months. On the first of August, 1834, the attorney Mr Grant, said she must go into the field. She said she was not able, and showed him her back; but he said that was nothing, and for her refusal she was sent three times to the workhouse ... This woman is an individual of superior intelligence for her station, and bears a very high character as a person of amiable and mild disposition, and consistent in her deportment as a professor of religion. She is almost blind from the effects of flogging; the upper part of her back is covered in white patches, where the *rete mucosum* has been entirely obliterated by the horrid punishment.[100]

She went on to speak of the continued hardships under the system of apprenticeship that replaced slavery in Jamaica between 1834 and 1838. She gave details of the lack of proper sustenance, hard labour and intrusions on the workers' free time. 'The Magistrate', she lamented, 'won't hear what we have to say.'

Robert junior's Jamaica-born cousin Robert consolidated the family interest in western Jamaica through the purchase of two estates in Hanover. Georgia was acquired from the heirs of Richard Brissett at the same time that Robert junior purchased Great Valley in 1815. In 1817 there were 380 enslaved people on the plantation – 195 women and 185 men.[101] Dundee, with its workforce of 226 enslaved people, was bought just over a decade later from Walter Murray.[102] As with his cousin, the acquisition of Georgia resulted in Robert becoming involved in the abolition controversies. In 1817 he sent a Unitarian missionary, the Reverend Thomas Cooper, to his estates to preach to the enslaved workers. The move, conceived of as an ameliorative gesture of benevolent plantership, backfired when Cooper published a critical account of his time in Jamaica. Initially the issues he raised were focused on the lack of access to religion and education, as opposed to extreme brutality. In 1832, when Cooper gave evidence to the House of Lords, he also detailed an incident in which:

> A young woman came up to him and told him to look at her. She turned around, and all across she was cut in a dreadful manner, and the blood

running. They were removing dung and she could not keep up with the rest. She had no idea the driver did it out of spite; he might or he might not.[103]

Cooper's testimony was damning in that it was not an exposé of the worst abuses of the system of slavery, but rather an example of the way in which even on plantations which were considered progressive amelioration was doomed to failure.[104]

Robert not only owned plantations, he also wrote about them, and in 1825 published *Hints to the young Jamaica sugar planter*. The manual offered wide-ranging advice on everything from the right age to embark on a colonial career to the correct clothes to bring, the structure and management of the plantation, agricultural tips, animal husbandry and sugar and rum production. Robert clearly viewed himself in the mould of the paternalistic planter, referring to himself as a 'kind master'.[105] Patience, gentleness and humane treatment were all advocated both as a means of securing labour and as a Christian duty. He advised the inexperienced planter to 'avoid making sport' of the enslaved 'or wantonly wounding their feelings'.[106] He stressed that 'A new-comer cannot be too much impressed with the impropriety of striking a negro.' Instead the young colonist should 'treat the negro with respect; this behaviour will insure respect from them, and will strengthen more exalted feelings of humanity'.[107]

Robert's idealised vision of relations on the plantation did not hold up to scrutiny. He was an absentee by the time of the pamphlet's publication and therefore reliant on his attorney for information regarding conditions on his estates. For all his fine words and elevated sentiments, according to Cooper the standards to which Robert aspired were not enforced on his plantations. Although as an absentee Robert could have laid the blame for these activities at the door of his attorney, in fact superintending his plantations was George Hibbert Oates, the son of his cousin Mary Oates (née Hibbert). Oates was accused by Cooper of being an 'open and avowed fornicator'.[108] Oates was not the only member of the family to have engaged in these kinds of sexual practices: his uncles Robert junior and Thomas junior as well as his great-uncles Thomas senior and John senior had all fathered illegitimate children. Robert's pamphlet, much like Hakewill's print, was a fantasy of life and labour in Jamaica – the orderly and civilised façade behind which lurked the brutality of colonial exploitation.

Born in Leeds in 1791, Oates was one of the last of the extended Hibbert family to settle on the island. In 1807, the year of the abolition of the slave trade, his mother, Mary, wrote to her brother, Robert junior, to request his thoughts on a living for her son on the island. Robert replied, telling her that 'I should not deceive you very much, if, with my knowledge of that Country, I should tell you that such a Plan is unattended with risqué in respect to health, or that a Fortune is to be acquired there without Industry and Abilities.'[109] He commented that there should be 'Life Love and Spirit in the Boy himself; he should not simply consent to go, but go with his whole heart.' When discussing whether the young man should pursue a career as a planter or merchant, Robert junior noted that the latter might lead to a 'rapid fortune' but the former 'is perhaps upon the whole surer and a Competency is generally attained if the Candidate be lucky enough to keep his health and possess moderate abilities joined to great Patience and great Industry'. To this end he determined that:

> If George gave out in the planting Line I would recommend his going to the Care of Mr. William Nembhard my Wife's Brother, who has the care of a Number of Properties in a healthy part of the Island, and who would I am sure bring him forward in preparation to his attainments. This I think would be better than to go to Agualta Vale because tho I am sure my Cousin would do everything in his Power to assist and recommend him, the Person who has the Management there tho very clever is a perfect Stranger to all of us.[110]

A trusted personal connection was always preferable to a stranger, especially in the matter of training a relation to take on the family interest. Oates was duly dispatched to Jamaica to learn his profession. In 1817 it was noted by his uncle George that he 'was about to return to Jamaica with the advantageous prospect of taking on himself the management of the Estates in Hanover that belong to my Brother and cousin R. H.'.[111] By the early 1820s Oates was acting as attorney on Coventry, Georgia and Great Valley plantations, as well as acting as agent for Haddington, Welcome and Williamsfield.[112] In 1823 the combined population on the plantations for which he was responsible was 1,481 enslaved people. It was Oates's family networks which enabled him to secure the positions; Haddington and Welcome were owned by the Purrier family, the London business partners of his uncles Thomas junior and George. Williamsfield was owned by James Hay, though mortgaged to the family merchant house of Hibbert, Fuhr & Purrier. When the partnership decided to foreclose and sell in 1823, Oates was appointed as the receiver. In 1829 he was acting as receiver for York Pen, a property associated with the Purriers in the slavery compensation claims.[113] Three years later Oates became both the agent and receiver for Adelphi, a plantation which had been a long-standing source of problems for the Hibberts, who had lent its former owner William Hillary £19,607 15s 8d which he did not pay back. The same year Oates also took on the management of two properties unconnected to the rest of his family – Riley's in Hanover and Thomas River in Clarendon. As attorney Oates had full rein to make decisions affecting agricultural practice and the plantation management structure. He claimed a fee for all of the estates he supervised, enabling him to purchase his own 270-acre property in 1831 – Morven near Lucea, the Hanover parish capital.[114] George died in Jamaica in 1837, a year before the system of apprenticeship came to an end.

Conclusion

Three generations of Hibberts made their livings through the system of slavery in Jamaica. The last British-born family member to leave for the colony was George's youngest son, Henry Robarts Hibbert. He arrived in 1825, just over ninety years after his great-uncle Thomas senior made the journey. In the century that had passed, thousands of enslaved Africans had been bought and sold by the Hibberts, accruing them a fortune that ran into the millions in today's money. The Hibberts' presence on the island is still tangible: many Jamaicans share the family surname and Hibbert Street in Kingston serves as a reminder of the family's historic connection to the city. Kingstonians continue to call the urban mansion on Duke Street 'Hibbert House'. Today the building serves as the headquarters of the Jamaica National Heritage Trust. Thomas senior's portrait still adorns the wall and the house retains many of the features that would have been recognisable to the family when they occupied the property. A less familiar and likely less welcome presence is Edna Manley's 1965 sculpture of Jamaican national hero Paul Bogle – one of the leaders of the Morant Bay Rebellion in 1865. Situated in the garden courtyard of the Hibberts' former home, the imposing statue of Bogle stares forcefully out, hands clasped around the hilt of a machete. It was from Hibbert House that Governor John Eyre coordinated the brutal repression which resulted in the deaths of 439 emancipated Jamaicans. Nicholas Draper has described the Eyre controversy as one of the persistent 'fault lines in British society over slavery'.[115] It is no surprise that amongst Eyre's defenders was Thomas senior's great-nephew, John Hubert Washington Hibbert.[116] The presence of the statue in the home of one of Jamaica's foremost slave traders tells us much about the shifting power structures which came with independence from British colonial rule.

There is very little archival trace of the lives of those enslaved Africans whose bodies and labour generated such extraordinary wealth for the Hibbert family. The accounts we have are mediated through official bureaucracy and abolitionist narratives. 'Some things remain unrecoverable,' write Brian Connolly and Marisa Fuentes. 'We have irretrievably lost the thoughts, desires, fears, and perspectives of many whose enslavement shaped every aspect of their lives.'[117] The memory of those who perished under, and survived, enslavement is present throughout the Caribbean. As Hilary Beckles has stated, 'The pain of enslavement and the injury of its injustice haunt citizens and weaken their capacity to experience citizenship as equals with the descendants of slave owners.'[118] Traces of slavery can be found everywhere in Jamaica; etched into the landscape, inscribed on memorials, it can be read in the naming practices of both people and place. It is no surprise that this history has manifested itself in recent calls for reparatory justice. Following the publication of CARICOM's ten-point plan for reparations, the then Prime Minister of the UK, David Cameron, addressed the issue of slavery on a visit to Jamaica in 2015.[119] He urged Jamaicans to 'move on from this painful legacy and continue to build for the future'.[120] For a country whose population, history, culture and identity have been forged through the experience of enslavement and colonialism it is impossible to break with this past. The unequal position in which Jamaica finds itself in relation to the great wealth of its former colonial master serves as a reminder of the unjust enrichment that transatlantic slavery represented. Agualta Vale, the Hibberts' great estate in St Mary, passed out of the family's hands and is now part of a vast 3,000-acre farm owned by Jamaica Producers Group. Thomas senior's funerary monument continued upon its perch overlooking the estate until 1980, when the urn was vandalised by looters 'searching for gold'.[121] The enormous profits that the Hibberts enjoyed from the system of slavery were not buried in the ground. For the most part they were redirected back into Britain itself. The flow of wealth from colony to metropole paid for position, power and land at home in the imperial centre, far away from its disturbing origins in the slave societies of the Caribbean.

Notes

1 Diary of Curtis Brett, quoted in Trevor Burnard and Emma Hart, 'Kingston, Jamaica, and Charleston, South Carolina', *Journal of Urban History*, 39:2 (2012), p. 220.
2 Trevor Burnard, '"The grand mart of the island": The economic function of Kingston, Jamaica, in the mid-eighteenth century', in Kathleen E. A. Monteith and Glen Richards (eds), *Jamaica in slavery and freedom: History, heritage and culture* (Kingston: University of the West Indies Press, 2001), pp. 225–41.
3 Burnard and Hart, 'Kingston, Jamaica', pp. 217–18.
4 *Ibid.*, p. 219.
5 *Ibid.*, p. 218.
6 Trevor Burnard and Kenneth Morgan, 'The dynamics of the slave market and slave purchasing patterns in Jamaica', *William and Mary Quarterly*, 58:1 (2001), p. 209.

JAMAICA

7 Burnard and Hart, 'Kingston, Jamaica', p. 222.
8 Olaudah Equiano, *The interesting narrative of the life of Olaudah Equiano or Gustavus Vasssa, the African* (New York: Dover Publications, 1999), p. 35.
9 Burnard, ' "The grand mart of the island" ', p. 226.
10 Letter from Henry Bright to Richard Meyler III, 25 July 1750, quoted in Kenneth Morgan (ed.), *The Bright–Meyler papers: A Bristol–West India connection, 1732–1837* (Oxford: Oxford University Press, 2007), p. 222.
11 Simon Taylor, quoted in Nicholas Radburn, 'Guinea factors, slave sales, and the profits of the transatlantic slave trade in late eighteenth-century Jamaica: The case of John Tailyour', *William and Mary Quarterly*, 72:2 (2015), p. 283.
12 Burnard and Morgan, 'The dynamics of the slave market', p. 205.
13 *Ibid.*, p. 212.
14 Richard Pares, 'A London West-India merchant house', in Richard Pares and A. J. P. Taylor (eds), *Essays presented to Sir Lewis Namier* (London: Macmillan, 1956), p. 103.
15 Danielle Goodman, Sophia Seebom and Chloë Stewart, 'Headquarters House, Kingston, Jamaica, 1755–1990' (unpublished manuscript, Jamaica National Heritage Trust, 1989), p. 4.
16 *Ibid.*
17 Trevor Burnard, 'Credit, Kingston merchants and the Atlantic slave trade in the eighteenth century', unpublished paper for British Group of Early American Historians, Stirling (3 September 2009), p. 23.
18 Burnard and Morgan, 'The dynamics of the slave market', p. 212.
19 Merseyside Maritime Museum, Liverpool, Earle Collection, Shipping Papers 1751–1781, D/EARLE/1/1, Letter to Captain Earle, 22 May 1751.
20 Extract from the books of Hibberts & Jackson, Part III, Jamaica Appendix, in *Reports of the Lords of the Committee of Council appointed for the consideration of all matters relating to trade and foreign plantations; submitting ... the evidence and information they have collected in consequence of His Majesty's Order in Council, dated the 11th of February, 1788, concerning the present state of the trade to Africa, and particularly the trade in slaves, etc.* (London, 1789).
21 Richard B. Sheridan, 'The commercial and financial organisation of the British slave trade, 1750–1807', *Economic History Review*, 11:2 (1958), p. 255.
22 Eli Faber, *Jews, slaves and the slave trade: Setting the record straight* (New York: New York University Press, 2000), pp. 119–20.
23 HFAC, Diary of Robert Hibbert junior, 6 August 1772.
24 Sherry Johnson, *Climate and catastrophe in Cuba and the Atlantic world in the Age of Revolution* (Chapel Hill: University of North Carolina Press, 2011), p. 114.
25 HFAC, Diary of Robert Hibbert junior, 20 April 1774. John Nixon owned Mullett Hall estate (138 enslaved people) in St Thomas in the East and Albion estate (211 enslaved people) in St David's. Robert junior eventually purchased the latter. Richard B. Sheridan, 'Simon Taylor, sugar tycoon of Jamaica', *Agricultural History*, 45:4 (1971), p. 290.
26 HFAC, Diary of Robert Hibbert junior, 22 November 1775.
27 *Ibid.*, 13 November 1775.
28 *Ibid.*, 20 June 1774.
29 *Ibid.*, 20 December 1773.
30 *Ibid.*, 12 April 1780.
31 Burnard and Morgan, 'The dynamic of the slave market', p. 212.
32 Radburn, 'Guinea factors', p. 255.
33 HFAC, Diary of Robert Hibbert junior, 2 October 1787. Details from the diary match the voyage details listed on the Trans-Atlantic Slave Trade Database. www.slavevoyages.org/voyage/80666/variables [accessed 13 April 2017].
34 HFAC, Diary of Robert Hibbert junior, 21 June–3 July 1787.
35 *Ibid.*, 2 December 1775, 15 July 1778.
36 For further detail on the these figures see Sheridan, 'Simon Taylor'; Clare Taylor, 'The journal of an absentee proprietor, Nathaniel Phillips of Slebech', *Journal*

of Caribbean History, 18 (1984), pp. 67–82; Elizabeth A. Bohls, 'The gentleman planter and the metropole: Long's *History of Jamaica* (1774)', in Gerald Maclean, Donna Landry and Joseph P. Ward (eds), *The country and the city revisited: England and the politics of culture, 1550–1850* (Cambridge: Cambridge University Press, 1999), pp. 180–96; Sarah Pearsall, 'The old husband and the young wife: Scandal, feeling, and distance', in *Atlantic families: Lives and letters in the later eighteenth century* (Oxford: Oxford University Press, 2010), pp. 210–39; Catherine Hall, 'Whose memories? Edward Long and the work of re-remembering', in Katie Donington, Ryan Hanley and Jessica Moody (eds), *Britain's history and memory of slavery: The local nuances of a 'national sin'* (Liverpool: Liverpool University Press, 2016), pp. 129–49.

37 HFAC, Diary of Robert Hibbert junior, 18 June 1773.
38 Burnard and Morgan, 'The dynamic of the slave market', p. 216.
39 NLW/SPD, 9212, Letter from Thomas Hibbert junior to Nathaniel Phillips, 20 August 1772.
40 Radburn, 'Guinea factors', p. 271.
41 NLW/SPD, 9212, Letter from Thomas Hibbert junior to Nathaniel Phillips, 20 August 1772.
42 HFAC, Diary of Robert Hibbert junior, 20 June 1774.
43 Burnard, 'Credit, Kingston merchants and the Atlantic slave trade', p. 3.
44 Marguerite Curtin, 'Mr. Hibbert of Stanton Street' (unpublished manuscript, Jamaica National Heritage Trust, 1983).
45 Radburn, 'Guinea factors', p. 283.
46 Burnard, 'Credit, Kingston merchants and the Atlantic slave trade', p. 24.
47 HFAC, Diary of Robert Hibbert junior, 17, 24, 26 June 1773.
48 *Ibid.*, 2 July 1773.
49 *Ibid.*, 2 June 1772.
50 Evidence of Hercules Ross, in *An abstract of the evidence delivered before a Select Committee of the House of Commons in the years 1790, and 1791; on the part of the petitioners for the abolition of the slave-trade* (London: James Phillips, 1791), pp. 154–5.
51 Vincent Brown, *The reaper's garden: Death and power in the world of Atlantic slavery* (London: Harvard University Press, 2008), p. 189.
52 Hercules Ross, quoted in Sheridan, 'The commercial and financial organisation', p. 255.
53 Curtin, 'Mr Hibbert of Stanton Street'.
54 Frank Cundall, *Historic Jamaica* (London: Ballatine, Hanson & Co., 1915), p. 179.
55 For an account of the life of Theresa Constantia Philips see Kathleen Wilson, 'The black widow: Gender, race and performance in England and Jamaica', in *The island race: Englishness, empire, and gender in the eighteenth century* (London: Routledge, 2003), pp. 129–69.
56 Goodman *et al.*, 'Headquarters House', p. 4.
57 Cundall, *Historic Jamaica*, p. 179.
58 Hall, 'Whose memories?', p. 138. For a further discussion of the role of the colonial assembly see Jack P. Greene, 'Liberty, slavery and the transformation of British identity in the eighteenth-century West Indies', *Slavery & Abolition*, 21:1 (2000), pp. 1–31.
59 Michael Craton, 'Property and propriety: Land tenure and slave property in the creation of a British West Indian plantocracy, 1612–1740', in John Brewer and Susan Staves (eds), *Early modern conceptions of property* (London: Routledge, 1996), p. 510.
60 Letter from Simon Taylor to Chaloner Arcedekne, Kingston, 11 July 1765, quoted in Betty Wood and Martin Lynn (eds), *Trade, travel and power in the Atlantic, 1765–1884*, Camden Miscellany 35 (Cambridge: Cambridge University Press, 2002), pp. 19–20.
61 HFAC, Diary of Robert Hibbert junior, 1 January 1788.
62 *Ibid.*, 24 August 1776.
63 *Ibid.*, 13 August 1773.

JAMAICA

64 Charity Harry and Thomas senior's relationship is discussed in Chapter 6 (part I).
65 HFAC, Diary of Robert Hibbert junior, 9 September 1775.
66 *Ibid.*, 13 July 1776.
67 *Ibid.*, 4 June 1778.
68 *Ibid.*, 19 November 1777.
69 *Ibid.*, 25 January 1780, 25 May 1791, 31 January 1796.
70 *Ibid.*, 2 April 1776.
71 *Ibid.*, 2 March 1779.
72 *Ibid.*, 10 March 1777.
73 *Ibid.*, 20 May 1780.
74 *Ibid.*, 22 May 1780.
75 James Hakewill, *A picturesque tour of the island of Jamaica from drawings made in the years 1820 and 1821* (London: Hurst & Robinson, 1825).
76 Goodman *et al.*, 'Headquarters House', p. 15.
77 *Ibid.*
78 *Marly; Or, a planter's life in Jamaica*, ed. Karina Williamson (Oxford: Macmillan Education, 2005), p. 41. For a discussion of the cultural significance of horsemanship within Caribbean slave societies see David Lambert, 'Master–horse–slave: Mobility, race and power in the British West Indies, c.1780–1838', *Slavery & Abolition*, 36:4 (2015), pp. 618–41.
79 HFAC, Diary of Robert Hibbert junior, 14 February 1777.
80 *Ibid.*, 6 May 1777.
81 *Ibid.*, 21 December 1772.
82 *Ibid.*, 11 August 1789.
83 *Ibid.*, 25 July 1791.
84 Jamaican National Archives, Hanover Slave Court Records, 1A/2/1/1, *The King v. Patrick Hibbert*, Agualta Vale Pen, 7 July 1830. My thanks to Michael Becker for supplying me with a transcription.
85 For a discussion of Hakewill's work in relation to slavery see Charmaine Nelson, *Slavery, geography and empire in nineteenth-century marine landscapes of Montreal and Jamaica* (Abingdon: Routledge, 2016) in particular 'James Hakewill's *Picturesque Tour*: Representing life on nineteenth-century Jamaican sugar plantations', pp. 277–340.
86 Brown, *The reaper's garden*, p. 239. For a discussion of Agualta Vale in relation to the idea of the 'planter picturesque' see Elizabeth A. Bohls, *Slavery and the politics of place: Representing the colonial Caribbean, 1770–1833* (Cambridge: Cambridge University Press, 2014), pp. 21–3.
87 Nick Hibbert Steele, 'The price of sugar' (unpublished manuscript, undated), p. 39.
88 Brown, *The reaper's garden*, p. 240.
89 Hakewill, *A picturesque tour of the island*.
90 Bohls, *Slavery and the politics of place*, p. 22.
91 Centre for Buckinghamshire Studies, Aylesbury, D107/44, Lease and release, Thomas Hibbert junior to Robert Hibbert junior, 1785.
92 HFAC, Diary of Robert Hibbert junior, 27 January 1791.
93 B. W. Higman, *Jamaica surveyed: Plantation maps and plans of the eighteenth and nineteenth centuries* (Kingston: Institute of Jamaica Publications, 1988), p. 139.
94 'Albion', Legacies of British Slave-ownership database. www.ucl.ac.uk/lbs/estate/view/1629 [accessed 18 January 2019].
95 The Rev. R. Bickell, *The West Indies as they are; Or a real picture of slavery: But more particularly as it exists in the island of Jamaica* (London: J. Hatchard & Son, 1824), p. 74.
96 Evidence of James Simpson, in *Analysis of the report of the committee of the House of Commons on the extinction of slavery* (London: J. Hatchard & Son, 1833), pp. 148–9.
97 Jamaican National Archives, Hanover Slave Court Records, 1A/2/1/1, *The King v. Raynes Waite*, 8 January 1822. My thanks to Michael Becker for supplying me with a transcription.

98 The National Archives, Kew, Colonial Office and Predecessors (TNA/COP), CO 142/185, TNA/COP. My thanks to Rachel Lang for supplying the documents.
99 Ibid.
100 Joseph Sturge and Thomas Harvey, *The West Indies in 1837* (London: Hamilton, Adams & Co., 1838), Appendix F, 'Jamaica', pp. l–li.
101 'Great Valley', British Slave-ownership database. www.ucl.ac.uk/lbs/estate/view/1890 [accessed 17 April 2017].
102 'Dundee', Legacies of British Slave-ownership database. www.ucl.ac.uk/lbs/estate/view/1891 [accessed 17 April 2017].
103 Evidence of the Reverend Thomas Cooper, in *Abstract of the report of the Lords committee on the condition and treatment of the colonial slaves and of the evidence taken by them on that subject* (London: J. Hatchard & Son, 1833), p. 114.
104 The public dispute between Cooper, Robert Hibbert and George Hibbert is discussed in Chapter 5.
105 Robert Hibbert, *Hints to the young Jamaica sugar planter* (London: T. & G. Underwood, 1825), p. 16.
106 Ibid., p. 8.
107 Ibid., p. 9.
108 Thomas Cooper, *A letter to Robert Hibbert Jun. Esq., in reply to his pamphlet, entitled, 'Facts verified upon oath, in contradiction of the report of the Reverend Thomas Cooper, concerning the general condition of the slave in Jamaica* (London: J. Hatchard & Son, 1824), p. 7.
109 GA/BFDP, D1799/C153, Letter from Robert Hibbert junior to Mary Oates, 7 August 1807.
110 Ibid., Letter from Robert Hibbert junior to Mary Oates, undated.
111 JFSGRL, Diary of George Hibbert, 6 July 1817, transcription by Mabel Nembhard. http://jamaicanfamilysearch.com [accessed 4 August 2013].
112 'George Hibbert Oates', Legacies of British Slave-ownership database. www.ucl.ac.uk/lbs/person/view/19116 [accessed 26 April 2017].
113 'York Pen', Legacies of British Slave-ownership database. www.ucl.ac.uk/lbs/estate/view/8340 [accessed 23 April 2017].
114 'Morven', Legacies of British Slave-ownership database. www.ucl.ac.uk/lbs/estate/view/7410 [accessed 19 April 2017].
115 Nicholas Draper, *The price of emancipation: Slave-ownership, compensation and the British society at the end of slavery* (Cambridge: Cambridge University Press, 2010), p. 21.
116 Ibid., p. 337.
117 Brian Connolly and Marisa Fuentes, 'Introduction: From archives of slavery to liberated futures', *History of the Present*, 6:2 (2016), p. 105.
118 Hilary Beckles, *Britain's black debt: Reparations for Caribbean slavery and native genocide* (Kingston: University of the West Indies Press, 2013), p. 1.
119 'Reparations ten-point plan approved unanimously by meeting of Caribbean nations in St Vincent', Leigh Day, 11 March 2014. www.leighday.co.uk/News/2014/March-2014/CARICOM-nations-unanimously-approve-10-point-plan [accessed 18 August 2017].
120 David Cameron, 'PM's speech to the Jamaican Parliament', 30 September 2015. www.gov.uk/government/speeches/pms-speech-to-the-jamaican-parliament [accessed 18 August 2017].
121 *Nature's jottings: Newsletter of the Natural History Society of Jamaica* (October 2015). http://naturalhistorysocietyjamaica.org/nature/NaturesJottings2015-10.pdf [accessed 18 August 2017].

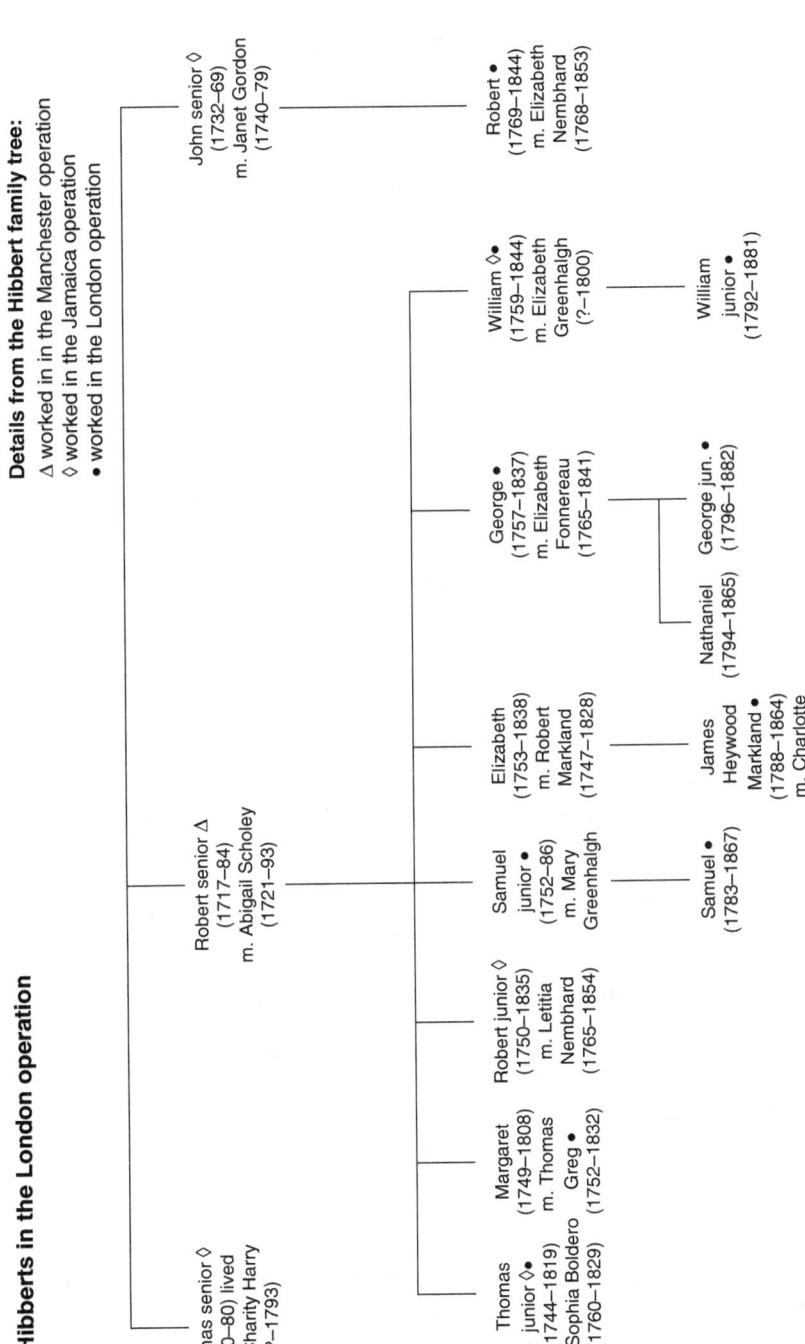

Family tree 4 The Hibberts in the London operation

CHAPTER THREE

London

I have observ'd those Countries where Trade is promoted and encouraged, do not make Discoveries to destroy, but to improve Mankind through Love and Friendship; to tame the fierce and polish the savage; to teach them the Advantage of honest Traffick, by taking from them, with their own Consent, their useless Superfluities; and giving them, in Return, what, from their Ignorance in mutual Arts, their Situation, or some other Accident, they stand in need of.

George Lillo, *The London merchant*, act III, scene I (London: John Gray, 1740), p. 35

The British merchant sitting in his accompting-house, and arranging the concerns of his extensive commerce, is an object, whether we consider him in a political or philosophical view, of the first respect and consideration. At the moment he commands the produce of the distant world to flow into his warehouses, he forwards the cultivation of his own country, sets the wheels of the British manufacturer in motion, holds forth the rewards of industry to the active, and animates by his encouraging liberality, the exertion of genius; while every wind that blows, serves to quicken the progress of his numerous ships to some or other of the various destinations in the different quarters of the globe.

William Coombe, *The devil upon two sticks in England*, vol. I (London: Logographic Press, 1790), pp. 178–9

In 1770 Thomas senior wrote to the Jamaica planter Nathaniel Phillips to announce a new co-partnership between his nephew Thomas junior and the London merchants John Purrier senior and Thomas Horton. Having established one of the most profitable slave factorage businesses in Jamaica, the Hibberts set their sights on the wealth being generated through the merchant houses of the City of London. London in the eighteenth century was both the capital of Britain's expanding empire and, for the mercantile elite, an empire of expanding capital.

LONDON

Commerce was the lifeblood of the city and flowing through it was that great artery of trade – the Thames. Connecting London to the regions, as well as to the global market, the international traffic on the river was a visible marker of Britain's growing position as one of Europe's dominant maritime trading powers. The notion of an 'empire of the sea' was embedded within ideas about the role of commerce within the nation.[1] The merchants of London were making the world knowable, and consumable, through trade and colonisation. Their efforts were to be lauded as improving the condition of humanity through the civilising effects of commerce both at home and in the empire. This ennobling of British economic activity masked the exploitation and brutality that accompanied commercial imperialism. Writing during a period of rapid expansion of the slave trade, Lillo's concept of trading as a means 'to tame the fierce and polish the savage' anticipated some of the arguments made by the proslavery lobby in later years.[2] In the mid-eighteenth century the slavery business was thriving, the respectability and riches of its elite participants holding 'forth the rewards of industry to the active'.[3]

Viewed with both admiration and suspicion, the rise of the commercial classes transformed the social, economic, political, cultural and imperial landscape. This trend was nowhere more pronounced than in the capital, although other centres of transatlantic mercantile influence were highly visible in Bristol, Liverpool and Glasgow. Largely divided by their respective geographic interests, the merchants of London were a powerful faction. Overseas trade exploded during the eighteenth century with the volume and tonnage of the Port of London 'greater than all the outports combined'.[4] By the 1750s London was increasingly recognised as *the* centre for the financing and organisation of a variety of different aspects of the slave economy. As Richard Sheridan noted, 'Here was a large and growing market for sugar; an important source of plantation supplies; a financial, exchange and shipping centre; and the seat of imperial Government.'[5] The credit, insurance and commodity markets that developed to accommodate overseas trading were all intensively cultivated within the City. Access to political decision making and the exertion of influence on policy was centralised on the capital, making a presence in London highly desirable for elite merchants. Opening a London counting house enabled the Hibberts to deepen their stake in the economic and political world of the slavery business, earning them the title of 'the first house in the Jamaica trade'.[6]

The Hibberts' commercial operation was based on years of steady consolidation. Utilising networks that had been nurtured in Liverpool, Manchester and Jamaica, Thomas junior called on his uncle's connections to establish an initial portfolio of correspondents. Having earned a reputation for financial probity, the Hibberts' branch house in London was able to build on the trust vested in them by their Jamaica clients to develop a truly transatlantic business enterprise. Family members were stationed at each of the counting houses, combining a recognisable name and face with an intimate working knowledge of the trade. Thomas junior had been trained by elite slave traders on both sides of the Atlantic; meanwhile his new partners brought knowledge and experience in the area of ship management. Alongside the cultivation of trust, the Hibberts also offered an ease of convenience through the provision of an integrated service which eventually took in not only the sale of enslaved people but also credit, plantation supplies, shipping, warehousing, insurance and distribution. For their elite clients they also catered to more personal needs such as the provision of lodgings and schooling for their children in England.

As their business flourished the Hibberts entered into a series of partnerships, sometime with each other and sometimes with outsiders. With the passage of time the family structure of the merchant house reconfigured; following the death of Thomas senior in 1780, his nephew Thomas junior became head of the family business. Thomas junior left Jamaica shortly afterwards, leaving his brother Robert junior and his Jamaica-born cousin Thomas to manage affairs in Kingston. Keen to abandon the exertions of trade and pursue the life of a country gentleman, by the early 1800s Thomas junior had handed over the reins of the London house to his younger brother George. The family firm continued on for a further six decades, with George's sons and nephews replacing the older generation. Increased success and visibility within the capital's merchant community enabled the Hibberts to influence policy and drive through large-scale initiatives of benefit to West Indian commerce. George's involvement in spearheading the building of the West India Docks cemented his position as one of *the* leading members of the London West India interest. Still standing today, the site is a lasting memorial to London's extensive engagement with the business of slavery.

The partners

The personnel of the Hibberts' London partnerships drew on both family members and trusted associates. Initially the merchant house of Hibbert, Purrier & Horton was a quintessentially transatlantic affair. Thomas junior remained in Jamaica throughout its establishment. He visited England for a year in 1777 but it was not until his uncle's death that he returned permanently to Britain in 1780. The two London-based partners were John Purrier senior, a former ship's captain, and Thomas Horton.[7] Thomas junior's return proved to be timely as Horton died shortly afterwards. In February 1781 Purrier wrote to Nathaniel Phillips to inform him that Edward Fuhr had been taken into the co-partnership of Hibbert, Purrier & Fuhr. He reassured Phillips that Fuhr had been working alongside the partners for many years, 'during which time he hath behaved much to our satisfaction – Independent of his connections with my Family by his Brothers being married to Mrs Purrier's Sister.'[8] The admittance of the intimate relation was countered by Purrier's vouching for Fuhr's good behaviour and long-standing service. The appointment was a relief for Purrier, who noted that he had been 'wanting assistance in the compting house from a Principal for sometime past'. Purrier also announced in his letter that Thomas junior's younger brother George had arrived from Manchester to commence working for the new co-partnership. He enthused that in time if it 'please God will by and by' George would 'be added to our firm'.

In 1785 John Purrier senior died, leaving an opening for a new partner, and in 1788 George wrote to Phillips to inform him that he had been elevated to the position in the new firm of Hibbert, Fuhr & Hibbert:

> I have the pleasure to tell you that our co-partnership is settled in a very harmonious manner and very advantageously for me. The merit and Service of my Friend Fuhr entitle him to a third of the Profits of the new House and my Brother has very generously put me on the same footing. I trust we shall prosper and not discredit the Character we have established under our old Fellow Labourer, nor lose the Countenance of Steady and valuable Friends like yourself.[9]

By the early 1800s a new partnership was being discussed; this coincided with Thomas junior's withdrawal from commercial life, and was in the wake of a financial crisis which rocked the counting house. George explained to the planter Simon Taylor that 'a very unjust and totally misguided attack has been made upon the Credit of our House originating as I think in the failure of our next door neighbour in Mincing Lane, thank God we stand though sorely pelted'.[10] The Hibberts wanted to wind up their old house which had become encumbered by a slew of bad debts. The proposed partnership consisted solely of family members: George, his Jamaica-born cousin Robert, his brother William and his brother-in-law Thomas Greg. In October of 1801 George's brother Robert junior detailed the opening of the negotiations over the new venture.[11] A month later, when deliberations were concluded, Robert junior wrote that 'my Bro. William comes to talk over T.G.'s [Thomas Greg] declining the new co-partnership'.[12] Eventually the co-partnership of Geo., Rob. & Wm. Hibbert pushed ahead without Greg. A number of different co-partnerships existed simultaneously at various times, including several with the son of their former business partner John Vincent Purrier.

The later partnerships of Geo., Rob., Wm. & Sam. Hibbert (1811–18), G., W., S. Hibbert & Co. (1820–38) and Hibbert & Co. (1839–63) involved the next generation of Hibberts. The family business provided a means of supporting sons, nephews and broader kin. Their reputation was established and its continuity over time and across distance was key to maintaining the firm's prosperity. Keeping the business within the family meant the Hibberts exerted a greater degree of control over its handling and took a larger share of the profits. This was part of an inheritance which allowed elite mercantile families to maintain their wealth and position. The first of the younger Hibberts to join the merchant house was George's nephew and son-in-law Samuel. Samuel's father died in 1786 when he was three, and the family counting house provided the living the boy would need to make his way in life and support George's daughter Caroline, whom he married in 1808. A further two additions were made in the 1820s when George's third son, George junior, and his nephew, William junior, joined the family business. The three cousins all went on to become highly successful in their own right. Whilst the counting house remained committed to the West Indies, the younger men diversified their interests. Perhaps as a result of their relationship with their uncle Thomas Greg, the next generation took a particular interest in the lucrative insurance industry. Following the Marine Insurance Bill of 1824 the monopoly held by Lloyd's and the London Royal Exchange was finally broken and the market opened up to newcomers. George junior became a Director of the Indemnity Marine Assurance Company, taking out its first ever policy on 4 August 1824.[13] This company went on to become part of the insurance providers Aviva, a now familiar household name. Aviva's online heritage section mentions George junior, though his association with the slave economy is absent. Both Samuel and George junior were Directors of the Imperial Life Insurance Company and the Imperial Fire Assurance Company. William junior was a Director of the Royal Exchange Assurance Corporation and a Director of the Canada Company. He was also involved in the establishment of the Colonial Bank of the West Indies. Samuel was appointed as a Director of the Bank of England five times between 1820 and 1833. George junior eventually left behind a personal estate valued at £70,000 in 1877.[14] Samuel prospered to an even greater degree, leaving £90,000 in his will of 1867.[15] It was William junior who accrued the greatest fortune, leaving a personal estate of £165,288 1s 11d on his death in 1881.[16]

LONDON

The counting house

A merchant's counting house served as more than simply a place in which to conduct business – it was a site for the construction and performance of mercantile identity. Status and respectability were signalled through both the location and appearance of the premises. In an economy that relied so heavily on reputation and the flow of information, having a recognisable address close to the thick of the action was an important part of establishing one's position. In 1772 the *New complete guide to London* listed Hibbert, Purrier & Horton as merchants with premises at Scotch Yard, Bush Lane, Cannon Street.[17] By 1777 they had relocated to 9 Mincing Lane to a property that remained their business address for the next thirty-five years. The move marked a shift in status, placing the Hibberts more firmly within a core of elite traders. Situated in the heart of London's commercial district, the property was a short walk to the Royal Exchange, the Bank of England, the Lloyd's and Jamaica Coffee House, Customs House, Trinity House and Wiggins Quay – the Hibberts' private dock. Mincing Lane had been associated with the slave trade since one of its inhabitants, John Hawkins, became the first Englishman to transport captive Africans in 1562. Later residents included Humphrey Morice, perhaps the most prolific slave trader of the mid-eighteenth century, and his partner in the Bance Island slave factory, John Sargeant. Francis Baring's accepting house at 7 Mincing Lane provided credit finance for slave-trading voyages. George and Baring shared a love of art and became good friends, working closely together on the founding of the London Institution. In 1812, the same year that George quit Parliament to become the Agent for Jamaica, the Hibberts left Mincing Lane under the partnership Geo., Rob., Wm. & Sam. Hibbert for a fashionable new address at 1 Billiter Court, Billiter Square. The area was described as 'a very handsome, open, airy place, graced with good new brick buildings, very well inhabited'.[18] The premier location within this space was Billiter Square, a sought-after address deemed to be the 'chief ornament of this place'. For the Hibberts the move put them in the same location as George's close friend William Manning, a Member of Parliament, West India merchant and Agent for Grenada. It also placed them in the vicinity of the offices of the West India Dock Company, which George served as Chairman. The desirability of the address reflected George's new station and confirmed the Hibberts as *the* premier Jamaica merchant house.

The interior of the counting house was also a crucial element in the construction of mercantile identity. The merchant house was both a private and a public space, entered variously by the partners, friends, family, employees, clients, suppliers and domestic staff. The space needed to project a sense of mercantile respectability suitable to the station of its occupants. David Hancock has pointed to the paucity of information on the material culture of the counting house, although he provided a lengthy description of John Sargeant's premises at 38 Mincing Lane.[19] His description is worth consideration, given that many of the houses in the area were built in a uniform style. The arrangement and number of rooms across three floors denoted a spacious property, including: multiple work rooms for the partners and junior employees, a kitchen, pantry, dining room, large and small drawing rooms, library, bedrooms and a laundry. As visitors ascended the heights of the building they moved further into its intimate spaces. Hancock has suggested that the middle section of the property was where 'private life and business life merged, as clerks and workers were more or less forced into the family mould'.[20] The house was decorated in the mode of polite respectability rather than ostentatious excess. This was not an aristocratic residence coded with the symbols of luxury and opulence, but rather a place of business in which the interior signified moral judgement and prudent restraint.

The Hibberts lived through an important shift in the division of work and home life. In the early 1780s the separation was still incomplete and the Purriers resided intermittently at the Mincing Lane property. Details of the interior were occasionally mentioned in the firm's letters. Features included wine vaults and storage space for their correspondents' luxury goods. In the wake of Purrier's death in 1785, Edward Fuhr informed Nathaniel Phillips of an imminent redecoration. He wrote, 'as our poor friends Pictures were ordered by his Will to be sold I was under the necessity of having the House in Mincing Lane new furbished and put into Repair it is now completed and ready to receive our friends'.[21] The ownership of artworks conformed to the culture of conspicuous consumption. It demonstrated good taste and the civilising effects of commerce by elevating the mercantile character through an appreciation of the arts. Details like this helped to distinguish the elite merchant from the grubby small-time trader. With the paintings removed it was important for the counting house to compensate as a slip in standards might be interpreted by their clients as signifying financial trouble. Just as those lending credit might attempt to 'read a debtor's personal worth and character from their clothing, their marital relations, their spending patterns and their perceived social status', these methods could be used to judge the standing of the counting house.[22] As demonstrated by the Hibberts' financial crisis in 1803, rumours could spread quickly, impacting on the house's hard-won credibility. In an age where bankruptcy was a frequent occurrence, attention to outward appearances was important for maintaining character and trust.

The correspondents

The calibre of a merchant's clients impacted on the reputation of the merchant, and as Sherylynne Haggerty has argued, 'reputation ... is a form of capital'.[23] If a man were to be taken seriously in the world of commerce his correspondents should reflect both the height of his station and the depth of his purse. The Hibberts were able to attract key figures from within the Jamaica plantocracy, men who were both large-scale landowners in their own right and also attorneys for other absentee planters. Capturing the business of the island's powerful attorneys increased the Hibberts' access to multiple plantations because the attorney had the power to consign sugar from all of the estates under his control to his chosen agent in Britain.[24] Attracting and retaining these prized connections was a ruthless business which relied on a combination of personal networks, opportunism and skilful communications. Relationships with clients were established and maintained through the flow of letters that traversed the Atlantic.[25] These epistolary exchanges served different functions: on a practical level they were a means of conveying important commercial and political information, and alongside this they operated as a vehicle for the construction of the mercantile self.[26] Neither public nor private, these letters formed part of a performance of the key virtues of moral trade as outlined by Adam Smith – probity, prudence and punctuality.[27] Among the correspondence that survives, there is a wealth of information about the Hibberts' business dealings in the archives of three of their most prominent clients – Nathaniel Phillips, Simon Taylor and John Tharp.

On 29 April 1770 the eminent West India merchant Vincent Biscoe died unexpectedly whilst taking the waters at Bristol Hot Wells. Word of his demise travelled quickly – on 4 May 1770 Hibbert, Purrier & Horton wrote to Phillips in Jamaica to inform him of the news.[28] Phillips was already known to the Hibberts from their time on the island, but Biscoe was Phillips's London agent and his death represented an opportunity to win over a prize client for the new co-partnership. David Hancock described how Biscoe's untimely death led to a scramble by agents to secure his correspondents:

> Dogged persistence in finding contacts in the colonies was critical. Two days after the death of London merchant Vincent Biscoe of Austin Friars, who had enjoyed 'many of the most valuable correspondents all over the island', Grant [Sir Alexander Grant of the trading company Grant,

Oswald and Co.] commanded his Jamaica superintendent to seek out Biscoe's contacts, and would not rest until he had secured the custom of three of them.[29]

Hibbert, Purrier & Horton had an advantage in the race, given that Biscoe's executors included Thomas senior's former slave-trading partner Nathaniel Sprigg. Sprigg was well placed to help his old friend, having left Jamaica and set himself up as a country gentleman at Barn Elms, just outside London. Hancock has argued that associations of this kind were vital in a trade where 'commercial linkages to men with established, tested skills were culled and cultivated from a collection of blood, ethnic, and neighbourhood connections'. With rival firms looking to pilfer Biscoe's lucrative connections, the initial correspondence sent out by Hibbert, Purrier & Horton was suitably gushing. 'We flatter ourselves', they wrote, 'that you will continue to favour us with the transaction of your Business assuring you that we will make it our Study to render you Satisfaction.'[30] To shore up the new co-partnership's bid for Phillips's custom, Thomas senior wrote to him again in August 1770 to 'express my zeal for its promotion'.[31] Using the personal prestige he had built up over the years, he personally assured Phillips that the partners had 'each advanced a very respectable capital for carrying on West India Business under the Auspices and Patronage of my good friend ... Mr. Sprigg'. The overtures paid dividends and over the following decades Phillips became one of the Hibberts' closest clients.

What survives of Phillips's mercantile correspondence suggests a good relationship which spilt over into friendship. George's letters to Phillips were framed by a sense of masculine sociability, with details spanning family matters, friends and foes, as well as the standard trade news of markets and shipping. The inclusion of what George termed 'chit chat' was fairly unusual for business correspondence, which had grown increasingly formalised during the eighteenth century.[32] In contrast, the slave trader and merchant Alexander Grant demanded that business letters 'should have no political or personal news in them; such material should be reserved for personal letters'.[33] Like his uncle Thomas senior, George engaged in both business and bawdy in his letters to Phillips. On one occasion he wrote to Phillips lamenting his decision not to come to England as it would 'deny us your Company here and ... deny yourself the comfort of a Fair and Elegant English Bedfellow'.[34] The letters entertained Phillips with descriptions of dinners, drinking and gambling with their mutual acquaintances. The Hibberts played an important role in encouraging Phillips to settle in London. In 1788 George urged him:

Come on this side the Water; an Honest well meaning Man and a Gentleman can here at least live in Peace and Protection and be suffered to enjoy without offence, the harmless pleasures of Society. We look for you impatiently and no one will be happier to take you by the hand.[35]

In 1789 the Hibberts loaned Phillips £20,000 to facilitate his relocation.[36] The loan was made in conjunction with the banking firm of the Boldero family, with whom the Hibberts shared a close connection following the marriage of Thomas junior to Sophia Boldero in 1784. After Phillips settled in London the co-partnership extended the use of their offices on Mincing Lane as a new business headquarters for him.[37]

Crucially for the Hibberts, they also secured a share of the commission business of the planter Simon Taylor.[38] Described by Christer Petley as one of 'the most opulent and powerful people in Jamaica', Taylor provided the Hibberts with a key political ally, as well as an extremely lucrative commercial connection.[39] Taylor was born on the island in 1740 and had made his money initially as a plantation attorney. He invested in property and at one time owned six sugar estates and three cattle pens.[40] As attorney Taylor decided which sugar commission houses in London he would consign produce to: for example, in 1775 he sent Hibbert, Purrier & Horton 374 hogsheads of sugar from two estates he managed as attorney and acting executor for John Nixon.[41] George calculated that in terms of the hogsheads produced by Taylor 'I should presume not less than 1,000 of his own nor less than 2,000 which he controuls.'[42] Taylor occupied a number of political, civic and military positions; he was a member of the Jamaica Assembly for Kingston between 1763 and 1781 and for St Thomas-in-the-East between 1784 and 1810. He also served as Custos, Chief Justice of the Court of Common Pleas and Lieutenant-General of the Militia.[43] Taylor's patronage enhanced the Hibberts' commercial reputation and facilitated their political ambitions, including George's drive to become Agent for Jamaica. As George noted, Taylor's 'kindness in protecting our interest in Jamaica in most essential to us'.[44] This became all the more important in later years when most of the Hibberts relocated to England. When George announced the new co-partnership of Geo., Rob., & Wm. Hibbert to Taylor, he wrote: 'I know that you will give me your good wishes and I am anxious too that we should have a share of your patronage – as for myself I shall always feel indebted for your past friendship and anxious to merit a Continuance of it.'[45] George's sense of indebtedness was both an expression of gratitude and a statement of fact. The firm Hibbert, Fuhr & Purrier borrowed £15,750 from Taylor's cousin Robert Taylor – a partner in the London West India house of Taylor & Renny.[46] It took them over five years to pay the sum back, during which time George offered his brother Thomas junior's country residence, Chalfont House, as security on the loan.[47] The debt was eventually paid in 1803 using the compensation money the Hibberts received as private quay owners following the West India Dock Act of 1799.

The letters to Taylor were much more formal than those to Phillips, with George adopting a deferential tone. While family news was still included in their correspondence, it was trade and politics, however, that dominated. George used his communications to circulate information about the sugar duties, the rise of the East Indians, American trade and the abolition campaigns. The material on the slave trade is illuminating of the differences in opinion between the proslavery lobby in the metropole and the colonies. George had been attending the meetings of the Society of West India Planters and Merchants (SWIPM) since 1782 and kept Taylor abreast of the prevailing opinions of the absentees and London merchants. Taylor in turn acted as a barometer for the political mood amongst the planters and merchants in Jamaica. In the years following his entry into Parliament, George reported faithfully on his efforts to promote the interests of those invested in the slavery business. This exchange of information formed a different, but no less vital, series of transactions between merchant and client.

Together with Taylor and Phillips, John Tharp was also counted as one of the firm's most valued relationships. Described by Sarah Pearsall as having inherited 'one of the greatest of Jamaican fortunes', Tharp claimed ownership in 3,000 enslaved people, seven sugar plantations and three pens representing over 20,000 acres of land.[48] His properties included Good Hope, which today is one of the best-preserved plantations in Jamaica.[49] Tharp also held political position: he was elected to the House of Assembly in 1772 and served as both a Justice of the Peace and as Custos of Trelawny. Tharp had been consigning his sugar to Hibbert, Purrier & Fuhr since 1782. When he died in 1804, George was appointed by the Court of Chancery as consignee, thus ensuring that the London partnership would continue to receive sugar from Tharp's estates.[50] The Hibbert firm maintained this position until 1835.[51] According to A. E. Furness the average production of Tharp's estates between 1795 and 1800 'was just over 1,500 hogsheads of sugar a year, which should have brought him the clear income of £30,000 a year'.[52] Furness has estimated that the Hibbert partnership made around £2,500 a year in fees and commission from their involvement with Tharp's plantations.[53]

Tharp's estate was willed to his infant grandson, with trustees appointed to take care of the property until he came of age, George Hibbert, Simon Taylor and the banker Philip John Miles among them.

As he grew older it became apparent that Tharp's grandson suffered with mental health problems and he was eventually committed to an asylum. When Taylor died in 1813 his role was taken on by brothers John and William Shand. This proved to be a poor choice when they defrauded the estate, resulting in significant losses. In a later court case George offered a series of alternative explanations for the spiralling costs incurred during the Shands' tenure. Furness has suggested that George's support for the brothers stemmed from his 'obligation to John Shand for his help in persuading the Assembly in Jamaica to appoint Hibbert as its Agent in London in 1812'.[54] The Shands were eventually dismissed, but the fortunes of Tharp's estates went into terminal decline. By the early 1820s the estates were heavily indebted to both the Hibberts and Miles. What began as a £20,000 debt in 1818 had increased to the sum of £107,000 by 1831. The Court of Chancery agreed to let the debt be serviced through insurance policies taken out by the creditors. When slavery compensation money was awarded to the Tharps it was put in a trust against which the Hibberts and Miles were able to draw an annual income from the interest.[55]

The business

The Hibbert mercantile partnerships in Manchester, Jamaica and London specialised in different but interconnected aspects of the slavery business. The London house focused on shipping, insurance, credit and the sale of slave-produced commodities. Despite these shifts in emphasis the houses were part of an integrated commercial concern. George explained the system to the Parliamentary Select Committee in 1790:

> The planters often draw bills on the merchants to whom their produce is consigned, to pay for the slaves they may buy. The planter has often credit in the island for the slaves he buys. When he draws on his merchant, at the expiration of that credit, he draws at the island usance, or, if for a longer time, interest for such time is included in the bill. Bills for Jamaica are usually drawn at 90 days sight.[56]

The family nature of the Hibberts' business offered some security for their clients. As John Fletcher remarked to his slave-ship captain Peleg Clarke in 1774: 'Hibberts and Co. Bills are as good as the bank and will tell well here, which is very Material in our Large Concern.'[57] The firm was so well thought of that Fletcher entreated Clarke not to charge interest to the Hibberts, 'as all their Bills are Guaranteed and no fear of their returning'. Although the London partners enjoyed a degree of separation from the day-to-day realities of slave trading, there were references to it within their mercantile correspondence. In a letter to Taylor in 1806, just a year prior to the abolition of the trade, George wrote that:

> Sir Simon Clarke certainly is thought to have got Welcome and Haddington with Negroes and stocks a great bargain ... but He wants Negroes very much indeed and he cannot reasonably look to supply from Imported Negroes for tho he might help himself that way a little, yet he wants more in November than it would be prudent to buy at once, or than he can expect to buy by degrees while the trade is open. It seems therefore that his interest is to buy and ours is to sell.[58]

The connection to the slave-trading operation run by his family allowed George to broker a deal to supply Clarke with enslaved labourers through Taylor. Later in the year George again used his connection to Taylor to facilitate the purchase of enslaved people. This time it was for his Jamaica-born cousin Thomas, who had bought out George's elder brothers' interests in the family plantation of Agualta Vale. George indicated to Taylor that his cousin had set out conditions for the sale and 'has given some instructions to Robert Markland'.[59] Markland was George's nephew and acted as both a slave factor and the Hibberts' attorney in Jamaica.

The primary concern of the London co-partnership was the sale of sugar. In 1790 George stated that 'We import from 5,000 to 6,000 hogsheads of sugar, besides other articles, the gross value of which may be from £200,000 to £250,000.'[60] For their services the partnership received a commission of 2.5 per cent.[61] Sugar agents required an expert knowledge of every aspect of production and of domestic and international markets, as well as political and military affairs affecting trade. For elite merchants the ability to influence these areas rendered them all the more useful. As with the sale of enslaved people in Jamaica, sugar agents could withhold their precious commodity until the highest possible price was achieved. During periods of war when shipping was dangerous and infrequent, the value of sugar soared; similarly, in periods when the markets became glutted profits could sink. A good agent could judge the quality of the consignment and price it according to its purity and market value. Insider information enabled the successful sugar agent to secure the best terms for their customers. George's Chairmanship of the Society of West India Merchants gave him access to privileged information, as well as the ability to influence trade policy. He was regularly involved in high-level deputations to Government to discuss commercial matters. The issue of sugar duties was a subject of intense interest, with George lobbying hard to keep the taxes down. During the debates over both the slave trade and slavery,

George served as a Member of Parliament (1806–12) and later as Agent for Jamaica (1812–30). His access to political power and the circuits of knowledge that came along with that made his firm a highly desirable choice for the discerning planter.

The Hibberts were unusual in that they owned their own ships, as well as investing in part shares of vessels. This provided the family and their associates with a greater degree of control over the movement of produce. As shipping agents the co-partnership could charge an additional fee of 2.5 per cent. Despite naming their first vessel *Hibberts* in 1763, initially the family did not hold the principal interest in the ship.[62] Having ships built bespoke for the trade was an expense that very few merchants could afford, so part-ownership spread both the cost and the risk. Marguerite Curtin has described how Thomas senior and his brother John senior overcame this problem during the conflict with France in the mid-eighteenth century:

> From time to time, a French prize ship purchased by the brothers in the Kingston harbour at a good price would add to the growing Hibbert fortune. The ship refurbished, renamed, and carrying a valuable cargo of brown and white sugar, coffee and indigo would make a handsome profit for the Hibberts, when it reached the Port of London.[63]

By 1772 the Hibberts were commissioning the building of their own ship on the Thames. So impressed was Taylor by their fleet that he advised his cousin Robert Taylor that he would 'win respect to resemble the ships in the Hibbert employ'.[64] In evidence given to a Select Committee in 1823 George stated that he had personally owned or held a part share in eight ships in the West India trade.[65] The calibre of the Hibberts' captains was also noted – most had been Younger Brethren of Trinity House and all served the family dutifully for long periods of time.[66] Captains Philip Stimpson, John Boyd and Benjamin Raffles (father of Sir Thomas Stamford Bingley Raffles, the 'founder' of Singapore) were regularly referenced in Robert junior's diary. The speed of the Hibberts' ships was also renowned – the *Hibberts* broke a record in 1785 by sailing from the Downs to Port Royal in just over thirty days.[67] Having the edge in terms of speed meant that the Hibberts could assure their clients that their produce would reach the market quickly. It was also a matter of pride and prestige that theirs was the fastest West Indiaman on the sea. When the vessels were spent the Hibberts sold them on; the *George Hibbert*, for example, ended life as a convict ship, transporting prisoners to Australia.[68]

The slave trade and the trade in slave-produced commodities were dangerous ventures which left both the ship owners and those who had cargo on board exposed to risk. As a result, the marine insurance industry developed to provide some form of protection for investors. In sourcing insurance for their clients the Hibberts could claim an additional 0.5 per cent in commission.[69] Insurance rates could double if the ships failed to leave Jamaica before 1 August and the onset of the hurricane season. Insurance was at the discretion of the planter and cargos were not always covered. The Hibberts experienced the loss of uninsured goods themselves. In 1791 Robert junior noted in his diary that 'I go down to the Store early this morn'g & hear the news of the loss of the *Simon Taylor Watt* in which I had 100 Hhds of Albion Sugars & 1/16th of the Ship totally uninsured.'[70] The Hibberts had a personal connection within the insurance trade; in 1780 Robert junior's sister, Margaret, had married Thomas Greg, a broker for Lloyds who provided insurance for some of the family's correspondents. The degree to which Greg was involved in the Hibberts' commercial affairs can be deduced from their desire to incorporate him into a co-partnership.

Once the West Indiamen arrived safely back to London they faced additional problems in terms of docking and storage. The ships were too deep to moor in the shallow waters by the quayside, so goods had to be transported onto lighters and carried to the numerous private docks that dotted the Thames. A lack of space resulted in sugar being stacked and left in the open, leading to spoilage and theft. When the Hibberts' vessels arrived into the Port of London their ships had private access to Wiggins Quay and a warehouse on Lower Thames Street. These facilities were owned by the family for the exclusive use of their clients, meaning that their produce could be securely stored and delivered to market more efficiently. Fees were charged on each aspect of the process: a lighterage and wharfage fee for transferring the cargo from the ship to the quay and on to the warehouse, plus a subsequent warehousing charge. The warehouse offered ample storage space – the basement was 124ft long, the crane house and wharf measured 52ft by 20ft. The frontage facing away from the Thames was 64ft wide with two further storeys above the basement.[71] In the 1790s the Hibberts threw their weight behind the scheme to build the West India Docks, which did away with the need to keep a private quay.

The London merchant house was involved with the supply of credit on a significant scale. The issue of West India indebtedness was well known: in 1790 George valued colonial debt as no less than £20 million.[72] If the colonial planters were the face of the system of slavery, the metropolitan merchants were the backbone. It was the huge sums of finance they were willing to pump into the Caribbean that sustained and grew the economy. Debt was incurred for a number of reasons, as George himself explained: 'in settling new, and extending and improving old estates ... in new machinery and modes of manufacture ... to repair damage made in hurricanes ... to buy negroes and other relief'. In some instances, as was the case with the Tharps, the only way for the Hibberts to see a return on a loan was for them to lend yet more money, particularly in the case of a natural disaster or a bad harvest. They loaned money to ensure that planters could make their consignments, they also did it to make sure the estates remained productive enough for their debtors to pay the mortgage money that was owed to them. The extension of credit allowed the Hibberts to accrue interest on debts – the interest on the Tharp debt was 5 per cent.[73] If the borrower defaulted the Hibberts could foreclose, resulting in an increase in their Jamaica holdings. The acquisition of plantations was not viewed favourably by the London house, especially after the advent of abolitionism. As George informed Taylor, 'I have expressed it to H T and M [Hibbert, Taylors & Markland] how anxious we are to diminish the Stake we are likely to be obliged to hold in the soil and how earnestly we wish to seize every opportunity of liquidation.'[74] With so much of the family's money tied up in mortgages in Jamaica it is easy to see why George campaigned so stridently for the payment of compensation in the event of abolition. The extent of the Hibberts' credit networks can be read in the very substantial amounts of compensation money they claimed as mortgagees, which came to the value of at least £20,948 16s 3d.[75] In today's money a conservative estimate would put the worth of this sum at £1.89 million.[76]

Lending money to the planters could be a long-drawn-out affair which grew increasingly complicated as time passed. In 1790 George stated that the house had debts on its books that had been there for forty or fifty years.[77] When the Hibberts formed a new partnership in 1801 George was determined that the new house 'will avoid all large advances, or money engagements'.[78] The issue of bad debt continued to be a worry. In 1806 George wrote to Taylor informing him that some debts owed to the Hibberts had 'grown too unwieldy for their first pledge' although he assured him that they had 'as few very bad or desperate debt as any house that had been so long in business'.[79] He went on:

> [O]ur large concerns were with Parties who had the greatest right to expect large reversions from their Properties indebted to us. And yet even this Circumstance we cannot collect a quarter of what is due to us without plunging into utter ruin our best connections and even so doing we are often only changing our Risque and the nature of our trouble.

Occasionally the Hibberts ran into difficulty in securing their debts – in one instance their client fled to avoid payment. Sir William Hillary and his brother had an interest in the Adelphi plantation in Jamaica and had borrowed £19,607 15s 8d from the Hibberts. Following Hillary's flight, George wrote to Taylor:

> Sir William Hillary is gone to pieces and has absconded and his Brother, who was of no better Character, is dead; we have I fear nothing but the Rights of the Brother in Adelphi Estate to look to for my demand which is very large ... Sir William Hillary has scandalously treated and deceived us and we have therefore no obligation to him but indeed his most sanguine creditor cannot look for any eventual advantage to his Estate from the demand on or Right in Adelphi after our Demand should be paid upon it.[80]

This was outrageous behaviour for a gentleman and the attack on Hillary's character was designed to blacken his name among the elite in Jamaica. The two men eventually put their differences aside to work together to found the National Institution for the Preservation of Life from Shipwreck in 1824. Despite their joint philanthropic endeavour, the financial dispute over Hillary's debt rumbled on even after George's death in 1837. The slave compensation register documented two claims awarded for 154 and 79 enslaved people on the Adelphi estate. The claims were contested on behalf of the Hibberts by their former partner John Vincent Purrier and another interested party, Isaac Lascelles Winn. In 1843 Purrier was eventually awarded £2,819 8s 11d compensation money as receiver in the suits *Hibbert* v. *Hillary* and *Hillary* v. *Winn*.[81]

The West India Docks

With their growing influence amongst the London mercantile elite, the Hibberts turned towards the promotion of a transformational project that would bring them authority, position, revenue and a lasting imprint on the capital's landscape. In 1793 George became involved in plans to build new docks for ships in the West India trade. The process of mooring, customs inspection and moving Caribbean produce to warehousing space was too slow. George estimated the resulting cost in terms of theft and spoilage was around £500,000 per annum.[82] The Hibberts' co-partnership had personal experience of this type of crime; they appeared in the records of the Old Bailey in 1796 in the case of Patrick Fallon who was indicted for 'feloniously stealing, on the 15th of November, fifty pounds weight of sugar, value 16s. the property of Thomas Hibbert, Edward Fuhr, and George Hibbert'.[83] Fallon was a Custom House Officer – he claimed that the actual perpetrator had made his escape through a cabin window and swam for shore. Whether part of a conspiracy or an innocent bystander, Fallon was acquitted.

His case demonstrated the difficulty in apprehending and convicting thieves, especially when the possibility of corruption from within the system was present. Reflecting back on these circumstances George recalled that 'The plunderage was extensive ... it was carried on by combination, and with very great art ... it was easy to commit it, and very difficult to detect it.'[84] Concerns over the theft of property led the SWIPM to fund the Marine Police Office, which was established in 1798.

The West India interest wanted a permanent resolution to the problem. With the onset of war with France the issue became a pressing one, as 'foreign trade, hitherto one of the chief mercantile activities of the country, became a matter of national survival'.[85] A scheme emerged to build London's first enclosed wet docks exclusively for the use of vessels in the West India and slave trade at the Isle of Dogs. Moving the West India Docks initiative forward proved to be a complicated issue thanks to the existence of a competing scheme.[86] The London Dock Company was set on building a free port at Wapping. The two bids divided financial backers in the City and have been described by Walter Stern as being framed by 'different political philosophies ... the London Dock Company represents democracy, the West India Dock Company benevolent autocracy'.[87] Having initially supported the former, George was persuaded to back the latter by his fellow merchant and slave trader Robert Milligan. As 'a leading West India merchant, an important wharfinger, and, from 1798, a City Alderman' George was 'a vital convert' for the scheme.[88] He had access to the political and commercial connections that were necessary to unify the City and raise funds in support of the plan for an enclosed dock at the Isle of Dogs.

In 1799 the West India Dock Act passed through Parliament. As stipulated in the legislation the Government agreed to compensate those affected by the building works, including private quay owners. The architect Sir John Soane was a member of the compensation commission and was sent to assess the claims. In 1804, following lengthy negotiations, the Hibberts received £33,408 in compensation for Wiggins Quay.[89] The finances required to pay for the construction of the docks was vast; the funds were acquired from 353 subscribers, who collectively invested £500,000.[90] Nicolas Draper has identified the investors as both those with interests in the West Indies as well as City men with no attachment to the Caribbean.[91] George invested £2,000 and owned 5,000 shares.[92] His brothers Thomas junior and Robert junior, brother-in-law Thomas Greg, partner John Vincent Purrier and client John Tharp all provided financial backing for the dock.[93] The shareholders were paid dividends capped at 10 per cent.[94] To ensure the scheme's success all ships in the West India trade were compelled to use the new facility. The monopoly was a controversial aspect of the West India Dock Act and a Select Committee was convened to discuss its renewal in 1823.

In 1802 George proudly wrote to Taylor to announce that 'At my request sent you a framed plan of our new Docks which will be ready for the Reception of a part of this year's crop.'[95] To ensure the goods were expedited to market George also served as Chairman of the Commercial Road Company. The road, which opened in 1804, ran through the suburbs of Whitechapel and linked the docks to the City. His championing of these endeavours made him the obvious choice for the position of Chairman of the West India Dock Company, a title he held eight times between 1799 and 1815.[96] The Chairman and the Court of Directors exerted control over the practical running of the docks, including, for example, setting the rates for using the facilities. The Company also provided a position for the next generation of Hibberts: George's son George junior, his son-in-law Samuel and his great-grandson Sydney served as Chairman and Directors. In 1838 the West India Dock Company merged with its neighbour, the East India Dock Company. George junior was appointed to the board and remained in position until 1877.[97] One of the East and West India Dock Company's major works of improvement was

Figure 6 *An elevated view of the new docks & warehouses now constructing on the Isle of Dogs near Limehouse for the reception & accommodation of shipping in the West India Trade ...,*
William Daniell, 1802

the building of the London and Blackwall Railway. The plans were underway by 1836 and completed by 1840 with George junior acting as Deputy Chairman.

The building of the docks completely transformed the area, leaving a lasting physical legacy of London's links to slavery. David Hancock has suggested that 'Through activities that were polite, industrious, and moral, with programs that combined a practical, commonplace approach with a visionary intent' the powerful merchants of London 'reshaped people's lives.'[98] Construction of the docks was on an epic scale – the site measured 2,508ft by 478ft. The complex opened for business in 1802, though the works were only finally completed in 1806. The project provided a large number of jobs both during the construction and afterwards, when men were needed for the daily operations of the new facility. Employment at the docks has been described as 'precarious ... the working conditions were harsh'.[99] When improvement came it was a 'fear of disorder more than compassion that motivated the Company's concern for its work-force'. The ruthless pursuit of profit, as Peter Linebaugh has argued, meant 'The international circuit of sugar brought the violence of its social relations back to London.'[100] The docks remained in operation until 1980, when they finally closed to commercial traffic.

Conclusion

The opening of the West India Docks was a crowning moment for George, it demonstrated his position as a leader of the mercantile elite and created a visible legacy that remains today. Traces of the family were inscribed into the very fabric of the structure; in 1803 at George's personal request, the gate leading to the docks was adorned with a model of the ship *Hibberts*.[101] Although the original gate was dismantled in 1932, a replica was reinstalled in 2000 by the Canary Wharf Group. The decision was defended in a text panel for an accompanying exhibition marking the bicentenary of the founding of the West India Docks:

> It is historically incorrect to believe that the name 'Hibbert Ship Gate' in some way was meant to be a memorial to the man – even in his time, and the re-erection of the Main Gate, complete with the model ship ... certainly does not represent any support for the practice of slavery or the part that George Hibbert played in it.[102]

Instead the exhibition claimed that the installation should be understood as 'a symbol, an important symbol, of the Island's mercantile past. At a time of change it is right to reflect, with pride, on that past.' An insistence on a mercantile past as separate to the history of slavery is a somewhat misplaced distinction, particularly in the context of the West India Docks, a place built at the request of West India merchants specifically to facilitate the slave economy. This uncomplicated veneration of mercantile endeavour is continued around the corner from the gate, where the dock's foundation stone remembers George as one 'distinguished among those chosen to direct AN UNDERTAKING, Which, under the favour of GOD, shall contribute Stability, Increase, and Ornament, to BRITISH COMMERCE.' A statue of Robert Milligan can be found in front of the old sugar warehouses with a base depicting the allegorical scene 'Commerce bringing prosperity to Britannia'. Echoing this sentiment, in 2018 an exhibition exploring the history of the docks was mounted on the hoarding on a construction site for the new Spire luxury residential tower. The narrative celebrated the docks and the West India trade as bringing 'prosperity to the area'. The text never once mentioned slavery, effectively erasing the enslaved from local history and memory.[103] The challenges posed by the tangible inheritance of slavery in a place which is now home to a multicultural demographic has been examined by Georgie Wemyss, who has argued that the docks are coded with the symbols and language of 'the invisible empire'.[104] Despite the presence of the Museum of London, Docklands, which includes the 'London, Sugar, Slavery' exhibition, these street-level signifiers remain untroubled by any contextualisation and instead reinstate uncritically the relationship between slavery, commerce and the empire of the seas.

The Hibberts' London merchant house was part of a system of trading that connected the capital to the colonies. Its operations demonstrate the flow of money from the Caribbean into the City via the interconnected networks of commercial activity that made up the slavery business. Without ever having to visit the slave societies they depended on, the London merchants could profit at a distance. The vast wealth generated was converted into political capital, which was then used to preserve trade privileges and defend the system against the rising tide of abolitionism. The Hibberts' success was such that by 1816 George was described as 'an eminent West India Merchant, whose family has long been considered as the head of the principal commercial house in Jamaica.'[105] The figure of the metropolitan West India merchant, whilst less familiar in the popular imaginary than his whip-wielding colonial counterpart, was no less implicated in slavery's structures. Shielded from the everyday realities of plantation life, polite mercantile culture provided a civilising veneer for slavery's depredations. Abstracted into the tidy rows and columns of the merchant's ledger the human cost of colonial productivity was transformed into profit and loss in pounds, shillings, and pence.

Figure 7 'Hibbert Ship Gate'

Notes

1 Kathleen Wilson, *The island race: Englishness, empire, gender in the eighteenth century* (London: Routledge, 2003), p. 15.
2 George Lillo, *The London merchant*, act III, scene I (London: John Gray, 1740), p. 35.

3 William Coombe, *The devil upon two sticks in England*, vol. I (London: Logographic Press, 1790), p. 178.
4 Christopher J. French, '"Crowded with traders and a great commerce": London's domination of English overseas trade, 1700–1775', *London Journal*, 17:1 (1992), p. 27.
5 Richard B. Sheridan, 'The commercial and financial organisation of the British slave trade, 1750–1807', *Economic History Review*, 11:2 (1958), p. 252. See also S. G. Checkland, 'Finance for the West Indies, 1780–1815', *Economic History Review*, 10:3 (1958), pp. 461–9.
6 R. G. Thorne, *The history of Parliament: The House of Commons, 1790–1820* (London: Secker and Warburg, 1986), p. 193.
7 Anthony Partington, 'A memorial to Hibberts', *Mariner's Mirror*, 95:4 (November 2009), p. 449.
8 NLW/SPD, 9061, Letter from John Purrier to Nathaniel Phillips, 24 February 1781.
9 NLW/SPD, 9092, Letter from George Hibbert to Nathaniel Phillips, 29 March 1788.
10 ICS/SHL/TVAP, M965/17/47, Letter from George Hibbert to Simon Taylor, 5 September 1803.
11 HFAC, Diary of Robert Hibbert junior, 20 October 1801.
12 *Ibid.*, 10 November 1801.
13 www.aviva.com/about-us/heritage/companies/indemnity-marine-assurance-company/ [accessed 8 August 2017].
14 *Illustrated London News*, 81:2254 (15 July 1882), p. 74
15 England & Wales, National Probate Calendar (Index of Wills and Administrations), 1867.
16 *Ibid.*, 1881.
17 *New Complete Guide to London* (London, 1772), p. 225.
18 Henry B. Wheatley, *London, past and present: Its history, associations, and traditions*, vol. I (London: John Murray, 1891), p. 185.
19 David Hancock, *Citizens of the world: London merchants and the integration of the British Atlantic community, 1735–1785* (Cambridge: Cambridge University Press, 1995), pp. 94–102.
20 *Ibid.*, p. 99.
21 NLW/SPD, E9101, Letter from Edward Fuhr to Nathaniel Phillips, 6 September 1786.
22 Margot Finn, *The character of credit: Personal debt in English culture, 1740–1914* (Cambridge: Cambridge University Press, 2003), p. 21.
23 Sherylynne Haggerty, *'Merely for money'? Business culture in the British Atlantic, 1750–1815* (Liverpool: Liverpool University Press, 2012), p. 99.
24 For a discussion on the role of the attorney see Barry Higman, *Plantation Jamaica, 1750–1850: Capital and control in a colonial economy* (Kingston: University of the West Indies Press, 2005), pp. 41–93.
25 Eve Tavor Bannet, *Empire of letters: Letter manuals and transatlantic correspondence, 1680–1820* (Cambridge: Cambridge University Press, 2006).
26 Toby Ditz, 'Formative venture: Eighteenth-century commercial letters and the articulation of experience', in Rebecca Earle (ed.), *Epistolary selves: Letters and letter writers, 1600–1945* (Aldershot: Ashgate, 1999), p. 62.
27 Adam Smith, 'Lecture on the influence of commerce on manners', quoted in Haggerty, *'Merely for money'*, p. 110.
28 NLW/SPD, 8889, Letter from Hibbert, Purrier & Horton to Nathaniel Phillips, London, 4 May 1770.
29 Hancock, *Citizens of the world*, p. 140.
30 NLW/SPD, 8889, Letter from Hibbert, Purrier & Horton to Nathaniel Phillips, London, 4 May 1770.
31 NLW/SPD, 8897, Letter from Thomas Hibbert senior to Nathaniel Phillips, London, 20 August 1770.
32 NLW/SPD, 9079, Letter from George Hibbert to Nathaniel Phillips, 4 May 1785.
33 Hancock, *Citizens of the world*, p. 103.
34 NLW/SPD, 9078, Letter from George Hibbert to Nathaniel Phillips, 4 August 1786.
35 NLW/SPD, 9093, Letter from George Hibbert to Nathaniel Phillips, 5 November 1788.

36 Kenneth Morgan, 'Jamaican material in the Slebech Papers: Introduction to the microfilm collection' (Wakefield: Microform Academic Papers, 2004), p. 2.
37 Clare Taylor, 'The journal of an absentee proprietor, Nathaniel Phillips of Slebech', *Journal of Caribbean History*, 18 (1984), p. 70.
38 For a biographical account of Simon Taylor see Christer Petley, *White fury: A Jamaican slaveholder and the age of revolution* (Oxford: Oxford University Press, 2018).
39 Christer Petley, *Slaveholders in Jamaica: Colonial society and culture during the era of abolition* (London: Pickering & Chatto, 2009), p. 17.
40 Richard B. Sheridan, 'Simon Taylor, sugar tycoon of Jamaica', *Agricultural History*, 45:4 (1971), p. 286.
41 Ibid., p. 290.
42 George Hibbert, quoted *ibid.*, p. 289.
43 Ibid., p. 286.
44 ICS/SHL/TVAP, M965/17/47, Letter from George Hibbert to Simon Taylor, 5 September 1803.
45 ICS/SHL/TVAP, M965/17/26, Letter from George Hibbert to Simon Taylor, 8 October 1801.
46 Sheridan, 'Simon Taylor', pp. 294–5.
47 ICS/SHL/TVAP, M965/17/47, Letter from George Hibbert to Simon Taylor, 5 September 1803.
48 Sarah Pearsall, '"The late flagrant instance of depravity in my family": The story of an Anglo-Jamaican cuckold', *William and Mary Quarterly*, 60:3 (2003), p. 555.
49 For a full list of properties associated with Tharp see 'John Tharp', Legacies of British Slave-ownership database. www.ucl.ac.uk/lbs/person/view/2146642249 [accessed 22 January 2019].
50 A. E. Furness, 'The Tharp estates in Jamaica' (unpublished manuscript, London, 2018), p. 36.
51 Cambridge Record Office, Tharp Family of Chippenham Records, Part III, Bacon Collection, R.55.7.133, no. 90.
52 Furness, 'The Tharp estate', p. 16
53 Ibid., p. 36
54 Ibid., p. 32.
55 Ibid., p. 52.
56 *Abridgement of the minutes of the evidence: Taken before a committee of the whole house, to whom it was referred to consider of the slave-trade* (London, 1789–91), p. 155.
57 John Fletcher to Peleg Clarke, 30 July and 22 December 1774, quoted in Sheridan, 'The commercial and financial organisation', p. 262.
58 ICS/SHL/TVAP, M965/17/68, Letter from George Hibbert to Simon Taylor, 1 October 1806.
59 ICS/SHL/TVAP, M965/17/71, Letter from George Hibbert to Simon Taylor, 3 December 1806.
60 *Abridgement of the minutes of the evidence*, p. 145.
61 Ibid., p. 154.
62 Partington, 'A memorial to *Hibberts*', p. 449.
63 Marguerite Curtin, 'Mr. Hibbert of Stanton Street' (unpublished manuscript, Jamaica National Heritage Trust, 1983).
64 Letter from Simon Taylor to Robert Taylor, 3 December 1798, quoted in Partington, 'A memorial to *Hibberts*', p. 449.
65 Evidence of George Hibbert, in *Report from the Select Committee into the means of improving and maintaining the foreign trade of the country* (London, 1823), p. 145.
66 Partington, 'A memorial to *Hibberts*', p. 449.
67 Ibid., p. 452.
68 www.convictrecords.com.au/ships/george-hibbert [accessed 11 August 2017].
69 *Abridgement of the minutes of the evidence*, p. 154.
70 HFAC, Diary of Robert Hibbert junior, 10 June 1791.

71 Sir John Soane's Museum and Collection, London, Soane Office, London, drawer no. 7, no. 57b, set 5, Elevation towards Thames Street of warehouse adjacent to Wiggins Quay, 1804.
72 *Abridgement of the minutes of the evidence*, p. 146.
73 Furness, 'The Tharp estate', p. 40.
74 ICS/SHL/TVAP, M965/17/68, Letter from George Hibbert to Simon Taylor, 1 October 1806.
75 Mortgages were held on Halse Hall, Hanbury Pen, Windsor Lodge, Paisley Estate and Hopewell Estate and Pen. This figure excludes the chancery cases and awards made to John Vincent Purrier on behalf of the partnership, Legacies of British Slave-ownership database. www.ucl.ac.uk/lbs/search/ [accessed 11 August 2017].
76 Calculated to the value of money in 2016 using 'Real price', which measures the value of a range of goods and is linked to RPI. www.measuringworth.com/ppoweruk/ [accessed 11 August 2017].
77 *Abridgement of the minutes of the evidence*, p. 146.
78 ICS/SHL/TVAP, M965/17/26, Letter from George Hibbert to Simon Taylor, 8 October 1801.
79 ICS/SHL/TVAP, M965/17/68, Letter from George Hibbert to Simon Taylor, 1 October 1806.
80 ICS/SHL/TVAP, M965/17/81, Letter from George Hibbert to Simon Taylor, 7 July 1808.
81 'Adelphi', Legacies of British Slave-ownership database. www.ucl.ac.uk/lbs/claim/view/14974 [accessed 11 August 2017].
82 Walter Stern, 'The first London dock boom and the growth of the West India Docks', *Economica*, 19:73 (1952), p. 61.
83 Proceedings of the Old Bailey London, T17961130-34, Trial of Patrick Fallon, November 1796, www.oldbaileyonline.org [accessed 15 August 2017].
84 George Hibbert, quoted in Peter Linebaugh, *The London hanged: Crime and civil society in the eighteenth century* (London: Penguin Books, 1991), p. 424.
85 Stern, 'The first London dock boom', p. 59.
86 *Ibid.*, pp. 64–8.
87 *Ibid.*, p. 74.
88 'The West India Docks: Historical development', in Hermione Hobhouse (ed.), *Survey of London: Poplar, Blackwall and Isle of Dogs*, vols 43 and 44 (London: Athlone Press for the RCHME, 1994), pp. 248–68. www.british-history.ac.uk/survey-london/vols43-4/pp248-268 [accessed 15 August 2017].
89 ICS/SHL/TVAP, M965/17/52, Letter from George Hibbert to Simon Taylor, 3 May 1804.
90 'The West India Docks: Historical development'.
91 Nicholas Draper, 'The City of London and slavery: Evidence from the first dock companies, 1795–1800', *Economic History Review*, 61:2 (2008), pp. 432–66.
92 Walter M. Stern, 'The Isle of Dogs canal: A study in early public investment', *Economic History Review*, 4:3 (1952), pp. 359–71.
93 Draper, 'The City of London', Appendix I, p. 464.
94 Stern, 'The first London dock boom', p. 77.
95 ICS/SHL/TVAP, M965/17/30, Letter from George Hibbert to Simon Taylor, 3 March 1802.
96 Evidence given by George Hibbert, in *Report from the Select Committee into the means of improving*, p. 142.
97 'The West India Docks: Historical development'.
98 Hancock, *Citizens of the world*, p. 20.
99 'The West India Docks: Offices, works and housing', in Hermione Hobhouse (ed.), *Survey of London: Poplar, Blackwall and Isle of Dogs*, vols 43 and 44 (London: Athlone Press for the RCHME, 1994), pp. 313–26. www.british-history.ac.uk/survey-london/vols43-4/pp313-326 [accessed 6 July 2018].
100 Linebaugh, *The London hanged*, p. 412.
101 Partington, 'A memorial to *Hibberts*', pp. 445–7.

102 Georgie Wemyss, *The invisible empire: White discourse, tolerance and belonging* (Farnham: Ashgate, 2009), p. 33.
103 My thanks to Kristy Warren for drawing this exhibition to my attention.
104 Wemyss, *The invisible empire*, pp. 21–49.
105 John Watkins, Frederic Shoberl and William Upcott, *A biographical dictionary of the living authors of Great Britain and Ireland* (London: Henry Colburn, 1816), p. 155.

PART II

Family politics: defending the slave trade and slavery

CHAPTER FOUR

Defending the slave trade

> This bill ... puts into hazard existing establishments, which though imperfect, confer much public and private benefit, with a promise of substituting what exists only in visionary theory. If so, the measure must be the occasion of just jealousy to a wise legislature, as approaching, in feature and character, to those wild projects of reform, to which the spirit of modern philanthropy has given birth, and of which the civilised world has lately seen the results – projects, Sir, that have universally proved subversive of their objects, and have collaterally caused a mass of misery and destruction, of which, to give even a faint and imperfect description, will puzzle the most eloquent of those who shall attempt to convey to posterity a record of the present times.
>
> George Hibbert, Slave Trade Abolition Bill, House of Commons, 23 February 1807, *Parliamentary debates from the year 1803 to the present time*, vol. VIII, cc. 945–95 (London, 1812)

On 22 May 1787 twelve men met at 2 George Yard in the City of London to form the Society for Effecting the Abolition of the Slave Trade (SEAST). The task ahead involved challenging not only one of the most powerful commercial groups of the period, but a settled orthodoxy which had remained largely untroubled by any popular clamour for reform.[1] The eighteenth century was 'characterised by Atlantic domination, with North America and, more critically for British wealth, the West Indies at the imperial centre'.[2] Prime Minister William Pitt estimated the value of Caribbean produce at £4 million as compared to £1 million from all other global trade.[3] Slavery generated an entire industry incorporating varied elements including finance, shipping, insurance, distribution and manufacturing. The combination of both primary and subsidiary interest groups enabled the development of a powerful moneyed lobby intent on preserving the system. Upsetting the balance of trade and destabilising the lucrative Caribbean possessions in pursuit of African liberty was not a cause deemed likely to succeed. Writing a year after SEAST was established, Thomas junior gave voice to the belief held by many that abolitionism was simply a short-lived fad which would dissipate when the next political drama swept on to the stage. In a letter to the Jamaica planter Nathaniel Phillips, he assured him that:

> There must be always some Tub thrown out to the Whales. Hasting's trial is the play thing of this Winter, & before the next there will be some other India Squabble; some petty Dispute on the Continent, or perhaps a general Election to amuse the People; so that I hope we shall not again be alarmed by any Thing that comes so directly Home to ourselves.[4]

Thomas junior's sentiment was shared by large numbers of planters and merchants who simply could not imagine a situation in which Britain would imperil either its national economic or imperial interests.

Initial abolitionist efforts were focused on ending the slave trade rather than slavery. In separating out the two issues the abolitionists hoped to avoid the thorny issue of state interference with private property. This allowed them to rebuff accusations of radicalism, whilst side-stepping the demand for compensation. Abolitionist rhetoric shifted the parameters of public dialogue away from economics and instead embraced an emerging language of humanitarianism. The West Indians, particularly those who were resident in the colonies, were slow to realise that the terms of the debate had changed, their arguments tended to focus on the trade's value and legitimacy. George, a rising figure amongst the planters and merchants in London, was quick to react to these developments and attempted to shape strategies and rhetoric which reflected the mood of the metropole. He responded to the challenge of abolitionist representations by presenting enslavement as part of the empire's civilising mission. The question of Britain's imperial identity was writ large in the slave trade debates. The bloodshed of the American Revolution and the unease over the power of the East India Company formed the political backdrop to the campaign.[5] What Thomas junior failed to understand when he wrote to Phillips was that the trial of Warren Hastings, rather than displacing the controversy over slavery, was part of a broader conversation over what kind of empire Britain wanted to be. Would Britain rule by the sword or through commerce, culture and 'civilised' governance?

For five decades George was at the forefront of defending slavery. Trust in his expertise and political acumen meant he was at the centre of orchestrating anti-abolition activities. Utilising a network of personal relationships with leading political figures, George marshalled support in both the Commons and the Lords. In recognition of the family's position within the West India interest, both George and his brother Robert junior were invited to give evidence to Parliament in 1790. As a powerful commercial man with a skill for political manoeuvring, George was increasingly recognised as a leading anti-abolitionist figure. Attuned to the political temperature of the imperial centre, occasionally his distinctly metropolitan mercantile position put him at odds with the colonial plantocracy. These moments of divergence allow us to see the West India lobby as a heterogeneous body with competing interests and world views. Having proved himself capable as a spokesman, George entered Parliament unopposed in 1806 using his position to try and block, then delay, the passing of the Abolition of the Slave Trade Act. His speeches outlined in full the key anti-abolition arguments, offering a window into the thinking which underpinned British involvement with, and support of, transatlantic slavery.

Society of West India Planters and Merchants (SWIPM)

Described as 'the institutional heart of the West India interest' in London, attendance at the Society of West India Planters and Merchants was essential for any merchant seeking to represent both his own interests and those of his Caribbean correspondents.[6] The SWIPM lobbied the Government on 'all aspects of the sugar policy. Military protection, island security, trade to North America, tax policy, the sugar market, agricultural practices and abolition.'[7] Its rise to political influence was inextricably bound to the value of the West Indian sugar economy and the payment of duties. As Alexandra Franklin has noted, 'This dependence of governments on the revenues of West Indian trade, as on East Indian trade, gave the West Indian interest in Britain its *entrée* into lobbying power.'[8] Whilst the British West Indies remained the jewel in the crown of empire, the interest could exert pressure on the Government to ensure that their investments were protected by the careful manipulation of new legislation effecting the colonies.

Dominated by those with interests in Jamaica, the SWIPM's membership included powerful absentee planters, merchants, and the island Agents.[9] The men who made up its ranks were highly mobile, they moved between metropole and colony, or alternatively they had family, kin and commercial partners who were resident in both. Membership often encompassed more than one family member, and in the case of the Hibberts it spanned the generations. The Hibberts rise to power within the SWIPM was a combined result of their dominant position in Jamaica and the timing of their breakthrough into the London market. With the emergence of abolition as a serious threat, George discovered a platform from which he could demonstrate his qualities as a leader. He became an entrenched part of the SWIPM – between 1785 and 1807 he was the third most regular attendee and was present at 122 of 136 of their meetings.[10] Over the years he was joined by his brothers Thomas junior, Robert junior and William, his cousin Robert, his sons Nathaniel and George junior and his nephews Samuel and William junior. Having attended meetings since 1824, George junior was made treasurer in 1835. A number of the Hibberts' extended kin were also members, most notably George's nephew James Heywood Markland, who served as the SWIPM's solicitor. George's family by marriage were also a useful presence: his wife Elizabeth's brother-in-law George Woodford Thellusson and his family were occasional attendees, as was his sister Margaret's husband, Thomas Greg. The Hibberts' co-partners had attended meetings since 1771, with Thomas Horton and the senior and junior Purriers and Fuhrs all listed in the minutes.

The nature of the West India interest – its size, its members and its lobbying influence – have been discussed at length.[11] George alluded to contemporary suspicions about the West Indians in a speech to Parliament in 1807. He rather disingenuously stated that:

> Alas, Sir, who ever heard of them as combined into a political phalanx or squad, displaying in this or in the other House a compact and regular front in critical moments of the battle, and, by judicious manoeuvres and co-operation with other bodies, giving and receiving mutual assistance and support? I will not say whether, had they done so, they would have stood here now defenceless as they do; but I have known the West India body long, and never seen them thus arrayed and disciplined.[12]

Whilst the SWIPM undoubtedly encompassed a diverse group of people and opinions, it was an organised entity with internal hierarchical structures and policy processes. It could draw on the support of similar institutions in the main transatlantic ports of Liverpool, Bristol and Glasgow. The SWIPM and the colonial assemblies discussed the coordination of their actions, although they did not always agree on what course to take. On 7 June 1785, just five years after he arrived in London, George was appointed as a member of the SWIPM's elite Standing Committee. The Committee formulated resolutions on subjects which were of concern to the interest enabling its members to influence which issues were a priority and to shape the terms of the debate. The importance of the Committee was articulated by George, who urged the wider membership to 'confine themselves to the business of the day, passing the resolution that be brought before them ... and leaving the rest to be managed by their committee and agents, who well know what ought to be done, and how to set about it'.[13] The Committee regulated the flow of information by acting as the sole 'authorised channel of communication with His Majesty's Ministers'.[14] Senior members formed deputations to call on the Prime Minister, the Chancellor of the Exchequer, the Board of Trade, and the Secretary of State for War and the Colonies. George was a familiar presence at these meetings, so much so that Markland wrote that 'Mr Pitt was accustomed to say, that "he never got so clear a view of the objects of a Deputation, as when he saw Mr. George Hibbert at the head of it".'[15] With both family members and clients in positions of political influence in Jamaica, George was well placed to discuss issues affecting trade from a colonial perspective. Interactions with British ministers gave him firsthand access to powerful politicians and privileged information which was then reported back to the SWIPM. Useful titbits from these talks made their way into his commercial letters. In recognition of his seniority, from 1794 onwards George regularly took on the role of the Acting Chairman for the SWIPM and was permanently appointed as the Chairman of the Society of West India Merchants.

The founding of SEAST in 1787 exposed the West India interest to public scrutiny, forcing it to find new methods for pressing its case. Despite a healthy disdain for the 'popular clamour',[16] the SWIPM was under increasing pressure to engage with a newly formed notion of 'the people', whose interest had been awakened by abolitionist campaigning.[17] In 1788 the SWIPM created a Sub-Committee on the slave trade specifically mandated to counter abolitionist propaganda.[18] In March of 1792 the original group was expanded to include George and allocated a £300 budget to fund its work.[19] The Sub-Committee was engaged in producing and distributing publications and George took a lead in both editing and writing material. Challenging abolitionist cultural productions proved difficult for the West Indians, whose arguments did not translate easily into the mobilising rhetoric and aesthetics of the abolitionist campaign. There could never be a proslavery equivalent with the visual impact of the slave ship *Brookes* – an image which must have infuriated the Hibberts, given that they had purchased the enslaved people on board. Instead the Sub-Committee chose to focus its defence on arguments relating to commercial authority, national and imperial security and the economic benefits of participation in the slave economy.

Personal networks

Private lobbying was the traditional way in which the West India interest operated in the eighteenth century. As the turn of the century approached, the increased bureaucratisation of the state changed the way in which the anti-abolitionists could access the Government and influence policy. Andrew O'Shaughnessy has suggested that although 'dinners and private friendships continued to be a critical feature of the West India lobby ... procedures became more rigid and a rising breed of career administrators showed less willingness to share information'.[20] Despite a move towards more formalised interactions, cultivating personal connections remained an important part of political culture. The Hibberts had developed an extensive Atlantic network which helped them to promote both their own concerns and those of the wider West India interest.

There were key figures within the Government whom the West Indians relied on to champion their cause. The Scottish Member of Parliament Henry Dundas, Secretary of State for the Home Department, had been a friend to the West Indians and they looked to him for a sympathetic hearing. The Glasgow West India merchants held particular sway with Dundas (who in turn controlled the Scottish voting bloc), and this, combined with his position within the Admiralty, secured his support for anti-abolition.[21] George attempted on at least one occasion to nurture this relationship: in 1791 he wrote to Phillips, stating that the Captain of the *Britannia* 'had delivered us a middling siz'd lively Turtle for you which we have sent up to Mr. Dundas in your name [original emphasis]'.[22] Dundas proved to be most useful – in a letter to Taylor written on 7 April 1792 George noted, 'I am glad the negotiation is begun with Mr. Dundas. I think it may be the means of escaping our entire destruction.'[23] There can be little doubt, given the timing of the letter, that George was referring to Dundas's amendment to William Wilberforce's motion of 2 April 1792 on the abolition of the slave trade. Dundas's insertion of the phrase 'gradually abolished' was widely recognised as having contributed to delaying the process for another fifteen years. Dundas's elevation to the House of Lords in 1802 added to an already sizeable group of anti-abolition members in the upper house.

The West India interest had a greater influence in the Lords than in the Commons. This was commented on in a letter from Hibbert, Fuhr & Purrier, who wrote that the 'Commons seems much inclin'd to give way to Popular delusion and we must look for safety in the upper House where there may perhaps be found less pretended, but more real Patriotism'.[24] The Hibberts shared a personal relationship with the Duke of Clarence, who was a vociferous supporter of the West Indians, having spent time in the Caribbean whilst in the Royal Navy. During both the period in which the Duke served in Jamaica and on his return to London, he met Robert junior on several occasions. George's relationship was apparently close enough for him to take the Duke's advice and place his son Edward in the Royal Navy.[25] George approved of the Duke and wrote to Taylor in 1804 praising his 'great information' on the slave trade question. George reported that the Duke was

> glad the question has thus gone by for that before another session something or other may turn up more favourable to us: He alluded to the Prince of Wales coming forwards more as a Political Character if even he should not be in Power as Regent or King. He says that the Prince is most diametrically adverse to all views of the abolitionists whom he looks upon as equally enemies in the event to the monarchy and to the Peace of the Kingdom. This I had from him a few days ago at the House of Lords when I waited on him respecting the Merchants Petition.[26]

George's words revealed the degree to which the anti-abolitionists were supported by the royal family, who were extremely influential in the Lords. Wilberforce commented on this with bitter disappointment: 'it was truly humiliating to see, in the House of Lords, four of the Royal Family come down to vote against the poor, helpless, friendless slaves'.[27] The Duke's loyalty to the interest was consistent throughout the abolition campaign – in 1794 he personally presented a petition to the House of Lords on behalf of the SWIPM. He attended their meeting on 14 February 1805, when they declared 'their sincerest gratitude to His Royal Highness for the distinguished and valuable services rendered to the West India Body by his judicious, indefatigable, zealous and able exertions displayed in various occasions in supporting their interests, particularly on every Question in Parliament relative to the Slave Trade'.[28] As the abolition debates of 1807 progressed and it became clear that the Bill would pass in the Lords, George reassured Taylor of the Duke's continued support. He wrote that 'The Duke of Clarence tells me ... that nothing on the part of himself the Duke could be wanting to stem the prevailing madness in the House of Lords.'[29]

The Hibberts were also well acquainted with leading members of the Admiralty, including the naval heroes Admirals Rodney and Nelson. Whilst staying in Kingston, Robert junior recalled an instance in which 'Adml. Rodney calls to pay his respects to my Uncle but cannot see him'.[30] Nelson had served on one of the Hibberts' West India ships as a boy. The tradition of hospitality meant that the Hibberts encouraged the naval elite to enjoy the luxurious surroundings of their town house when visiting the city. They entertained Admiral Gayton, Admiral Sir Peter Parker and Admiral Cornwallis (then a captain). This attention continued across the Atlantic, with the Hibberts maintaining this practice in London. Robert junior's diary recorded that on 25 May 1795 'sundries dine, viz. Admiral Affleck ... Mr. & Mrs. W. Mitchell,

B. Edwards, Sewell, Mr. & Mrs. Allardyce & George H.'.[31] The mixture of guests demonstrates the role of sociability in the sustaining networks of commercial and political power. Aside from Robert junior's brother George, the party included Admiral Affleck, a Lord of the Board of Admiralty; William Mitchell and Bryan Edwards, elite members of the SWIPM; Alexander Allardyce, a Jamaica slave trader turned Scottish politician; and Robert Sewell, the Agent for Jamaica. Supporting the notion that the slave trade was the 'nursery of British seamen', four Admirals, one Commodore and Lord Rodney himself all testified to the Select Committee in 1790 in support of the West India interest.

As a consummate pragmatist George – himself a Whig – courted favour from across the political spectrum. This included cultivating a relationship with the radical pamphleteer William Cobbett. The relationship between English radicalism and slavery was a complicated and contradictory one.[32] Whilst there were some obvious connections between the experiences of enslaved Africans and exploited English workers, it did not necessarily follow that this led to the fermentation of transatlantic solidarity.[33] George quickly realised that the anti-abolitionists could use these divisions to their advantage by playing on the lack of reformist zeal for the improvement of conditions in England for the working poor. George saw the potential for Cobbett's *Journal* to become more fully engaged with the debates over abolition. He commented to Taylor that Cobbett 'enters more fully and more intelligibly into the general Commercial Question and into the particular dispute of Jamaica with Government here than I could have expected'.[34] He added that he would 'make Cobbett a present of a puncheon of good old Rum for the spirit and ability with which he has taken up our Cause'. A year later the two men were evidently still in communication. George relayed to Taylor that he had written to Cobbett to thank him for 'his exertions in our Cause'.[35] It seems Cobbett's response to this praise was guarded – George reported that Cobbett had stated that he 'was in Principle a friend to the West India Cause or rather to the cause of the country as connected to the West Indies'. This is an interesting distinction and supports Marcus Wood's claim that radical patriotism could accept the notion of unfreedom, providing that it was not British people who were subjected to such tyranny and that the West India colonies continued to enrich the metropole.[36] George told Taylor that Cobbett had assured him that 'we had not lost ground in the House of Commons and that on the contrary Wilberforce was losing the confidence and regard of the Members who were ... disgusted with what Cobbett called his damned Hypocrisy'.[37] As Wood has pointed out, the issue of slavery allowed Cobbett to indulge in some of his 'favourite hobby horses' which included 'the sacred status of the British farmer, and of the land, the religious hypocrisy of the Clapham sect, and the superiority of the British labourer over any foreign rival black or white'.[38] Writing to Taylor in 1805, George set out the advice given to him by Cobbett, which was that 'you should learn to try and obtain your just rights by licking the dust off the shoe of a clerk or an under-secretary'.[39] George also mentioned that Cobbett's 'publication was at our service and that he would not be paid for anything he inserted there'. His final titbit from his conversations sounded a note of warning in that Cobbett had cautioned that although the West Indians had 'flapped a wasp from the window with a handkerchief we must set our foot on it immediately or it will with redoubled rage sting us'. This sentiment was echoed by George, who added that 'Mr W. [Wilberforce] will I fear prove the wasp and rise again very anxious to Insert his sting if he can find the opportunity.'

Expert evidence

Following abolitionist pressure a Parliamentary Select Committee was convened to hear evidence on the slave trade in 1789. Since the emergence of SEAST, the SWIPM had developed a series of standardised positions on the key issues raised by their opponents. From the outset George was heavily involved with co-ordinating their strategy. He was one of fifteen men appointed 'to prepare and select such Evidence and take such other measures' to ensure the interest's position was represented in Parliament.[40] The solicitor Robert Cooper Lee, himself a Jamaica slave owner, attended a meeting of the SWIPM at which he chose the members who would be called upon to give evidence to the inquiry.[41] George and his brother Robert junior were selected, Robert junior in his capacity as both a Jamaica planter and merchant, and George as a spokesman for 'merchants, mortgagees, annuitants, and other creditors of the sugar colonies'.[42] The West India interest were convinced that the social standing of their witnesses would lend their testimony greater weight than that of their opponents. Writing in 1789, Gilbert Franklyn stated that Robert junior's reputation was such that it carried 'more authority than the journals, or pretended journals, of twenty such surgeons of Guinea ships'.[43]

Of the two brothers it was Robert junior who was the first to give evidence. He travelled from Jamaica in November of 1789 and in January 1790 he began attending Parliament in preparation for the delivery of his testimony in February.[44] The occasion was marked in his diary with the brief words 'Friday I attend the Committee of the House of Commons'.[45] Despite the seeming ordinariness of this encounter with the British state, Robert junior was thoroughly primed in advance. His diary contained a handwritten questionnaire which closely followed the official version of his evidence. The possession and preservation of this document suggests the level of preparation which was required before an individual was put before the Committee. Evidence was heard from 10 a.m. until 3 p.m., with witnesses and petitions presented by the counsel for the petitioners, before being handed over to the Committee for cross-examination. Acting on behalf of the West India interest were Arthur Piggott and George Trower. Piggot came from a Barbadian family and had formerly acted as attorney-general for Grenada.[46] Trower was a less prominent figure but was identified as the executor of Thomas Nash Kemble in the slave compensation registers.[47]

Robert junior's testimony focused primarily on conditions on the plantations; in a revealing reframing of his commercial activities he described himself as a merchant and plantation owner, despite the fact he was still heavily involved in slave trading. In his evidence Robert junior, unlike his brother George, engaged to a greater extent with the construction of race as an ideological justification for the slave trade. His statement opened with a consideration of the suitability of replacing African labour with European. Drawing on climatic constructions of racial difference, Robert junior insisted that 'no European could bear constant exposure to the heat, still less when labouring'.[48] Although he did not express the view in his official evidence to the Committee, in his private notes Robert junior rejected the idea that Europeans would travel to the Caribbean to undertake agricultural or domestic labour. In his opinion:

> Such white persons ... must be the very scum & refuse of Europe. The effect which the climate would have on such characters would be to make men drunkards, and the women whores, if they were not so already. From instances I have seen I would rather wait upon myself than be plagued with such people.[49]

This damning indictment drew on middle-class assumptions about the character of the white working poor. Given his sympathy for the labouring classes one wonders what Cobbett might have made of this representation. Employing the trope of the lazy African, Robert junior informed the Committee that 'there were a great number of free negroes and tradesmen, of whom many do nothing ... Never knew free negroes offer to do field labour.'[50] These words served as a warning – without the iron discipline of violent compulsion an emancipated workforce would not work on the plantations. In his written notes Robert junior offered a different explanation in regard to the use of force. He noted that 'The number of Whites in Jamaica are about 20,000 ... The number of Negroes is about 250,000. Where the disproportion is so great, a strictness of discipline is absolutely necessary.'[51] According to Robert junior neither a voluntary European nor a free African workforce could provide the labour necessary to maintain productivity or settle new estates. Without the means to clear and plant, the abolition of the slave trade would result in 'Immediate ruin to some and eventual ruin to all'.[52]

Robert junior's evidence on mortality rates among the enslaved offers an insight into the ways in which race, class, gender and sexuality intersected within proslavery rhetoric. His admission that the annual rate of decrease on the plantation could run as high as 5 per cent raised the issue of population decline and negative birth rates. This was something that abolitionists had attributed to the brutality of slavery, allowing them to frame slave trade abolition as a pro-natalist policy which would force the planters to ameliorate conditions for the enslaved. Here counsel was quick to ask for clarification, offering Robert junior the opportunity to direct blame away from the planter class. Thus prompted, he cited a pronounced gender imbalance in Jamaica, where enslaved males outnumbered females. Additionally he also argued that the spread of disease was related to the fact that 'the young women have indiscriminate intercourse with the men'.[53] Given his personal engagement in sexual relationships with women in Jamaica (including fathering illegitimate children and contracting venereal disease), the racial framing of his representation was particularly hypocritical. The characterisation of African women as sexually promiscuous formed part of a recognisable trope of the exoticised and erotised Other which served to justify the sexual abuse which was rife within slave societies.[54] In contrast to his evidence to the Committee, in his written notes Robert junior stated that 'The young women during their prime wish to make the most of their person and are not fond of breeding and settling.'[55] He suggested that it was the 'invariable custom amongst them to keep it [the baby] at the breast two sometimes three years, during which time they abstain from all commerce with the opposite sex'. This custom, which Robert junior characterised as African, was not considered by him to be 'favourable in propagation'. When mulling over the idea that enslaved women might be persuaded or compelled to abandon the practice, Robert junior was adamant that 'the women have ever claimed and exercised the right of disposing of themselves as they think proper ... It is a fact well known by persons who have resided in Jamaica that Masters dare not interfere.' Given the prevalence of rape and coercion this claim rang hollow. In reference to the treatment of pregnant women, Robert junior remarked that 'their natural indolence prompts the pregnant women to take advantage of their situation, and to claim exemption from labour when, I have understood, exercise would rather be of service to them'. This attitude was in stark contrast to the treatment his wife received during her pregnancies. Robert junior recorded in his diary that his wife Letitia had spent a twenty-two-day period in May 1800 either confined to bed or lying on the 'sopha' in the hopes she would carry the baby to full term.[56] Despite a regime of rest she suffered a miscarriage, after which Robert junior sent for the physician and noted that his wife 'remains in bed'.[57] Robert junior's assertion that pregnant African women would benefit from hard agricultural labour is an indication of the extreme racial differencing necessary to disavow any responsibility for the destruction of human life.

A month after Robert junior appeared before the Committee, George was called to give evidence. His testimony was substantially more detailed than his brother's, with the focus on issues of commerce. George's statement articulated the key anti-abolition themes summarised by Ian John Barrett as the value, legitimacy, humanity and utility of the slave trade.[58] George framed his arguments using a discourse of 'proslavery patriotism' which emphasised the mutually beneficial relationship between the metropole and colony.[59] He asserted his authority to speak by comparing his own extensive practical experience with the idealistic naivety of the abolitionists. His use of facts and figures underscored his claims to expertise, as well as making clear the scale of the economic value of Caribbean commerce. He estimated the worth of West India imports at £6.8 million (with a customs revenue of £1.8 million) and the slave trade at £547,995 per annum.[60] He also gave figures for shipping, insurance and wharfinger fees. In terms of the wealth generated by the colony, George argued that 'in my own time and that of my predecessors ... there is a very small portion of it indeed that I cannot follow home'.[61] Not only were duties paid on colonial commodities, but returning planters and metropolitan merchants spent their fortunes within the domestic economy as conspicuous consumers, investors and employers.

George carefully intertwined the issue of colonial debt – which he estimated at £20 million – with a call for compensation.[62] Speaking as a creditor, he informed the Committee that security for a loan was based on 'an estate with Negroes thereon, or Negroes alone; land without Negroes thereon, or without an immediate prospect of buying them for the purpose of cultivating that land, would be considered by a merchant as no security at all'.[63] The enormity of the colonial debt left an inevitable question mark over the issue of compensation. As Julian Hoppit has explained, 'to abolish the slave trade undermined that property by preventing the replenishment of labour stocks, damaged the property of merchants tied up in the trade and contradicted previous commitments'.[64] Should an estate fail as a result of a labour deficit then the merchant would foreclose on the debt and take ownership. Since it was impossible to sell the plantation or render it productive, terminal decline would be inevitable, leaving those involved to 'look forward to an entire loss of that commerce which they have hitherto found a maintenance to themselves, and have looked forward to as an inheritance to their children'.[65] George equated slave trade abolition with the effective forfeiture of the loans, arguing that if the merchants were to accept these losses then the Government must compensate them.

George presented the slave trade as not only a respectable form of commerce, but one legally sanctioned by the British Government. Parliament had recognised the right of individual merchants to trade in enslaved Africans by abolishing the monopoly of chartered slave-trading companies.[66] Legitimacy had been conferred through extensive legislation passed by the Government, 'during all which time no public censure was passed upon the trade'.[67] Investors had acted in good faith by participating in a state sanctioned economy. As George argued:

> I was not ignorant that the trade I am engaged in, those plantations in the West Indies which afford me security for my advances, that trade to Africa which supports the cultivation of those plantations, and even the very loans I have made, have all been repeatedly encouraged, protected and sanctioned by repeated acts of the British legislature ... [list of acts] The leading feature in them all is encouragement to the Sugar Colonies, as inhabited by British Subjects, and very advantageous to Great Britain.[68]

George's rehearsal of successive laws passed by the British Parliament made the case for the slave trade's legitimacy as a recognised commercial enterprise. In raising the lawfulness of the trade, George also implicated the British state in its operations. The use of the term 'British Subjects' served as a reminder to the Committee of where the British Government's duty lay – not with the imported African workforce but with those steadfast colonists who had forged an empire which continued to enrich the mother country.

Unlike many others within the West India interest, George recognised the need to engage with the rhetoric of humanitarianism. To do this he needed to create an alternative construction of victimhood which would appeal to a metropolitan audience. Using the emotive example of estates in trust for minors he argued that 'the estates of infants, or others, so situated, could not possibly be improved or kept up, without new negroes'.[69] Vulnerable children and widows were used to represent the sympathetic face of the slaveholder – a more palatable image than the despotic tyrant depicted by the abolitionists. By emphasising the plight of helpless dependants as the white victims of abolition, he was echoing the criticisms levelled at the abolitionists that philanthropy for the people of Africa was misplaced – charitable sentiment was better directed at the worthy of the mother country. Perversely George hinted at a moral responsibility to maintain the slave trade for the sake of the enslaved. He told the Committee that 'I am connected with several planters, who have assured me that they wish to purchase new negroes without any view to the extension of their plantations, but merely that the labour of their present stock be lightened.'[70] He argued that those advocating an end to the trade as an act of humanitarian conscience would in fact succeed in adding to the suffering of those already under the yoke of slavery.

George's performance in front of the Committee proved him an able public speaker and soon afterwards he was elevated to the SWIPM Sub-Committee convened to counteract the abolitionists. During evidence George told the Select Committee that 'I confess that the abolition of the Slave Trade was a measure not in my contemplation as not believing it probable.'[71] Despite these words of confidence he recognised the seriousness of the threat posed and the need to develop additional strategies to make the West Indians' commercial structures more resilient.

Anti-abolition reform

By the early 1790s a conservative backlash against the French Revolution was under way. Even more damaging to the cause of abolition in Britain were the events which unfolded in Saint-Domingue, when, under the leadership of Toussaint L'Ouverture, the enslaved claimed their freedom by force. George was a shrewd man, and recognised that these external distractions would dissipate sooner or later. He prepared by advancing new approaches to the issue of slave trading which took into consideration the ways in which the abolitionists had shaped their arguments. In 1796 he wrote a letter to William Manning, the Agent for St Vincent, setting out 'a Plan for benefitting Humanity in respect to the Slave Trade'.[72] 'Considering the matter Philanthropically' he wished that an experiment might be undertaken which would test the 'Principles of freedom and Religious Instruction' by instituting a colony where 'young Africans' might be taught 'the rudiments of Civilisation'. To this end he wrote that 'I do most sincerely wish Success to the beneficent Views of the Sierra Leone Company.' George followed events in Sierra Leone carefully, for although he considered society in Africa to be inherently 'Cruel and abominable', he added that 'the interests of the West Indies must be made to Square as well as possible with so Indispensible a claim of moral obligation'. If the colony failed then the West Indians would be proved correct in their claims about the nature of the African and any 'moral obligation' would be satisfied.

In the spirit of compromise which characterised George's style of political negotiation, he put forward the idea that a limited suspension of the slave trade, or a system of quotas, might satisfy the public clamour for reform. He recognised that 'some Steps in regulation or restriction of the Trade must take place' and suggested that the West Indians seize the initiative. This would allow them to control the scale and pace of the change by acting of their own volition 'to cooperate with the intensions of Government'. If the colonial legislatures could be persuaded to pass their own laws to regulate the slave trade they could perhaps mitigate the damage done to their reputation and continue their operations without further intervention. George went even further in his plans to rebrand the sullied image of the West Indies by suggesting that the colonial assemblies should 'adopt new regulations as to the Government of the Negroes – favourable to humanity'. In suggesting this strategy George anticipated the abolitionists' next target – the institution of slavery itself. 'The West Indians ... have done well in general', he wrote, 'to keep their Cause distinct from that of the African Traders', but he suspected they too would eventually become a target.

George took a risk in articulating these measures; the colonists were vehemently against anything that might be interpreted as a concession to either the abolitionists or the meddling imperial Government. George had aspirations towards becoming Agent for Jamaica that could be fatally hurt if his influential friends believed he was wavering in his commitment. In 1800 George tentatively introduced the idea to Taylor. Given Taylor's bellicose and intractable nature, as well as his significant political and economic power on the island, this strategy was potentially personally damaging. Cautiously, George wrote in general terms that:

> Another idea lately spoken of is that of suspending the trade for a few years, to let it open again if the Islands should prove to need it, and if it should appear foreigners go into the trade on our leaving it. This tho it proceeds in their Principle of Abolition I think the less evil of the two; for it would quiet men's minds here about the question and I am perfectly convinced the experience would prove that no good could be done by abolition.[73]

Taylor, who had threatened to abandon Jamaica for America if abolition was successful, clearly disapproved and George was forced to clarify his position by writing that:

> You may assure yourself that you have from me the whole of my Sentiments and Conduct respecting Mr. Pitt's idea of suspending the Slave Trade. I did both to him and Publically utterly discourage the idea of the West India Interest taking a part in that or any other project for the abolition – but for reasons I have expressed to you I did think and still do think that the suspension, supposing it to have taken place some years ago, would have been less hurtful to the <u>old</u> Colonies [original emphasis] than other Projects which were then thought of and I disclaim entirely and positively deny having once suggested to any Minister whatsoever nay, even the least interference with the Slave Trade is just as respects the West India Colonies.[74]

As a metropolitan man George knew that the 'national wish' and the imperial Government must eventually prevail.[75] He wanted to find a solution which would enable the West Indians to keep the trade for as long as possible, whilst avoiding a constitutional clash which would pit the colonial assemblies against the imperial Government. In his letter to Manning he described the threat of abolition as 'the Hydra' which needed to be attacked 'at both its formidable heads'. By this he meant that abolition could be defeated, but only if the West Indians proved their commitment to public concerns by firstly reforming the trade and secondly adhering to the principles of the civilising mission. George's conciliatory approach might have worked, especially given the support of Pitt, but the difference in opinion between the anti-abolitionists proved too great to overcome and the plan fell by the wayside.

Parliament

In 1806 George entered the House of Common to take his place as 'a leading Parliamentary spokesman for the West India interest'.[76] His career as a public man had been building up to this moment: having been made a Master of the Clothworkers' Company in 1796, he was elected Alderman for the City of London Bridge Within in 1798. George planned to use this position as a stepping stone on the way to becoming the parliamentary representative of the City. The timing coincided with a particularly unstable period in the counting house's finances and in 1803 he 'resigned his alderman's gown "to avoid the expensive offices of sheriff and lord mayor" which would soon have fallen to him'.[77] In 1806 George gained a seat in the House of Commons as 'the paying guest' of Sir John Leach, one of the controlling patrons of the rotten borough of Seaford.[78] George was the only one of the Hibbert brothers who took an interest in becoming a Member of Parliament. As Robert junior remarked to his sister Mary in 1807, 'George is at Seaford electioneering. His elder Brothers are waiting for a Call to the upper House.'[79] By George's own admission his 'sole inducement' to enter Parliament was 'to lend my best aid to the Cause of the Colonies' although he was far from optimistic over what could be done.[80]

Entering Parliament in the lead-up to the slave trade debates of 1807, George was uncertain as to 'what sort of Muster we shall make in the House' but was determined that the bill to abolish the slave trade would 'receive the most determined opposition from a few among which I will be one'.[81] Aware of the gravity of the situation, in 1806 George wrote to Taylor decrying the lack of coordinated action on the part of the West India interest and blaming the disarray on a lack of strong leadership. He complained that:

> [A]las we want a Head of union, compact steady union! Is it possible, I am sure it is, even yet, to make an impression in our favour upon such administrations as we are likely to see, to make ourselves at least respected somewhat more than we have been; but it would require that somebody should take the lead and every friend to the West Indies set his Shoulders to the wheel.[82]

The subtext was that George was the leader that was wanting and he was determined to show Taylor that he could mount a rigorous, if ultimately unsuccessful, defence of the slave trade. By January 1807 George had privately admitted to Taylor that 'I have no doubt that the Abolition will pass both Houses and receive the Royal Assent.'[83] Realising that the numbers were stacked against them, George focused on strategies which might delay or derail the legislation. In particular he viewed the issues of compensation as a potential sticking point. He mused that 'such a clause might be worked' and if introduced could 'prove fatal to the Bill', although he foresaw that 'for this reason if for no other, it will be undoubtedly opposed'. Convinced of the impending abolitionist victory, George wrote that at least 'I have the small consolation of having done my duty.'

George made three speeches to the Commons during February and March 1807, later published in full so that the colonists in Jamaica would 'know the cause of the colonies has been sustained more diligently ... than it appears to have been by any report of these debates that has been hitherto published'.[84] Aware that he needed to be seen to deliver a convincing performance by his allies on both sides of the Atlantic, he was concerned that his oratory had not received adequate coverage. George's second speech was delivered at such a late hour

(2.30 a.m. by his reckoning)[85] that 'all the Reprinters were asleep and therefore gave a very imperfect account of what I said'.[86] Drawing on themes from his previous evidence, George expanded on his arguments, introducing new ideas which had been developed in the intervening period. These included colonial rights and liberties, misplaced philanthropic sentiment, the threat of slave revolts, the condition of Africa and philosophical, biblical and classical justifications for the practice of slavery. Once again proslavery patriotism was central to his position. For George the West Indians represented a particular concept of Britishness; bold, manly, maritime and commercial, with a deep-seated consciousness of the imperial dynamics of national identity. He lauded 'the adventurous spirit which has created and sustained the commercial character of this country, which has "raised other fruits beneath another sun" and rendered every quarter of the world the theatre of British industry, and the source of British wealth'.[87] The colonists had helped to make the country great and the empire profitable – they expected to have their rights recognised.

For George the national interest would be best served by setting aside sentimentality and religiosity in favour of practical reason. To this end he called for 'calm and solemn deliberation', his inference being that the abolitionists placed too great a weight on irrational emotion.[88] He urged that 'no popular sentiment out of doors, however assiduously and enthusiastically excited, ought to effect their deliberations'. In opening his arguments with these words George asserted the power of the Commons as beyond the influence of popular opinion. He continued by stating that Parliament was not 'a mere organ of the voice of the multitude, but a deliberate body, limited in their number that they might the better deliberate'. The masses were not to be trusted, as events in France had demonstrated. Parliament had the right to 'dictate for the good of the whole' on the basis of 'dispassioned investigation'. George set himself up as the voice of reason in the face of dangerous idealism. Summoning his authority as a merchant, he challenged Wilberforce to 'descend and fight this battle upon the level plain of fact and experience', criticising the 'delusive promise of good' which the abolition of the slave trade offered.

The issue of the proper application of philanthropy threaded through George's interventions. He cautioned against the hazard to 'existing establishments' with 'a promise of substituting what exists only in visionary theory'.[89] He compared the abolitionist measures to 'those wild projects of reform, to which modern philanthropy has given birth, and of which the civilised world has lately seen the results'. This was a reference to both the French Revolution and events in Saint-Domingue. George attacked the idea that abolition would improve the condition of the enslaved in the West Indies. He insisted that 'the treatment of the slaves has been progressively ameliorated'. Building on his depiction of the philanthropic nature of the West Indians, George contrasted it with the lack of improvement in the conditions of the industrial poor in Britain. Drawing a parallel with the economic rationale for tolerating the slave trade, he noted that whilst conditions in the factories of the 'northern counties' were 'highly advantageous in a commercial view' they 'are fatal to the health and morals of His Majesty's subjects'. In raising the status of the factory worker as a British subject, he was drawing an implicit comparison with the enslaved, who to his mind would never be part of the nation. Pushing the point further he raised the issue of child labour, asking why regulations not been passed to prevent 'one more ruddy-cheeked boy or blooming girl' from being immured 'in your putrid haunts of vice and disease'. Mocking the abolitionists' insistence on ameliorating conditions in the colonies, he argued 'Tell us not of your ventilators and artificial gasses; the thing is contrary to the first principles, and it must be discontinued.' Appealing directly to men like Cobbett who prioritised British interests over and above both the colonists and the enslaved, George pointed to the poverty and wretchedness to be found in the metropolis. Describing children with 'their countenances pale, their limbs emaciated, and their bodies swollen with famine', George asked why 'our Philanthropists do not make it the theme of declamation or the object of reform'. In answer, he declared that:

> This is too near and obvious for them; their aim is more distant, their scope is larger; the spirit of modern philanthropy does not act, sir, like the rational principle of self-love ... which first puts the centre in motion, and then extends itself in progressive circles of beneficence to the extremities; the spirit of modern reform attacks at once the connecting chain of the system, and, if the whole do not fall to pieces at its touch, it works inwards till it shakes the centre.

With this statement George articulated an early version of the idea of 'telescopic philanthropy'. This concept was picked up on by Isaac Robert Cruikshank in his satirical cartoon 'John Bull Taking a Clear View of the Negro Slavery Question' (1826) and later popularised by Charles Dickens in his novel *Bleak House* (1852–53). Ultimately, according to George, this misplaced sense of benevolence would send 'the Blacks into a phrenzy' and turn 'the Whites into despair'.

The nature of Africa and Africans received a lengthy treatment from George. Foremost in his mind was a need to dismantle the 'Utopia in Africa which the imagination of the abolitionists has projected'.[90] He argued that slavery was endemic throughout the continent and an important part of the local economy. As such the imposition of British morals, values and laws broke with traditional practice. For George the rights and liberties which were being asserted in Europe did not apply to African societies, which, he insisted, were fundamentally different. Thus, he inquired:

> Is it pretended, that the mere possession, or use, or transfer of a slave in Africa, is unjust or inhuman? ... By all the laws and customs of Africa, existing from the remotest antiquity, it is authorised; and the abstract rights of man cannot be profitably applied to societies existing under established laws. What is consistent with those laws must be accounted just. Is the same thing in Africa inhuman?

Implicit in his statement was a different, but no less critical question – is African humanity comparable to European? Depicting Africa as a place characterised by savagery and blighted by barbarism, George was gesturing towards slavery as a civilising force. This argument was made explicitly by his brother Thomas junior, who considered that 'the Removal of the Negroes from their own Country, governed as it is, must, under <u>any</u> Circumstances [original emphasis], be a change for the better'.[91] George supported his depiction of Africa by quoting Leo Africanus and Mungo Park. Of Park's work, George stated that 'what he tells us of the Negro nations does not lead to a conviction that we shall better their condition by abandoning this trade'.[92] There had been some controversy over Park's publication. It was edited by the Jamaica slave owner Bryan Edwards, and there was a rumour that 'Mr. Edwards foisted those opinions into the book'.[93] George, however, reported that during a conversation with Park at a meeting of the Linnean Society, he had been assured that the sentiments contained within his text were his own.[94] In contrast, in the second edition of Park's *Journal of a mission to the interior of Africa* (1815), he was described as an 'enemy of slavery' who regretted that his descriptions of Africa had been used to undermine abolition.[95]

George compared Park's text with the writings of Thomas Malthus in *An essay on the principle of population* (1798).[96] Malthus's description in the section 'Of the Checks to Population in different parts of Africa' drew on Park's report on the state of the country.[97] It described a population devoid of Adam Smith's markers of civilisation – production and commerce. It was these characteristics which elevated the British nation above a primitive agrarian subsistence, allowing them to develop technology, science and culture. Malthus wrote: 'What the negro nations really want is security of property, and its general concomitant, industry; and without these, an increase of people would only aggravate their distresses.'[98] George argued that a population surplus justified the slave trade, although he admitted that 'I do not, sir, know the sentiments of Mr. Malthus upon the subject.'[99] Wilberforce corrected him by stating that Malthus had 'expressed his surprise to have learned, that in some publications of the day he was regarded as in favour of the slave trade'.[100] The Malthus family had direct connections to the slave economy, having invested in both the Royal African Company and the South Sea Company. Malthus's cousin Marianna eloped with William Leigh Symes, who inherited the Oxford plantation in Jamaica. This marriage entangled the Malthus family with the Hibberts, who acted as consignees for the estate. Malthus himself took an active role in helping Marianna secure the jointure owed to her when her husband died. Alison Bashford and Joyce E. Chaplin have argued that this familial connection was a 'pertinent context' for Malthus's 'reluctance to engage in robust public discussion on the political economy (and demography) of the slave trade and slavery'.[101] For Malthus, as for the Hibberts, 'Lines of connection – familial, commercial, political, legal – crossed, as public and private worlds folded into one another.'[102]

Despite his efforts George knew the battle was lost and this left him with a palpable sense of anger. To the House he stated that 'if in what I have said I have expressed myself at any time with unbecoming warmth, I shall tomorrow be sorry for it; the House will, I trust, regard it as the effort of an expiring flame, the spasm before dissolution'.[103] George was furious with the way that the slave owners had been represented. He was also scathing towards those within the West India interest who had voted for the bill, assuring them that:

> [T]hey will soon find themselves undistinguished from us who have from the first withstood these innovations – undistinguished, excepting by the bitter consciousness of having been aiding and consenting to their own destruction; and they must be contented with us to walk through the empire with a brand upon their backs; if they enjoy a short prosperity, it will be prosperity blasted by obloquy and reproach; if they fall, on the contrary, as I believe they will, they will fall unpitied and unprotected.[104]

The use of the term 'brand' was deliberately incendiary, and was not the first time George had framed legislation restricting his economic freedoms using the language of slavery. Earlier in the debate he had claimed that he 'bore the burthen of a slave; for he had embarked all his property in our West India colonies; he felt the shackles of the slave about him, and he no longer enjoyed the freedom he was before possessed of'.[105] In private George made sure that his correspondents in Jamaica knew who had voted in favour of the bill. He wrote to Taylor informing him of 'the miserable minorities we were left in' and lambasting the 'Renegade conduct of the chief Planters and Merchants in the House' naming and shaming 'Manning, Barham, Dawkins, Long ... Dudley, Sam Boddington, Sharpe'.[106] To those who had betrayed the colonists he asked publicly in Parliament if they would 'demand compensation at least, as the condition for their passive concurrence'.[107] He stated that the bill ought to be 'accompanied with a liberal pledge of compensation to those whose property, hitherto protected by the laws, may be injured by its enactments'. Failure to compensate the West Indians would in effect put 'out of the protection of the law a large class of British subjects' and that would be 'repugnant to every principle of justice, humanity and sound policy'. Adopting once again the mantle of the merchant he prompted the House to remember that it was mercantile capital which had been laid out to cultivate the colonies and yet 'the security of those who lent money in faith ... is, without compensation, to be violated'. The bill passed without a clause for compensation on 23 March 1807 and came into effect a year later in 1808.

Conclusion

In recognition of his exertions in defence of the slave trade, the SWIPM resolved 'that the thanks of the Meeting be given to Mr. George Hibbert' for his 'zealous & unremitted attention to the interests of the West India body, on this & many former occasions'.[108] George's performance won him the respect and admiration of his fellow merchants and planters, setting him on a course to play a crucial role in the coming struggles over slavery. George continued on in the Commons, acting as a 'useful but not brilliant parliamentarian' in the service of the West India interest.[109] In 1810 he supported Brougham's motion to put an effective end to the slave trade, explaining his turnaround by claiming that 'he had opposed abolition on practical grounds' but 'had never questioned its desirability on humanitarian ones'.[110] He also used the opportunity to 'point out that the motion itself vindicated his former argument that abolition would merely encourage the foreign slave trade'. Despite his words, it was arguably economic rather than humanitarian concerns which prompted George's newfound enthusiasm for abolition. As a sugar agent with an eye on the European re-export market, George doubtless wished to find ways of reducing the competitiveness of those producers who still benefited from an unlimited supply of enslaved labour. Concern over the issue of labour replenishment led George to support Foster Barham's proposal of 1811 to furnish the West India colonies with free labour from the East Indies, a move which anticipated the system of indenture which replaced slavery in the 1840s.[111]

DEFENDING THE SLAVE TRADE

In 1812 George left Parliament in order to take on the role of Agent for Jamaica. It was from this position, as the most powerful representative of the largest of Britain's Caribbean possessions, that George fought to preserve his family's business and way of life. In 1807 George had warned his fellow West Indians that the next target for the abolitionists would be the institution of slavery itself. 'Have they not heard', he asked, 'the alarm bell of further innovations yet ringing in their ears?'[112] Following a five-year period in which there was a lull in campaigning efforts, the abolitionists regrouped before entering into a new phase of antislavery activism. Having been convinced for many years of the certainty of this development, George was ready to play his part.

Notes

1 Srividhya Swaminathan, 'Developing the proslavery position after the Somerset decision', *Slavery & Abolition*, 24:3 (2003), p. 43.
2 Philippa Levine, *The British empire: Sunrise to sunset* (Harlow: Pearson Education, 2007), p. 13.
3 Hugh Thomas, *The slave trade: The history of the Atlantic Slave Trade 1440–1870* (London: Picador, 1997), p. 515.
4 NLW/SPD, 9096, Letter from Thomas Hibbert senior to Nathaniel Phillips, winter 1788.
5 For a discussion of the role of the American Revolution see Christopher Leslie Brown, *Moral capital: Foundations of British abolitionism* (Chapel Hill: University of North Carolina Press, 2006).
6 Roger Anstey, *The Atlantic slave trade and British abolition 1760–1810* (London: Macmillan, 1975), p. 287.
7 David Beck Ryden, *West Indian slavery and British abolition, 1783–1807* (Cambridge: Cambridge University Press, 2009), pp. 36–7.
8 Alexandra Franklin, 'Enterprise and advantage: The West India interest in Britain 1774–1840' (PhD thesis, University of Pennsylvania, 1992), p. 26.
9 Ryden, *West Indian slavery and British abolition*, pp. 40–82.
10 *Ibid.*, p. 53. Ryden added that he had not included in this figure instances where the name 'Hibbert' appeared without a forename. He suggested that if these instances had been counted George Hibbert would have been the most frequent attendee.
11 Lillian Penson, 'The London West India interest in the eighteenth century', *English Historical Review*, 36:143 (1921), pp. 373–92; Lewis Namier, *England in the age of the American Revolution* (London: Macmillan, 1961); Barry Higman, 'The West India "interest" in Parliament, 1807–1833', *Historical Studies*, 13:49 (1967), pp. 1–19; Andrew J. O'Shaughnessy, 'The formation of a commercial lobby: The West India interest, British colonial policy and the American Revolution', *Historical Journal*, 40:1 (1997), pp. 71–95.
12 George Hibbert, HC Deb., 23 February 1807, vol. VIII, cc. 945–95.
13 George Hibbert, quoted in T. S. Winn, *A speedy end to slavery in our West India colonies by safe, effectual and equitable means for the benefit of all parties concerned* (London: J. Hatchard & Son, 1825), p. 111.
14 Institute of Commonwealth Studies, Senate House Library, London, West India Committee Papers (ICS/SHL/WICP), M915/2, General Meeting, Society of West India Planters and Merchants (SWIPM) Minute Book, 8 May 1806.
15 J. H. Markland, *A sketch of the life and character of George Hibbert Esq., F.R.S., S.A., and L.S.* (London, 1837), p. 5.
16 George Hibbert, HC Deb., 16 March 1807, vol. IX, cc. 114–40.

17 John Oldfield, *Popular politics and British anti-slavery: The mobilisation of public opinion against the slave trade, 1787–1807* (London: Routledge, 1998).
18 ICS/SHL/WICP, M915/2, SWIPM, Meeting of the Standing Committee, London Tavern, 1788.
19 *Ibid.*, SWIPM, Meeting of the Sub-Committee, London Tavern, 19 January 1792.
20 O'Shaughnessy, 'The formation of a commercial lobby', p. 76.
21 William Hague, *William Wilberforce: The life of the great anti-slavery campaigner* (London: Harper Press, 2008), p. 146.
22 NLW/SPD, 9143, Letter from George Hibbert to Nathaniel Phillips, 20 July 1791.
23 ICS/SHL/TVAP, M965/17/2, Letter from George Hibbert to Simon Taylor, 7 April 1792.
24 Letter from Hibbert, Fuhr, & Hibbert to Nathaniel Phillips, 1 July 1788, quoted in Ryden, *West Indian Slavery*, p. 193.
25 Captain Edward Hibbert, Obituary, *Gentleman's Magazine* (London: John Nichols, 1824), p. 185
26 ICS/SHL/TVAP, M965/17/54, Letter from George Hibbert to Simon Taylor, 4 July 1804.
27 William Wilberforce to Lord Muncaster, quoted in Thomas, *The slave trade*, p. 549.
28 ICS/SHL/WICP, M915/2, SWIPM Minute Book, General Meeting, 14 February 1805.
29 ICS/SHL/TVAP, M965/17/72, Letter from George Hibbert to Simon Taylor, 8 January 1807.
30 HFAC, Diary of Robert Hibbert junior, 7 April 1772.
31 *Ibid.*, 25 May 1795.
32 For a general discussion see Michael J. Turner, '"Setting the captive free": Thomas Perronet Thompson, British radicalism and the West Indies, 1820s–1860s', *Slavery & Abolition*, 26:1 (2005), pp. 115–32.
33 For a discussion of working-class attitudes towards slavery see Seymour Drescher, 'Cart whip and billy roller: Antislavery and reform symbolism in industrializing Britain', *Journal of Social History*, 15:1 (1981), pp. 3–24; Ryan Hanley, 'Slavery and the birth of working class racism in England, 1814–1833', *Transactions of the Royal Historical Society*, 26 (2016), pp. 103–23.
34 ICS/SHL/TVAP, M965/17/55, Letter from George Hibbert to Simon Taylor, 1 August 1804.
35 ICS/SHL/TVAP, M965/17/58, Letter from George Hibbert to Simon Taylor, 6 March 1805.
36 Marcus Wood, 'William Cobbett, John Thelwall, radicalism, racism and slavery: A study in Burkean parodics', *Romanticism on the Net*, 15 (1999). www.erudit.org/revue/ron/1999/v/n15/005873ar.html [accessed 10 April 2018].
37 ICS/SHL/TVAP, M965/17/58, Letter from George Hibbert to Simon Taylor, 6 March 1805.
38 Wood, 'William Cobbett', p. 9.
39 ICS/SHL/TVAP, M965/17/58, Letter from George Hibbert to Simon Taylor, 6 March 1805.
40 ICS/SHL/WICP, M915/2, SWIPM Minute Book, General Meeting of the Merchants, Mortgagees, Annuitants and Other Creditors of the Sugar Colonies, London Tavern, 11 February 1790.
41 For a history of Robert Cooper Lee see Anne Powers (ed.), *A parcel of ribbons: The letters of an eighteenth-century family in London and Jamaica* (lulu.com, 2012).
42 *Select Committee appointed to take the examination of witnesses respecting the African slave trade. Minutes of the evidence taken before a committee of the House of Commons appointed for the purpose of the examination of such witnesses who have petitioned against the abolition of the slave trade* (London: House of Commons, 1790), p. 359; hereafter *Minutes*.
43 Gilbert Francklyn, *Observations occasioned by the attempts made in England to effect the abolition of the slave trade* (London: Logographic Press, 1789), p. xv.
44 HFAC, Diary of Robert Hibbert junior, 27 January 1790.
45 *Ibid.*, 19 February 1790.

46 R. A. Melikan, 'Pigott, Sir Arthur Leary (1749–1819)', *Oxford dictionary of national biography* (Oxford: Oxford University Press, 2004). www.oxforddnb.com/view/article/22249 [accessed 3 February 2011].
47 'Thomas Nash Kemble', Legacies of British Slave-ownership. www.ucl.ac.uk/lbs/person/view/1222646969 [accessed 10 April 2018].
48 *Abridgement of the minutes of the evidence: Taken before a committee of the whole house, to whom it was referred to consider of the slave-trade* (London, 1789–91), p. 134.
49 HFAC, Diary of Robert Hibbert junior.
50 *Abridgement of the minutes*, p. 134.
51 HFAC, Diary of Robert Hibbert junior.
52 *Ibid.*
53 *Abridgement of the minutes*, p. 135.
54 Henrice Altink, 'Forbidden fruit: Proslavery attitudes towards enslaved women's sexuality and interracial sex', *Journal of Caribbean History*, 39:2 (2005), pp. 201–35.
55 HFAC, Diary of Robert Hibbert junior.
56 *Ibid.*, 11–23 May 1800.
57 *Ibid.*, 23 May 1800.
58 Ian John Barrett, 'Cultures of pro-slavery: The political defence of the slave trade in Britain c.1787–1807' (PhD thesis, King's College London, 2009), pp. 90–116.
59 Christer Petley, '"Devoted islands" and "That madman Wilberforce": British proslavery patriotism during the age of abolition', *Journal of Imperial and Commonwealth History*, 38:3 (2011), pp. 393–415.
60 Evidence of George Hibbert, in *Minutes*, p. 392.
61 *Ibid.*, p. 393.
62 *Ibid.*, p. 386.
63 *Ibid.*, p. 388.
64 Julian Hoppit, 'Compulsion, compensation and property rights in Britain, 1688–1833', *Past & Present*, 210:1 (2011), p. 118.
65 Hibbert, *Minutes*, p. 397.
66 For a detailed discussion see William Pettigrew, *Freedom's debt: The Royal African Company and the politics of the Atlantic slave trade, 1672–1752* (Chapel Hill: University of North Carolina Press, 2013).
67 Hibbert, *Minutes*, p. 391.
68 *Ibid.*, p. 390.
69 *Ibid.*, p. 389.
70 *Ibid.*, pp. 387–8.
71 *Ibid.*, p. 390.
72 Devon Archives and Local Studies Centre, Exeter, Political and Personal Papers of Henry Addington, 1st Viscount Sidmouth, 152M/C1796/OC2, Letter from George Hibbert to William Manning, 23 March 1796.
73 ICS/SHL/TVAP, M965/17/17, Letter from George Hibbert to Simon Taylor, 2 April 1800.
74 ICS/SHL/TVAP, M965/17/25, Letter from George Hibbert to Simon Taylor, 3 September 1801.
75 Devon Archives and Local Studies Centre, Exeter, Political and Personal Papers of Henry Addington, 1st Viscount Sidmouth, 152M/C1796/OC2, Letter from George Hibbert to William Manning, 23 March 1796.
76 R. G. Thorne, *The history of Parliament: The House of Commons, 1790–1820* (London: Secker and Warburg, 1986), p. 193.
77 'George Hibbert (1757–1820)', History of Parliament. www.historyofparliamentonline.org/volume/1790-1820/member/hibbert-george-1757-1837 [accessed 30 May 2018].
78 Thorne, *The Commons*, p. 479. For an analysis of the relationship between the unreformed Parliament and the West India interest see Izhak Gross, 'The abolition of negro slavery and British parliamentary politics 1832–3', *Historical Journal*, 23:1 (1980), pp. 63–85; Thomas C. Holt, *The problem of freedom: Race, labour and politics in Jamaica and Britain, 1832–1938* (London: Johns Hopkins University Press, 1992), p. 29.

79 GA/BFDP, D1799/C153, Letter from Robert Hibbert to Mary Oates, 5 May 1807.
80 ICS/SHL/TVAP, M965/17/70, Letter from George Hibbert to Simon Taylor, 5 November 1806.
81 ICS/SHL/TVAP, M965/17/72, Letter from George Hibbert to Simon Taylor, 8 January 1807.
82 ICS/SHL/TVAP, M965/17/68, Letter from George Hibbert to Simon Taylor, 1 October 1806, M965/17/68.
83 ICS/SHL/TVAP, M965/17/72, Letter from George Hibbert to Simon Taylor, 8 January 1807.
84 George Hibbert, *The substance of three speeches in Parliament, on the Bill for the Abolition of the Slave Trade, and on the petition respecting the state of the West India trade, in February and March, 1807, by George Hibbert Esq. M.P. for Seaford* (London: Lane, Darling & Co., 1807), p. vii.
85 *Ibid.*, p. 4.
86 ICS/SHL/TVAP, M965/17/74, Letter from George Hibbert to Simon Taylor, 7 March 1807.
87 George Hibbert, HC Deb., 16 March 1807, vol. IX, cc.114–40.
88 George Hibbert, HC Deb., 10 February 1807, vol. VIII, cc. 717–22.
89 George Hibbert, HC Deb., 23 February 1807, vol. VIII, cc. 945–95.
90 *Ibid.*
91 NLW/SPD, 9096, Thomas Hibbert junior to Nathaniel Phillips, winter 1788.
92 George Hibbert, HC Deb., 23 February 1807, vol. VIII, cc. 945–95.
93 Hibbert, *Substance of three speeches*, pp. 24–5.
94 George Hibbert, HC Deb., 23 February 1807, vol. VIII, cc. 945–95.
95 Mungo Park, *The journal of a mission to the interior of Africa in the year 1805*, 2nd edn (London: John Murray, 1815), p. 351.
96 George Hibbert, HC Deb., 23 February 1807, vol. VIII, cc. 945–95.
97 Thomas Malthus, *An essay on the principle of population, Or a view of its past and present effects on human happiness; with an inquiry into our prospects respecting the future removal or mitigation of the evils which it occasions*, 5th edn, vol. I (London: John Murray, 1817), pp. 203–11.
98 *Ibid.*, pp. 210–11.
99 George Hibbert, HC Deb., 23 February 1807, vol. VIII, cc. 945–95.
100 William Wilberforce, HC Deb., 23 February 1807, vol. VIII, cc. 945–95.
101 Alison Bashford and Joyce E. Chaplin, *The new worlds of Thomas Robert Malthus: Rereading the 'Principle of Population'* (Oxford: Princeton University Press, 2016), p. 186. My thanks to Catherine Hall for this reference.
102 *Ibid.*, p. 187.
103 George Hibbert, HC Deb., 16 March 1807, vol. IX, cc. 114–40.
104 *Ibid.*
105 George Hibbert, HC Deb., 27 February 1807, vol. VIII, cc. 1040–53.
106 ICS/SHL/TVAP, M965/17/74, Letter from George Hibbert to Simon Taylor, 7 March 1807.
107 George Hibbert, HC Deb., 16 March 1807, vol. IX, cc. 114–40.
108 ICS/SHL/WICP, M915/2, SWIMP Minute Book, General Meeting, 26 February 1807.
109 A. E. Furness, 'George Hibbert and the defence of slavery in the West Indies', *Jamaican Historical Review*, 5:1 (1965), p. 60.
110 Thorne, *The Commons*, p. 194.
111 For a detailed history of indenture see Madhavi Kale, *Fragments of empire: Capital, slavery and Indian indentured labour in the British Caribbean* (Philadelphia: University of Pennsylvania Press, 1998).
112 George Hibbert, HC Deb., 16 March 1807, vol. IX, cc. 114–40.

CHAPTER FIVE

Defending slavery

> Mr H. is gliding down the vale of years, and hath grown grey in the West India service. – Great is the propensity of Man to excuse and cajole himself even in his greatest aberration from plainest duties. – What qualms of conscience, or peradventure what degree of satisfaction, Mr H. may experience from the review of a long life spent in support of the slave system, I cannot pretend to know – or how far at the close of the scene, when he finds this world receding from him, and he verging on another state of Retribution, he may hope the welcome greeting, 'Come thou good and faithful servant, enter into the joy of thy Lord'.
>
> T. S. Winn, *A speedy end to slavery in our West India colonies by safe, effectual and equitable means for the benefit of all parties concerned* (London: J. Hatchard & Son, 1825), p. 112

In 1812 George became Agent for Jamaica – a role he had long desired and which it had taken him ten years of careful political lobbying to achieve.[1] His aspirations for the agency were narrow in their focus: 'I have only two objects in respect to the Agency, the weight and authority it would give me with the West India Interest at home and the administrations and that it should repay to me the expense of a seat in Parliament.'[2] The Agent acted as a bridge between the colonial assembly and the imperial Government, giving him access to both. As A. E. Furness has described, 'the Colonial Office in London gave the Agent an almost complete monopoly of representing the views of the colonists to them ... This made him almost a competitor with the Governor of Jamaica for the ear of the Secretary of State.'[3] It also gave George a means of increasing his wealth as the position paid £1,500 per annum. As Agent for the largest and most powerful of the Caribbean possessions, George became *the* leading spokesman for the West India interest in Britain. His appointment came at a crucial time; with the campaign to defend the slave trade lost, the planters and merchants were left in a precarious situation. Metropolitan consciousness had been awakened and it followed that the next target for the abolitionists would be the institution of slavery itself.

The abolitionists renewed their campaign with a call for the implementation of slave registers. While this innovation was ostensibly to monitor the illegal slave trade, it also recorded population fluctuations on the plantations, providing accurate data which could be used to make claims about the treatment of the enslaved. Following this the abolitionists established the principles of amelioration, which included the regulation of conditions on the plantation as well as an emphasis on the 'civilisation' and Christianisation of the enslaved. These measures were a test of the West Indians' appetite for reform; failure to act would confirm to both the British Parliament and people that the colonists could not be trusted to act in the interests of humanity. It was within this context that George conducted the work of staving off abolition. He authored pamphlets, wrote to the newspapers and pressed his case with the Secretary of State for War and the Colonies. In private he was convinced that the abolition of slavery would eventually come and was determined to buy as much time as he could through a policy of compromise with the British Government. Describing his own tactics, George noted that 'by moderation on our part' the interest could 'place ourselves in favourable contrast with our hot headed opponents'.[4] George advocated for the Jamaica Assembly to pass legislation which would improve the conditions of slavery. Acting of their own volition would increase their moral capital and divert a potentially embarrassing confrontation with the imperial Government over who had the right to legislate on the internal operations of the colony. At the same time George made dire predictions at home about the danger of infringing on the colonists' rights. Maintaining the delicate balance between these two governing bodies allowed George to wring concessions from both. His reputation for political manoeuvring led the abolitionist T. S. Winn to describe him as 'Mr George Hibbert, agent for Jamaica, a shrewd and knowing man, well versed in the mystery of West India policy, and very dexterous in the management.'[5]

With George championing the slave holders as active agents in the civilising mission, he attracted the attention of the abolitionists, who sought to undermine this rhetoric. As the debates intensified in the 1820s, the Hibberts became involved in a public spat which left them open to accusations which were both personally compromising and politically damaging. The incident formed part of what Catherine Hall has described as the 'war of representation' – a bitter contest over the 'truth about the system of slavery' and the character of 'the African'.[6] A constituent part of that process involved intense scrutiny of the character of plantocratic society, making 'white colonial identities ... a site of struggle during the age of abolition'.[7] Antislavery literature and visual culture depicted the colonies as spaces of transgression in which both the enslaved and their oppressors were degraded by the institution. The West Indies were cast as a place devoid of morality; gluttony and excess, whether imagined through the gross consumption of food and alcohol or sexual incontinency, were presented as the societal norm in the colonies.[8] This lack of restraint, combined with a reputation for irreligiosity and cruelty, allowed the abolitionists to question 'whether white slaveholders could be classed as fully "English" and whether slavery was compatible with "English" conceptions of liberty and morality'.[9] Characterised as a despot reigning over his personal tropical fiefdom, the planter was imagined as the antithesis of enlightened metropolitan modernity. For George this was not simply a political campaign but a matter of personal and familial integrity. He rejected the image that the abolitionists had presented to the world, although in the end he was unable to persuade Parliament and the public that his vision of slavery justified its continued existence.

George's most lasting political legacy stemmed from his longstanding support for compensation. He lobbied for the measure for over forty years and ultimately the Government agreed that any state-mandated change to the status of property must be compensated for. A. E. Furness remarked that 'His persistence helped to strengthen the Government's resolve not to yield thoughtlessly to irresponsible philanthropists, and thus be beguiled into an act of massive confiscation.'[10] Respect for property and a wish to see slavery ended quickly led many abolitionists to acquiesce on the issue. The Hibberts were, of course, materially interested, given that they both owned enslaved people and had extended large amounts of credit to slave holders in Jamaica. A significant proportion of their claims were related to the payment of debt which had been accrued over the course of their long commercial relationships. The compensation money not only validated George's claims regarding the legitimacy of 'property in people', it also provided the family with the capital necessary to maintain their status and diversify their business interests in the wake of abolition.

Slave Registry Bill

George's first major crisis as Agent came in 1815 when the abolitionists introduced the Slave Registry Bill. George immediately met with the Prime Minister, Lord Liverpool, to discuss the proposals. Christer Petley has noted that 'Liverpool recognised the constitutional delicacy of the situation', yet at the same time also issued a 'gentle threat to try to strike a compromise' by warning that any failure to act would result in 'acts of the parent legislature more directly and offensively militating against the rights claimed by the colonial legislatures'.[11] The SWIPM met to discuss the matter and urged its membership to see their 'Friends who may be Members of either House of Parliament & endeavour to engage their attention to all Questions which materially affect the West India Interest, particularly to the measure now in contemplation for a Registry of Slaves'.[12] The bill was despised by the planters, who considered it a challenge to their legislative independence and a definitive sign that the abolitionists were moving towards a campaign for emancipation. The colonists' strongest objection to the bill was set out in terms of its encroachment on their constitutional rights and liberties as freeborn Englishmen. The language bore a striking resemblance to the rhetoric of the American Revolution, with the Assembly arguing that since they had no parliamentary representatives they should not be bound by laws imposed without their assent. Once again, in the words of Samuel Johnson, the 'loudest yelps for liberty' were emanating from 'the drivers of the negroes'.[13]

George personally intervened in the debates following the publication by Zachary Macaulay of a review of James Stephen's *Reasons for establishing a registry of slaves in the British colonies* (1815). George's response was recorded in his diary:

> I have written and published two tracts on this subject, the one entitled Brief Remarks on the Slave Registry Bill and upon a Report of the African Institution recommending that measure, the other, written in animadversion upon a coarse and scurrilous Article in the Xtian Observer for Jany., is published under the name of Thomas Venables and entitled the Reviewer Reviewed. I am told that the Article I here attack has been written by Mr. Macaulay.[14]

The reviewer reviewed was published in January and 'Brief remarks' in March 1816. Writing under a pseudonym enabled George to adopt a more impassioned tone whilst avoiding censure from the abolitionist press. He noted that 'I have had some civil things said to me concerning my Brief Remarks and among the rest Mr. Wilberforce came to me in the House of Commons the other day purposely as he said to thank me for being the only one of his opponents who had treated him like a Gentleman.' 'Brief remarks' was described as 'well timed' by Wilberforce, in comparison to a publication by Joseph Marryat which was characterised as 'violent and rude'.[15] George's ability to harness the power of gentlemanly sociability was part of what made him such an effective opponent; he used his cultured reputation and mannered politeness as a means of rebuffing detractors who claimed that the West Indians were brutes devoid of English sensibility.

Both publications engaged with the issue of representation, mounting a robust defence of the character of the West Indian. George opened *The reviewer reviewed* with the lines:

> [T]he advocates of this Bill have created a monster of the imagination, and have dressed it in every shape of horror, that they the more easily reconcile the public and the legislature to measures which they recommend as necessary for the destruction of this chimera, but which have in truth other ultimate objects.[16]

The depiction of the planter as a cruel tyrant was dismissed by George as a political construct designed to manipulate the sympathies of a metropolitan audience. Stephen's original work had insinuated that the bill was necessary in order to monitor the planters, not only in terms of the prohibition of the slave trade, but also their treatment of the enslaved. George decried the use of 'presumptive evidence' to present the slave owner as 'destitute of every principle which could control his criminal propensities'.[17] Instead he insisted that the condition of the enslaved was 'in progressive amelioration' as a result of the 'humane spirit' of the legislation passed by the Jamaica Assembly regulating 'their food, their clothing, their punishments'.[18] He argued that 'generally speaking, the slaves in the colonies are contented in their situation; their labour is lighter far than millions of men in Europe gladly undergo for their daily bread'.[19] With this comparison George once again appealed to men like William Cobbett, who believed that the abolitionists should focus their reformist energies on conditions in Britain. In highlighting the legislation already enacted by the Jamaica Assembly, George insisted that the colonists were capable of dealing with issues of internal reform. This framing implicitly raised the thorny spectre of the constitutionality of imperial interference in the internal workings of the colony. Building on the theme, George warned that this kind of meddling led inexorably to 'the disenfranchisement of our colonial legislatures'.[20]

In contrast 'Brief remarks' opened with a paragraph which was designed to align it with metropolitan sentiments. 'There was reason to hope', George opined,

> that all European powers would ere long abolish that trade. The colonies would probably, if a little time were allowed them, see the propriety of adopting, of themselves, this or any measure which might be necessary to give effect to that abolition. He wished abolition to be complete and effectual, and wished eventual success to this or any other measure that might be found necessary for that end.[21]

On behalf of his constituents he was happy to report that 'Jamaica, since the abolition law passed, has not imported, by illicit practice, a single slave.'[22] He listed the improvements undertaken in the 'spirit of amelioration ... operating in concurrence with, or guided by, the local legislatures in our colonies, without any interference of the Imperial Parliament in their internal regulation'.[23] He pointed out that 'Laws directed to this object have been passed by the colonial legislatures, both previous to, and subsequent to, the abolition' and that 'many wholesome and humane provisions respecting the slaves' had been made.[24] He also noted that the yearly decrease in the population had dropped from 2 per cent to 0.2 per cent. George's consideration of the treatment of the enslaved moved beyond simply regulating the conditions of labour. Additionally he adopted the language of the civilising mission, gesturing towards efforts made to promote Christianity on the plantations. He informed his reader that in this sacred mission 'no impediment is given to the zealous efforts of religious pastors'. However, he cautioned that these meetings were sometimes used as an excuse for 'indecencies and disorders'.[25]

The collective national trauma at the loss of the Thirteen Colonies still carried political weight, and one of the major issues in 'Brief remarks' was the constitutionality of interfering with the internal regulation of the colony. George warned that 'Although the Imperial Parliament may acknowledge no concession of its supremacy, beyond that which it has already made in regard of taxation, every prudent man would deprecate the unnecessary introduction of a question which separated this country from the United States of America.'[26] George considered the imposition of the registers as both a constitutional challenge and a threat to civil order. He wrote that:

> Order and security in the colonies entirely depend upon that confidence which all classes of the population there repose in the local governments; to control their municipal jurisdiction, is to do away their influence; suspicion and alienation will take place of respect and deference, and insubordination, with all its dreadful train, must follow.[27]

The whites ruled in a tiny minority and were dependent on the perception of their power as absolute. To have the limits of that power exposed was not only humiliating but dangerous. The West Indians feared that divisions between themselves and the imperial Parliament might be interpreted by the enslaved as an incitement to open rebellion. The colonial legislature had still 'to prepare the civilisation of the subordinate race' and whilst they remained in a barbarous state, exciting their passions 'will be the signal for commencing a convulsion similar to that which eventually severed from France its greatest and most valuable colony'.[28] For the colonists, the bloodshed of Saint-Domingue continued to cast long shadows. When Bussa's Rebellion broke out in Barbados in April 1816, George no doubt felt vindicated in this sentiment. On hearing the news the SWIPM immediately formed a deputation to see Earl Bathurst, Secretary of State for War and the Colonies, to discuss the 'dangerous consequences ... of the mischievous effect that have arisen from the mistaken Opinion entertained there on the subject of the proposed Registry Bill'.[29] Despite their obvious distaste for the measure, the colonial assemblies passed their own legislation for the triennial registration of slaves. Whilst this allowed them to resist 'the imposition of an abolitionist-inspired measure from London', it also demonstrated the degree to which 'their opponents were shaping the political agenda'.[30] The legacy of this legislation was the creation of one of the most comprehensive sources of information on the enslaved in the Caribbean. Whilst the information contained within is framed by the demands of colonial bureaucracy, the documents nonetheless form a precious resource for recording and remembering the lives lived under slavery.

Amelioration

By the early 1820s the issue of amelioration had become entangled with a wider call for the total abolition of slavery. In 1823 the Society for the Mitigation and Gradual Abolition of Slavery throughout the British Dominions was formed, initially under the leadership of William Wilberforce, with Thomas Fowell Buxton replacing him in 1825. Several months before the organisation formed, Buxton introduced a motion into the House of Commons demanding the amelioration of slavery in preparation for its gradual abolition. Interfering with the colonial legislature was not something that the British Government undertook lightly.[31] Instead they sought a compromise which would enable them to effect the changes desired but without arbitrarily imposing the will of Parliament on the colonial assemblies. As William A. Greene has suggested, the Government was in consultation with the West India interest in London.[32] In a letter to the Under Secretary, Robert Wilmot-Horton, George reported that Earl Bathurst had conceded the slave owners' rights to compensation.[33] This reassurance led George to signal that the colonial interest 'will act in concert on efforts for their own preservation' and that to this end 'I shall not, you may rest assured, be found wanting in my duty'.

When Buxton moved his resolutions in the Commons on 15 May 1823 he was out-manoeuvred by George Canning, the Foreign Secretary and Leader of the House, who countered with his own measures. Canning pushed for an end to the use of the whip, an improvement in religious instruction, the prohibition of market days on the Sabbath, the protection of enslaved people's property, the promotion of marriage and family, the introduction of enslaved people's evidence in court, a stop to the practice of selling enslaved people and estates separately and the facilitation of manumission. He also introduced an amendment to the motion which stated that the 'house is anxious for the accomplishment of this purpose, at the earliest period that shall be compatible with the well-being of the slaves themselves, with the safety of the colonies, and with a fair and equitable consideration of the interests of private property'.[34] With this, 'Canning committed the Government to a policy of working with the West Indians, exhorting reform from them rather than imposing it'.[35] Following a short debate Canning's resolutions were passed.

Opinion was divided among the West India interest as to this approach; those members of the leadership within the metropole looked on it favourably, whilst their counterparts in the colonies expressed dismay at what they perceived as the failure of their members to challenge the resolutions. Overall, George was pleased with Canning's speech. He wrote to Wilmot-Horton, stating that:

> Mr Canning's speech was most eloquent, and in some respects subverted in a Masterly Manner the Arguments advanced by Mr. Buxton – but, in consistency with a determination which the Cabinet Ministers had previously adopted it holds out in express terms – a pledge for the adoption of measures which, at a time more or less distant, is to terminate in a general emancipation of all the Slaves in the Colonies.[36]

From Canning's speech it was clear that slavery as an institution could not be sustained indefinitely. The public articulation of this made the need for committed reform of paramount necessity. George promised Wilmot-Horton that 'I have exerted my utmost ability, in recommending that the West India Body should declare itself favourable now, as it has been ever to all such Amelioration of the Condition of our Slaves.' He did not go back on his word. The SWIPM immediately agreed to Canning's resolutions and sent them to the colonial assemblies, urging them that the survival of slavery as a system depended 'upon the measures which shall be adopted (and without delay) in the Colonies'.[37] Their willingness to implement the policies would decide whether the attacks that had 'recently been so unjustly made upon their Property and Rights (and which will not fail to be renewed and continued) shall or shall not be frustrated in future; and the protection of the Government secured to them against such attacks'.

The Chairman of the SWIPM, Charles Rose Ellis, wrote to George articulating his dismay over the reaction of the planter class to Canning's resolutions. The letter was indicative of the difference between metropolitan and colonial attitudes. The colonists had expressed 'a feeling of dissatisfaction and jealousy with respect to the course pursued by the West India Body in England, in reference to Mr. Buxton's motion'.[38] Ellis believed that 'Such a feeling could only have arisen from a complete misconception of both the motive and effect of that line of conduct.' He sought George's backing, stating that 'no other course could have given the Colonial Legislatures even a voice in the question, you will yourself, I am sure, not hesitate to vouch'. Ellis worried that colonial intransigence would thwart the efforts of those who were best placed to judge 'the temper, either of the Publick throughout England, or of the House of Commons'. Now more than ever the West India interest was reliant upon 'the conduct of our friends in the Assembly of Jamaica', for there had never been 'a moment when the temper, and discretion, and a cordial understanding with the Executive Government were so essential to the deepest Interests of Jamaica'. The colonists saw compromise as capitulation, and Ellis urged George as Agent for Jamaica 'to employ your utmost efforts to remove so fatal and so ill founded a misconception'. For Ellis the planters had failed to understand that 'there was another class whom it was [original emphasis] of the most essential importance to conciliate – the impartial independent mass of the Publick, who were well disposed to the West Indies, but who were of opinion that things could not be left as they were'.[39] If the colonial assemblies were to win popular support they must demonstrate 'substantial and sincere co-operation in the benevolent intensions of the British Publick'. Both George and Ellis had accepted the impact of public opinion on slavery, which George described as an 'impelling tide which it is impossible to resist'.[40] They understood that the representation of the institution was central to its preservation. Only through the careful management of its public image could the West India interest buy itself time and levy concessions from the imperial Government.

The war of representation

As conditions on the plantation took centre stage, the abolitionists needed to demonstrate that the colonial assemblies were remiss, if not outright negligent, in their ameliorative duties. During this period 'colonial reform, mission work and emancipation' became deeply intertwined, forming a central site for the contestation over slavery.[41] George was determined to prove that the colonists were taking an active part in the civilising mission. To this end he had been in communication with the Bishop of London, William Howley in order to develop the Curates Act, which was passed by the Jamaica Assembly in 1817. The Act required curates on the island to spend two days a week visiting the plantations and offering religious instruction to the enslaved, although permission from the plantation owner had to be sought beforehand. Members of the West India interest began to take a more active role in the promotion of Anglican missionary work. The Society for the Conversion and Religious Instruction and Education of the Negro Slaves in the British West India Islands was established in 1794, with the Bishop of London, Beilby Porteus as its President. The Society's work was limited, with very few curates recruited to go out to the Caribbean. Its deeply conservative nature appealed to the planters, who were able to control the clergymen through the stipends they paid for. In 1823, the same year as Canning's resolutions, the proslavery lobbyists George Hibbert, Charles Rose Ellis, Charles Pallmer and William Manning were all listed as Governors of the Society. Their abolitionist opponent William Wilberforce was also a subscriber. The SWIPM donated £1,000, purchasing with it what they hoped would be the moral high ground. The Bishop of London, William Howley's letter of gratitude articulated exactly the response that the charitable gift was designed to elicit. He begged 'leave to express the great satisfaction I have felt in observing the spirit of enlightened humanity which directed the proceedings of the Committee'.[42]

Attempts to highlight the plantocracy's newfound religious zeal suffered a setback following an uprising by the enslaved in Demerara in August 1823. Reverend John Smith, a Wesleyan Methodist sent by the London Missionary Society, was accused of inciting rebellion among his congregation and was subsequently arrested and sentenced to death. Before he received a pardon from Britain he died of consumption in prison. Christer Petley has argued that Smith's death provided the abolitionists with a narrative of religious martyrdom in the face of the 'godless planters'.[43] This representation was given added weight by the treatment of the Reverend William Shrewsbury, a Methodist minister. In October 1823 a mob of colonists in Barbados burned down his church, forcing him and his pregnant wife to flee for safety to St Vincent. The damage done to the planters' reputation in the wake of these events meant that two years later George was still having to defend their actions. In a letter to Wilmot-Horton, George enclosed two newspaper cuttings penned by Thomas Venables, the same pen-name he used for *The reviewer reviewed*. The articles lamented that events in Demerara and Barbados had been linked to the 'general indisposition of the inhabitants of the colonies towards the means of affording to the negroes religious instruction'.[44] It insisted that the colonists 'have shown a most liberal disposition to afford the utmost possible facilities to the labours of missionaries of varying descriptions, when those labours have been directed simply and purely to the means of religious instruction'. Implicit in George's construction was the notion that both Smith and Shrewsbury had in fact been engaged in subversive abolitionist politicking rather than the pious work of proselytising.

It was against this backdrop that the Hibbert family were drawn into a very public political scandal over the nature and efficacy of ameliorative policies. In reference to the events that unfurled in the press, Lowell Ragatz noted that this 'war of pens lent spice to the whole question and was eagerly followed by the British public'.[45] The episode began in 1817 and centred on George's Jamaica-born cousin Robert. Whilst studying at Emmanuel College, Cambridge in the late 1780s, Robert had struck up a friendship with the radical reformer William Frend. Frend had recently converted to Unitarianism and it was perhaps this shared religious non-conformity which brought the two men together. The pair debated the morality of slavery, but Robert was unconvinced by the arguments against it. According to Jerom Murch it was after consultation with Frend that Robert 'resolved in 1817 to send out a Missionary, whose duty it should be to mitigate as far as possible the lot of his slaves, then about four hundred; especially by such religious instruction as would be suited to their uncultured minds'.[46] Robert appointed the Reverend Thomas Cooper, a Unitarian minister, to undertake the task. Cooper was enjoined by Robert 'to consider myself perfectly at liberty to adopt my own plans in every thing, and gave instructions to the authorities upon the estate that my labours should not be opposed under any pretence'.[47] This was qualified, however, by the condition that his ministrations 'should in no respect be found incompatible with the order and management of the plantation'.[48] Cooper and his wife Ann were sent to Robert's estate Georgia in Hanover, where they lived for three years. In a letter to Murch, Cooper praised Robert as 'generous and liberal, far beyond most of the owners of similar property, very bountiful in sending out yearly supplies to his estate, and spared no expense in anything that could lighten the terrible chain'.[49] Despite these commendations, the experiment proved to be a disaster that further tarnished, rather than rehabilitated, the character of the planter.

On his return to England, Cooper wrote about his experiences in the *Monthly Repository* in April 1822. A version of Cooper's testimony was then republished in *Negro slavery* by Zachary Macaulay in 1823. The timing of this was crucial – Canning's resolutions had just been passed in Parliament. Cooper's evidence was damning in that it was not an exposé of the worst abuses of the system but rather an example of the way in which even on the most progressive of plantations amelioration was doomed to failure. The article was at pains to present Robert as 'a man of great benevolence'.[50] Rather than focusing on extreme examples of cruelty which could be dismissed by the proslavery lobby as isolated incidents, in depicting Robert as a model slave owner the account focused attention on the systemic failings. As the text pointed out, Georgia was 'not singled out for its harshness or inhumanity of its treatment, but such an estate as would be as likely as any other to have been selected in order to convey the most favourable representation of Negro bondage; being an estate the owner of which is conspicuous for his benevolence'.[51] In framing the narrative in this way the text exposed the limits of planter paternalism in the face of an institution which was inherently cruel and dehumanising. As the abolitionist T. S. Winn wrote in relation to events on Robert's plantation, 'such is the nature of Slavery, it must be Abolished, it cannot be Improved'.[52]

Cooper's evidence covered a range of issues including the restrictions on religious provision for the enslaved, the absence of education and culture, the working conditions on the plantation, the lax morality and sexual conduct of the planter class, the breakdown of family life, the use of the whip and the difficulty of securing manumission. His initial comments focused on the lack of time given over for religious practice. During crop season the exhausted workers had a single day off – Sunday – which was also their only opportunity to attend to their provision grounds and visit the market. Religious instruction was also impeded by the lack of education among the enslaved. 'Ignorance, gross ignorance', claimed Cooper, 'is conceived to be the grand prop of Negro slavery.'[53] Cooper wrote to Robert to inform him of what he viewed as the incompatibility of education, religion and slavery. He received a reply stating that 'As you yourself, therefore, are of the opinion that an ability to read would render the Slaves discontented with their situation, I have to request of you to discontinue your labours.'[54] Cooper commented on the degraded state of morals and religion among both the black and white inhabitants of the island. He was critical of the Curates Act, so prized by George, stating that 'it was generally held there to have been passed for the satisfaction of England, and not for any good it was likely to produce'.[55] He claimed that he 'does not recollect to have seen a single White man there, who showed any serious concern about religion, excepting some Missionaries'.[56] He gave details of lascivious relations between white men and enslaved women. This contributed towards the breakdown of family life among enslaved people, who were also subjected to being sold away from loved ones both as a form of punishment and in order to fulfil debt obligations. In contrast to the evidence given by George and his brother Robert junior to Parliament in 1790, Cooper blamed population decrease on the brutality of life on the plantation. The misery and violence inherent in daily life 'causes the women to be extremely careless of themselves when breeding, so that miscarriages are very common; and it produces also the most miserable neglect of their children'.[57] The casual and extensive use of the whip was detailed by Cooper in a passage which described the methods of discipline on Georgia. The whip was used for minor and major breaches of plantation order, including on both the elderly and pregnant women. Cooper 'never saw a Negro who, when uncovered, did not exhibit marks of violence, that is to say, traces of the whip, on his body'.[58] Recourse to the law for unwarranted punishments was woefully inadequate and consistently abused. Looking forward to emancipation, Cooper condemned the race prejudice of Jamaica's slave society, pointing to its dismal treatment of the free people of colour.

Robert's cousin George was appalled at the picture painted within the pages of *Negro slavery*. Aware of what was at stake both politically and personally, he weighed in and wrote two anonymous letters to *John Bull* in an attempt to discredit Cooper. George was extremely fond of his cousin; he had grown close to him when he had acted as a guardian to the young boy when he was sent to England for his education in 1784. He was also perceptive enough to realise the damage that would be done to both the proslavery cause and his own reputation if Cooper's claims went unchallenged. In George's letter he described Cooper's testimony as having been 'coloured' by the editorial work undertaken by Macaulay.[59] He criticised Cooper for not reporting the allegations to his cousin so that he might intercede. George took particular umbrage at the claim that Cooper had not met with a single religious white man in Jamaica. This was a personal slight, given that his nephew George Hibbert Oates was Georgia's attorney. In a second letter George tried to hang the blame for conditions on the plantation on a single corrupt individual – the estate overseer, Adam Arkinstall – who, he noted, Robert had dismissed.[60] He drew attention to Cooper's non-conformist beliefs, although he disingenuously insisted that there should be no prejudice against him on that score. He suggested that Cooper was seeking vindication for his own failure to Christianise the enslaved. As George became increasingly drawn into the debate with Cooper he left himself and those he was close to open to attack.

Cooper soon discovered who his detractor was and the resulting war of letters was spread across *John Bull*, *The Times* and the *Morning Chronicle*. As a measure of public interest, the whole correspondence was also published in a consolidated pamphlet. The incident caused deep embarrassment to both parties as each side sought to prove the veracity of their position. Matters worsened when the press in Jamaica became aware of Cooper's testimony. In July 1823, in support of the Hibberts, the *Jamaica Royal Gazette* published a scurrilous piece containing shocking accusations which were directed not just at Cooper but also his wife Ann.[61] The *Gazette* did its best to blacken the reputation of the Coopers by claiming that they behaved in an immoral and even criminal fashion and that their beliefs were inimical to true Christianity. They stated that Cooper had refused to baptise or bury the enslaved and had preached to them that Jesus was not the son of God. The *Gazette* implicated the Coopers in the illegal sale of Georgia's sugar to the enslaved; it suggested too that they had requisitioned books which had been purchased for use in the school the Coopers had established; it accused them of being drunken and Ann of having stolen a bottle of brandy. The *Gazette* even went so far as to insinuate that an improper relationship had existed between Ann and a white carpenter. The Coopers were maligned as cruel adherents to the whip, with the article describing their summary recourse to violence as shocking even to the plantation overseer. This wholesale defamation was beyond what even George himself had been willing to articulate. Cooper generously noted that as far as he was aware the Hibberts had nothing to do with the sentiments contained within the piece.[62] In the wake of the ill treatment suffered by Smith and Shrewsbury, the abuse of a missionary and his wife was unlikely to curry favour in Britain.

Disgusted at the public defamation of himself and his wife, Cooper chose to publish all the correspondence relating to the matter in 1824. This caused Robert to respond by writing a pamphlet, *Facts verified upon oath, in contradiction of the report of the Reverend Thomas Cooper, concerning the general condition of the slave in Jamaica*. The document contained the sworn affidavits of George Hibbert Oates, the replacement overseer Alexander McKenzie and the estate surgeon, Mr Skirving. Paula Dumas has described Robert's intervention as 'a fine example of a West Indian contesting abolitionist propaganda and appealing to the putatively objective testimony of sworn witnesses'.[63] This proved to be a mistake when Cooper replied with *A letter to Robert Hibbert Jun. Esq., in reply to his pamphlet, entitled, 'Facts verified upon oath, in contradiction of the report of the Reverend Thomas Cooper, concerning the general condition of the slave in Jamaica'*. In this piece Cooper had clearly decided the gloves were off. 'I kept back until the last moment', he wrote, 'from an idea that my accusers might see the propriety of quietly withdrawing.'[64] He expressed his regret that the dispute had become so personal and so rancorous, contending that 'This is surely an indication that the West Indians have a bad cause to defend.' He blamed George for his decision to carry on the debate in the press and thus expose his friends to public scrutiny.[65] Cooper stated that it was the decision to swear an oath that had finally provoked him to tell the whole truth of what he had witnessed on Georgia. He reiterated his claim that the whites of Jamaica were devoid of proper religious and moral sentiment. He accused both George Hibbert Oates and another planter, Samuel Vaughan, of being 'open and avowed fornicators. They kept their mistresses without any disguise or shame.'[66] On this point Ann, whose letter was also included in the publication, went even further in giving the detail that a 'girl in the house, a Quadroon, about sixteen years of age, was pregnant by Mr. Oates'.[67] The Coopers insisted that the inclusion of this salacious information about George's nephew was the result of their treatment at the hands of the West India interest. Cooper denied that the conditions on the plantation were the result of Adam Arkinstall's behaviour alone, suggesting this was a ruse thought up by George, and condemned the institution of slavery in its entirety.

The whole affair was poisonous for attempts to resuscitate the image of the West Indian. Aside from that the incident was personally humiliating for George, given that he had set himself up as a champion of the religious cause in the colonies. In addition the respectable and upwardly mobile Hibberts were faced with one of their own being publicly named as a fornicator. To add to George's chagrin, another publication came out that year, this time singling him out for public criticism in reference to the estate Albion. In 1824 the Reverend Richard Bickell published *The West Indies as they are*. In it he gave a scoffing description of George as 'a gentleman who wishes (as I have been informed) to afford his people every facility, that they may attend to religious duties, and encourages them to go to church as often as possible'.[68] He then went on to describe a conversation with Albion's head bookkeeper in which the man had said that in Ireland he was a regular church attendee, but since he had been on the estate it had not been possible because he was engaged on a Sunday morning 'superintending the Negroes whilst they were potting the sugars'. Bickell noted that the man 'spoke with regret' at the loss of his spiritual life.[69] That not only the enslaved on the estate, but also white people, were denied the opportunity to worship on a Sunday was in direct contradiction to the way in which George had been positioning the colonists. The fact that Albion actually belonged to his brother Robert junior was inconsequential – the damage to George's public image had been done. This combined with the Cooper scandal seriously undermined his efforts to refashion the planter as an instrument for the moral and spiritual improvement of the enslaved. It also demonstrated to the reading public that even the most progressive of metropolitan slave owners fell far short of the promise of reform.

Compensation

George was politically intuitive enough to know that the fight was lost. He was also shrewd enough to make sure that he was in a position to capitalise on defeat. George had supported the principle of compensation since he first gave evidence to the Select Committee in 1790 and was determined that abolition would only come about on the payment of a financial settlement. He repeated the claim in 1807 during the slave trade debates.[70] In 1823, ten years before the Slavery Abolition Act was passed, George wrote a revealing letter to Wilmot-Horton. He informed him that Earl Bathurst had communicated that 'it will not now be endured to give out that the Slaves and their progeny are to remain in a state of Slavery for ever ... a time must be looked to when they or their Posterity may, by gradual means and without injuring the Property of their Masters, be liberated'.[71] George added that Bathurst had confidentially assured him that 'our Property in our Slaves is entitled to exactly the same protection as every other Property which a British Subject can possess ... that by those Laws we hold them as Slaves and cannot consistently with the faith of the Legislature, have our Property taken from us without compensation'. Three years later in 1826, George wrote to Wilmot-Horton again to press his point, stating that 'a more just measure of Compensation cannot I think be devised than that which you have admitted & that is, not the value of the liberated Slave, simply considered, but the injury which the Property of the Owner must sustain by the Act of power which frees him'.[72] The following year George sent yet another letter, in which he explained to Wilmot-Horton that 'An Appraiser may measure a Man & ascertain his strength – but it is impossible that he could adequately estimate the importance of the Man in every relation to the Plantation.'[73] George wondered if the true value of compensation would make the cost of emancipation prohibitive. This thinking mirrored his delaying tactics during the 1807 debates, in which he fancied that the introduction of a debate on compensation would impede, if not wholly derail, the abolition process.

Citing old age and increasing infirmity, in 1830 George resigned from his post as the Agent for Jamaica and a year later from his role as the Chairman of the Society of West India Merchants. Despite his relinquishment of his leadership positions, George entered into a final war of words over slavery compensation. In March 1833, five months before the Slavery Abolition Act received royal assent, the Society

DEFENDING SLAVERY

of Friends forwarded him a copy of their reflections of the subject of slavery. Showing no signs of diminished resolve, George replied, addressing himself to the points they raised. The short correspondence was printed in *The Times*.[74] The Friends had initiated the letter with a plea for the slave owners to come to an agreement which would see slavery ended quickly. They denounced the practice as unchristian and a 'disgrace to our country'. They pitied the West Indians – especially those who had inherited their property – on the grounds that slavery degraded both the enslaved and the slave owners. The Friends warned that the judgement of God would be upon those who wilfully sought to protract its existence. Whilst stopping short of outright support for compensation they admitted the colonists' right to 'judicious and equitable provisions' as part of the process of abolition. The Friends viewed abolition as God's work and believed Providence would raise the man who acted with justice and humanity.

George was not so sanguine in his estimation of the bountiful nature of Providence. He asked incredulously if the Friends would really demand that 'I should sign away the security I have legally acquired ... in expectation that Providence will make it up to me in some other way?' Freed from his obligations to his Jamaica constituents, George admitted that there was now a consensus that slavery should be got rid of 'wholly and speedily'. However, he advised caution and compromise, for the success of emancipation rested not only on legislation but also on the cooperation of the colonists. He believed that the only way to carry the colonial proprietors along with abolition was to offer them compensation for their loss in property and some form of Government guarantee in the event the colonies should fail as a result of its reforms. He criticised the Friends for their 'feebly and timorously' expressed sentiments in regard to compensation. In contrast to the piety of the tone taken by the Friends, George stated that 'It may be unchristian, that the cooperation of the colonial proprietors should depend upon the terms which are held out to them; but you must take man as he is, with all the self-interested motives which, for the most part, actuate his conduct.' Whilst he acknowledged 'Our Saviour's' teachings to 'offer our scrip to the man who robs us of our purse', he was adamant that 'men never have acted on such principles, and, it is to be feared, never will'.

Property in people had been sanctioned under law and it was to the laws of the country that men looked to be governed. For George, those who had entered into a lawful commerce should be entitled to protection. He stated that in times of need, when a proprietor could no longer afford to pay for supplies for the enslaved, it was merchant men like himself who had paid the deficit, having made a security on either the estates or the enslaved. As a result, 'upon the values of these securities depends the maintenance or the beggary of myself and of my family'. He went on to implicate the Quakers themselves, whom he cited as active participants in the networks of trade which made up the slavery business. He opined that if they had been paid as agents and ship owners, why then should he be expected to forfeit his investments? In George's mind emancipation was fraught with danger; not two years previously his brother Robert junior's plantation Great Valley had been burned in the Baptist War.[75] He believed that a peaceful transition to a free-labour economy would only be possible if the enslaved perceived the planters to be willing participants in their freedom. The right path to liberty lay in the application of 'gentleness and intelligence', which considered the needs of both the planter and the enslaved, because when all was said and done it would be those resident in the colonies who would undertake the practical task of making freedom work.

As an anonymous opponent of compensation wrote, 'Admit the slave-holders claims to compensation, and you admit the justice of slavery.'[76] Yet this was precisely what occurred – as part of the measures taken to bring about emancipation in the Caribbean, Mauritius and the Cape of Good Hope, the slave owners were awarded £20 million in compensation. Alongside this they negotiated an additional period of apprenticeship in which the formerly enslaved were forced to continue labouring on the plantations for free. Initially intended to last for twelve years, this system was brought to an end prematurely in 1838 following increasing levels of unrest among the workers. Given the scale of the Hibberts' involvement with all aspects of the slavery system it is unsurprising that George lobbied so hard for the payment of compensation. Collectively the family received over £103,000 – a conservative estimate for the value of that payment in 2018 is £8.5 million. The Hibberts made claims as trustees, owners-in-fee, mortgagees, judgement creditors, devisees in trust and executors. The variety of their claims is demonstrative of the different ways in which Britons became entangled in the complicated legal and financial structures that supported slavery. George died in 1837, before the compensation process could be completed. He recognised that he would be a significant recipient – he received £63,000 – and made provisions in his will stating, 'My estates in Jamaica, compensation monies, stock, leaseholds, dock, canal and other shares, and all residue of personal est. to my Ex'ors on trust to sell.'[77] By the time compensation was awarded the Hibberts had already secured a place for themselves in British society. The money was no doubt of practical use, but more than that it confirmed the family in their claims to respectability. It was an admission by the Government that George's arguments around the legitimacy of 'property in people' were held to be true.

Conclusion

In a pamphlet published in 1830 entitled *A letter to the most honourable the Marquis of Chandos*, a passage was devoted to George's tireless support of the West Indians.[78] The author wrote of his 'unwearied *exertions* [italics original] for their prosperity and welfare for a period approaching *to half a century'*. He claimed that 'a more intelligent, honourable, experienced, or indefatigable advocate, could no where be found ... to him, indeed, every person who has any connection whatever with the West India colonies, is bound by the strongest feelings of gratitude'. He was presumably discounting the sentiments of the enslaved. The author lamented that George had not 'quite *subdued* [italics original] the enemies of the colonies before he had retired from active life', so that 'like an old warrior of former days he may have hung up his weapons with this motto, "Hic Victor, cestum artemque depono"'. Written at the end of George's long service in the West India interest, the text is demonstrative of his centrality to the proslavery defence. His contemporaneous detractors were not so generous in their estimation of George's achievements. The abolitionist T. S. Winn wrote that 'Mr H ... has laboured hard, and long, and adroitly in his vocation' and 'hath grown Rich by the slave system'.[79] However, he cautioned that 'naked came we into this world, and naked we must go out of it, stripped of everything but Virtue, the only current coin in the world to come'. Winn's reflections on George's career suggest the degree to which the abolitionists viewed him as a long-standing obstacle to their cause.

The SWIPM knew well the value of a man like George, and at a meeting in 1831 the assembled men paid tribute to him. They applauded his 'talent, zeal, and firmness' as well as 'the conciliatory tone and speech with which he has supported and maintained the constituted authorities of the Colonies.'[80] George's greatest political strength was his ability to mediate between the varying positions which made up the colonial interest. His was a measured voice, one which encouraged tactical thinking and compromise in order to achieve results. George was a pragmatic realist and his was a game of prolongation: the longer abolition could be staved off the longer he could turn a profit. George's feeling towards his years spent as a proslavery lobbyist can be read from his response to the SWIPM's gift of a solid silver candelabra awarded to him 'as a mark of their esteem, and ... high respect they entertain'.[81] George wrote a note thanking them for

> the presentation of a splendid Piece of Plate, a Compliment from the West India Body: in real worth far more than an adequate acknowledgement of any exertions of mine in support of our Common interest and which as expressing the sentiment of that respectable Body to whose welfare I must during life remain dutifully and warmly attached is to me invaluable.[82]

George's humble acceptance belied his significant contribution to the proslavery cause. His inclusion of the term 'respectable Body' is indicative of a commitment undiminished by any evidence the abolitionists had produced on the evils of slavery. Writing just five years before his death, George remained proudly attached to the cause of the colonists, believing them to be lawful, productive and loyal imperial subjects. If George had served the cause of proslavery well over the years, then it was certainly true that slavery had rewarded him and his family for those years of faithful service. Involvement with slavery had transformed the Hibberts' fortunes and even its abolition continued to yield further fruit in the form of compensation. Whilst the battle over slavery was finally lost, the financial benefits accrued across multiple generations enabled the family to elevate themselves from the instability of mercantile life, providing an inheritance which maintained their position for generations to come.

Notes

1 George first expressed his desire to become the Agent for Jamaica to Simon Taylor in 1802. ICS/SHL/TVAP, M965/17/31, Letter from George Hibbert to Simon Taylor, 5 May 1802.
2 ICS/SHL/TVAP, M965/17/47, Letter from George Hibbert to Simon Taylor, 5 September 1803.
3 A. E. Furness, 'George Hibbert and the defense of slavery in the West Indies', *Jamaican Historical Review*, 5:1 (1965), p. 61.
4 Agent's letters to the Committee of Correspondence, 10 June 1822 and 4 July 1815, quoted *ibid.*, p. 64.
5 T. S. Winn, *A speedy end to slavery in our West India colonies by safe, effectual and equitable means for the benefit of all parties concerned* (London: J. Hatchard & Son, 1825), p. 111.
6 Catherine Hall, *Civilising subjects: Metropole and colony in the English imagination 1830–1867* (Cambridge: Polity, 2002), pp. 98–115.
7 David Lambert, *White Creole culture, politics and identity during the age of abolition* (Cambridge: Cambridge University Press, 2005), p. 2.
8 Christer Petley, 'Gluttony, excess and the fall of the planter class in the British Caribbean', *Atlantic Studies*, 9:3 (2012), pp. 85–106.
9 Lambert, *White Creole culture*, p. 2.
10 Furness, 'George Hibbert and the defense of slavery', p. 70.
11 Christer Petley, *Slaveholders in Jamaica: Colonial society and culture during the era of abolition* (London: Pickering & Chatto, 2009), pp. 87–8.

DEFENDING SLAVERY

12 ICS/SHL/WICP, M915/2, SWIPM Minute Book, Select Committee, 28 June 1815.
13 Samuel Johnson, *Taxation no tyranny: An answer to the resolutions and address of the American congress* (London: T. Cadell, 1775), p. 89.
14 JFSGRL, Diary of George Hibbert, 30 March 1816. www.jamaicanfamilysearch.com/Members/bcarib28.htm [accessed 24 May 2018].
15 Robert Isaac and Samuel Wilberforce, *The life of William Wilberforce* (London: Seeley, Burnside & Seeley, 1834), p. 450.
16 Thomas Venables, *The reviewer reviewed; Or some cursory observation upon an article in the Christian Observer for January 1816, respecting the Slave Registry Bill in a letter to a Member of Parliament* (London: J. M. Richardson, 1816), p. 5.
17 Ibid., p. 11.
18 Ibid., p. 29.
19 Ibid.
20 Ibid., p. 30.
21 George Hibbert, 'Brief remarks on the Slave Registry Bill and upon a special report of the African Institution, recommending that measure', *The Pamphleteer*, 7:14 (March 1816), pp. 546–7.
22 Ibid., p. 553.
23 Ibid., p. 560.
24 Ibid., p. 557.
25 Ibid., p. 559.
26 Ibid., p. 548.
27 Ibid., p. 570.
28 Ibid., pp. 573–4.
29 ICS/SHL/WICP, M915/2, SWIPM Minute Book, Standing Committee, 4 June 1816.
30 Petley, *Slaveholders in Jamaica*, p. 89.
31 Andrew Porter, 'Trusteeship, anti-slavery and humanitarianism', in Andrew Porter (ed.), *Oxford history of the British empire*, vol. III: *The nineteenth century* (Oxford: Oxford University Press, 1999), p. 205.
32 William A. Green, *British slave emancipation; The sugar colonies and the Great Experiment, 1830–1865* (Oxford: Oxford University Press, 1991), p. 101.
33 Derbyshire Record Office, Matlock, Wilmot-Horton of Osmaston and Catton Papers (DRO/WHOCP), D3155/WH/2814, Letter from George Hibbert to Robert Wilmot-Horton, 9 April 1823.
34 George Canning, HC Deb., 15 May 1823, vol. IX, cc. 257–360.
35 Green, *British slave emancipation*, p. 102.
36 DRO/WHOCP, D3155/WH/2814, Letter from George Hibbert to Robert Wilmot-Horton, 11 June 1823.
37 ICS/SHL/WICP, M915/4, SWIPM Minute Book, Sub-Committee Meeting, 5 June 1823.
38 Derbyshire Record Office, Matlock, Confidential Papers on the West India Question, D3155/WH2939, Letter from Charles Rose Ellis to George Hibbert, 23 October 1823.
39 Ibid.
40 George Hibbert, quoted in Petley, *Slaveholders in Jamaica*, p. 90
41 Petley, *Slaveholders in Jamaica*, p. 92
42 ICS/SHL/WICP, M915/4, SWIPM Minute Book, Standing Committee Meeting, 24 November 1823, Letter from the Bishop of London to the SWIPM, 7 August 1823.
43 Petley, *Slaveholders in Jamaica*, p. 94.
44 TNA/COP, CO 137/161/103, Letter from George Hibbert to Robert Wilmot-Horton, 5 July 1825.
45 Lowell J. Ragatz, *The fall of the planter class in the British Caribbean 1763–1833* (London: Century Co., 1928), p. 422.
46 Jerom Murch, *Memoir of Robert Hibbert, founder of the Hibbert Trust: With a sketch of its history* (Bath: William Lewis, 1874), p. 16.
47 Ibid., p. 17.
48 Thomas Cooper, in Zachary Macaulay, *Negro slavery; Or a view of some of the more prominent features of that state of society, as it exists in the United States of America*

and in the colonies of the West Indies, especially in Jamaica (London: Richard Taylor, 1823), p. 36.
49 Murch, *Memoir*, pp. 18–19.
50 Cooper, in Macaulay, *Negro slavery*, p. 36.
51 *Ibid.*, p. 54.
52 Winn, *A speedy end to slavery*, p. 84.
53 Cooper, in Macaulay, *Negro slavery*, p. 46.
54 Letter from Robert Hibbert to Thomas Cooper, 7 March 1820, in Thomas Cooper, *A letter to Robert Hibbert Jun. Esq., in reply to his pamphlet, entitled, 'Facts verified upon oath, in contradiction of the report of the Reverend Thomas Cooper, concerning the general condition of the slave in Jamaica'* (London: J. Hatchard & Son, 1824), p. 25.
55 Cooper, in Macaulay, *Negro slavery*, p. 43.
56 *Ibid.*, p. 41.
57 *Ibid.*, p. 42. For a discussion of reproduction as a site of resistance see Barbara Bush-Slimani, 'Hard labour: Women, childbirth and resistance in British Caribbean slave societies', *History Workshop Journal*, 36:1 (1993), pp. 83–99.
58 Cooper, in Macaulay, *Negro slavery*, p. 50.
59 Thomas Cooper, *Correspondence between George Hibbert, Esq., and the Rev. T. Cooper: Relative to the condition of the negro slaves in Jamaica, extracted from the Morning Chronicle, also a libel on the character of Mr. and Mrs. Cooper, published in 1823, in several of the Jamaica journals; with notes and remarks* (London: J. Hatchard & Son, 1824), p. 1.
60 *Ibid.*, p. 5.
61 *Jamaica Royal Gazette*, 26 July 1823.
62 Cooper, *Correspondence between George Hibbert, Esq., and the Rev. T. Cooper*, p. iv.
63 Paula Dumas, *Proslavery Britain: Fighting for slavery in an era of abolition* (Basingstoke: Palgrave Macmillan, 2016), p. 65.
64 Cooper, *A Letter to Robert Hibbert*, p. iv.
65 *Ibid.*, p. iii.
66 *Ibid.*, p. 7.
67 Ann Cooper to Robert Hibbert, 17 August 1824, quoted in Cooper, *A Letter to Robert Hibbert*, p. 20.
68 Reverend Richard Bickell, *The West Indies as they are; Or a real picture of slavery: But more particularly as it exists in the island of Jamaica* (London: J. Hatchard & Son, 1824), p. 74.
69 *Ibid.*, p. 73.
70 George Hibbert, HC Deb., 23 February 1807, vol. VIII, cc. 945–95.
71 DRO/WHOCP, D3155/WH/2814, Letter from George Hibbert to Robert Wilmot-Horton, 9 April 1823.
72 *Ibid.*, Letter from George Hibbert to Robert Wilmot-Horton, 25 February 1826.
73 TNA/COP, CO 137/166/78, Letter from George Hibbert to Robert Wilmot-Horton, 2 April 1827.
74 *The Times*, 21 March 1833.
75 *Jamaica as it was and as it may be: Comprising interesting topics for absent proprietors, merchants, &c., and valuable hints to persons intending to emigrate to the island: Also an authentic narrative of the negro insurrection in 1831* (London: T. Hurst, 1835), p. 284.
76 *Letters on the necessity of a prompt extinction of British colonial slavery ... to which are added thoughts on compensation* (London: J. Hatchard & Son, 1826), p. 195.
77 Will of George Hibbert, 29 February 1836, quoted in Vere Langford Oliver, *Caribbeana: Being miscellaneous papers relating to the history, genealogy, topography, and antiquities of the British West Indies*, vol. IV (London: Mitchell Hughes and Clarke, 1919), p. 199.
78 *A letter to the most honourable the Marquis of Chandos* (London: T. Brettell, 1830), pp. 70–1.
79 Winn, *A speedy end to slavery*, p. 111.

80 ICS/SHL/WICP, M915/4, SWIPM Minute Book, Special General Meeting, 21 February 1831.
81 *Ibid.*, SWIPM Minute Book, Standing Committee Meeting, 16 May 1832, Letter from the Marquis of Chandos to George Hibbert, 3 May 1832. The candelabra was sold by Christie's auction house (lot 124, sale 7108) on 14 June 2005 and achieved a sale price of £12,000.
82 *Ibid.*, SWIPM Minute Book, Standing Committee Meeting, Letter from George Hibbert to the SWIPM, 16 May 1832.

PART III

Family culture: domesticating slavery

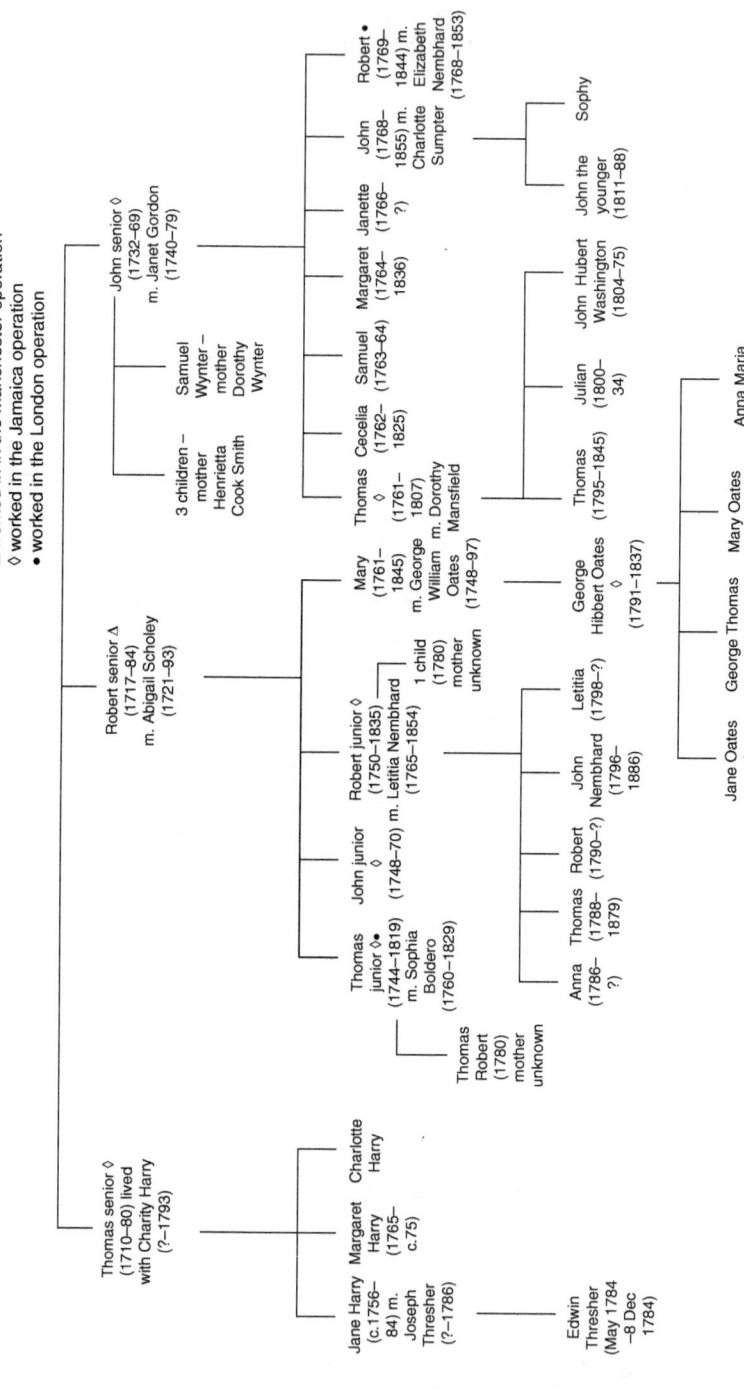

Family tree 5 The Hibbert family in Jamaica

CHAPTER SIX

Part I Intimate relations: the colony

> Every unmarried white man, and of every class, has his black or his brown mistress, with whom he lives openly; and of so little consequence is this thought, that his white female friends and relations think it no breach of decorum to visit his house, partake of his hospitality, fondle his children, and converse with his *housekeeper* ... the most striking proof of the low estimate of moral and religious obligation here is the fact, that the man who lives in open adultery, – that is, who keeps his brown or black mistress, in the very face of his wife and family and of the community, has generally as much outward respect shown him, and is as much countenanced, visited, and received into company, especially if he be a man of some weight and influence in the community, as if he had been guilty of no breach of decency or dereliction of moral duty!
> John Stewart, *A view of the past and present state of the island of Jamaica* (Edinburgh: Oliver & Boyd, 1823), p. 173

'Thomas Hibbert, the Eldest, of Jamaica ... died a bachelor 20 May 1780' read the entry in the 'Pedigree of Hibbert' compiled for *Caribbeana*.[1] With a thriving business, wealth, property and political position, Thomas senior was extremely marriageable and yet according to the published genealogical record he died unmarried, with no mention of any children. In truth Thomas senior had conducted an intimate relationship for over thirty years with a mixed-heritage woman called Charity Harry. Together they had three daughters, Jane, Margaret and Charlotte. The sprawling family tree, spread out over four pages, documented multiple generations of the Hibberts, giving details of their marriages, children and accumulated property. The representation of family relations prioritised masculinity, whiteness and legitimacy; excluded from its branches were any details of daughters and their marriages, as well as any mixed-heritage or illegitimate children. The Hibbert men, like many of their colonial counterparts, engaged in sexual relations with both free and enslaved women in Jamaica. Barbara Bush has stated that the practice was 'regarded as an integral part of plantation life, inextricably woven into the social fabric'.[2] For the merchant classes this behaviour extended beyond the plantation to the urban environs of the city. Kingston's population included 40 per cent of all white females resident on the island but they made up just 7 per cent of the population total.[3] This feature of Jamaican society was noted by Robert junior, who lamented 'Most of the ladies married or widows'.[4] This, combined with an unfettered access to the bodies of enslaved women, helped to create a climate in which inter-racial sex was commonplace. As John Stewart noted, neither the presence of a wife nor the traditional boundaries of respectability served to halt these practices. Enslaved women were vulnerable to sexual abuse and exploitation – rape and sexual violence were endemic. Relationships like that of Thomas senior and Charity raise difficult questions about agency and consent.[5] The unequal raced and gendered power structures within the slave societies of the Caribbean complicated women's ability to exercise free will. That said, some of these relationships, including that of Thomas senior and Charity, offered women a degree of influence which would otherwise have been unthinkable.

The ways in which systems of concubinage were structured, as well as attitudes towards it, were geographically and temporally specific. As Adele Perry has explained, 'Heterosexual intimacies were honed to particular colonial economies and societies ... they were also informed and interpreted through wider discussions and insurgencies.'[6] Whist women of colour and their children were a common sight in every echelon of Jamaican society, their presence was commented on by metropolitan visitors to the country. Lady Nugent, the wife of the Governor of Jamaica, wrote in her journal about her encounter with 'a little mulatto girl' at Simon Taylor's plantation Golden Grove. She commented that 'Mr. T. appeared very anxious for me to dismiss her, and in the evening, the housekeeper told me she was his own daughter, and that he had numerous family, some almost on every one of his estates.'[7] His response to seeing his daughter with the wife of the Governor suggests that Taylor was aware of his transgression from metropolitan norms of respectable behaviour. As the movement to abolish slavery intensified in the 1820s, the treatment of enslaved women and its implications for the character of the slave owners became a focus for the campaign.[8] The accusations of sexual impropriety levelled at George Hibbert Oates by the Reverend Thomas Cooper were indicative of the moral condemnation increasingly being directed at slave-holding societies. To his damning indictment of the practice of inter-racial sex, John Stewart added that 'This profligacy is,

I: INTIMATE RELATIONS: THE COLONY

however, less common than it was formerly.'⁹ Pressure exerted from the imperial centre was designed to force slave owners into reforming the system, or at least appearing to do so. Writing in 1824 in his capacity as Agent for Jamaica, George informed Earl Bathurst, the Secretary of State for War and the Colonies, that the island Assembly had passed a bill 'declaring it a felony to commit a Rape upon a Slave not ten years of Age'.¹⁰ The need for this kind of legislation and the exclusion of children over the age of ten is indicative of the vulnerability of enslaved people to this form of exploitation.

Legitimate family relationships were also established by the Hibberts in Jamaica. Marriage played a key role in reinforcing their presence within the island elite. As with the family in Manchester, the production of children was necessary for the provision of a trusted workforce capable of maintaining their newly established interests in the management and ownership of plantations. With Thomas senior's refusal to enter into the bonds of matrimony, it was his brother John senior and his nephews that helped to cement the family's place. These unions changed the nature of the Hibberts' engagement with Jamaica: the island was no longer simply a place of commercial opportunity as relationships of flesh and blood reconfigured their ties to it, solidifying their status as a transatlantic family. Marriages with Creole women raised the issue of colonial difference. Robert junior's mother Abigail was a key conduit of family communications, and throughout her lifetime she kept up a correspondence with her children. Her letters reflected a degree of ambivalence towards her West Indian daughter-in-law; subtle forms of othering gave a clear sense of her belief in the superiority of metropolitan social mores. Suspicions of the negative effects of prolonged colonial contact were also cast upon Abigail's grandchildren. The Hibbert matriarch's shock at witnessing the ministrations of an enslaved nanny underscored the relative distance both physically and psychologically that separated the two worlds that the family inhabited.

The Hibberts had to negotiate family politics within the context of both metropole and colony. Their intimate relations were transformed through their engagement with slavery; it created new structures and changed the ways in which family was both imagined and lived. Great distances separated what had been a close-knit network in Manchester. New kinds of relationships developed to take the place of physical proximity. Paper bonds became substitutes for embodied family exchanges. Letters circulated within the family, acting as both the carriers of important personal information and as the material traces which confirmed the relationships between different members. Their contents reveal the shifting patterns of allegiances, the private squabbles, the fears, the humanity of these long-dead figures. Unlike those who faced the forced migration of the Middle Passage, the Hibberts chose to leave Britain for Jamaica. Whilst there can be no equivocation with the violent rupture that tore African families apart, leaving home sometimes represented a painful severance. Life in Jamaica could be brutally short, the pervasiveness of death, disease and violence was a constant worry for family members and their letters anxiously fretted about the safety of loved ones. Curtailed by war, the demands of the business and family obligations on the island, years might pass between visits to Britain. By his death in 1780 Thomas senior had lived in Jamaica for longer than he had lived in Britain. Of all the Hibberts it is perhaps he alone who embraced a sense of Creole identity, an affinity with island life that none of the other family members shared. By the end of the first half of the nineteenth century there were no legitimate Hibberts left on the island. If illegitimate offspring remained they have been lost to history and memory. Banished from both the official and private recollections of the family tree, they became a branch of colonial relations best forgotten.

Outside families

Thomas senior's relationship with his 'housekeeper' Charity Harry has fascinated historians for over a century.[11] Thomas senior arrived in Kingston in 1734 when he was twenty-four years old. By the 1750s he had begun a relationship with Charity. In 1756 Charity gave birth to their eldest daughter, Jane; a further two daughters followed, Margaret in 1765 and later Charlotte. What Charity's status was when she met Thomas senior is unclear, though an Act of Assembly in 1775 described her as a 'free mulatto woman' and gave her and 'the issue of her body hereafter to be begotten by White Men' the same rights and privileges as English subjects 'with certain restrictions' on holding office and voting.[12] As the legal wording made clear, the rights of Charity's children were contingent on their proximity to whiteness. In 1761 the Jamaica Assembly limited the property rights of the free coloured population. These limitations could be circumvented if a petition was made and granted. A large number of these petitions were sponsored by the island's slave-holding elites and they spoke to some of the complicated relationships that existed across both the class and colour lines. The granting of additional freedoms allowed Charity to amass increased property and wealth, and entitled her to a greater inheritance. Although Jane and her sisters were privately acknowledged by their father, he did not give them the Hibbert name and his name does not appear as a sponsor on the petition. Jane's sister Margaret was baptised in the

I: INTIMATE RELATIONS: THE COLONY

Anglican faith at Thomas senior's house in Kingston. *Rider's British Merlin* stated that Mrs Charles Hall, Miss Sally Gordon and Henry Croasdaile acted as godparents.[13] Charity's name and association was notably missing from the announcement. The brief entry described Margaret as 'Mr. Thomas Hibbert's Child', adding that she was given the name Margaret 'after Mr. Hibbert's mother'. One wonders what Thomas senior's family in Manchester, respectable trustees of the Cross Street Chapel, must have made of this tribute. This level of recognition was not enjoyed by all mixed-heritage children. If the mother was enslaved, her offspring inherited her status, so that any children born out of these sexual encounters represented a potential increase in property in people and labour. Some fathers could not afford to purchase the freedom of their offspring and others chose not to. In some remarkable instances manumitted children were given ownership of their enslaved mothers and siblings.[14]

Charity's relationship with Thomas senior 'propelled her into the upper ranks of Jamaica's society of colour'.[15] Framed by an official sense of public morality and respectability, Charity's petition to the Assembly reported that she had been baptised and attended church regularly. It also remarked that she was in possession 'of lands, Houses and Negroes in the Town of Kingston in this Island to a very Considerable Amount and Value so as to put her above the Common level of Free Negroes and Mulattoes'.[16] Discourses of culture and class intersected to strengthen Charity's claims for preferential treatment before the law. In 1777 she was living in one of the Hibberts' properties within sight of their grand house in Kingston on Mark Lane.[17] The free coloured population tended to concentrate in urban areas as they afforded greater opportunities for making a living and socialising. Thomas senior was free to see Charity whenever he pleased – he never married, enabling him to associate with his young family unencumbered by the emotional conflict which could accompany liaisons where a wife and legitimate offspring were involved.[18] 'Miss Charity' or 'Mrs Harry', as Robert junior uniformly called her, was mentioned on numerous occasions in his diary. She was part of daily life: she socialised with the family and their friends, accompanied them to Agualta Vale, she even took an active interest in Robert junior's affairs of the heart. When he showed a liking for a 'Miss G', she became 'the eternal theme' of conversation for Charity.[19] She maintained contact with the Hibberts after Thomas senior's death and was invited to take part in the christening of Robert junior's illegitimate child.[20] Despite her material comfort and good relations with the Hibberts, the fact remained that her relationship with Thomas senior 'involved the unequal status of male and female, colonizer and colonized'.[21]

In 1771 Jane and her sister Margaret were sent to England for their education.[22] Owing to the colonists' preference for schooling their children in the English style, few quality educational facilities existed in Jamaica. Many who sent their children back to Britain believed in the innate superiority of home, viewing life in the colonies as a means to an end, with the ultimate badge of success a return to the mother country. Parents wanted their children to acquire the social finesse of a metropolitan education, in some instances to fit them for life there. There is nothing to suggest that Thomas senior felt this way; he never purchased property in Britain, choosing to live and die in Jamaica. Perhaps his decision regarding his daughters stemmed from a realisation of the limits placed on free people of colour in a slave society. In a culture obsessed with racial lineage and gradations of skin colour his children's 'quadroon' status would have elevated their position in relation to blackness, but knowledge of their parentage might have circumscribed hopes of a respectable marriage. Whiteness was a form of power, and anxieties around the destabilisation of racial hierarchies were present in the writings of a number of slave owners. In a letter to Thomas senior's nephew George, Simon Taylor recounted that:

> When I returned from England in the year 1760 there were only three Quadroon Women in the Town of Kingston. There are now three hundred, and more of the decent Class of them never will have any commerce with their own Colour, but only with White People. Their progeny is growing whiter and whiter every remove ... from thence a White Generation will come.[23]

A fear of racial slippage could also be read in the work of the historian of Jamaica Edward Long. Long viewed inter-racial sex as a pollutant of racial purity. Describing the practice as a 'venomous and dangerous ulcer', he wrote despairingly that 'The nation already begins to be browned with the African tint.'[24] As Catherine Hall has noted, in the eyes of Long, 'English blood, every English family, was in danger of contamination.' Henrice Altink has argued that the 'quadroon' woman in particular 'threatened Jamaica's social structure more than Coloured women because they were so similar to White women that they could easily pass as White and also because their offspring of relations with White men were four generations removed from their Black ancestors and hence were legally free'.[25] An ability to transcend, or at least subvert, the colour line would perhaps have been more effective in England, where racial categorisations were, according to Roxann Wheeler, still a 'paradigm in transition' and therefore less socially limiting than in Jamaica.[26]

What Charity felt about the removal of two of her daughters to England is unknown. Jane was fifteen and Margaret was six – their departure marked the last time they would ever see Jamaica or their mother. Charity and Jane continued to correspond, and when Jane wanted to marry she and her husband-to-be Joseph Thresher wrote to her to ask for her blessing. Daniel Livesay has argued that the 'couple's desire for Charity's permission demonstrates that the mothers of mixed-race migrants could remain actively involved with their children'.[27] Charity's will reveals that she kept a token of her daughter – a painting by Jane – bequeathing it to a free woman of colour named Sarah Wynter.[28] Despite the majority of the Hibbert family residing in England, the two children were not sent to live with them. Thomas senior instead arranged for his daughters to reside with his old partner in the Kingston slave trading firm, Nathaniel Sprigg, who had left Jamaica, married and settled into the life of a country gentleman at Barn Elms in Surrey. In a discussion of the mixed-heritage family of John Tailyour, Livesay posits a number of reasons why he chose not to send his illegitimate child to live with his relatives. The discomfort Tailyour felt about his son meeting his family can be read in his own words:

> [A]s soon as he has Sense to know the disadvantages with which he has been ushered into Life, & by keeping him at a distance from his own Relations I think there is the greater chance of concealing from him his Inferiority and preventing the Mortification of being slighted by relations who from early habits he might consider himself perfectly upon a footing with.[29]

Despite Wheeler's contention that racial categorisations in Britain were more elastic than those in the colonies, race and legitimacy still mattered for metropolitan families. Respectability was at the heart of the Hibberts' claims to social position, and whilst some members certainly indulged in affairs in the colonies, it was quite a different matter to bring the offspring of such liaisons into the bosom of the family at home.

Jane's life at Barn Elms was comfortable and she reported to her father that 'Mr. and Mrs. Sprigg ... were very kind and friendly to me'.[30] Jane described herself as 'of a grave and solid turn of mind' with a 'great thirst for learning', although she 'could not easily pursue this inclination for reading and study at Cheltenham'.[31] Like many young women of her status she was expected to focus on the niceties of polite society. She wrote that 'I did not exempt myself from the fashionable amusements of the place I lived in', although by her own inclination these pursuits did not hold great interest for her.[32] She complained that 'I loved retirement rather than the company of those who delight in trifling conversation.' Her preferred enjoyments included 'hearing a few select friends discourse on moral subjects': this to Jane was 'the highest entertainment in the world'. Schooling Jane in the art of female sociability was part of the process of fitting her for marriage. Painting was an area in which she excelled and was encouraged, as she told her father: 'Mr. Sprigg, finding I had a Taste and genius for drawing, was so kind to let me have a drawing Master.' Paid for by Thomas senior, her teacher was Sir Joshua Reynolds. Such was Jane's success with the brush that in 1778 she was awarded a gold medal from the Society for the Encouragement of Arts and Commerce.

In around 1775 Jane's sister Margaret died, leaving her disconsolate with grief. Jane wrote of Margaret's death that 'When she died I no longer wanted to live', feeling that she had 'lost a part of myself'.[33] Her loneliness was perhaps exacerbated by the isolating sense of difference which she must have felt as a relative outsider in England. This marked a turning point in Jane's life; it was the moment at which 'Religion at length (and for a time) presented herself.' She began to study the Scriptures, commenting that 'I knew little of them before ... thinking, as alas! the generality of people do, that the Bible was a Book for Priests only to study.'[34] This led her to critique the Church of England, arguing that 'the ceremonial observations of the established Church were but the remains of Popish superstition'.[35] In the wake of the trauma of loss, an interest in religion provided Jane with a period of reflection which 'blunted the edge of sorrow'.[36]

At around the same time, Jane was introduced by the Spriggs to the Quaker artist and wit Mary Morris Knowles. The two women shared a love of art and Knowles advised Jane on improving her skills.[37] The friendship transformed Jane's life, significantly influencing her burgeoning interest in religious non-conformity. Mary brought Jane to London to meet her circle of literary friends. On her return to Barn Elms she confessed to Sprigg that she wished to convert to Quakerism. Jane had been baptised as an Anglican by her father and in choosing her own spiritual path she was acting in defiance of both her guardian and her family by challenging the authority of the men in her life upon whom she relied. A number of the Hibberts were dissenters, and the distinctions between non-conformist denominations 'while ostensibly based on doctrinal issues ... often covered latent social distinctions'.[38] The Hibberts' religion formed part of a wider identification with the mercantile classes, who were strongly represented in the elite ranks of Unitarianism. Religious sentiments aside, the Hibberts may have wondered how Jane – an illegitimate mixed-heritage female dependant – could have been so impudent as to flout her father's choice of religion. The autonomy of Jane's decision displayed a liberty of mind which subverted her status as both a woman and the descendent of enslaved Africans. Recognising that her actions might well lead to an

I: INTIMATE RELATIONS: THE COLONY

estrangement, Jane wrote to her father pleading that 'I hope you will not also be irreconcilable, for I have much need of your parental love, and who have I else in this World to look unto?'[39] Thomas senior's reply has been lost. In the wake of her conversion Jane left Barn Elms and her father's day-to-day financial support was withdrawn. She did remain in her father's will, suggesting that the parental tie was not completely lost. After a brief stay with the Knowles family in London, Jane went to Birmingham to work as a governess for the Quaker Lloyd family. Samuel Lloyd recalled 'the courageous'[40] Jane Harry in his family biography, lamenting that she was 'very cruelly treated by her father, quite in the old spirit of persecution to which the early Lloyds were accustomed'.[41]

Jane's conversion is one of the reasons that historians still have access to her life and letters, a number of which were carefully transcribed by the Quaker historian Joseph Green. Her connection to the London literary scene has also helped to secure her memory. Jane's apostasy featured in James Boswell's *Life of Samuel Johnson* following an altercation in 1778 between Knowles and Johnson on the subject of women's liberties. According to the poet Anna Seward, Jane 'came home in tears' after Johnson snubbed her when she encountered him on the street in London.[42] At Jane's request Knowles interceded in the matter at a dinner hosted by Charles and Edward Dilly. Johnson was incensed and raged that 'I hate the arrogance of the wench for supposing herself to a more competent judge of Religion than those who educated her' and that she 'ought not to have presumed to determine for herself in so important an affair'.[43] Situated within a wider discourse on the position of women, Johnson's words are indicative of the expectations of gender; as a woman and a dependant, Jane should have been content to allow decisions of import to be made for her by those (men) who knew better. Jane recognised that her shunning was a result of her choice to live against the grain. She wrote to her father, wryly noting that 'I am not put away from my friends for entering into the pursuits and pleasures of this World, but because I scrupled to conform to them.'[44]

On 20 May 1780 Charity was at Agualta Vale with Thomas senior when he died. She remained there for over a month afterwards and on her return to Kingston Robert junior recorded that 'Mrs Harry talks business with my Bro'.[45] It is possible that she had some matters to settle as a result of the will. Thomas senior provided an inheritance for both Charity and Jane. Charity received 'a small House to live in, and 1000 pounds Jamaican currency, payable in ten annual instalments', as well as a number of enslaved Africans.[46] This was deemed by the executors of the will to be 'inadequate to the Wants, as well as the

Merits of the Person to whom it was bequeathed', therefore the annuity was increased. Jane received £2,000, the maximum amount a person of colour could legally inherit under Jamaican law. Although significant sums, their portion was dwarfed by that of Jane's cousins Thomas junior, Robert junior and Thomas, who inherited the bulk of her father's estate. Jane disputed both her own and her mother's share, describing the disparity as 'a Privation of the several Rights of Justice'.[47] In response she received a letter from her cousin Thomas junior which spoke to the precarity of family bonds within the context of 'outside' relations. Thomas junior informed Jane that his uncle had been mindful 'of the Obligations of a Parent to a Child' and that he had made provisions for her that were 'equal to the Fortune, which any person, in the Rank of Life *he* [italics original] had no wish to take her out of, ought to expect in Marriage'. According to Thomas junior, the money was intended to help Jane secure a decent marriage. In a passage designed to remind Jane of her inferior status, Thomas junior stated that:

> [I]f this should be a Legacy inadequate to your Estimation of my Uncle's Fortune, permit me to call to your Recollection, how many Daughters of some of the best Families in England, with whose Education and Style of Life and Company you yourself would not compare your own, are little better portioned.

In an effort to distance Jane from any familial claim on his uncle's wealth, Thomas junior did his best to cast doubt on the validity and intimacy of the parental relationship. Becoming increasingly spiteful in his tone, Thomas junior wrote that his uncle

> never claimed the parental Relation: for how freely soever you may have used the word 'Father', you will not find, that in speaking of you he ever used the word 'Daughter' ... So far was my late uncle from desiring that you should be 'held up to the world as his child', that no consideration gave him more uneasiness, than that of your being so publically known to be so; of which the Change of your name is of itself sufficient proof.[48]

The advertisement of Jane's sister Margaret's christening would suggest that perhaps Thomas senior's attitude towards his mixed-heritage children was more nuanced than his nephew implied. With Thomas senior dead the remaining Hibberts were free to reconfigure the boundaries of familial belonging. Jane's claim on her father's estate was a challenge, albeit merely rhetorical, to the ways in which power was structured in a patriarchal, racially stratified society. It was rejected out of hand and with a venom that represented a severance of any notion of familial obligation outside of the parental relationship that had expired with Thomas senior. There is no further record of any contact between Jane and the Hibbert family in either England or Jamaica.

I: INTIMATE RELATIONS: THE COLONY

In 1782 Jane met and married Joseph Thresher, a Quaker doctor. The couple lived with Joseph's brother Ralph at an address on Foregate Street, Worcester. In May 1784 Jane gave birth to their son Edwin. In August of the same year she died and was buried at the Friends' Burial Ground, New Meeting House, Worcester. For Joseph the blow of his wife's death was compounded when four months later Edwin also died. Within two years Joseph himself was dead following a brief illness. Jane's death was commemorated with an obituary by her friend and mentor Mary Morris Knowles that revealed that prior to the birth of her son she had 'formed an idea of going to Jamaica, the residence of her mother, with a view to procure the freedom of her mother's Negroes'.[49] The American Revolution forced Jane to abandon the idea. However, the text went on to state that 'she has requested her husband that, if the said Negroes be liberated at her mother's decease, he will pay the premium to the island for such liberation'. It is fascinating to imagine what might have been had Jane survived. The Society for Effecting the Abolition of the Slave Trade was founded in 1787, with Mary Morris Knowles an early supporter. Given Jane's personal convictions, alongside her connection to one of Jamaica's most prominent slave-trading families, she could have been deeply embarrassing for the Hibberts. With Jane's death it was her cousin George who became the family's foremost spokesperson on the subject.

Charity died in 1793 in Kingston. Her will revealed that she was a wealthy woman and a slave owner in her own right. The size of her estate enabled her to 'bequeath hundreds of pounds to her family, as well as several plots of land'.[50] Her possessions included: 'a gold watch, clothes, furniture, linen, mahogany furniture, silver, and enslaved men, women and children ... a map of England, jewellery made with her daughters' hair, and paintings, drawings, and a sampler by her daughter, presumably Jane'.[51] Over twenty years after she had last seen her daughters, the inclusion of these tokens of her children amongst the inventory of her personal possessions stands testament to the ways in which the bonds of family were sustained across time and distance. These objects embodied, quite literally in the case of the jewellery, the physical and emotive ties that bound mother to child. Charity's will also contained a request that the enslaved people she held should be manumitted. Charity's youngest daughter Charlotte had died in 1774 and she also outlived her son-in-law, Joseph Thresher. This left the question of who might fulfil the request for manumission. She appointed John Boyd of Britain, likely one of the Hibberts' ship's captains, to take care of this final wish. There is, however, no evidence either way to indicate whether this request was carried out. With Charity's death the last of Thomas senior's 'outside' family died with her. Thomas senior had raised a fortune but it would be his brothers' children and not his own who would enjoy the full benefits of his legacy, being what his own daughters could never be – white, male and legitimate.

Thomas senior was not the only family member to have children outside of marriage in Jamaica; John senior, Thomas junior, Robert junior and George Hibbert Oates all fathered illegitimate children. In 1757 an entry in the parish records of Kingston noted the birth and baptism of Samuel Wynter, the son of John senior and Dorothy Wynter, a 'free mulatto'.[52] Nicholas Hibbert Steele has documented that John senior fathered a further three children with Henrietta Smith.[53] Robert junior noted some of his sexual liaisons in his diary, in particular with Sally, Jenny and Molly. There is no indication as to the status of the women, but Sally's and Molly's repeated presence at the Hibberts' Agualta Vale Pen suggests they could have been enslaved women. Both Robert junior and his brother were sexually interested in Sally; Robert junior recorded that 'I go to the Pen at night. My Bro. merry seizes Sally' and for his own part Robert junior noted he got 'home late; attempt Sally but am disappointed'.[54] A 'romp' with Jenny Boswell took place at 'Mrs Harry's'.[55] Charity owned enslaved people so it is possible that Jenny could have belonged to her. By 1776 Robert junior had contracted a venereal disease, something noticed and commented upon by the Hibberts' client Nathaniel Phillips.[56] His symptoms made horse-riding uncomfortable and after a day in the saddle Robert junior complained that 'This ride retards my cure much ... Have a wretched sleepless night.'[57] Both Thomas junior and Robert junior fathered illegitimate children in 1780.[58] Robert junior's diaries between 1780 and 1787 are missing, however, and later entries made no further reference to this child. There are, however, three mentions of an enslaved woman called Harriet and her two children. 'I very uneasy about Harriett's child, but it wears off and I hear no more about it', wrote Robert junior.[59] Following a gap of three years he noted, 'I then return to Town being uneasy about Harriet.'[60] Finally two days later he commented, 'Sell Harriet & her two children.'[61] It is impossible to say with any certainty what the cause of his unease was; by the time he wrote these entries Robert junior was married, and the presence of an enslaved mistress and illegitimate children could be a source of family tension. It is interesting to note that the decision to sell Harriet and her children came within a week of his wife, Letitia, having been delivered of a daughter who died after just a couple of hours.[62] Any connection is, however, purely speculative. Thomas junior also had a son – 'christened Thomas Robert' – the child's mother was not documented.[63] Three weeks after the christening Robert junior wrote, 'My Bro's little boy very ill. Melancholy quartetto dinner. My Cousin & I down soon. In returning are informed the child

I: INTIMATE RELATIONS: THE COLONY

is dead.'[64] The next day Thomas junior's son was buried in the family vault in the garden of the house in Kingston.

John senior's legitimate son Thomas left an indication that he had a connection to a free woman of colour and her children. In his will of 1805 Thomas left annuities to both Jeanott Smith and William Oakum, the children of Harriet Cook Smith, 'a free mulatto of Kingston'.[65] He also left a bequest of £100 for Harriet herself. Thomas later removed the clause relating to Harriet, although this could have been on account of her death rather than a breakdown in the relationship. Was there any connection to the Harriet and her two children that Robert sold in 1793? Or perhaps Harriet Cook Smith was related to the woman his father John senior had two children with? Were Henrietta Smith and Harriet Cook Smith the same person, making Jeanott and William his half-siblings? Thomas also inserted an additional codicil which entitled Sarah Winter – 'a free quadroon of Kingston' – to £50. Although no further detail is given as to Sarah's identity, she shared the same surname as Thomas's mixed-heritage half-brother Samuel and could possibly have been a relation. Sarah was certainly close to the Hibberts' extended family circle – Charity also remembered her in her will. Thomas's legitimate family received considerably more: his wife Dorothy was entitled to £300 annuities with an additional £1,000, plus furniture and plate. His legitimate children received £10,000 each on reaching twenty-one, and for each son who lived to twenty-five a further £10,000 was settled on them. Laid out in bald monetary terms the difference between the acknowledged Hibbert family members and those who were denied the family name is clear.

The last of the Hibbert men to father illegitimate children in Jamaica was George Hibbert Oates. His sexual practices became the source of notoriety following a public exposé by the Reverend Thomas Cooper in the mid-1820s.[66] Ann Cooper accused Oates of impregnating a sixteen-year-old girl on the Georgia plantation, where he was the attorney. Oates's will confirmed that he did in fact have a 'reputed' daughter called Mary Oates who was 'a free girl of colour formerly a slave on Georgia estate'.[67] Oates used the Hibberts' connections to different plantations to gain access to the bodies of enslaved women. His will detailed a further set of intimate relationships which spanned various properties the family were linked to. He had a daughter Jane Oates who was 'formerly a slave on Whitney', where his brother Hibbert Oates was the attorney. There was a son – George Thomas Oates – who was 'formerly a slave on Hals Hall', a property of which the Hibberts were mortgagees. Finally the will documented a 'mulatto child' called Anna Maria. Her mother Elizabeth Williams was 'formerly a slave on Great Valley', a plantation owned by Oates's uncle Robert junior and for which he acted as attorney. Oates left £100 to each of his children and land to Elizabeth. The bulk of his fortune was split between his brother Hibbert Oates and sister Anna Maria, who both received £2,000, with an annuity settled on his mother Mary.

Inside families

With his elder brother Thomas senior eschewing matrimony, John senior was the first of the Hibberts to make a match in Jamaica. Having arrived in Kingston in 1754, after six years of bachelor life John senior married twenty-year-old Janet Gordon in 1760. The Gordons were originally from Scotland but had emigrated to Jamaica to overcome the prejudices that circumscribed their prospects at home.[68] Evidence of the enmity directed towards the Scots can be read in comments made by Janet's brother Thomas, who wrote that 'In spite of the great disadvantage of being a Scotch man I have made very genteelly by my profession.'[69] By the time of the marriage Thomas was both the Assembly member for Port Royal and the Attorney General, as his father Samuel had been before him.[70] John senior and Janet began a family immediately and had seven children – four boys and three girls. John senior died in 1769 aged thirty-seven, leaving Janet pregnant with their youngest son Robert.

Janet stayed in Jamaica for a further three years. However, in May 1772 she prepared to depart for Britain. Robert junior's diary noted that Janet was engaged in a passionate affair with Dr David Grant, the son of another Scottish *émigré* family. Two days before Janet left, Robert junior noted that 'Dr. G is here very early in the morning and makes violent love almost till dinner time.'[71] On the night of her departure the family gathered on board the ship to say their goodbyes before leaving her with Grant. Despite Janet's flouting of the usual rules of morality attached to women, her dead husband's nephews were saddened at her leaving. Robert junior wrote: 'The Ship gets under way and we take leave of Mrs H ... My spirits depressed beyond what I never before experienced ... My Bro and self indulging separately our feelings, decline supper and retire early.'[72] The brothers discussed Janet a few weeks later. There seemed to be some disapproval registered at her behaviour, although the language was ambiguous: 'My Bro. Mentions to me some instances of Mrs H.'s conduct which confirms me in the opinion I had of her disinterestedness.'[73] Over the years the Hibberts continued to do business with Janet's family, acting as mortgage holders for their plantations Windsor Lodge and Paisley. Hibbert & Co., a later branch of the London-based operations, successfully counterclaimed against the Gordons for their slave compensation money. They were eventually awarded £6,252 12s

I: INTIMATE RELATIONS: THE COLONY

for 353 enslaved people attached to Windsor Lodge and £3,135 for 167 enslaved people on Paisley.[74] They also had further dealings with Janet's lover, Dr David Grant; her youngest son Robert acted as his attorney and managed his estate Spring Garden for several years.[75]

When Janet left for England, she took her daughters Cecelia and Margaret and her youngest son Robert with her. Her son Samuel died in Kingston in 1764 and it seems she may have left her eldest son Thomas in Jamaica with his uncles. It is not clear where her son John junior and her daughter Janette spent their youth. There is also some mystery over why it was that John junior, who was born in Manchester in 1768, was 'unprovided for' in his father's will. According to Janet's own will, this circumstance led to her coming to an agreement with her brother-in-law Thomas senior, her nephew Thomas junior and their former business partner Samuel Jackson, who paid '£1000 and £100 apiece for his [John junior's] education'.[76] In 1778 Janet added a codicil requesting that in the event of her death her daughters should be cared for by her sister-in-law Abigail Hibbert and Arabella Sprigg, the wife of Thomas senior's former slave-trading partner. She entrusted her two youngest sons to her brother Samuel Wilkinson Gordon, a London merchant. Janet died at Mortlake in Surrey in 1779. Having only recently dispatched Jane Harry from their house, Arabella and her husband took in Janet's daughters. Neither Cecelia nor Margaret married and they remained living with the Spriggs for the rest of their lives. Though not a blood relation, Arabella cared for Janet's daughters until her death in 1824. In her will she bequeathed her home to her only living charge, Margaret.[77]

Between 1784 and 1787 Janet's youngest son Robert was educated at Warrington Academy in Nottingham, under the tutelage of Gilbert Wakefield, at a cost of £200 per year.[78] Wakefield remembered Robert fondly in his *Memoirs*, stating that 'The society of this ingenious and amiable youth was a source of perpetual satisfaction, and he usually passed his vacations with me till the completion of his academical career.'[79] The two men remained close; when Wakefield was imprisoned in 1801 for writing a pamphlet in support of the French Revolution, Robert sent him £1,000.[80] During his time in England, Robert's older cousin George took on a parental role, acting as his guardian. George spoke highly of his young charge, writing to Simon Taylor that 'Your ... good opinion of young Robert Hibbert is very pleasing to me ... I have known him intimately from his infancy and have always found him acute, attentive and honourable.'[81] As Robert grew and matured he was eventually taken into the London family partnership by George.

Following on from his brother John senior's marriage, Thomas senior looked next to his nephews Thomas junior and Robert junior to make advantageous matches. Both men harboured aspirations towards marriage, with Robert junior documenting some of their early attachments. Thomas junior formed a serious relationship with a Miss Reeves, to whom he was engaged in 1772. To his deep sadness Miss Reeves fell ill and died. Robert junior described the event in his diary:

> Miss Reeves ... Very ill on Wednesday, but recovers a little, and addresses all her friends in a very pathetic & sensible manner, acquits my Brother of any breach of promise, etc. On Thursday morng. a little better, but relapses in the aftn. & dies at night, to my Brother's and, I may add, to my unspeakable regret.[82]

Her death was a blow to Thomas junior, whose brother George recorded in his diary that 'My Bro. T. writes in very bad spirits. The Lady whom of all others he lik'd best and to whom he was engag'd had died abo't 10 days before he wrote he had sat up with her 5 Days and 3 nights and this join'd to the lowness of his spirits we are afraid will bring on some illness.'[83] Such was his grief that in the days following Miss Reeves's death Thomas junior told his uncle that he wanted to return to England.[84] In the end he finally left Jamaica still a bachelor in 1780.

In 1775 Robert junior took an interest in a Miss Goulburn (possibly Sarah Goulburn, the daughter of Edward Goulburn and Thomasin Roberts) – the 'Miss G.' that Charity had taken such a keen interest in. Thomas junior met with the lady and her mother when they arrived from England, following which the brothers had 'some talk on the subject'.[85] Having seen Miss G. at a play a couple of days later Robert junior confided in his diary that 'I think her very handsome.'[86] Three days after this encounter Robert junior proclaimed that 'I was to have dined on board *Boyd* but cannot yet relish society but where she is the theme.'[87] The next day he added that he was 'rather touched and sick with wine & love combined'.[88] Despite Robert junior's private declarations of love, nothing transpired of this infatuation.

A decade later on 3 September 1785 Robert junior was married to twenty-year-old Letitia Nembhard. Letitia was the daughter of Dr John Nembhard and his wife Ann Payton Hamilton. The Nembhards owned the 300-acre Konigsberg estate in St Mary's, the same parish where the Hibberts' Agualta Vale plantation was situated. The family were of good social standing and on his death in 1777 John left each of his four daughters £1,200.[89] The year after their marriage and with a newborn daughter, Anna, Robert junior purchased Whitehall plantation. He pulled down the old house and made plans to build a new home for his family.[90] From entries in Robert junior's diary it seemed the couple enjoyed a good relationship; they attended the usual social functions of people of their station, including social calling, balls, exhibitions, auctions, theatre performances, church and family occasions. When

I: INTIMATE RELATIONS: THE COLONY

Letitia was pregnant or ill, Robert junior was attentive and concerned. In his earlier diaries he had written about his sexual encounters with women, venereal diseases and an illegitimate child. The diaries spanning 1787–1802 contained two references, in 1787 and 1788, to Robert junior sleeping at the Spanish Town property of a woman named Kitty Hinks, although the nature of this relationship is unclear.[91] After that there were no more references to this kind of behaviour, although that is not necessarily to say that it did not persist.

Robert junior and Letitia had five living children. In his diary and private letters Robert junior recorded his wife's seven miscarriages (including one during a voyage to England). In addition there were two babies that died within a day of their birth. Between 1786 and 1802 Letitia went through fourteen pregnancies. In 1790 Robert junior wrote to his sister Mary on the impending birth of his son Robert. His description indicated that constant pregnancy and miscarriage had taken a physical toll on Letitia: 'My Wife is as well as Ladies so <u>weighty</u> [original emphasis], in general are', adding that they would soon return to England as 'Mrs. H's health requires cold weather.'[92] Robert junior's diaries recorded the many weeks of illness both leading up to and after his wife miscarried. Eight days after a miscarriage in 1797 Letitia was 'again seized with violent discharges'.[93] During June 1798 she suffered from sustained periods of breast pain. Robert junior attended to his wife, summoned the doctor and cancelled their engagements.[94] In July 1790, 'Mrs. H. taken ill about 5 o'clock with a violent headache & lowness of spirits ... Saturday morn'g she complains of violent spasms in her stomach.'[95] In August 1800, a year after suffering another miscarriage, Letitia was again experiencing problems with her reproductive health. Robert junior noted that 'Mrs. H. not well; her disorder an inflammation so near the womb as to frighten her.'[96] The impact of multiple miscarriages and child deaths was emotional as well as physical. Robert junior noted periods in which both he and his wife were 'low spirited' following these events.[97] Robert junior's diary was littered with anxious references to his wife's ill health, although in the end she outlived him by nineteen years, dying at the age of eighty-nine.

By his own admission Robert junior loved children. Writing to his sister Mary he enthused, 'I am so fond of Children that if I was in England I should be loading my Nephews and Nieces with Whistles and Trumpets and Dolls etc.'[98] He shared a loving relationship with his sons and daughters, using his diary to note down each of their births, and as they grew he kept a record of their heights. As a proud father Robert junior recalled that at a dinner party at Whitehall 'little Anna is brought and exhibited in crossing the table'.[99] Letitia was supported in motherhood by her mother and sisters, as well as the enslaved women who served her. When Letitia was nearing the birth of their first son Thomas, Robert junior waited eagerly for the new arrival. There was a false alarm on 15 June, but the danger of a premature birth passed and after weeks of anticipation Thomas was finally born on 29 July 1788.[100] A month later the child was given over to the care of a nurse.[101] The children's health was a serious and regular concern for both parents. Sore throats, disorders of the bowel, fever, chicken pox, boils, thrush in the mouth, prickly heat, measles and scarlet fever were just some of the childhood ailments that Robert junior documented in his diary. Proving himself a thoroughly modern father he insisted that his son Robert was inoculated against smallpox after an outbreak in Jamaica in 1791, his son John followed suit in 1796.[102] The image of Robert junior as a gentle and caring father is difficult to reconcile with the hard-headed business of slavery – a business responsible for the dismantling of enslaved family units. Did Robert junior believe that enslaved men and women were incapable of the kind of parental affection he felt for his own offspring, or was it simply commercially expedient to adopt this mentality? There is nothing in his diaries, letters or evidence to Parliament that reflected on how the practice of slavery emotionally affected the families who laboured under it. Perhaps he never thought of it at all.

Following the births of his children Robert junior's family structure became increasingly transatlantic. As they grew their parents determined to send them to England for their schooling. In contrast to Thomas senior's daughters Jane and Margaret, the children were cared for by their immediate Hibbert family. Letitia and Robert junior visited as often as they could and eventually settled at Birtles Hall in Cheshire, a country house which Robert junior purchased in 1791. Breaking up the family unit was difficult; with three generations of Nembhards in Jamaica, the family bonds were strong. Unlike Robert junior, this was the only place that his wife knew as home. Letitia was very close to her mother and sisters and they were very involved with family life. In 1790 as his young family prepared to visit England, Robert junior wrote to his sister of his concern for his wife stating that 'I almost dread the parting between her and her Mother which in all human probability will be a final one. Nothing can reconcile such sacrifice to the mind but the prospect of meeting and living with those dearest of all Relations Children.'[103] His fears did not come to fruition and in the end both Letitia's sister and mother chose to relocate to London rather than break up the family.

In 1791 Robert junior handed his two eldest children Anna and Thomas into the care of his English relations. Having left both his wife and his youngest son sick after an inoculation in Jamaica, Robert

I: INTIMATE RELATIONS: THE COLONY

junior reflected on the conflicting emotions of living between metropole and colony:

> I hardly recollect any voyage where, all things considered, I had greater cause for anxiety & apprehension than at present. The unsettled situation in which I left my new purchase, Birtles, the state of Fuhr's health & dread of the consequences in case of accident to George, the leaving of my two children; the reason I have to apprehend injury from dry weather – fire; or what of worse than all, Insurrection of Negroes. All these and a thousand others are swallowed up by fears for the health and welfare of my wife & child.[104]

Robert junior's sentiments expressed the way in which business and family were absolutely enmeshed within the transatlantic world. George was both his younger brother and the head of the Hibbert counting house in London; with their business partner Fuhr sick, any accident or illness that affected George could have a serious impact on their commercial enterprise. Parts of Robert junior's life – his new country house and his eldest children – were anchored to Britain. Yet he had left his wife and younger child in Jamaica, where he owned multiple properties (including human 'property'), held political position and had a business of his own. It was his involvement with slavery that sustained his family life, but reliance on such a volatile and violent practice caused deep uncertainty. Both merchant capitalism and transatlantic slavery were risky trades; the angst that Robert junior expressed was not related to any moral uneasiness with his situation, but rather a realisation that despite his great wealth, his style of life was reliant on the maintenance of two interlocking systems that were inherently unstable.

In 1792 the bonds between the Hibbert and the Nembhards were strengthened when Robert junior's cousin Robert married Letitia's sister Eliza. Having returned from England in 1791 to take his place in the family business, Robert was in a good position to provide for a wife and any children. In spite of the pre-existing connection it seems that Robert's initial marriage proposal was rejected by Eliza's mother.[105] Whatever the reason for this refusal, the obstacle was overcome and four months later the families were preparing for the wedding. In a return to the bawdy language of his earlier years Robert junior reported that on 12 September 1792 'my Cousin storms poor Eliza's fort'.[106] The couple remained childless, but were devoted to their 'darling adopted Child Sophy', the daughter of Robert's brother John.[107]

Despite the multiple marital ties that bound them, there remained a lingering sense of difference between the colonial and metropolitan branches of these families. Robert junior's mother Abigail expressed some of these perceived divergences in her letters to her own daughters.

The discourse within which Abigail situated her criticisms spoke to some of the prevailing suspicions about the un-English nature of the Creole.[108] West Indians were not viewed as transplanted Englishmen and women, prolonged colonial contact had distanced them from the social mores and habits of their metropolitan counterparts. Richard Cumberland's play *The West Indian* (1771) is perhaps the best-known literary example of the ways in which the Creole was constructed in the English imagination. Fiery, generous and idle, they were considered prone to overindulgence, gluttony, irreligiosity and promiscuity. The climatic influence of the Torrid Zone, alongside extended periods spent in the company of enslaved Africans, created a sense of colonial difference that was expressed by both residents of, and visitors to, the Caribbean. Edward Long criticised Creole women in particular as corrupted through their contact with the enslaved. He wrote disdainfully of 'a very fine young woman aukwardly [sic] dangling her arms with the air of a Negroe-servant, lolling the whole day upon beds or settees ... her speech is whining, languid and childish'.[109] These views were repeated in the journal of Lady Nugent, who penned a passage outlining some of her opinions on Creole society:

> It is extraordinary to witness the immediate effect that the climate and habit of living in this country has on the minds and manner of Europeans ... In the upper ranks, they become indolent and inactive, regardless of anything except eating, drinking and indulging themselves ... The Creole language is not confined to the negroes. Many of the ladies, who have not been educated in England, speak a sort of broken English, with an indolent drawling out of their words, that is tiresome if not disgusting.[110]

Abigail's letters articulated some of these tropes in relation to Letitia and her children. Letitia's ill health was scrutinised by her mother-in-law; in response to her delicate constitution, Abigail recommended bathing in the sea at Blackpool. The letter relating to this expedition was dated 29 September – a bracing time of year to enjoy the restorative powers of the Irish Sea, particularly for someone used to the warmer waters of the Caribbean. Abigail reported to her daughter Mary that 'Mrs. R. H. bathed 4 times, but not a word of what effect it had.'[111] Letitia's response was immediately compared to that of Abigail's other daughter-in-law, her son Samuel junior's wife, Mary Greenhalgh. 'Mrs. S. H.', Abigail reported, 'had bathed the day before merely for the pleasure of it, but had found such benefit that she meant to Continue.' Mary's family hailed from Horton in Lancashire – good, hardy northern stock comparable to Abigail's own family background. Dismissing Letitia's health problems, her mother-in-law added that 'Mrs. R. H. complaints are merely from a weak, relaxed habit.' In the

I: INTIMATE RELATIONS: THE COLONY

figure of the Creole woman, Abigail, Lady Nugent and Edward Long all identified unwelcome deviations which marked her out as inferior.

Letitia's mothering skills were also called into question by Abigail. She disapproved of her daughter-in-law's practice of letting her children suckle for too long. This was a habit that Robert junior associated with enslaved mothers in a questionnaire he wrote in order to prepare for giving evidence to Parliament in 1790.[112] In one of her letters Abigail wrote about a communication she had received from Letitia giving an update on the progress of her grandson. Abigail relayed the information that 'all was well, her little boy has ten teeth & speaks many words quite plain, but she does not tell the whole truth, for I find he was not wean'd when his father returned, & perhaps sucks yet, as she avoids saying anything about it'.[113] If Letitia suckled the child herself is it possible that having lived her whole life in Jamaica she was aware of the lactational amenorrhea method of birth control practised by African women on the plantations? Katherine Paugh's work on slavery and reproduction has suggested that the planter class were well aware of the link between breastfeeding and a reduction in fertility.[114] Does this explain why Letitia chose to breastfeed for long periods? Perhaps she simply took pleasure from this form of maternal bonding. Abigail was firm in her condemnation and urged the letter's recipient not to follow Letitia's example.

Abigail's opinions about her Jamaica-born grandchildren were also inflected with the language of Creole difference. She wrote that 'I have a poor heart of my Guests, the Children are delicate, & have not had the small pox, the boy suffers much from his teeth, & has a Negro Nurse.'[115] The tone of disapproval in Abigail's letter is notable. The presence of an African woman in the household, fulfilling such an intimate family role, would have been entirely alien to Abigail. Although her husband, sons and nephews were heavily involved in the slavery business, the 'Negro Nurse' was neither a tidy entry in a ledger book nor one of the fearful savages conjured in the newspaper reports of such events as the revolution in Saint-Domingue. This was transatlantic slavery brought into the heart of the metropolitan home. Writing from Manchester a month afterwards, Abigail relayed yet more troubling news about her Creole granddaughter Eliza. A friend of the family, Miss Parker, had informed Abigail that she 'observed Eliza with great attention when with her & cannot find that she uses her tongue at all in speaking, neither is her Language in the least intelligible but to those who are Constantly with her'.[116] Again this differencing of accent and pronunciation can also be found in both Edward Long's and Lady Nugent's writings. On her return to England, Lady Nugent presented her children to their metropolitan relations and reported that they 'amuse all the family very much, by their little funny talk, and Creole ideas and ways'.[117] Abigail, it seemed, was more alarmed than entertained. With the children safely ensconced in England there would be time enough to correct the habits they had learned in Jamaica. Coming of age during the tumultuous period of abolition, none of Robert junior and Letitia's children returned to the island to settle there.

Conclusion

The Hibberts, like so many other families forged under the shadow of slavery, were transformed both as economic agents but more intimately as private individuals – as mothers, fathers, sons and daughters. The existence of an inside–outside dynamic based on legitimacy and skin colour, and shaped by religion and place, created a hierarchy which enabled the wealth and privileges of the plantation system to circulate within defined boundaries. Jane and Margaret existed on the periphery of the Hibberts' family circle. When they arrived in England they were sent to live with business associates and not with their family. Their position was entirely contingent on the status of their father, Thomas senior. On his demise Jane's ties to the family were effectively severed. Her decision to flout the raced and gendered rules that dictated acceptable behaviour made this estrangement a more straightforward decision, though it was her claims to financial equality that triggered the final separation. Despite her family's rejection, Jane's social position as the daughter of a powerful merchant with private wealth of her own mitigated the worst effects of her disownment. Having enjoyed some of the privileges of class prior to her expulsion from the family, she was able to access elevated figures within the elite circles of the metropolitan cultural world. Helped by the bonds of religion, her relationship with Mary Morris Knowles gave her the opportunity to fashion an identity of her own. None of the Hibberts attended Jane's wedding in 1782, instead Mary and her husband acted as witnesses. In the absence of, or perhaps more properly in preference to, her blood relations, the Knowles became the family of Jane's choosing. As a Quaker, an abolitionist and a woman of colour she was a remarkable figure for her time, becoming visible where the majority of mixed-heritage children born during slavery have fallen into obscurity.

Jane was absent from both the public and private accounts of the family lineage. In amongst the Blathwayt papers there is an extensive handwritten family tree in which it is stated that 'Thomas Hibbert died unmarried'.[118] Despite the Hibberts' efforts to exclude Jane from the family story, her archival erasure was not complete. Her life intertwined with the lives of influential friends and in this way her memory was preserved. When her extraordinary story came to the attention of the

I: INTIMATE RELATIONS: THE COLONY

Quaker historian Joseph Green, he continued to search for further fragments with which to piece together her narrative. He was particularly interested in Jane's paintings, but he wrote that 'Upon the break-up of the Kingston establishment they disappeared, and never reached England; and possibly the Hibbert family, from the sad circumstances of Jenny Harry's birth, would hardly care to perpetuate her memory by retaining such mementoes.'[119] On the other hand Jane's husband's family kept and treasured one of the single surviving objects that had been owned by the couple – their silver wedding spoons. Passed down a somewhat convoluted family line they made their way into Green's hands. He wrote of them that they 'are greatly valued as a memorial of a most interesting and excellent personality – Jenny Harry'. Just over a hundred years on from when Green wrote his article, Jane has been reclaimed by Hibbert family historian Nicholas Hibbert Steele. His website, whilst focusing primarily on Jane's cousin George, has a section in which Jane is acknowledged as part of the family story.[120] The stigma of illegitimacy and race is perhaps no longer the barrier it once was to intimate recognition, although the ability to grapple with the slaving past remains a difficult personal issue for some families.

The archival presence of elite planter-merchant families contrasts sharply with the absences faced by those who attempt to document enslaved ancestors. The lack of official records between the last of the triennial slave registers and the first census in the West Indies has created a gap in our knowledge. The Solomon and Elizabeth Hibbert Network is a family website that has tried unsuccessfully to trace relations back into the period of enslavement.[121] The families have been in contact with Hibbert Steele to try and ascertain if their forebears were once the property of the family. Despite their efforts they have been unable to find any evidence documenting the lives of their relatives under slavery. The asymmetry of the historical record is a reflection of both the power structures of society and of the archives that they create. Recovering enslaved families – their humanity and agency – is extremely difficult, given the nature of the sources that historians have to work with. Slave registers, plantation accounts, attorney letters and reports all occasionally offer some skeletal information about the connections that bound people to one another on the estates, but in most instances they lack the detail that would allow a deeper penetration of enslaved family life. Colonial intimacies radically altered the experience and meaning of family – the legacies of these shifts continue to shape the lives of people in both the former spaces of empire and the former metropole. The Hibberts' story serves as a reminder of what is gained through an analysis of imperial family relations, what is lost and also, for some, what is ultimately unrecoverable.

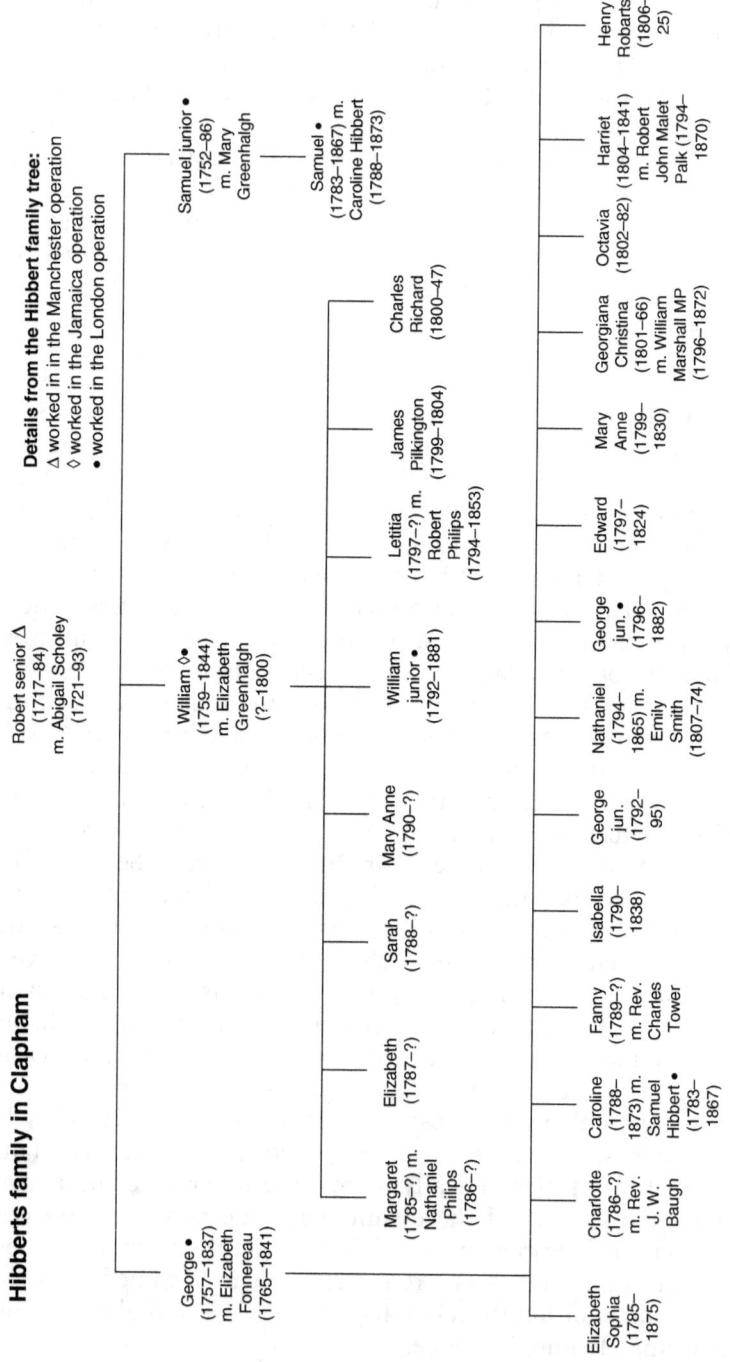

Family tree 6 The Hibbert family in Clapham

CHAPTER SIX

Part II Intimate relations: the metropole

People in middle age are not so strongly tempted to be thoughtless, and idle, and licentious. From excess of this sort they are sufficiently withheld, particularly when happily settled in domestic life, by a regard to their characters, by the restraints of family connections, and by a sense of what is due to the decencies of the married state. *Their* probation is of another sort; they are tempted to be supremely engrossed by world cares, by family interests, by professional objects, by the pursuit of wealth or ambition.

William Wilberforce, *A practical view of the prevailing religious system of professed Christians in the higher and middle classes of this country, contrasted with real Christianity* (London: T. Cadell & W. Davies, 1797), p. 277

A character not uncommon among his countrymen, who by an active and persevering industry, have risen from the lowest situation of menial service, to the highest rank of the mercantile profession ... and lives in luxury and splendour. His country-house was purchased of a nobleman, who had lately built it, and whose title it still retains; – he has his park and his hot-houses, – he sees, in spring, the fruitage of summer on his walls, and is rolled in a coach and six from his accompting-house to his villa. While his son figures as a fine gentleman about town, and his daughters rival, in manners and accomplishments, the best education of the great world.

William Coombe, *The devil upon two sticks*, vol. I, 3rd edn (Dublin: Zachariah Jackson, 1790), p. 190

In 1793, with his wife Elizabeth pregnant with their sixth child, George removed his family to an 'elegant and commodious Residence' on the North Side, Clapham Common.[122] When they were first married, the couple lived at 12 New Broad Street, close to the merchant house on Mincing Lane. As both his brood and his status as a merchant grew, George required more suitable accommodation. Away from the dirt and menace of the City, Clapham combined the trappings of gentility with the everyday demands of a working merchant. Its draw for respectable families was articulated by E. M. Forster: 'The Clapham area had become civilised, there was no danger from highwaymen, the merchants and politicians who were beginning to settle there could leave their families in safety when they drove the four or five miles to Westminster or to the City.'[1] That sense of security came not only in the form of physical safety, but also from the moral and spiritual character of its middle-class residents, who included William Wilberforce and his close-knit circle of Evangelical antislavery reformers. As a prosperous enclave of middle-class respectability Clapham's appeal transcended the political boundaries between pro and antislavery, creating a community in which the opponents coexisted.

For the Hibberts in Britain their experiences of family life were radically different from those of their colonial counterparts. Metropolitan ideas about gender and the family shifted notably from the later eighteenth century, prefiguring the development of the cult of domesticity that characterised the Victorian period. With the rise in influence of Evangelicalism, middle-class notions of the family and home were increasingly refracted through the prism of Christianity. According to John Tosh, 'Family life was expected to reflect Christian belief – to be moral and decorous and enlightened.'[2] The idea of a companionate marriage based on 'companionship as well as authority' took root.[3] The home was framed as a sacred space in which men and women harmoniously performed the gendered rituals of domesticity, creating a place of succour and retreat from an outside world that was conceived of as corrupt and corrupting. As Catherine Hall and Leonore Davidoff have argued, this was a period in which the notion of 'separate spheres' was gaining cultural currency.[4] Unlike Abigail Hibbert's experience in Manchester, her sons' wives were shielded from day-to-day commercial operations. John Tosh has explored the 'deeply contradictory associations' that this separation entailed for the middle-class man:

> [O]n the one hand, pride in climbing the ladder of success, providing for his family, and acquiring the esteem of his peers; on the other, resentment of time and toil required, fear of failure at the impersonal hands of the market, and revulsion from the morals of the business world. Home served to mitigate the brashness of these reactions, it could not soften the fear of failure. But it did explain and justify the labours of the breadwinner, and perhaps even the moral depths to which he must stoop, in order to sustain his dependants.[5]

II: INTIMATE RELATIONS: THE METROPOLE

One wonders if any of the Hibbert men similarly counterbalanced their domestic comforts with the ethical implications of involvement in the business of slavery. Work, of course, did more than simply explain and justify domesticity – it paid for it. In this way the profits of participation in the system of slavery were abstracted in the elegance of the polite mercantile home. Distanced from the violence of the plantation, the labour of the enslaved was domesticated and remade into the signifiers of respectability, taste and status.

'Family and domesticity were central to a man's being', Catherine Hall has written in relation to the abolitionist Macaulays; they were 'the essential underpinning of a public life'.[6] Whilst George disagreed with the Saints on the subject of slavery, he placed similar value on the importance of home and family, although it is difficult to reconcile the notion of George as a gentle father and loving husband with a man who was complicit in the destruction of so many enslaved families. A self-confessed 'family man',[7] George embraced the domesticity that characterised concepts of middle-class manhood.[8] The degree to which he aspired to this ideal can be read in his nephew James Heywood Markland's description of his character. He wrote that 'Distinguished, as Mr. Hibbert was, by the active powers of his mind, and valuable as were his services as a public man, his social and domestic qualities are those upon which his friends and family must always dwell with the greatest satisfaction.'[9] George 'was happy in his family', wrote Markland. They allowed him to display the 'cultivated understanding and gentle temper' which the commercial world all too often denied a man of feeling. Recalling his uncle's parental virtues, Markland noted that 'he was the kindest and most generous of fathers, contributing by every possible means to the gratification of his children'.[10] Alongside his evident affection for his wife and children they also served a very necessary practical purpose. Elizabeth provided George with important family connections, the promise of property and heirs to continue the family interest. Their children were modelled from a young age to conform to middle-class expectations of gender: for the boys the law, the navy and the merchant house, for the girls an advantageous marriage.

The public image of his family was political for George; living a lifestyle which in many ways shadowed the Clapham Saints was a direct challenge to their depiction of the slave owner as a Creolised tyrant. Unlike the vision of the Caribbean planter presented by the abolitionists, George was every inch the respectable metropolitan man. He lived in the same refined domestic world, he subscribed to similar ideals of masculinity and family life, he even attended the same church as his abolitionist counterparts. George conformed to the dictates of polite middle-class society and in doing so visibly demonstrated the ways in which reputable English families were maintained by an engagement with the slave economy. Of course, his representation of his own relations relied on the suppressed family narrative of sexual exploitation and illegitimacy in the colonies. For the Hibberts the personal was political; domesticity, respectability and a Christian family life were an integral part of the justification for, and legitimisation of, the continuation of transatlantic slavery.

Marriage, networks and property

Whilst middle-class women were increasingly excluded from the physical places of work, they were vital to the intangible labour of network building. A prudent match might strengthen old connections or draw in new associates. George's wife Elizabeth was the eldest daughter of Philip Fonnereau and Mary Parker. Her mother's family were wealthy and landed, having previously served in both Parliament and at the royal court. Elizabeth's father was a prominent London banker, politician and land owner. Like the Unitarian Hibberts, the Huguenot Fonnereaus had arrived in London as relative outsiders, having come to England from France following the revocation of the Edict of Nantes. The Fonnereaus had historically been involved with the cloth trade and commerce, before moving into finance. Elizabeth's grandfather, Zachary Philip Fonnereau, was wealthy and connected enough for the Duke of Newcastle to seek his assistance with financing the Seven Years War.[11] Her father served as a Director of the Bank of England between 1771 and 1783. By 1732 the family had acquired the manors of Christ Church and Wicksufford, as well as a large estate in Edmonton. They purchased the rotten borough seats of Sudbury and Aldeburgh, returning family members including Philip Fonnereau, his father, uncle and brother, continuously between 1747 and 1784. Crucially Elizabeth was an heiress – she was set to inherit Munden estate in Hertfordshire through her uncle Rogers Parker. George and Elizabeth's marriage would eventually transform him from a merchant into a country gentleman. The coverture laws which existed effectively meant that the property would be entailed to George once he and Elizabeth were married. The promise of a family seat had important implications for the social trajectory of their eldest son and heir, increasing his eligibility by guaranteeing him a position within the landed gentry. Marriage to Elizabeth therefore represented the combined attributes of political and commercial connections, alongside the acquisition of land and property.

The marriage of Elizabeth's younger sister Mary Ann in 1790 also brought with it access to important financial, mercantile and imperial networks. Her husband, George Woodford Thellusson, served as a

II: INTIMATE RELATIONS: THE METROPOLE

Director for the East India Company between 1796 and 1807, Director of the Imperial Insurance Company between 1803 and 1811 and as a Member of Parliament in 1796 and then continuously between 1804 and 1811. The Thellussons were also a French Huguenot family, and had left Paris for Geneva, before settling in London in 1761.[12] George Woodford's father Peter Thellusson was a merchant with links to the premier finance houses of Paris, Geneva and Amsterdam.[13] He had reputedly made 'great sums' from remittances deposited by Frenchmen who perished on the guillotine.[14] Peter had invested heavily in the West India trade and owned plantations in Grenada and Montserrat.[15] George Woodford's older brother, Peter Isaac, was an associate of London's largest slave trading company, Camden, Calvert & King, a Director of the Bank of England between 1787 and 1806, a Member of Parliament between 1795 and 1808 and was eventually awarded the title Baron Rendlesham.[16] George Woodford's cousin, Sir Ralph Woodford, served as Governor of Trinidad and Tobago between 1812 and 1828. Following the abolition of the slave trade, Sir Ralph was a 'leading exponent of "free labour" from the East Indies' into the Caribbean, perhaps as a result of the family's interests in both the West and East Indies.[17] The mutual interests of the Woodfords, Thellussons and Hibberts can be traced in George's support of Joseph Barham's 1811 proposal to supply Indian labour to the Caribbean.[18] George was close enough to the Thellussons to have been asked by Peter to act as trustee in the event of the death of any of the original appointees.[19] George Woodford also made George an executor of his will.[20]

Domestic masculinity and a companionate marriage

As Davidoff and Hall have argued, 'The significance of marriage for middle-class men cannot be overestimated. It profoundly affected their economic, social, spiritual and emotional life as well as everyday standard of comfort.'[21] Elizabeth's powerful connections and her status as an heiress made her an ideal match for a young man intent on establishing himself as a leading figure within the City. George was aided along the path to matrimony when his father died on 12 January 1784. The death of Robert senior, in itself a severing of boyhood ties, provided George with the means to embrace full manhood through marriage. Financially cautious middle-class men tended to wait until they were capable of supporting a household and dependants before contemplating matrimony. Having previously furnished his son with £1,500, Robert senior left George land in Holbeck, Leeds, and a further £1,000.[22] The land and capital given to George, alongside his position in the family's West India counting house, secured his independence. On

31 August 1784 at St George's Church, Bloomsbury, George married his nineteen-year-old bride Elizabeth. It was, wrote Markland, a 'union which mainly contributed to the happiness of his life'.[23]

George grew to manhood during a period in which middle-class men 'placed a high value on a harmonious marriage and on domesticity'.[24] George's commonplace book is a fascinating window into how he conceptualised marriage and fatherhood. The act of commonplacing was itself an indication of his desire to embrace an enlightened masculine sensibility.[25] That both of the opening passages were dedicated to the subject of marriage suggests that George spent time thinking about the proper form of matrimonial behaviour. The first was an extract from a letter by Samuel Johnson on the death of his wife.[26] Describing her as a 'friend', Johnson's text placed heavy emphasis on the feminine virtues of piety, simplicity, patience and submissiveness. George also expressed admiration for these characteristics; in reference to Simon Taylor's niece, he praised her 'Beauty' and 'modest manner'.[27] When commenting on the marriage of his business partner John Vincent Purrier, he wrote 'Purrier is married; a prudent and sensible woman and he seems the more ... diligent from it.'[28] For George, marriage to a woman whose qualities improved her husband provided the solid foundation for him to succeed in both his public and private life.

Despite these expressions of admiration for demure feminine qualities, George's wife was not expected to remain sequestered within the home. Aside from the usual engagements expected of a couple of their social standing, Elizabeth also accompanied George on some of his public duties. In 1798, after he became an Alderman of the City of London, George was involved with organising a militia 'for the protection of private property'.[29] A report in *The Times* informed its readers that:

> The Inhabitants request of their worthy Alderman to communicate their sincere and grateful acknowledgements to Mrs. Hibbert, for her polite attention to the Corps, by presenting them with a Pair of very elegant and expensive Colours, and which were greatly enhanced in value by the truly correct and energetic Speech which accompanied her kind present.[30]

In this instance Elizabeth was far from a silent domestic presence; not only was she presented to the crowd, but she was also given a platform to speak. The terms in which her intervention was framed give the impression of Elizabeth as a capable and lively performer. In the few remaining examples of her private correspondence she was similarly forthright. Writing to Lady Byam Martin in 1831, Elizabeth commiserated with her when her husband – Sir Thomas Byam Martin – lost his position as Comptroller of the Navy. She wrote in the strongest terms that 'I am so vexed and chagrined at the <u>vile ministers, whom I hate and detest</u> [original emphasis] more than is becoming a Christian should hate anything.'[31] Expressing her opposition to the Government, she declared 'they are <u>vile</u> and have <u>ruined</u> the country'. In 1833 Admiral Byam returned the favour when he publicly defended the West India colonists.[32] For Elizabeth the boundary between the public and the private world was blurred: political decisions affected the lives of her family and friends. Rather than cut herself off through a retreat into the domestic realm, she embraced respectable feminine strategies for expressing her beliefs and exerting her influence.

The second passage in George's commonplace book – 'A noble Lord to a young Lady on the eve of Marriage' – indicated that he was aware of the limitations of subscribing to an ideologically fixed representation of gender. The text parodied the ways in which lived experience exposed the gap between the ideal and the reality of marriage. The author suggested that if an argument arose the prudent wife should ask herself if she had

> philosophy enough to scratch [her] ribbon and smile good humouredly, when [her] mighty Lord struts in all his dignity across the room and gabbles his importance like an angry turkey-cock ... If you be equal to such fortitude, to such heroism, you are in my estimation a great philosopher:– in that of your turkey-cock, you will be an angel.[33]

Anticipating and undermining the mid-nineteenth-century notion of the angel in the house, the author good-humouredly subverted dominant stereotypes of masculinity and femininity by revealing the performative nature of these constructs. Whilst the text poked fun at some of the more banal conventions of gender identity, the issue of respectability was treated with greater gravity. 'Let respectability be your aim and object', the author admonished; 'be respectable in your connections, in your acquaintance, in the management of your family; but above all in your choice of intimates'. Demarcating the boundaries of acceptable behaviour for both men and women was an important part of policing middle-class respectability. The text warned against men who wrongly equated 'roughness, illmanners and brutality' with 'frankness, courage, and manliness'. Remembering George after his death, Markland wrote that 'His presence ever diffused cheerfulness. His countenance was the index of the gentleness, urbanity, and good temper, which in him were unfailing. His manners were simple and to everything which savoured of ostentation, or parade, he felt the strongest dislike.'[34] Whether in the home or the counting house, a man should display the correct forms of gentility, refinement and sensibility.

These idealised gendered and classed attributes were considered to be essential for the making of a companionate marriage which was the bedrock of harmonious family life.

Parenthood: raising daughters

The provision of children was at the heart of a Christian marriage. Elizabeth's life was dominated by pregnancy and child-rearing for over twenty years. She carried five boys and nine girls to full term – her first in 1785 and the last in 1806. Childbearing was a dangerous time for both mother and child; George's brother William lost his wife just a week after the birth of their son Charles in 1800, leaving him a widower with eight young children. In 1786, when Elizabeth was waiting to give birth to their second daughter Charlotte, George wrote anxiously to Nathaniel Phillips that 'I only wait for my Wife's being bought to Bed as please God that event is well got over.'[35] In June of 1787 Elizabeth found herself pregnant again; however, a month later the entire family contracted measles. The disease was a serious one, especially for young children. In a letter to Phillips, George noted that 'I saw Mrs Cameron [Phillips's daughter] the other day but she was afraid to come near me, when I told her our Malady.'[36] The combination of adult measles and pregnancy left Elizabeth melancholy and incapacitated. Her mother-in-law Abigail wrote to her daughter Mary regarding Elizabeth's health. In the letter she stated that:

> Dr. P is against her having any unnecessary hurry, & her own spirits are so low ... Her bodily Complaint is a Constant Confusion in her Head which followed the Measles & had Continued in a greater or less degree ever since, this is bad enough – yet the apprehension of being so soon again in the family way, gives her more Concern & together renders her unfit for general Company at present.[37]

Elizabeth eventually gave birth to a daughter, Caroline, on 21 March 1788. George wrote to Phillips to announce the birth: 'I have another Girl born, this makes the third. Where the husbands are to come from I know not.' He joked that 'my Eldest girl will be about ready for you by the time you come home; unless there should appear in a short time some very active Symptoms about you'.[38] George knew Phillips well enough to tease him about his sexual habits and the mention of 'active Symptoms' was probably a reference to venereal disease.[39] He ended the paragraph by saying he had purchased 'a good new [original emphasis] Wine that will be drinkable about the time Eliza is marriageable and we doubt not you will take care to be in time for them'.[40] Despite George's jovial tone, Phillips was a close business associate with large plantations in Jamaica. Although there was an age gap of fifty-two years between Eliza and her father's associate, he still presented an interesting prospect for consolidating the family interest. In the end Phillips married Mary Dorothea, a women who was forty years his junior.[41] As George's letter made clear, from the moment of their birth the expectation was that his daughters would be destined for marriage.

The first five of Elizabeth's pregnancies resulted in female children. On the birth of their fifth daughter, Isabella, in 1790, Abigail wrote that Elizabeth

> has brought George another fine Girl & both Mother & Child in a promising way when the letter was written. Tis rather singular that every Child she has were born upon a Friday, the little stranger I fear would have a Cool reception, but will soon make itself friends. Mrs Boardman says the next Child will be a girl also.[42]

Abigail's allusion to a 'Cool reception' for Isabella was likely owing to the couple's desire for a son. Given the structure of the family counting house, George must have been acutely aware that if he did not produce boys then the commercial empire he was building would not be passed down through his own line. George's older brothers and cousin had inherited their uncle Thomas senior's estate precisely because he had failed to produce a legitimate male heir. To George and Elizabeth's great delight, Mrs Boardman's prediction of another girl proved to be wrong and their next child was a much longed-for boy. The couple's huge brood of girls was a source of amusement for George. In 1804 he wrote to Taylor exclaiming that 'Mrs G Hibbert has given me a ninth daughter! both doing well. You see that let the times be good or bad, some trades will flourish!'[43] Despite his good humour, having nine daughters had significant financial implications. George commented to Taylor that the additional income he would receive on becoming Agent for Jamaica was for 'a man with eleven children and more on the Stork ... a consideration'.[44] Given George and Elizabeth's social aspirations, the couple sought good matches for all their children. The burden of having such a large number of daughters lay in first finding suitable alliances and then providing the financial incentives to make them marriageable. Unlike his sons, who took on professions to support themselves, the Hibbert girls would be dependent on their father until married.

George and Elizabeth instilled in their daughters a sense of correct middle-class morals and manners. Like all young girls of social standing they needed impeccable reputations to make good marriages. Respectability and virtue were highly prized when combined with a decent marriage portion and useful family connections. George's commonplace book sheds light on some of his parental expectations. It contained a number of his own original compositions, ranging from morally instructive to sentimental poetry dedicated to his daughters. For Eliza's twenty-eighth birthday in 1813 he wrote a poem, 'To be spoken by her four youngest sisters, on presenting a wreath of roses'.[45] The poem likened his daughter to a rose in bloom, full of youthful blushes and 'belov'd by virtue'. The text offers an insight into George's sense of the proper feminine character; Eliza was idealised as 'modest', 'genial' and 'mild'. George's poetry was designed to both elevate and educate his daughters. When his daughter Octavia lost her pet linnet he penned a poem to cheer her, which also acted as a cautionary tale on the perils of 'unguarded freedom'. He wrote:

> Will, let my dear Octavia treasure
> For e'en from this unpolished strain,
> An useful lesson she may gain.
> The wise restraint, the daily Task,
> Which Teachers on which Mothers ask,
> The dictates of experienced age,
> May seem too like the Linnet's Cage;
> And she too fain would wing her flight
> To scenes of unconstrain'd delight
> But, from unguarded freedom, flow
> Ills that Octavia cannot know;
> And girls who from their Parent's side,
> Rush on the dangerous world untried;
> Victims of one uncautious minute,
> Shall perish like the Truant Linnet.[46]

Not surprisingly for a man so heavily involved in the business of slavery, George regarded unfettered freedom as a dangerous state for those that he deemed unready or unable to negotiate it. Young girls should heed the wisdom of their elders and remain within the protective confines of their sphere of influence. Those that strayed incautiously into the world beyond the gilded cage faced a perilous future.

George's writings were not solely devoted to the moulding of his children. They also include examples of his warmth and genuine feeling. In 1814, when his fifteen-year-old daughter Mary Ann was ill, he composed a poem which he transcribed on to the back of his own miniature portrait. This intimate token of affection was designed to offer comfort and succour by reminding Mary Ann of her father's love and concern. He wrote:

> Should e'er the unwelcome couch of pain

II: INTIMATE RELATIONS: THE METROPOLE

> Thy throbbing limbs, dear Maid, sustain,
> Then look on this, and call to mind
> Thy cares in nursing, watchful, kind
> And still with pleasing smiles endear'd
> Which long a Father's anguish cheer'd –
>
> And may those thoughts with lustre bright,
> Like stars that guild the Winter's night,
> Beam on thy prayers relief divine,
> And pay the love that sustain'd mine.[47]

Both the poem and the method of its conveyance reveal George as a caring, thoughtful and devoted father. His gift would remind Mary Ann of his paternal presence and soothe her in her times of need.

George and Elizabeth's parental ministrations paid off, as the marriage records of five of their daughters show. The first to wed were the couple's second and third daughters, Charlotte and Caroline. The double wedding took place at Holy Trinity Church in Clapham in 1808. Charlotte married the Reverend Job Walker Baugh, the chancellor of the diocese of Bristol. Caroline married her cousin Samuel. As Davidoff and Hall have argued, the marriage of cousins 'provided a form of security' in that it acted as a 'guarantee of congenial views as well as trustworthiness in economic and financial affairs'.[48] Samuel's father died at Nantes in 1786 when his son was only three years old. George stepped into his brother's shoes and supported his widow Mary. She recounted in a letter that she preferred to have her children schooled in London because 'their uncles will act as parents to them'.[49] The marriage represented a way in which George could support both his dead brother's son and his own daughter. Samuel worked with his father-in-law in the merchant house, and marrying Caroline confirmed the bonds of business and kinship. Fanny, the couple's fourth daughter, married the Reverend Charles Tower, the perpetual curate of Brentwood, Essex, in 1814. That two of George's daughters were married to Anglican clergymen is indicative of George's determination to break with his family's dissenting identity. Anglicanism offered a greater degree of social acceptance, and whatever his private beliefs were, George subscribed to the established church and raised his children in the Anglican faith. Harriet and Georgiana both married in 1828. Harriet was wed to Robert John Malet Palk, the son of Sir Lawrence Palk and Lady Dorothy Elizabeth Vaughan. Georgiana married William Marshall of Patterdale Hall, a wealthy heir and at different times the Member of Parliament for Beverley, Carlisle and East Cumberland.[50] These were solid, respectable unions which added to the Hibberts' reputation and relieved George of the financial burden of so many dependent females.

At least two of George's daughters did not marry. Spinsterhood was not a condition that young women were encouraged to aspire to. In depleted circumstances unmarried females could fall on hard times. Very few opportunities for work were open to middle-class women, although some found the position of governess provided a means to sustain them. If their family could afford to support them they were saved from this indignity, but there was often the expectation that in lieu of having a husband and children of their own they should instead be in attendance for parents, brother and sisters. Unmarried or widowed relatives were often called upon to help care for young children, the sick or the elderly. Among George's own siblings only his sister Esther remained unmarried. She was the subject of several family letters, including one from her brother Robert junior, who displayed a distinct lack of compassion for her situation. Writing in 1790 to congratulate his sister Mary Oates on the birth of her first child Anna Maria, he warned that:

> Esther is fond of Children, and fond of kissing and having no object at Newton Heath to divide her attention will be apt to kiss it too much if you do not keep a sharp look out. Why does Esther not get married herself? ... if I am not much deceived she has no heart to lose.[51]

Esther's love of children was also noted by her mother Abigail, who described Esther's reaction to the birth of her niece as almost a kind of hysteria. She wrote that Esther was

> so violently agitated that Mrs. T. Robinson (to whom she ran as soon as possible) was quite angry with her for not having more self Command – I was thankful she had not fallen downstairs bringing the letter to me, and her trembling was so great she [could] neither stand nor speak, tears relieved her, but she did not rest.[52]

Did this outburst stem from an overwhelming joy for her sister? Did it spring from her sheer relief that Mary and Anna Maria had survived the dangers of childbirth? Or was it an uncontrollable expression of a deep, unfulfilled longing? There is no way of telling. In different ways both her mother's and her brother's letter gestured towards the ways in which single women were sometimes caricatured. In the first instance she was deemed hard-hearted and in the second borderline hysterical, her lack of a husband and children making her alternately both lacking in and overcome by emotion. Abigail worried about what would happen to Esther 'when I am gone'.[53] There was a plan for her to lodge at Halton in Cheshire but she fretted 'if the Halton scheme does not suit, she is quite alone'. The fate of unmarried women following the death of their parents could be a source of concern and provisions had to be made to ensure that they did not slip into genteel poverty.

In the case of George's unmarried daughters, the two women appeared to have led a comfortable life facilitated by his financial support. The independently minded owner of the absconded linnet, Octavia, initially lived at 105 St George's Road, Pimlico. By 1861 she had moved to Cookham in Berkshire, where her cousin John Hibbert of Braywick Lodge was an esteemed member of the community. The census for that year documented Octavia as an unmarried fifty-eight-year-old woman of private fortune. The record showed that she was head of the household, with four domestic servants – three women and one man – as her dependants.[54] She died at St Margaret's, Dorking, in 1882, leaving an estate of £37,506 17s 3d, which she divided among her nephews and nieces.[55] Octavia's eldest sister Eliza also remained unmarried. The 1871 census listed her as head of the household for a property at 11 Cavendish House, Bath.[56] Like her sister Octavia, Eliza was a woman of independent means and her occupation was listed as 'dividend fundholder'. The household consisted of six servants – four women and two men. Interestingly she also had her elderly widower brother-in-law William Marshall and niece Georgiana Marshall living with her. Despite William's presence in the house it was Eliza who was listed as head of the household. When she died in 1875 she left the substantial sum of £50,000.[57]

Parenthood: raising sons

On 23 September 1792 George and Elizabeth welcomed their first son into the world. George junior represented the continuation of the family name and business. Their joy, however, was short-lived. In 1795 Robert junior noted in his diary that 'George's little boy is taken sick. One day he is so bad that George cannot leave him.'[58] Five days later the couple's son died aged two. Having waited eight years for his arrival, his loss must have been devastating. In his commonplace book George had carefully copied out a poem by Herrick capturing a parent's private grief:

> But born, and like a short delight,
> I glided by my parent's sight:
> That done, the harder fates denied
> My longer stay, and so I died.
>
> If pitying my sad parents' tears,
> You'll spill a tear or two with theirs,
> And with some flowers my grave bestrew,
> Love and they'll thank you for't. Adieu![59]

The little boy was buried in St Paul's churchyard in Clapham. Positioned in a prominent plot, his chest tomb can still be seen today. Reflecting the social mixture of Clapham's inhabitants, the Hibberts shared the graveyard with both their abolitionist opponents and some of the African children that were brought from Sierra Leone to Clapham by Zachary Macaulay in 1799.[60]

Despite their loss George and Elizabeth might have taken comfort in the fact that their first son was followed by three boys in quick succession: Nathaniel in 1794, George junior in 1796 and Edward in 1797. The couple's final child, Henry, arrived nearly a decade later in 1806. Just as with their sisters, the boys were expected to conform to their parents' expectations. George had been 'destined from his boyhood to a commercial life', but he wanted more for his boys than the limited options of his own childhood.[61] One of the first changes he made was his decision to eschew the dissenting academies; instead George sent Nathaniel to Winchester and George junior to Eton. These prestigious schools were the training ground of the nation's elite. As Linda Colley has noted, by 1800 'over 70 per cent of all English peers received their education at just four public schools, Eton, Westminster, Winchester and Harrow'.[62] These institutions aimed to transform boys into men through the combination of rigidly gendered isolation, patriotic inculcation, manly sportsmanship and harsh corporal punishment. Following public school Nathaniel and George junior attended Trinity College, Cambridge for their bachelor's degree. George junior continued his studies and was eventually awarded a master's. Colley has linked an Oxbridge education to the moulding of British imperial masculinity, with undergraduates invited to write essays on topics such as 'the best means of civilising subjects of the British empire'.[63]

Having finished their studies, Nathaniel and George junior needed suitable professions. It was the duty of a middle-class father to select a career for his son that would offer respectability and the chance for elevation. George's brother Robert junior wrote to their sister Mary discussing the issue:

> George proposes to send his eldest Son to the East Indies and his third to the Navy. My Bro William also has a Son who in a very short time must be provided for some way or another, and my Second Son has now left Eton and I know not what to do with him. He is unfortunately very peaceably inclined or he should follow his Brother into the Army.[64]

Robert junior's revelation that George was considering sending Nathaniel to the East Indies is surprising, given that George had described India as a dumping ground for the 'younger Sons and bastards of Noblemen and Members of the House of Commons'.[65] It is possible that in the wake of the abolition of the slave trade in 1807, George recognised the necessity of diversifying the family interest. Perhaps he hoped to call on his sister-in-law's husband George Woodford Thellusson, a Director of the East India Company, to secure a position for Nathaniel. Given George's denunciations of the East India interest's encroachment on West Indian privileges, this could have been a politically awkward move. In 1809 George wrote to Taylor telling him that he was thinking of sending his eldest to Jamaica instead. Given the high rates of mortality, it was a difficult decision. Parental fear for a cherished child had to be balanced with the needs of the family business. The emotional bind of competing familial obligations can be read in George's letter:

> I am thinking of sending my eldest boy to Jamaica as soon as he is fit for it. He must take his chance and work for his Brothers and Sisters for all our hopes are there and we cannot expect Friends and Strangers to take a warm Interest in promoting that which we do not think it worth our while to put the hand to. I wish however we could see the Island somewhat more favourable to the health of newcomers than it has lately been.[66]

George knew the risks attached to colonial life, both his uncle John senior and his brother John junior had died young on the island. This experience left him anxious for the well-being of his son and heir. In the end it was George's youngest boy, Henry, who made the journey to Jamaica in 1825. Shortly after his arrival his father's worst fears were confirmed when Henry died, aged twenty. A memorial inscription commemorating his short life was installed in Kingston Cathedral.

As controversy swirled around the issue of slavery, George decided to keep his eldest son Nathaniel at a distance from the family's commercial affairs. The far less contentious profession of the law was settled upon instead. In 1814 Nathaniel moved to Lincoln's Inn, where he was called to the bar as a barrister-at-law. The separation was not entirely complete and he did occasionally involve himself with the family business. As heir to the estate at Munden, Nathaniel would eventually become a country gentleman. In 1828 he married Emily Smith, the daughter of the renowned wit the Reverend Sydney Smith. It seems that George was wise to keep his eldest boy away from the counting house. A letter from Smith to Lady Gray in 1827 betrayed a degree of anxiety regarding Nathaniel's association with the West Indies. As Nicholas Draper has pointed out, the letter 'characterised George Hibbert as "the Indian" rather than *West* Indian [italics original], merchant: Nathaniel he described as "Mr Hibbert of the North

Circuit ... a sensible high-minded young man who will eventually be well off".[67] Despite Smith's apprehensions regarding the source of Nathaniel's fortune, his future wealth was enough to convince the Reverend of his suitability. Nathaniel and Emily had a daughter Elizabeth in 1834 and it was through her line that Munden was passed along the generations.

Nathaniel's future was far more secure than that of his younger brothers, who could not look forward to the inheritance that their older brother would enjoy. As discussed in Chapter 3, after finishing university George junior joined the Hibberts' London counting house, eventually becoming a significant commercial figure in his own right. Unlike his two brothers, Edward did not attend university but instead fulfilled his father's ambition of having a son in the Royal Navy. On the advice of the Duke of Clarence, Edward entered the Royal Navy in 1810, aged thirteen.[68] The timing was inauspicious for new recruits, Britain was still locked into the Napoleonic Wars and in 1812 conflict with America also broke out. By putting his son in the Navy, George was able to demonstrate his commitment to the nation and the empire by making the ultimate sacrifice. During the period naval recruits were subject to heavy discipline, including the use of flogging. As the son of a wealthy merchant, Edward enjoyed his fair share of privilege and was spared the extreme forms of violence that lower-ranking seamen were subjected to. On discovering that his son had been posted to the *Ganymede* under Captain Robert Cavendish Spencer, George wrote to his brother, Lord John Charles Spencer, to secure an introduction for Edward. Lord Spencer and George knew each other socially through their shared membership of the bibliophile Roxburghe Club. In 1818 George informed Lord Spencer that 'Capt. Spencer kindly took my young Lieutenant to Rome and patronised him there. The story of "the Fortunate Youth" is not altogether a fable!'[69] Captain Spencer ensured that George's son was well treated; when Edward was ill he reported that Spencer 'sent me on board the *Creole* with such representations that the Commodore gave me up his After Cabin'.[70] Seemingly unaware of his father's intercession, Edward ended his letter asking, 'What have I done or can do to deserve all this kindness?'

George's pride in his son's naval exploits was evident from a poem he wrote in 1811 which gives an insight into George's notions of manliness and patriotism:

Our favourite indeed you will not find,
The objects round will bring him to your mind.
The gallant Boy, inspired by Nelson's story,

II: INTIMATE RELATIONS: THE METROPOLE

> Toils, under Britain's flags for naval glory.
> Perhaps, just now, the tedious watch to cheer,
> His fancy pictures what is passing here.
> And from the Sailor's heart a sigh may come
> At thoughts of distant friends and well remember'd home.
> Comrade go on – pursue thy destin'd way:
> The Muse prophetic hails the coming day
> When, on a nobler stage thy deeds may shine
> And plaudits from thy Country's hands be thine![71]

The Navy would transform the 'gallant Boy' into a 'Sailor', his masculinity forged in battle with a foreign enemy. Described by his father as 'Our favourite', Edward was the prodigal son whose absence was required for the higher purpose of defending the realm. There was no doubt in George's mind that naval service would lead to heroic glory. The Hibberts' close identification with the empire of the seas was evident throughout George's speeches on the slave trade. The Hibberts engaged in continuous overseas trade and owned a fleet of ships, and both in Jamaica and London they spent a good deal of time among the ranks of Britain's seafaring elite. Having a son in the Royal Navy further consolidated George's affinity with maritime culture, creating new networks of influence and patronage among the officer class of one of Britain's most powerful institutions.

George's poetic depiction of the scene on board the ship betrayed no hint of the horror of naval service during the period. In 1815 Edward nearly lost his eye during an attack against a battery in Algiers.[72] The reality of a live conflict finally penetrated the Hibberts' household. Absent from home for long periods, 'thoughts of distant friends and well remember'd home' no doubt entered Edward's mind. Family letters were a welcome link to the safety of domestic life. The correspondence was a form of emotional reassurance for George as well – in a letter to Lord Spencer he fretted over 'rather an unusual silence on the part of Edward'.[73] As with sending a son to the West Indies, George's anxieties stemmed from the very real prospect of him not returning. Eventually Edward did come back safely from the war, but was struck down by a fever in 1824 whilst in Edinburgh attending a lecture. His death, followed swiftly by that of his younger brother Henry in Jamaica, must have come as a heavy blow for the Hibberts. Their children were raised in the protected environs of leafy Clapham. Sheltered from the perils of the city they were reared in a genteel fashion; their education, surroundings and acquaintances were polite and ordered, as they themselves were expected to be. Whether at home or out in the empire, they could not be shielded from the great levellers of death and disease.

Abolitionist intersections

For twenty-eight years George and Elizabeth's family life centred on their home in Clapham. They were eventually joined in the area by George's widowed sister-in-law Mary in 1800 and his brother William in 1812. Clapham's social mixture tells a fascinating story of the intermingling between abolitionist and proslavery supporters. As a popular mercantile area, the Common was home to a number of those who derived a living from their involvement in the West Indies. Herman Sillem, a European and West India merchant, resided at 29 Clapham Common West Side between 1824 and 1848.[74] The Grange, Clapham Common West Side, was built in 1762 by the Antigua-born West India merchant Christopher Baldwin. Baldwin's family were early settlers on the island and owned plantations both there and in Dominica. They lived there until 1801.[75] In 1775 William Vassall leased Front Hall in Clapham following his departure from Boston in the wake of the American Revolution. Vassall owned plantations in Jamaica.[76] The Wedderburns also lived on the Common. They were both plantation owners in Jamaica and West India merchants in London. They traded through the mercantile partnership Wedderburn, Webster & Company. A tutor of the young James Webster Wedderburn – John Campbell, the future Lord Chancellor – remembered his time in the house:

> I found my situation from the beginning very irksome, and it became more and more unbearable. The company frequenting the house consisted chiefly of West India merchants and East India captains, and the conversation turned on the price of sugars, the rate of freights, and the trifling gossip of the day.[77]

Campbell's description gives an indication of the blend of social and commercial interactions that took place within the mercantile home. From his residence in Clapham, George played host to a similar mix of personal and professional visitors, including merchants, ship's captains, members of the admiralty, politicians and absentee Jamaica planters. George frequently conducted business meetings in his home including in his capacity as Chairman of the West India Dock Company.[78] It is extraordinary to think that as the Saints planned the abolition campaign from their homes in Clapham, simultaneously the business of slavery was being conducted by their neighbours.

A map of Clapham Common in 1800 demonstrates the close proximity within which the political opponents lived. The path leading to William Wilberforce's residence Bromfield House was sandwiched in between the abodes of Christopher Baldwin and John Wedderburn.

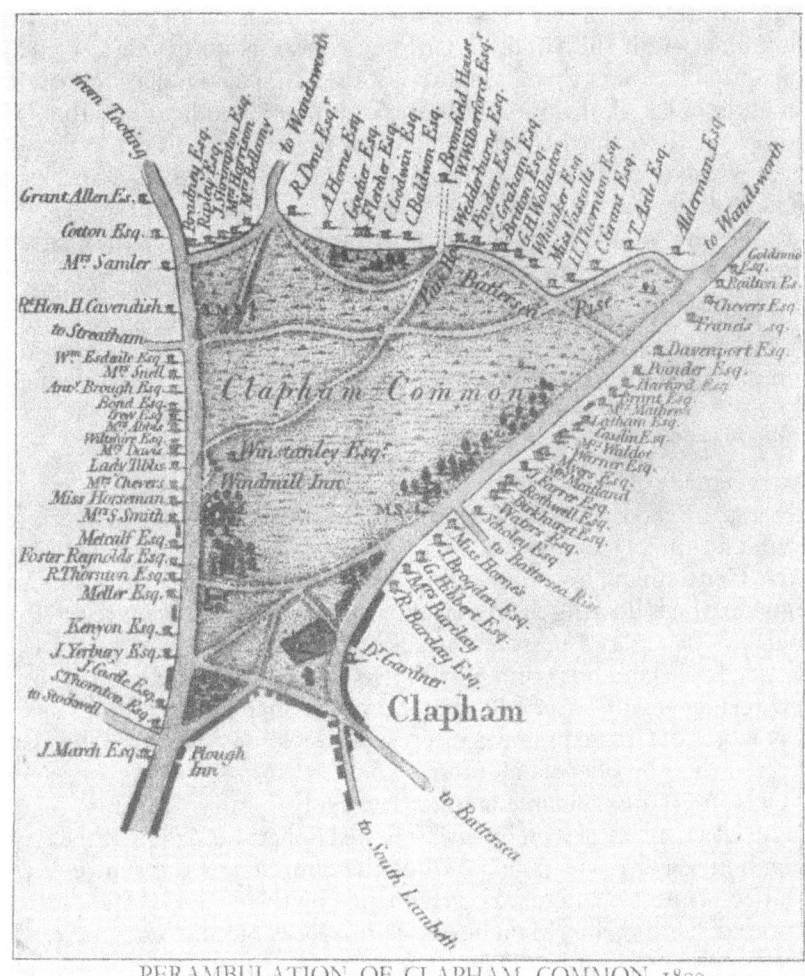

PERAMBULATION OF CLAPHAM COMMON 1800.

Figure 8 Perambulation of Clapham Common, 1800, in C. Smith, *The chronicles of Clapham Common, being a selection from the reminiscences of Thomas Parsons, sometime member of the Clapham Antiquarian Society*

Henry Thornton lived next door to the Vassalls. The Hibberts' neighbour was the Quaker brewer Robert Barclay, an active member of the London Abolition Committee. In the midst of her conversion, George's mixed-heritage cousin Jane Harry had visited Barclay at his home in Bury Hill before he moved to Clapham.[79] The Hibberts and their abolitionist neighbours inhabited the same space, they attended the same church and there was at least one occasion in which a visit took place with the Hibberts, although there is no evidence of what transpired between them. On 24 May 1812 Martha Frances Smith, the daughter of the abolitionist William Smith, noted in her diary that 'My Father went to the Hibberts'.[80] This was not their first interaction, in the midst of the slave trade debates in 1807 Smith had suggested to George that if his family had not been so entangled in the slavery business he would not support proslavery. George replied thanking him for his kindly meant letter, but stated that:

> It is possible that had I not been as you say, thrown on the Slave Trade Question I might not have taken a very active part in it. Having been so thrown, however I have given the Subject my best attention & during its discussion have never committed the sincere violation upon my Inclination or my Conviction.[81]

George made it clear that he believed himself to be acting rationally and in good conscience. Despite George noting that Wilberforce regarded him as 'the only one of his opponents who had treated him like a Gentleman', his relationship with the abolitionists grew increasingly hostile following the renewal of the campaign in the mid-1810s.[82] Zachary Macaulay's personal attack on the Hibbert family in *Negro slavery* (1823) did not come until after George had left Clapham for a new residence at Portland Place. Occupying such close confines as the cosy world of Clapham raises interesting questions over how the issue affected their broader social interactions.

One site of unavoidable contact was Holy Trinity Clapham, which was used as a place of worship by both the Hibberts and their antislavery neighbours. For respectable families the church was the centre of the local community, and regular attendance by the entire household was expected. Unlike his Manchester family, George did not outwardly practise non-conformity. There is no positive evidence that he ascribed to Unitarianism, although he appears in a list of 'supposed' dissenting politicians drawn up by D. W. Bebbington.[83] With legislation still in place to bar non-conformists from taking political office, adherence to the Anglican faith was crucial for George to join the parliamentary faction of the West India interest. An indication of his sympathy towards the position of dissenters can be traced in his parliamentary voting record, since on entering the Commons, George supported Catholic emancipation and political reform.[84] George's social and commercial circles embraced a number of influential dissenters, including Richard Sharp, Samuel Rogers, Samuel Boddington and Benjamin Vaughan. Despite this George chose to raise his children in the established church and had them baptised at Holy Trinity Clapham, St Boltoph's Bishopsgate

II: INTIMATE RELATIONS: THE METROPOLE

and St Dunstan's in the East.[85] As with his choices for their education, George made sure to place no potential barriers in the way of his children's social advancement.

In 1792 John Venn, a leading member of the Clapham Sect and a committed abolitionist, was appointed Rector of Holy Trinity Clapham. The church constituted a sacred space for this close-knit group of Evangelicals; it was their spiritual sanctuary, a place in which their beliefs were formulated and lived. Whilst there was no bar to the Hibberts using it as a place of worship, one must wonder how the Saints felt about the presence of a family who were so publicly in opposition to their stance on slavery. The social importance of church life can be read in a dispute between George and Peter Dobrée which broke out over who was the rightful claimant to a much-coveted pew. When George first started attending the church in 1793 he was relegated to pew 19, middle aisle. By 1798 he had moved closer to the altar by acquiring pew 12, middle aisle. In 1800 pew 9, south middle aisle, became vacant, a pew whose position was highly desirable and was the furthest forward anyone had ever been able to move, the front pews never having become available. The trustees noted that the pew would be awarded to whoever had moved to the area first and if neither could prove decisively when they arrived, then preference would be given to Dobrée, 'for the services he has rendered the Parish'.[86] In the end George was able to demonstrate that he had lived there longer and was duly awarded the prime seating. His prominent position within the church reflected his status; in claiming the disputed pew he was laying claim to his right to be seen and acknowledged as an established and important member of the congregation. George also paid for the use of eight seats for his servants. In 1801 the trustees' minute book contained a note that said he was not to be allocated any more. The comical round of musical chairs played by the great and good of Holy Trinity Clapham is indicative of the importance of the family's visibility in the religious life of the community. As George went to church each Sunday, accompanied by his wife, their ever-growing brood of children and their servants, he presented the picture of respectable Christian middle-class masculinity. In 1797 George's name appeared on a list of trustees responsible for 'the Act for Vesting a piece of Waste Ground within and Parcel of the Manor of Clapham in the County of Surrey, in Trustees, and for enabling them to Build a new Parish Church thereon'.[87] With a thriving congregation Holy Trinity Clapham needed to build a new chapel of rest to accommodate the dead of the parish. George was one of the subscribers who helped to fund what would eventually become St Paul's Clapham. It was here that his firstborn son and brother William were buried. George's attendance at,

THE BONDS OF FAMILY

and monetary contributions to, Holy Trinity Clapham implicated the church and its congregation in the web of financial beneficiaries of the Hibberts' involvement with slavery.

At home with the Hibberts

The Hibberts lived at 31 North Side Clapham Common. Clapham was a popular destination for those seeking to follow the eighteenth-century fashion for suburban villas, indeed George's brother Robert junior referred to the house as 'George's Villa'.[88] These properties were designed to approximate rural living, although in 1807 Wilberforce dismissed Clapham as a 'poor mimicry of the real (live) country'.[89] The fashion for suburban living was a subject treated by numerous satirists, including the writer Robert Lloyd, who penned 'The Cit's country box' in 1756. The poem was prefaced with the lines 'O Cit thrice happy, that canst range / To *Bow* or *Clapham* from the *'Change*; [italics original] / In whose spruce *Villa* is display'd / The plumb, thou hast acquir'd by trade!'[90] What these literary imaginings underscored was the central importance of the home as a site for the construction of identity. The grounds and the interior projected an intimate expression of personal taste to both the outside world and those who penetrated its inner sanctum. One of George's relations, Sir George Philips, described his abode as 'a beautiful house with books and pictures of great value, hot-houses, etc.'.[91] Although this period witnesses the emergence of separate spheres, the home cannot be characterised as simply a feminine space. As John Tosh's work on middle-class masculinity has demonstrated, the domestic realm was central to a man's sense of self.[92] The descriptions that exist of the Hibberts' residence documented the dominant influence of George's taste. Referring to George as Honorio, his friend and fellow bibliophile the Reverend Thomas Frognall Dibdin wrote:

> [T]he mansion of Honorio is both capacious and richly furnished. And his *Albanos* [italics original], his *Annibal Caraccis, Murillos, Berghems, Bassans*, and *Cuyps*! All these – in a Palladio-proportioned room, some twenty-five feet in height – are the rich accompaniment of his stained-glass book-vistos, and scattered and classically-embellished libraries.[93]

The sumptuousness of the decorative flourishes caused Dibdin to gush further: 'Or shall we recline in his membranaceous *Palace of Pleasure* [italics original]? Oh the luxury of that abode! The felicities which his taste and his well-replenished purse impart!' As an avid collector of books, art and botanical specimens, George was amply supplied with objects and plants to adorn his home and garden. Markland was at pains to emphasise the 'purity and discrimination' of George's taste, although he was quick to add that its demands 'never tempted him towards cupidity or selfishness'.[94] For the discerning patron of the arts there was a fine balance between the display of taste and vulgar exhibitionism.

A sales advertisement from 1820 gave a detailed account of the property, allowing a glimpse into how the family inhabited the space. Introduced as a 'capacious family home', the 'very commodious brick built residence' was offered as a freehold property set in 11 acres of grounds.[95] A separate lot of 5 acres and 2 perches stretching down to Wandsworth Road was also on offer. The estate commanded 'a Frontage to the Common of One Hundred and Seventy-seven Feet'. In 1795 it was recorded that 'Mr. Hibbert is allowed to fence in a piece of ground from the Common, opposite his house, and to plant trees for the ornament of the Common.'[96] Putting his reputation as an amateur botanist into practice for the collective good of the residents allowed George to demonstrate his neighbourly benevolence. In keeping with the semi-agrarian aspirations of his new home, George's property included pleasure grounds, gardens and rich meadow land. A professional gardener was employed to attend to George's famed collection of rare plants. The land was described as 'productive and extensive' and included a dairy, a range of forcing houses, grapery, greenhouse, kitchen garden, herb garden, melon ground, fruit trees, a tool house, outbuildings, a cow house, a piggery and a paddock. For 'a fair Valuation' purchasers also had the opportunity to buy 'Stoves, Coppers, Ranges, Bells, Pumps and Pipes, the Steam Apparatus, and usual Fixtures'. The property also had detached offices which housed 'Three Cellars for Wine, Ale Cellar etc.'. With its elegant blend of the ornate and the practical, George's property adhered to the requirements of a fashionable mercantile villa.

On entering the Hibberts' home visitors moved through the entrance hall and were ushered into a lobby fitted out as a library. This arrangement allowed George to impress upon his guests the cultural capital that his literary investments signified. Just off the lobby a further two ground-floor rooms had been similarly altered and upstairs on the first floor a purpose-built library was located, so that altogether four areas of the house were filled with George's prized possessions. There were several rooms for entertaining; friends and family members could socialise in the 25ft by 18ft dining parlour. More formal gatherings took place in an 'elegantly fitted up drawing room or saloon, 36ft. by 24ft. and 18ft. high', replete with 'costly marble chimney-pieces'. Its size allowed for large-scale dinner parties, dancing and theatrical performances. This room was without doubt the magnificent centrepiece of the Hibberts' abode. It was dominated by a specially commissioned painted frieze by Henry Howard RA depicting 'The Fable of Cupid and Psyche'. As a member of the Society of Antiquaries, the choice reflected George's love of classical civilisation.

The family's private rooms were on the upper floors. With fourteen children to house the living quarters were extensive. There were nine bedrooms, three on the first floor and a further six in the second storey, accessed via a grand double staircase. As the family rose in the morning to prepare for the day they had the use of three dressing rooms, house closets and a water closet, all of which were situated on the first floor. Two servants' bedrooms were situated on this floor so that they could be easily summoned to assist the family. The Hibberts' early hours might have been passed in what was described as 'a cheerful Morning Room'. With the sunlight streaming through the large windows on the first floor, this room provided Elizabeth with a place in which to entertain, write letters and spend time with her family. As Robert junior's diary recorded, there was a steady stream of relations calling at the house, including the Gregs, Thellussons and Fonnereaus as well as numerous Hibberts who came to visit from northern England. Whilst Elizabeth might be found in the morning room, her children were likely familiar with the music room, located on the second floor. With nine daughters, the couple would have been keen to make sure their girls were suitably endowed with the requisite feminine skills to make them marriageable. Playing an instrument and being able to hold a tune were just such desirable qualities.

The residence in Clapham also encompassed a wider household which included the domestic staff. The sales advertisement registered a 'neat Gardener's Cottage of Four Rooms', four servants' rooms, a 'Housekeeper's Room' and a 'Man's Room'. The records give no indication of how many people occupied the various spaces, though the inclusion of a separate 'Servant's Hall' gives an impression of the number of staff employed by the Hibberts. As the mistress of the house, overseeing the management of the domestic staff would have been one of Elizabeth's primary tasks. The functional aspects of the house were indicative of the types of labour required to ensure that the family's standards were maintained. Those features included a store room, kitchen, two sculleries, larder, washhouse, coal vaults and butler's pantry. Despite the house being 'excellently supplied with good Water', cleaning and cooking in a property of this size would have required monotonous hard work. With nine family bedrooms, the care of the linen alone was an arduous task. Alongside this there were another twelve rooms in use, not to mention all the servants' quarters to be kept clean and orderly. The support of the workforce (both in Britain and Jamaica) and of his wife was essential for George to be able to present his family as respectable and prosperous. George conceived of himself as the family patriarch and he remembered his senior servants in his will. The housekeeper, cook and bailiff each received between £20 and £25, whilst George's butler, James Bright, was bequeathed 'the sum of one hundred pounds and all my wearing apparel'.[97] These were generous legacies and an indication of the largesse that George considered to be the duty of the benevolent merchant. When contemplating how to remember his staff for their years of domestic service, one wonders if George ever spared a thought for those many thousands of enslaved people whose life-long labour went unrewarded.

Conclusion

The Hibberts' home in Clapham was an outward display of their identity – a sign of their wealth and status. It was filled with exotic plants, fine art and rare books, symbols of Enlightenment culture that created a sense of the family as fashionable and cosmopolitan. Materially rebutting abolitionist claims that slavery brutalised the enslaver, the house and gardens reflected a vision of urbane metropolitan civilisation. At the house in Clapham the degradation of slavery was transformed into a world of polite amusements, elegant furnishings and domestic harmony. George never visited the Caribbean, he never saw for himself the conditions under which people laboured and the ways in which family life was undermined. Distanced from the brutal means of production, the wealth generated through the slave economy financed the Hibberts' genteel aspirations, enabling them to create a family idyll within the abolitionist heartlands of Clapham.

Despite their differences, George lived amongst the abolitionists for nearly three decades. From his writings it is clear that he aligned himself with habits and manners which were shaped by the dictates of culture, gender, class and religion. His private life echoed that of his opponents much more closely than that of his family in Jamaica. The open toleration of illegitimate children and mistresses was not a feature of life for this metropolitan branch of the Hibberts. There was also a greater degree of stability for George and his family; unlike his brother Robert junior, who spent the best part of two decades traversing the Atlantic, George settled into the daily rhythms of home and work. When he returned from the merchant house he was attended to by the household servants and not a retinue of enslaved labourers. Respectability was central to George's public and private life, necessary for both his reputation as a merchant and for securing the prospects of his children. When he stood up in Parliament and lamented the decline of the family in the wake of industrialisation, George could turn and point to his own as a model of Christian middle-class domesticity. In making his case for the defence of slavery, George argued that it would be decent families, widows and children who would suffer as a consequence of abolition. In contrast to public representations of the slave owner as a colonial despot, the metropolitan Hibberts constructed a home and an identity that was polite and moral. Following a targeted abolitionist campaign directed towards the Hibberts in the 1820s, this carefully crafted visage became increasingly difficult to maintain. For the Hibberts their involvement with slavery was at once both the foundations that supported the edifice of respectability and the reputational crack that threatened to destabilise it altogether. Their image rested on their ability to control and contain the familial slippages that emerged as a result of their colonial transgressions.

In 1820 the house was put up for sale and the Hibberts relocated to 38 Portland Place. The geographic shift from Clapham to Marylebone, an enclave of absentee planters, saw the family move closer into the circles of West India influence. With the slavery debates reignited in the early 1820s, the move reduced the likelihood of uncomfortable social encounters. The departure of the slave owners from the Common paved the way for a forgetting of their presence, but markers remain to tell their stories. The 'Saints' of Clapham Common are now synonymous with the story of abolition. London County Council and English Heritage plaques celebrate the area's importance to British antislavery. The familiar names of Wilberforce, Macaulay, Stephen and Thornton are remembered in local histories and street names in the area. The Hibberts also have a road named after them – Hibbert Street, off York Road – although it is doubtful whether many current residents know of the Hibberts' history or their association with slavery. During the bicentenary of the abolition of the slave trade in 2007, historian Steve Martin produced a walking tour which reconnected the Hibbert family to the local area. Challenging an official narrative that emphasised Wilberforce and the Saints, Martin problematised the traditional memory of Clapham as simply the seat of pious abolitionism. In doing so he demonstrated the ways in which proslavery advocates and their slave-produced wealth penetrated into the social, financial, cultural and material fabric of London. In this way Clapham's history of abolitionist and proslavery entanglements, including both their commemoration and erasure, speaks to Britain's own historical identification as both enslaver and emancipator.

II: INTIMATE RELATIONS: THE METROPOLE

Notes

Part I Intimate relations: the colony

1 Vere Langford Oliver, *Caribbeana: Being miscellaneous papers relating to the history, genealogy, topography, and antiquities of the British West Indies*, vol. IV (London: Mitchell Hughes and Clarke, 1919), p. 194.
2 Barbara Bush, *Slave women in the Caribbean 1650–1838* (London: James Curry, 1990), p. 111.
3 Trevor Burnard, 'Credit, Kingston merchants and the Atlantic slave trade in the eighteenth century' (unpublished paper for British Group of Early American Historians, Stirling, 3 September 2009), p. 16.
4 HFAC, Diary of Robert Hibbert junior, 1 October 1779.
5 For an in-depth discussion of these issues in relation to Simon Taylor and Grace Donne see Meleisa Ono-George, '"Washing the Blackamoor White": Interracial intimacy and coloured women's agency in Jamaica', in Will Jackson and Emily Manktelow (eds), *Subverting empire: Deviance and disorder in the British colonial world* (Basingstoke: Palgrave Macmillan, 2015), pp. 42–60.
6 Adele Perry, *Colonial families: The Douglas-Connolly family and the nineteenth-century imperial world* (Cambridge: Cambridge University Press, 2015), p. 20.
7 Philip Wright (ed.), *Lady Nugent's journal* (Kingston: University of the West Indies Press, 2002), p. 68.
8 Henrice Altink, *Representations of slave women in discourses of slavery and abolition, 1780–1838* (Abingdon: Routledge, 2007).
9 John Stewart, *A view of the past and present state of the island of Jamaica* (Edinburgh: Oliver & Boyd, 1823), p. 173.
10 TNA/COP, CO/137/158/28, Letter from George Hibbert to Earl Bathurst, 5 February 1824.
11 Thomas senior described Charity as his housekeeper in his will. The historiography of their relationship, and that of their children includes; Joseph J. Green, 'Jenny Harry, later Thresher (circa 1756–1784)', *Friends Quarterly Examiner* (1913), pp. 559–82; Joseph J. Green, 'Jenny Harry, later Thresher (circa 1756–1784) (concluded)', *Friends Quarterly Examiner* (1914), pp. 43–64; Judith Jennings, 'A trio of talented women: Abolition, gender, and political participation', *Slavery & Abolition*, 26:1 (2005), pp. 55–70; Judith Jennings, *Gender, religion, and radicalism in the long eighteenth century: An 'ingenious Quaker' and her connections* (Aldershot: Ashgate, 2006); Judith Jennings, '"By No Means in a Liberal Style": Mary Morris Knowles versus James Boswell', in Ann Hollinshead Hurley and Chanita Goodblatt (eds), *Women editing/Editing women: Early modern women writers and the new textualism* (Newcastle upon Tyne: Cambridge Scholars Publishing, 2009), pp. 227–47; Judith Jennings, 'Jane Harry Thresher and Mary Morris Knowles speak out for liberty in Jamaica and England', in Amar Wahab and Cecily Jones (eds), *Free at last? Reflections on freedom and the abolition of the British transatlantic slave trade* (Newcastle upon Tyne: Cambridge Scholars Publishing, 2011); Katie Donington, 'Harry [married name Thresher], Jane, 1755/6–1784', *Oxford dictionary of national biography* (Oxford: Oxford University Press, 2016) https://doi.org/10.1093/ref:odnb/107509 [accessed 28 September 2017]; Daniel Livesay, *Children of uncertain fortune: Mixed-race Jamaicans in Britain and the Atlantic family, 1733–1833* (Chapel Hill: University of North Carolina Press, 2018).
12 TNA/COP 139/31, Jamaica Acts, 1774–75, quoted in Daniel Livesay, 'Children of uncertain fortune: Mixed-race migration from the West Indies to Britain, 1750–1820' (PhD thesis, University of Michigan, 2010), p. 61.
13 Green, 'Jenny Harry', p. 560.
14 Rachel Lang, 'The Whitemans of Grenada: Illegitimacy and the "ownership" of family members', Legacies of British Slave-ownership, October 2013. https://lbsatucl.wordpress.com/2013/10/11/the-whitemans-of-grenada-illegitimacy-and-the-ownership-of-family-members/ [accessed 31 August 2017].

15 Livesay, 'Children of uncertain fortune: Mixed-race migration', p. 61.
16 TNA/COP 139/31, Jamaica Acts, 1774–75, quoted *ibid.*
17 Danielle Goodman, Sophia Seebom and Chloë Stewart, 'Headquarters House, Kingston, Jamaica, 1755–1990' (unpublished manuscript, Jamaica National Heritage Trust, 1989), p. 11.
18 For a description, see the Rev. R. Bickell, *The West Indies as they are; Or a real picture of slavery: But more particularly as it exists in the island of Jamaica* (London: J. Hatchard & Son, 1825), pp. 27–9.
19 HFAC, Diary of Robert Hibbert junior, 5 May 1775.
20 *Ibid.*, 30 September 1780.
21 Jennings, 'Jane Harry Thresher and Mary Morris Knowles', p. 63.
22 There has been some speculation over the date of Jane and Margaret's departure. Thomas senior left Jamaica for London in 1771 and it is possible they travelled with him. Judith Jennings has suggested they might have left earlier, possibly in 1769. *Ibid.*, p. 64.
23 Letter from Simon Taylor to George Hibbert, 14 January 1804, quoted in Daniel Livesay, 'Extended families: Mixed-race families and the Scottish experience, 1770–1820', *International Journal of Scottish Literature*, 4 (2008), p. 1.
24 Edward Long, quoted in Catherine Hall, 'Whose memories? Edward Long and the work of re-remembering', in Katie Donington, Ryan Hanley and Jessica Moody (eds), *Britain's history and memory of slavery: The local nuances of a 'national sin'* (Liverpool: Liverpool University Press, 2016), p. 141.
25 Henrice Altink, 'Forbidden fruit: Pro-slavery attitudes towards enslaved women's sexuality', *Journal of Caribbean History*, 39:2 (2005), p. 211.
26 Roxann Wheeler, *The complexion of race: Categories of difference in eighteenth-century British culture* (Philadelphia: University of Pennsylvania Press, 2000), p. 177.
27 Livesay, *Children of uncertain fortune*, p. 180.
28 Island Record Office, Jamaica, Will of Charity Harry, Wills LOS 58 (fo. 71), 13 November 1793. Transcription provided in a private communication by Daniel Livesay, 5 August 2012.
29 Letter from Robert Taylor to John Tailyour, 27 August 1791, quoted in Livesay, 'Extended families', p. 7.
30 Letter from Jane Harry to Thomas Hibbert senior, date unknown, quoted in Green, 'Jenny Harry', p. 565.
31 *Ibid.*, pp. 563–4.
32 *Ibid.*, p. 563.
33 *Ibid.*, p. 564.
34 *Ibid.*, p. 565.
35 *Ibid.*, p. 567.
36 *Ibid.*, p. 565.
37 *Ibid.*, p. 566.
38 Leonore Davidoff and Catherine Hall, *Family fortunes: Men and women of the English middle class, 1780–1850* (London: Routledge, 2002), p. 23.
39 Letter from Jane Harry to Thomas Hibbert senior, date unknown, quoted in Green, 'Jenny Harry', p. 566.
40 Samuel Lloyd, *The Lloyds of Birmingham*, 2nd edn (Birmingham: Cornish Brothers, 1907), p. vii.
41 *Ibid.*, p. 118.
42 Anna Seward, quoted in Jennings, 'Jane Harry Thresher and Mary Morris Knowles', p. 70.
43 Several versions of the conversation exist: *Gentleman's Magazine* (London: John Nicholls, 1791), pp. 700–1; *Dialogue between Dr. Johnson and Mrs. Knowles* (London: J. & A. Arch, 1799); James Boswell, *The life of Samuel Johnson*, vol. III (London: Routledge, Warnes & Routledge, 1859), pp. 199–200; Lloyd, *The Lloyds of Birmingham*, pp. 114–19.
44 Letter from Jane Harry to Thomas Hibbert senior, date unknown, quoted in Green, 'Jenny Harry', p. 576.

II: INTIMATE RELATIONS: THE METROPOLE

45 HFAC, Diary of Robert Hibbert junior, 9 June 1780.
46 Letter from Thomas Hibbert junior to Jane Harry, 15 December 1780, quoted in Green, 'Jenny Harry (concluded)', p. 45.
47 Jane Harry, quoted by Thomas Hibbert junior, *ibid.*, p. 46.
48 *Ibid.*, pp. 45–6.
49 *Gentleman's Magazine*, p. 716.
50 Island Record Office, Jamaica, Wills LOS 58 (fo. 71), Will of Charity Harry, 13 November 1793.
51 Jennings, 'Jane Harry Thresher and Mary Morris Knowles', p. 79.
52 JFSGRL, Kingston Parish Registers 1722–1825. The record notes that he was born on 12 July 1756 and baptised on 26 October 1757. www.jamaicanfamilysearch.com/Samples/regkgn01.htm [accessed 31 August 2017].
53 www.georgehibbert.com/hibbertsjam.html [accessed 10 April 2011].
54 HFAC, Diary of Robert Hibbert junior, 15 July 1779, 5 April 1776.
55 *Ibid.*, 2 July 1773.
56 *Ibid.*, 28 May 1776.
57 *Ibid.*, 2 June 1776.
58 *Ibid.*, 30 September 1780.
59 *Ibid.*, 19 September 1790.
60 *Ibid.*, 23 January 1793.
61 *Ibid.*, 25 January 1793.
62 *Ibid.*, 15 January 1793.
63 *Ibid.*, 3 February 1780.
64 *Ibid.*, 25 February 1780.
65 Oliver, *Caribbeana*, p. 197.
66 Discussed in detail in Chapter 5.
67 'George Hibbert Oates', Legacies of British Slave-ownership database. www.ucl.ac.uk/lbs/person/view/19116 [accessed 8 July 2018].
68 Scotland's relationship to the Caribbean has recently received increased scholarly attention: see Douglas Hamilton, *Scotland, the Caribbean and the Atlantic world, 1750–1820* (Manchester: Manchester University Press, 2005); Michael Morris, *Scotland and the Caribbean, c.1740–1833: Atlantic archipelagos* (Abingdon: Routledge, 2015); Stephen Mullen, 'The Glasgow West India interest: Integration, collaboration and exploitation in the British Atlantic World, 1776–1846' (PhD thesis, University of Glasgow, 2015); T. M. Devine (ed.), *Recovering Scotland's slavery past: The Caribbean connection* (Edinburgh: Edinburgh University Press, 2016).
69 Letter from Thomas Gordon to Archibald Grant, 27 June 1752, quoted in Alan L. Karras, *Sojourners in the sun: Scottish migrants in Jamaica and Chesapeake, 1740–1800* (Ithaca, NY: Cornell University Press, 1992), p. 61.
70 J. M. Bulloch, *The making of the West Indies: The Gordons as colonists* (Buckie: W. F. Johnston & Sons, 1915), p. 36.
71 HFAC, Diary of Robert Hibbert junior, 24 May 1772.
72 *Ibid.*, 27 May 1772.
73 *Ibid.*, 22 June 1772.
74 'Windsor Lodge', Legacies of British Slave-ownership database. www.ucl.ac.uk/lbs/estate/view/1910 and 'Paisley', Legacies of British Slave-ownership database. www.ucl.ac.uk/lbs/estate/view/1916 [accessed 31 August 2017].
75 'Spring Garden', Legacies of British Slave-ownership database. www.ucl.ac.uk/lbs/estate/view/2783 [accessed 31 August 2017].
76 Transcription of the will of Janet Hibbert, in Oliver, *Caribbeana*, p. 193.
77 'Nathan Sprigg', Legacies of British Slave-ownership database. www.ucl.ac.uk/lbs/person/view/2146646049 [accessed 19 January 2019].
78 NLW/SPD, 9080, Letter from George Hibbert to Nathaniel Phillips, 5 March 1787.
79 Gilbert Wakefield, *Memoirs of the life of Gilbert Wakefield, B.A. late Fellow of Jesus College, Cambridge* (London: J. Deighton, 1792), p. 281.
80 Jerom Murch, *Memoir of Robert Hibbert, founder of the Hibbert Trust: With a sketch of its history* (Bath: William Lewis, 1874), p. 10.

81 ICS/SHL//TVAP, M965/17/30, Letter from George Hibbert to Simon Taylor, 3 March 1802.
82 HFAC, Diary of Robert Hibbert junior, 7 December 1772.
83 JFSGRL, Diary of George Hibbert, Monday 29 March 1773. www.jamaicanfamilysearch.com/Members/bcarib28.htm [accessed 6 October 2017].
84 HFAC, Diary of Robert Hibbert junior, 14 December 1772.
85 *Ibid.*, 1 May 1775.
86 *Ibid.*, 4 May 1775.
87 *Ibid.*, 8 May 1775.
88 *Ibid.*, 9 May 1775.
89 Mabel Nembhard, *Nembhard of Jamaica* (date and publisher unknown). https://archive.org/details/nembhardofjamaic00nemb [accessed 28 September 2017].
90 HFAC, Diary of Robert Hibbert junior, 1787–1802, Foreword.
91 HFAC, Diary of Robert Hibbert junior, 12 September 1787, 13 April 1788.
92 GA/BFDP, D1799/C153, Letter from Robert Hibbert junior to Mary Oates, Kingston, 9 November 1790.
93 HFAC, Diary of Robert Hibbert junior, 1 May 1797.
94 *Ibid.*, June 1798.
95 *Ibid.*, 9 July 1790.
96 *Ibid.*, 5 August 1800.
97 *Ibid.*, 9 February 1794.
98 GA/BFDP, D1799/C153, Letter from Robert Hibbert junior to Mary Oates, Kingston, 9 November 1790.
99 HFAC, Diary of Robert Hibbert junior, 11 February 1797.
100 *Ibid.*, 15 June 1788.
101 *Ibid.*, 31 August 1788.
102 *Ibid.*, 4 June 1796.
103 GA/BFDP, D1799/C153, Letter from Robert Hibbert junior to Mary Oates, Kingston, 9 November 1790.
104 HFAC, Diary of Robert Hibbert junior, 3 December 1791.
105 *Ibid.*, 5–6 May 1792.
106 *Ibid.*, 12 September 1792.
107 JFSGRL, Diary of George Hibbert, 6 November 1819. www.jamaicanfamilysearch.com/Members/bcarib28.htm [accessed 31 January 2018].
108 There is an extensive literature on the development of Creole society and identity; some key works include Kamau Braithwaite, *The development of Creole society in Jamaica, 1770–1820* (Oxford: Clarendon Press, 1972); Michael Craton, 'Reluctant Creoles: The planters' world in the British West Indies', in Bernard Bailyn and Philip D. Morgan (eds), *Strangers within the realm: Cultural margins of the first British empire* (Chapel Hill: University of North Carolina Press, 1991), pp. 314–62; Verene Shepherd (ed.), *Questioning Creole: Creolisation discourses in Caribbean culture* (Kingston: Ian Randle, 2005); David Lambert, *White Creole culture: Politics and identity in the age of abolition* (Cambridge: Cambridge University Press, 2005); Christer Petley, *Slaveholders in Jamaica: Colonial society and culture during the era of abolition* (Abingdon: Routledge, 2009).
109 Edward Long, quoted in Craton, 'Reluctant Creoles', p. 343.
110 Wright (ed.), *Lady Nugent's journal*, p. 98.
111 GA/BFDP, D1799/C153, Letter from Abigail Hibbert to Mary Oates, 29 September, no year recorded.
112 HFAC, a questionnaire written in the hand of Robert Hibbert junior and kept with his diary.
113 GA/BFDP, D1799/C153, Letter from Abigail Hibbert, Highfields, 16 April. No year or recipient included, although it is likely that the letter was intended for her daughter Mary Oates as part of a series of letters on the subject of breastfeeding.
114 Katherine Paugh, *The politics of reproduction: Race, slavery, and fertility in the age of abolition* (Oxford: Oxford University Press, 2017), pp. 85–121.

II: INTIMATE RELATIONS: THE METROPOLE

115 GA/BFDP, D1799/C153, Letter from Abigail Hibbert to Mary Oates, 19 August, no year recorded.
116 *Ibid.*, Letter from Abigail Hibbert to Mary Oates, Manchester, 12 September, no year recorded.
117 Wright (ed.), *Lady Nugent's journal*, p. 259.
118 GA/BFDP, D1799/149 and D1799/150.
119 Green, 'Jenny Harry (concluded)', p. 63.
120 'Hibberts in Jamaica'. www.georgehibbert.com/hibbertsjam.html [accessed 13 October 2017].
121 www.hibbertfamily.com/genealogy/ancestors-corner/solomon-augustus-hibbert/introduction [accessed 13 October 2017].
122 Surrey History Centre, Woking, G85/2/1/1/134, Sale particulars of residence on north side of Common in Clapham with 6a (George Hibbert Esq.) and 5a meadow on the Wandsworth Road.

Part II   Intimate relations: the metropole

1 E. M. Forster, *Marianne Thornton: A biography* (London: Edward Arnold, 1956), p. 16.
2 John Tosh, *A man's place: Masculinity and the middle-class home in Victorian England* (New Haven, CT: Yale University Press, 2007), p. 35.
3 *Ibid.*, p. 26.
4 Leonore Davidoff and Catherine Hall, *Family fortunes: Men and women of the English middle class, 1780–1850* (London: Routledge, 2002), pp. 149–92.
5 Tosh, *A man's place*, p. 34.
6 Catherine Hall, *Macaulay and son: Architects of imperial Britain* (New Haven, CT: Yale University Press, 2012), p. 144.
7 ICS/SHL/TVAP, M965/17/15, Letter from George Hibbert to Simon Taylor, 8 October 1799.
8 For a discussion of these shifts see Michael Roper and John Tosh (eds), *Manful assertions: Masculinities in Britain since 1800* (London: Routledge, 1991); Tim Hitchcock and Michèle Cohen (eds), *English masculinities, 1660–1800* (London: Longman, 1999); John Tosh, *Manliness and masculinities in nineteenth-century Britain: Essays on gender, family and empire* (London: Longman, 2005); Tosh, *A man's place*.
9 J. H. Markland, *A sketch of the life and character of George Hibbert Esq., F.R S., S.A., and L.S.* (London, 1837), pp. 18–19.
10 *Ibid.*, p. 21, pp. 19–20.
11 Reed Browning, 'The Duke of Newcastle and the financing of the Seven Years War', *Journal of Economic History*, 31:2 (1971), p. 356.
12 David Carnegie A. Agnew, *Protestant exiles from France in the reign of Louis XIV: Or, the Huguenot refugees and their descendants in Great Britain and Ireland*, vol. IV (London: Reeve & Turner, 1871).
13 E. I. Carlyle, 'Thellusson, Peter (1737–1797)', rev. François Crouzet, *Oxford dictionary of national biography* (Oxford: Oxford University Press, 2004). www.oxforddnb.com/view/article/27164 [accessed 10 January 2011].
14 R. G. Thorne, *The history of Parliament: The House of Commons, 1790–1820* (London: Secker and Warburg, 1986), p. 362.
15 'Peter Thellusson', Legacies of British Slave-ownership database. www.ucl.ac.uk/lbs/person/view/2146641147 [accessed 19 January 2019].
16 Ken Cozens, 'George Hibbert, of Clapham – 18th century merchant and "amateur horticulturalist"'. www.academia.edu/12319084/George_Hibbert_of_Clapham_18th_Century_Merchant_and_Amateur_Horticulturalist [accessed 14 May 2019].
17 *Ibid*. For a discussion of the intersection between family interests in the East and West Indies see Chris Jeppesen, 'East meets West: Exploring the connections between Britain, the Caribbean and East India Company, c.1757–1857', in Katie Donington, Ryan Hanley and Jessica Moody (eds), *Britain's history and memory*

of transatlantic slavery: The local nuances of a 'national sin' (Liverpool: Liverpool University Press, 2016), pp. 102–28.
18 'George Hibbert (1757–1820)', History of Parliament. www.historyofparliament online.org/volume/1790-1820/member/hibbert-george-1757–1837 [Accessed 18 May 2018].
19 Francis Hargrave, *Three arguments in the two causes in Chancery on the last will of Peter Thellusson Esq.* (London: G. G. & J. Robinson, 1799), p. xxi.
20 *London Gazette*, Part I (London: T. Neuman, 1812), p. 322.
21 Davidoff and Hall, *Family fortunes*, p. 324.
22 JFSGRL, transcription of the Hibbert family Bible made by Mabel Nembhard. http://jamaicanfamilysearch.com/ [accessed 19 December 2017].
23 Markland, *Sketch*, p. 4.
24 G. J. Barker Benfield, *The culture of sensibility: Sex and society in eighteenth-century Britain* (Chicago: University of Chicago Press, 1992), p. 248.
25 For a study of the function and practice of commonplacing see David Allan, *Commonplace books and reading in Georgian England* (Cambridge: Cambridge University Press, 2010).
26 British Library, London, George Hibbert's Commonplace Book (BL/GHCP), RP5573, Letter from Dr Johnson to Dr Taylor on the death of his wife (February 1794).
27 ICS/SHL/TVAP, M965/17/9, Letter from George Hibbert to Simon Taylor, 20 March 1798.
28 ICS/SHL/TVAP, M965/17/15, Letter from George Hibbert to Simon Taylor, 8 October 1799.
29 *The Times*, 24 December 1798.
30 *Ibid.*
31 British Library, London, Martin Papers, vol. XIII, Additional MS 41368, Letter from Elizabeth Hibbert to Lady Byam, Munden, 24 October 1831.
32 *The Times*, 28 May 1833, quoted in Nicholas Draper, *The price of emancipation: Slave-ownership, compensation and British society at the end of slavery* (Cambridge: Cambridge University Press, 2010), p. 34.
33 BL/GHCB, RP5573, A noble lord to a young lady on the eve of marriage, May 1785.
34 Markland, *Sketch*, p. 19.
35 NLW/SPD, 9078, Letter from George Hibbert to Nathaniel Phillips, 4 August 1786.
36 NLW/SPD, 9091, Letter from George Hibbert to Nathaniel Phillips, London, 4 July 1787.
37 GA/BFDP, D1799/C153, Letter from Abigail Hibbert to Mary Oates, undated but must have been in 1787, when George's family contracted measles.
38 NLW/SPD, 9092, Letter from George Hibbert to Nathaniel Phillips, 29 March 1788.
39 Clare Taylor, 'The journal of an absentee proprietor, Nathaniel Phillips of Slebech', *Journal of Caribbean History*, 18 (1984), pp. 72–3.
40 NLW/SPD, 9092, Letter from George Hibbert to Nathaniel Phillips, 29 March 1788.
41 'Nathaniel Phillips', Legacies of British Slave-ownership database. www.ucl.ac.uk/lbs/person/view/1330090056 [accessed 19 January 2019].
42 GA/BFDP, D1799/C153, Letter from Abigail Hibbert to Mary Oates, 31 December 1790.
43 ICS/SHL/TVAP, M965/17/51, Letter from George Hibbert to Simon Taylor, 8 March 1804.
44 ICS/SHL/TVAP, M965/17/47, Letter from George Hibbert to Simon Taylor, 5 September 1803.
45 BL/GHCB, RP5573, George Hibbert, 'For Eliza's birthday', 24 June 1813.
46 *Ibid.*, George Hibbert, 'To Miss Octavia Hibbert', June 1819.
47 *Ibid.*, George Hibbert to Mary Ann Hibbert.
48 Davidoff and Hall, *Family fortunes*, p. 221.
49 GA/BFDP, D1799/C153, Letter from Mary Hibbert (*née* Greenhalgh) to Mary Oates, 3 March (no year given).

II: INTIMATE RELATIONS: THE METROPOLE

50 'William Marshall, 1796–1872', History of Parliament. www.historyofparliamentonline.org/volume/1820-1832/member/marshall-william-1796-1872 [accessed 9 July 2018].
51 GA/BFDP, D1799/C153, Letter from Robert Hibbert junior to Mary Oates, 9 November 1790.
52 *Ibid.*, Letter from Abigail Hibbert to an unknown recipient, 7 May 1790.
53 *Ibid.*, Letter from Abigail Hibbert to an unknown recipient, 10 June (year unknown).
54 The National Archives, Kew, RG9/754, fo. 77, p. 12, roll 542696, Census Returns of England and Wales, 1861.
55 *Illustrated London News*, 81: 2257 (5 August 1882), p. 150.
56 The National Archives, Kew, RG10/2495, fo. 43, p. 36, roll 835198, Census Returns of England and Wales, 1871.
57 The National Archives, Kew, 1875 index to wills and administrations (1858–1995), p. 295.
58 HFAC, Diary of Robert Hibbert junior, 26 May 1795.
59 BL/GHCB, RP5573, 'Epitaph upon a child by Herwick [*sic*]'.
60 Catherine Hall, *Macaulay and son: Architects of imperial Britain* (London: Yale University Press, 2012), pp. 47–8.
61 Markland, *Sketch*, p. 1.
62 Linda Colley, *Britons: Forging the nation 1707–1837* (London: Vintage, 1996), p. 180.
63 *Ibid.*, p. 182.
64 GA/BFDP, D1799/C153, Letter from Robert Hibbert junior to Mary Oates, 7 August 1807.
65 ICS/SHL/TVAP, M965/17/38, Letter from George Hibbert to Simon Taylor, 6 January 1803.
66 ICS/SHL/TVAP, M965/17/90, Letter from George Hibbert to Simon Taylor, 3 April 1809.
67 Nowell C. Smith (ed.), *Selected letters of Sydney Smith*, 2nd edn (Oxford: Oxford University Press, 1986), p. 119, quoted in Draper, *The price of emancipation*, p. 19.
68 'Obituary of Captain Edward Hibbert', *Gentleman's Magazine* (London: John Nichols, 1824), p. 185.
69 British Library, London, Althorp Papers, Additional MS 76121, Letter from George Hibbert to Lord Spencer, 12 February 1818.
70 British Library, London, Althorp Papers, Additional MS 76126, Transcript of Edward Hibbert's letter included in a letter from George Hibbert to Lord Spencer, 5 September 1821.
71 BL/GHCB, RP5573, George Hibbert to Edward Hibbert.
72 'Obituary of Captain Edward Hibbert', p. 185.
73 British Library, London, Althorp Papers, Additional MS 76124, Letter from George Hibbert to Lord Spencer, 16 September 1816.
74 'Between the Commons: Part One', draft for *Survey of London*, vol. 50, ch. 17, p. 5 (2013). www.ucl.ac.uk/bartlett/architecture/sites/bartlett/files/50.17_between_the_commons_1.pdf [accessed 4 January 2017].
75 *Ibid.*, p. 8.
76 *Ibid.*, p. 12.
77 The Hon. Mrs Hardcastle (ed.), *Life of John, Lord Campbell, Lord High Chancellor of Great Britain*, vol. I (London: John Murray, 1881), p. 32.
78 Museum of London, PLA/WIDC/1/3/1, Journal of the Proceedings of the West India Dock Company, 1799–1800.
79 Green, 'Jenny Harry', p. 568.
80 Quoted in Jenny Handley and Hazel Lake, *Progress by persuasion: The life of William Smith* (Hazel Lake, 2007), p. 253.
81 Wilberforce Institute for the Study of Slavery and Emancipation, Hull, Abolition and Emancipation, Part 6: Sources from the Special Collections Library, Duke University, Reel 92, William Smith: Letters, 1787–1860, Miscellaneous, 1785–1833, HT/1031/A1, Letter from George Hibbert to William Smith, 24 February 1807.

82 JFSGRL, Diary of George Hibbert, 30 March 1816. www.jamaicanfamilysearch.com/Members/bcarib28.htm [accessed 24 May 2018].
83 D. W. Bebbington, 'Unitarian Members of Parliament in the nineteenth century: A catalogue', *Transactions of the Unitarian Historical Society*, Supplement, 24:3 (2009), p. 62 (notes that no allegiance to Unitarianism found but included in the 'Supplementary list of supposed Unitarian MPs').
84 'George Hibbert (1757–1820)', History of Parliament. www.historyofparliamentonline.org/volume/1790–1820/member/hibbert-george-1757-1837 [accessed 18 May 2018].
85 Nicholas Hibbert Steele, private communication, 1 March 2013.
86 London Metropolitan Archives, London, Records of Holy Trinity, Clapham Common (LMA/RHT), P95 TR11-1/X077/084, Trustee Minute Book of Holy Trinity Church, Clapham Common.
87 *Ibid.*, 19 July 1797.
88 HFAC, Diary of Robert Hibbert junior, 2 February 1794.
89 'Between the Commons', p. 26.
90 *The Connoisseur*, 135 (London: R. Baldwin, 1756), reprinted in Lionel Thomas Berguer, *British essayists; With prefaces biographical, historical and critical*, vol. XXXII (London: T. & J. Allman, 1823), p. 212.
91 George Philips, *The autobiography of George Philips*, pp. 334–7, quoted in David Knapman, *Conversation Sharp: The biography of a London gentleman. Richard Sharp (1759–1835) in letters, prose and verse* (Dorchester: The Dorset Press, 2003), p. 131.
92 Tosh, *A man's place*.
93 Thomas Frognall Dibdin, *Bibliographical Decameron; Or ten days pleasant discourse upon illuminated manuscripts, and subjects connected with early engravings, typography, and bibliography*, vol. III (London: W. Bulmer & Co., 1817), pp. 35–6.
94 Markland, *Sketch*, p. 16, p. 19.
95 Surrey History Centre, Woking, G85/2/1/1/134, Sale particulars of residence on north side of Common in Clapham with 6a (George Hibbert Esq) and 5a meadow on the Wandsworth Road.
96 *Clapham, with its common and environs: Containing an historical and topographical description of the parish and manor, principally extracted from parochial documents, with a catalogue of indigenous plants growing in the neighbourhood, list of population, rates, and other parochial occurrences, from 1603 to 1827, and a list of the inhabitants, corrected to 1841* (Clapham: D. Batten, 1841), p. 151.
97 The National Archives, Kew, Prerogative Court of Canterbury and related Probate Jurisdictions: Will Registers, PROB 11/1889/241.

CHAPTER SEVEN

Consuming passions: collecting and connoisseurship

Blest age! when all men may procure,
The title of a Connoisseur;
When noble and ignoble herd,
Are govern'd by a single word;
  Robert Lloyd, 'The Cit's country box' (1756)

I am apt to suspect the negroes and in general all other species of men (for there are four or five different kinds) to be naturally inferior to the whites. There never was a civilised nation of any other complexion than white, nor even any individual eminent either in action or speculation. No ingenious manufactures amongst them, no arts, no sciences ... Such a uniform and constant differences could not happen in so many countries and ages, if nature had not made an original distinction betwixt these breeds of men. Not to mention our colonies, there are negroe slaves dispersed all over Europe, of which none ever discovered any symptoms of ingenuity, tho' low people, without education, will start up amongst us, and distinguish themselves in every profession.
  David Hume, 'Of national characteristics', in *Essays and treaties on several subjects*, new edn (London: A. Millar, 1758), p. 125

Robert Lloyd's satirical representation of the pretensions of the wealthy man of trade is indicative of the ways in which culture demarcated the difference between traditional and emerging forms of wealth. Consumer culture, buoyed by capitalism and colonisation, created a new world of things and a new class of people able to participate in the market.[1] An anxiety around class can be read in James Heywood Markland's remembrance of his uncle George as a man who 'flattered himself that he was encouraging and setting an example of a love of the arts amongst persons of his own degree ... he loved to dwell upon the elevation of the mind which such pursuits had produced in his own time on the mercantile character'.[2] Whilst Markland's language reinforced hierarchical distinctions, George viewed the relationship between commerce and culture through the lens of the merchant princes of the Italian Renaissance. The legacies of the Medici family were a shining example of the ways in which trade could be ennobled through the arts. Like the Medici, George lived through a period in which new cultural and intellectual formations emerged. The age of Enlightenment brought with it an explosion of interest in science, philosophy and culture. The marriage of the arts, commerce and science encouraged technological experimentation which in turn revolutionised industry. Exploration and 'discovery', made possible through the violence and displacement of empire building, greatly expanded Western knowledge of, and interest in, the natural world. Crucially, new public arenas developed that allowed for the participation of the middle classes in the sphere of politics and culture.[3] The distinctly bourgeois nature of some of these spaces gave the man of commerce an *entrée* into Enlightenment culture. Roy Porter has described this shift in the balance of cultural power:

> The arts had always been watered by ecclesiastical, royal and noble patronage ... From the late seventeenth century, however, the cultural centre of gravity was conspicuously migrating away from Court into metropolitan spaces at large – into coffee houses, taverns, learned societies, salons, assembly rooms, debating clubs, theatres, galleries and concert rooms; formerly the minions of monarchy, the arts and letters were to become the consorts of commerce and the citizenry.[4]

With its concentration of new and old cultural institutions London became 'the metropolis *à la mode*'.[5] The elite merchants of the City were hungry to participate in a culture which was increasingly not only open to them, but actively shaped by them.

Combining the acquisition of knowledge with the acquisition of things, the figure of the collector occupied a fascinating position in the cultural history of Enlightenment. Collections ranged from art to anatomical specimens, antiquities to scientific instruments, natural history to rare manuscripts. They were both public and private entities; jealously guarded within the home yet deliberately exhibited to visitors as visible symbols of wealth, taste and expertise. Increasingly during the period some collectors began to offer their treasures for public delectation. On his death in 1753, Hans Sloane requested that his 'collection be preserved and kept and that the same may be from time to time, visited and seen by all persons desirous of seeing and viewing the same, as well towards satisfying the desire of the curious, as for the improvement, knowledge and information of all persons'.[6] Sloane's collection went on to form the British Museum. His story links the development of London's first public museum to the history of transatlantic slavery. In 1687 he travelled to Jamaica as physician to the Governor. His time there impacted hugely on both his intellectual interests and his collecting practices. In 1697 Sloane married Elizabeth Langley Rose, the widow of the Jamaica physician and planter Fulke Rose. The laws of coverture meant that Sloane was in receipt of 'Elizabeth's one-third share of the net profits from the Rose plantations' which totalled over 3,000 acres.[7] It was this revenue that helped to fund Sloane's collection.

No one knew better than the merchant man the power of possessing and displaying desirable commodities. The affluent mercantile classes did not simply sell, they were also enthusiastic buyers. The exercise of consumer power is an important and neglected facet of masculine identity. As Margot Finn has noted, 'the Hanoverian consumer market included highly acquisitive men as well as compulsively possessive women'.[8] The reasons for establishing a collection are many and varied:

> Collecting is often pursued in order to represent, sustain, or enhance the owner's social status; to signify economic achievement or to make an investment; to demonstrate the collector's cultural acuity, including to dignify the sources of recently acquired wealth; or for sheer love of art, the need for solace, or other subliminal motivations.[9]

On a more intimate level, 'The objects of collection reflect the taste values, knowledge, resources, and power of the collector, and become extensions of his or her selfhood. By selecting, ordering and re-presenting the objects of desire, the collecting subject re-creates the self.'[10] In consideration of the imperial dimensions of some collections, James Delbourgo has argued that 'Collecting a world of things meant collecting a world of people. Universal knowledge demanded universal acquaintance, up and down the social hierarchy and reaching across different cultures.'[11] In this construction, the social relations of the object stand in for the social relations between people, with the coloniser taking possession of the cultural signifiers of the colonised in order to produce knowledge about the Other.

The separation of the polite sphere of culture from the grubby world of trade was designed to reinforce the boundaries of class, although in reality the collector was thoroughly embedded within the commercial landscape. The market in collectibles was a lucrative one and merchants utilised their global contacts to purchase and ship the rarest of blooms, the finest examples of craftsmanship and the most sought-after works of art. Transnational webs of finance created relationships which were used to gain access to different markets, including the flourishing auction houses of continental Europe. Whilst all of the

Hibberts practised forms of conspicuous consumption, it was George who made the transition from consumer to connoisseur. He threw himself into a variety of gentlemanly pursuits, building up a significant collection of art, books and botanical specimens. With his reputation increasingly recognised, he gained access to the capital's elite social circles through both club and society membership. George's cultural practices were at once cerebral and practical; his acquisitions represented the delights of rational amusement, access to high society and the accumulation of appreciating commodities. In the longer term they also sustained an alternative memory of him which has at different times served to obscure and mitigate his involvement with the slavery business.

Slavery, race and culture

Slave-based wealth impacted on the development of European art galleries, museums and libraries, creating a tangible legacy that is still identifiable today. The importance of slavery to the culture of taste cannot only be measured in terms of the financial investment made in the accumulation of cultural treasures. As Simon Gikandi has explained, cultural norms and practices were not only gendered and classed, but importantly they were also raced, leading to 'the establishment of a realm of taste, or even the valorization of ideals of beauty, [that] depended on systematic acts of excluding'.[12] The discourse of taste was itself implicated in the construction of racial difference, playing an important role in the formulation and entrenchment of civilisational hierarchies. The production, consumption and judgement of art was one of the ways in which some commentators chose to distinguish between what they considered to be the separate races of man. Writing in the first half of the eighteenth century, Jonathan Richardson called for a history of mankind

> with respect to the place they hold among rational beings; that is, a history of arts and sciences; wherein it would be seen to what heights some of the species have risen in some ages, whilst at the same time, on other parts of the globe, men have been but one degree above common animals.[13]

Of course the standard by which culture was to be judged was formulated by Western philosophers like David Hume, a man who had pronounced, 'There never was a civilised nation of any other complexion than white.'[14] Private and public collections were founded on principles of taste which were embedded within a discourse of European cultural superiority.[15] Non-European objects were often treated as curios rather than high art, although a fetishisation of oriental culture was expressed in, for example, the craze for chinoiserie within the homes of the wealthy.[16] African art was considered neither fashionable nor desirable (if it was considered art at all). These kinds of cultural judgements reinforced an understanding of race predicated on the notion of civilisational progress.

During a period in which European empires were expanding, Enlightenment philosophers grappled with the issue of race, defining it variously through cultural, climatic and biological difference.[17] Stadial theories emphasised the importance of the law, governance and commerce in defining the 'progress' of different societies. Roxann Wheeler has argued that this definitional fluidity meant that skin colour alone was not necessarily the only, or dominant, marker of racial otherness.[18] There were some subscribers to theories of polygenesis, including the influential slave owner and historian Edward Long. In a now infamous passage in his widely read *History of Jamaica* (1774) he compared the Hottentot and the orangutan, even suggesting that 'I do not think an oran-outang husband would be any dishonour to a Hottentot female.'[19] Drawing on the discourse of natural history, this form of scientific racism found its roots in the Enlightenment impulse towards classification and categorisation. These ideas were not widely accepted during the eighteenth century, in large part because they posed a challenge to biblical monogenesis. The study of human nature formed a significant strand of Enlightenment thinking leading to a questioning of what it meant to be fully human. There was a political and commercial value in denigrating the humanity of the enslaved, who were designated as chattel and repeatedly likened to animals. This ambiguous status was reflected in their legal position; their humanity meant they could be punished for criminal offences, while their status as property also allowed them to be bequeathed in a will or offered as collateral on a loan.[20] For the abolitionists, with their campaigning slogan of 'Am I not a man and a brother?', the recognition of enslaved humanity was their gift to bestow. If the opposing sides differed in their views on slavery, they agreed that African culture was inferior and would be improved through prolonged contact (forced or otherwise) with European colonisers.

The absorption by slave owners of ideas relating to the construction of racial difference can be read in the pamphlet *Hints to the young Jamaica sugar planter* (1825) authored by Jamaica-born Robert Hibbert. In it he admitted that his ideas would be 'repugnant to some minds', but he felt compelled to give the prospective planter a 'recital of the whole truth ... instead of misleading him through false delicacy'.[21] Robert was clearly influenced by the controversial disciplines of phrenology and physiognomy. He wrote:

> Whoever has once seen a negro must notice his difference from all other men; his thick lips, wide nose, woolly hair and black skin, all mark him as a distinct race of man ... the negro and the European are as distinct in mind as in body ... You see in the children no playful fancy, no arch tricks, so frequent in English boys and girls, nor is there to be found one solitary instance of a negro man conspicuous for his mental powers.[22]

Referring authoritatively to Charles White's writings, he detailed the difference in 'the formation of the skull, the chin, the arms, the legs, the feet ... the texture and effluvia of the skin' as further evidence of 'a distinction' between the races.[23] White rejected the use of his theories in relation to the slave trade, writing that the 'Negroes are, at least, equal to thousands of Europeans, in capacity and responsibility; and ought, therefore, to be equally entitled to freedom and protection.'[24] White's polygenesis theories were controversial because they went against Christian teachings on the origins of man, and Robert was quick to add that he was not challenging the 'Mosaic account of creation'.[25] Despite this lip-service to the Bible, it was clear that Robert viewed Africans as a separate and unequal race.

It was not simply biological difference that interested Robert, his account was also invested in articulating the cultural divisions between Africans and Europeans. Quoting directly from Thomas Jefferson's *Notes on the state of Virginia* (first London edition, 1787), Robert stated that 'Never yet could I find that a black negro had uttered a thought above the level of a plain narration, never could I see even an elementary trait of painting and sculpture.'[26] Jefferson's writings were highly influential; Robert's cousin George also owned a copy of this work, which was included in his 1829 auction catalogue. Drawing on ideas of empirical knowledge and natural observation, Robert opined in his *Hints to the young Jamaica sugar planter* that 'experience convinces us of a slowness of intellect and an obstinacy in the negro, which no want of civilisation can explain'. Whilst he was prepared to admit that the 'state of slavery' was 'unfavourable to the exertion of intellect', he insisted that during the period in which the slave trade permitted the importation of formerly free Africans, he had 'never found any symptom of strong intellect amongst the best educated'.[27] He denied the existence of complex African societies prior to European contact, suggesting instead that it was the Greek, Egyptian (whom he thought of 'as much Asiatic as African') and Arabic peoples who had built the great monuments of civilisation on the continent.[28] According to Robert a 'consciousness' of European 'superiority of understanding' would enable the planter to exercise 'the greatest patience and forbearance towards the slaves, not to expect too much from them, nor to rely too much on them, to pardon many excesses, and to make many allowances which might be unreasonable to an equal'.[29] For Robert the racial differences between master and slave placed each in positions befitting their station. He had been born into a life of wealth and privilege, and whilst he believed that this position required of him certain duties and responsibilities, he never questioned that this was the natural order of things.

Art

George's participation in the art world involved collecting, dealing and patronage. He was not alone in these practices – many returning slave owners and West India merchants spent their accumulated fortunes on these pursuits. George's contemporary collectors included William Beckford, Charles Long, George Watson Taylor, James Hughes Anderdon, Ralph Bernal, William Young Ottley, Sir Simon Haughton Clarke, John Julius Angerstein and Samuel Boddington. George's collection of art is relatively well documented, but the extent of his activities as a dealer are less clear. Major sales of work from his collection took place in 1802, 1809, 1829 and 1833.[30] According to Markland, George's collection of paintings 'though not large, contained specimens of first rate excellence, particularly in the Dutch and Flemish schools, in which alone Mr. Hibbert professed to be a connoisseur'.[31] His extensive collection of prints 'comprised nearly all that is curious or interesting, from the earliest period of the art of engraving to the present time, and was particularly rich in the works of Marc Antonio and Rembrandt'. George collected some contemporary British art, including sketches by Gainsborough.[32] He acted as a patron of the arts, commissioning portraits as well as a frieze by Henry Howard RA for his home in Clapham. His patronage of Howard earned him entrance to the Royal Academy's exclusive annual dinner in 1813. Having money was not enough to merit an invitation – only those who had demonstrated a committed patronage of the arts were considered. George's invitation was secured after Howard wrote to the invitation committee to assure them that George had 'laid out much money with modern artists'.[33] The invitation confirmed his acceptance into the cultural elite, allowing him to take his place among the leading figures of the art world and their influential patrons.

The story of George's collection is one which entangles Caribbean slave-produced wealth, the British art market and the violent upheaval of the French Revolution. As a successful merchant with a trained skill for interpreting the markets, George chose an auspicious time to build up his collection. The French Revolution proved to be a boon for British art collectors. With the aristocracy in flight or facing execution, new possibilities opened up for making acquisitions from the most sought-after collections in Europe. Rather than criticise the art enthusiast for their macabre opportunism, British collectors were instead praised for seizing the chance to enrich the nation's cultural stores. William Buchanan's *Memoirs of painting* (1824) articulated precisely this form of cultural patriotism. He suggested that individuals who purchased works of art from the French were involved in a form of acquisitive nationalism. The movement of these cultural trophies from the continent to Britain offered material evidence of the superiority and stability of the British ruling elite. In 1792 gambling debts forced Louis Philippe, the duc d'Orléans, to sell part of the collection he had inherited from his great-grandfather Philippe II. Acknowledged as the most important private art collection in Western Europe, it held a special position within Parisian society owing to its availability for public viewing. In 1792 a large part of the collection – 147 Dutch, Flemish and German paintings – was purchased by a syndicate orchestrated by the London art dealer Thomas Moore Slade. Following the execution of Louis Philippe in 1793, his French and Italian painting were sold. They also ended up in London and were purchased in 1798 by another syndicate involving the Duke of Bridgewater and the Earls of Gower and Carlisle. The paintings were exhibited at Michael Bryan's gallery in Pall Mall, Bryan having acted as a broker for the sale. The auctions were spread out over 1798, 1800 and 1802, with the original buyers keeping a good portion of the prime works for themselves. Buchanan viewed the interest generated by the sale as disproving 'the assertion which foreigners had till then made, that we were a nation possessing no love for the Fine Arts, nor any knowledge of them'.[34]

The list of buyers for the Orléans collection was dominated by merchants, financiers and gentlemen amateurs. It also included men with direct connections to slave ownership – the Earl of Harewood, William Beckford and George Hibbert. Buchanan described George as an 'early and considerable' buyer.[35] Amongst the principle purchasers from the City were Sir Francis Baring and John Julius Angerstein, both of whom had links to the wider slave economy through the supply of credit and insurance. Buchanan opined that the sums paid by these men 'proves the ... liberality' which was the 'mark [of] the character of the British merchant'. Though they might have been lampooned as tasteless social climbers by the satirists, some commercial men successfully cultivated reputations as discerning art lovers. George's purchases from the Orléans collection included *Christ Bearing his*

Cross (150 guineas)[36] and *Virgin and Child* (500 guineas) by Raphael;[37] from the Roman school *The Holy Family* by Frederico Baroccio (100 guineas)[38] and the *Flight of Jacob* by Pietro da Cortona (450 guineas);[39] from the Lombard school *Christ and the Samaritan Woman* by Annibale Carracci (300 guineas),[40] *Ecce Homo* (150 guineas) and *The Sibyl* (300 guineas) by Guido Reni[41] and *Head of the Virgin* by Francesco Barbieri (50 guineas);[42] from the Venetian school *Sketch of a Concert* by Titian (100 guineas);[43] and finally from the Flemish school *The Game of Tric-Trac* by David Teniers the Younger (300 guineas).[44] Altogether he laid out 2,400 guineas at the auction.

Apart from the famed Orléans sale, George's name could be found amongst the list of purchasers at several of the major auctions of the period. On 23 March 1795 the sale of the art collection belonging to the French statesman Charles Alexander de Calonne commenced. At this auction George was able to add a partner for his previous acquisition with the purchase of *An Interior of a Flemish Farmhouse* by David Teniers the Younger (350 guineas).[45] Michael Bryan sold part of his collection at an auction which began on 17 May 1798. From this sale George acquired an 'exquisite cabinet jewel' depicting a pastoral scene by the Dutch artist Nicolaes Pieterszoon Berchem (336 guineas).[46] He also added to his collection of the works of David Tenier the Younger with a further two paintings, *Assemblage of Flemish Peasants* (357 guineas)[47] and *Le Bonnet Rouge* (367 guineas 10 shillings).[48] Finally he purchased *Dutch Cabaret* by Adriaen Jansz van Ostade (409 guineas 10 shillings).[49] In 1800 George made one extravagant purchase from the collection of Mr Day, an additional Titian – *The Madonna, Infant Christ and Saints* (1,000 guineas).[50] The auction of the Ottley collection in 1801 represented a double-layered connection to the slave economy. Formed by William Young Ottley whilst he was in Rome, it was sold after a downturn in his family's fortunes. The Ottleys made their money through slave and plantation ownership:

> William Young Ottley's means derived from slavery: he received £10,000 under the will of his mother Sarah Elizabeth Ottley which specified that it had come from the proceeds of the £20,000 of her marriage settlement, contributed equally by her father Sir William Young of Delaford and her husband-to-be Richard Ottley. Richard Ottley's own will stated that the £20,000 was to be invested in Tobago as part of the marriage settlement of Richard Ottley and Sarah Elizabeth nee Young. Warner Ottley and William Young Ottley both served as trustees of the will of Drewry Ottley late of the Island of St Vincent (proved 27/08/1807), who was probably their half-brother. William Young Ottley himself, with Sarah Elizabeth Ottley, was shown as the owner of 17 enslaved people on Antigua in the 1817 Slave Registration.[51]

In a further link to the cultural sphere, Ottley went on to become Keeper of Prints and Drawings at the British Museum in 1833. Nicholas Turner has suggested that Ottley was forced to accept the post 'for financial reasons, since the act abolishing slavery had reduced his income from the family's West Indian plantation'.[52] J. Allan Gere went further in arguing that his straitened financial position was due to Ottley's decision to reject the slave compensation payment.[53] George made a single purchase from Ottley's collection, *The Infant Jesus Sleeping Attended by Angels* by Annibale Caracci (700 guineas).[54] The same year George's brother Robert junior noted a 'Story of George having given £5,000 for Woodhouse's Pictures'.[55] This is probably a reference to the sale of John Woodhouse's collection of drawings by Giovanni Battista Cipriani on 27 February 1801.[56]

In 1801 George entered into a partnership with Sir Simon Haughton Clarke to acquire the renowned collection of Citizen Robit when it was auctioned in Paris. Clarke was also embedded in the slave economy, his father Sir Simon Clarke was married to Anne Haughton, a Jamaica heiress. The family owned five plantations and at the ending of slavery they were collectively awarded £21,048 18s 6d compensation money for 1,141 enslaved people.[57] Michael Bryan, who acted as a broker for the Bridgewater syndicate, was appointed as their agent and furnished with the credit necessary to make the purchase. According to Buchanan, Bryan had 'advised these gentlemen that it might be purchased by them upon the same principle as the Orléans ... with the view of enabling them to possess some capital pictures at a reasonable rate by the sale of others of the same collection'.[58] Bryan's selections from the painting segment cost upwards of 170,000 francs, which 'accounted for more than one quarter of the turnover of the entire sale'.[59] In the end Bryan secured 51 of the 182 catalogued pieces. George's treasures from this collection included *The Virgin Holding the Infant Jesus* by Albano;[60] three landscapes by Nicolaes Pieterszoon Berchem (300 guineas each);[61] *The Marriage Feast at Cana* by Bartolomé Esteban Murillo (1,200 guineas)[62]; *Le Corset Bleu* by Gabriël Metsu (700 guineas)[63]; two paintings of rustic cottages by Isaac Van Ostade (the first valued at 250 guineas and the second at 4,516 francs);[64] *The Holy Family* by Nicholas Poussin (1,200 guineas);[65] and two Rembrandt paintings depicting a warrior and a villager (500 guineas each).[66]

George and his partner sold part of Robit's collection in London. The auction took place on 14 and 15 May 1802 at John Christie's under the catalogue title *The united cabinet of Sir Simon Clarke, Bart. and George Hibbert, Esq*. The timing of the sale coincided with a period of financial instability for the Hibberts' London merchant house. This would perhaps explain why it was George who 'seems to have owned the majority' of paintings being auctioned.[67] There were 142 pieces for sale, some of which came from the Robit collection, others from the Orléans, Calonne and Gildemeester collections. The auction was hugely anticipated and included 'some of the most important old master pictures to be seen on the market during the early part of the century'. Given the desirability of the art on offer, 'the auction attracted unusual attention, resulting also in exceedingly high prices'. The auctioneer for the Excise Office's annotated copy of the catalogue noted that 75 per cent of the paintings remained unsold, a result of overly ambitious reserves rather than a reflection of the quality of the works. As with the Bridgewater syndicate, the choicest paintings were kept by the original buyers, with the sales from the rest of the collection subsidising their purchases. Using the sums recorded in Christie's catalogue, family historian Nicholas Hibbert Steele has calculated that the auction raised approximately £18,454 16s.[68]

The second major sale of George's art collection began on 17 April 1809 and lasted fifteen days. This auction focused on his print collection and represented around 10,000 etchings.[69] Among the lots were a large number of prints of works by Rubens and Rembrandt. An album by Wenceslaus Hollar after Adam Elsheimer attracted the attention of Samuel Woodburn, Lord Fitzwilliam's buyer. As curator Eleanor Ling has noted, the two men 'competed to buy prints; in the same year as the sale of the Orléans pictures, Hibbert and Fitzwilliam's agent, Thomas Philippe, were both bidding on prints at the auction of the great print collection of John Barnard'.[70] The book of prints was sold for £9 15s to Woodburn. In a demonstration of the ways in which cultural capital could be converted into social elevation, a year after the purchase Lord Fitzwilliam sponsored George's membership to the Whig affiliated gentleman's club Brooks's. The images went on display in the 2010 'Prized Possessions' exhibition at the Fitzwilliam Museum in Cambridge, where they form part of the permanent collection.[71] The presence of these prints in the Fitzwilliam Museum is just one example of the ways in which slave-based wealth aided the transfer of art objects into Britain's public collections, enriching its cultural repositories for many generations to come. In 1829 George sold off a portion of his art collection, though the limited nature of the sale frustrated his fellow enthusiasts. The collector and plantation owner James Hughes Anderdon remarked that 'One cannot fail to be greatly disappointed in the expectation of finding this a superior collection ... This can be only a part of that fine collection I had seen some years since in Portland Place.'[72] The sale consisted of seventy-three lots and included works by Federico Barocci, Jan Both, Sébastien Bourdon, Albert Cuyp, Antony Van Dyke, Henry Howard, Pier Francesco Mola, Raphael, David Tenier the Younger, J. M. W. Turner, five works by Rembrandt, two by Rubens and three by Bartolomé Esteban Murillo (including *The Marriage Feast at Cana*). The piece by Turner was bought by the artist himself, who paid £125 15s for it.[73]

According to a study of over 5,000 Dutch auction lots in the second half of the eighteenth century, George was investing in some of the most popular artists of the time.[74] The subjects of his paintings were often classical or biblical, with influences drawn from a Judeo-Christian Western tradition. The story of one of George's most expensive acquisitions – *The Marriage Feast at Cana* – presents a fascinating entanglement between European high art and transatlantic slavery. The painting by the Spanish Baroque artist Bartolomé Esteban Murillo was completed c. 1672 and depicted Jesus turning water into wine. Murillo lived in Seville, which had operated as a slave-trading port since the 1460s. The city had the second highest enslaved population in Europe and people of African descent made up around 10 per cent of the population.[75] It was a common practice for artists to use enslaved labour in their workshops and Murillo was himself a slave owner.[76] The artist depicted an African serving the guests, all of whom were represented as fair-skinned Europeans. The Reverend Thomas Frognall Dibdin noted that this painting hung in George's house at Clapham.[77] The image and its history raise interesting questions about George's emotional and imaginative relationship to the painting; when he looked at Christ accepting the servitude of the African boy did he feel vindicated in his assertion that the Bible authenticated slavery as a Christian practice? Did the romantic representation of the neatly clothed and well-fed black servant confirm for him that slavery was the benign institution he claimed it to be? As a slave owner himself did it remind him of the power he wielded, or did it ever perhaps trouble him? Today the painting is in the collection of the Barber Institute of Fine Arts, University of Birmingham.[78]

If George was able to imagine himself through the prism of his collection, he was also to represent himself in a more literal sense through the medium of portraiture. Peter Funnell has argued that the production of a man's portrait created 'a sense of the dynastic and of a wish to record for future generations his achievements and rise in social status'.[79] Portrait painting was an elite form of cultural consumption, the cost could be extravagant, depending on the calibre of the artist. Selecting a fashionable artist was a necessity – shared patronage was a way of claiming mutual taste with the most powerful cultural figures in the land. George sat for portraits by John Hoppner RA and Sir Thomas Lawrence PRA. Hoppner's sitters included George III, the Prince of Wales, the Duke of York and Lord Nelson. Lawrence was considered 'the leading portrait painter of his generation', whose work depicted 'the principal players of the Regency period'.[80] His portraits

Figure 9 *The Marriage Feast at Cana*, Bartolomé Esteban Murillo

captured the luxury of a society in which both new and old wealth were happy to invest in conspicuous cultural consumption. Both George and his abolitionist opponent Wilberforce sat for Lawrence, with the resulting portraits reflecting the very different characters of these men. Other patrons included George's friends John Julius Angerstein and Sir Francis Baring. According to Funnell, Lawrence felt more at home with these commercial men, whose 'uncertain' backgrounds put him at ease.[81]

Hoppner was commissioned to paint George and his wife Elizabeth in the years immediately following their wedding. The twin portraits were designed to be displayed together in the home, an image of husband and wife enjoying the complementarity of a companionate marriage. The furniture and costume created a sense of the couple's comfortable upper-middle-class lifestyle; expensive and tasteful, but far from flamboyant or excessive, a vision of polite mercantile respectability.[82] Visible behind Elizabeth were the rolling hills and pleasant vistas of the English countryside. Elizabeth's positioning emphasised her femininity, bringing her closer to nature and in doing so closer to the aesthetics of beauty and the sublime. The image of George captured

Figure 10 George Hibbert, James Ward after John Hoppner

Figure 11 Elizabeth Hibbert, James Ward after John Hoppner

his sense of himself as a domestic man, his relaxed pose and thoughtful expression indicative of a genteel sensibility. Hoppner's painting was subsequently turned into two engravings by James Ward and can be found in the collection of the National Portrait Gallery. Omitting any reference to either slavery or the West Indies, the sitter information records only that George was a 'merchant'.[83]

George sat for a second portrait in 1811, this time at the behest of the West India Dock Company, who spent 300 guineas commissioning Sir Thomas Lawrence to paint the portrait in recognition of George's role in founding the docks. In contrast to the intimate domesticity of the Hoppner image, this was a bold representation of George as a public figure. The difference in the two portraits also speaks to changing concepts of manliness. As John Tosh has noted, a characteristically late eighteenth-century emphasis on 'gentlemanly politeness' gave way to a preference for 'manly simplicity'.[84] Whilst gentlemen continued 'to value a certain refinement and sociability', increasingly ideas about 'manliness spoke to the virtues of rugged individualism'. Destined to hang in the exclusively male setting of the Company's boardroom, the portrait was a full-blooded celebration of mercantile masculinity and the commercial empire of the seas. Master of all he surveyed, here was the opulent merchant replete with all the trappings of commercial success. Clad in sumptuous velvet, standing tall with feet apart in a pose which exuded masculine authority, George was presented as a dominant force in the mercantile world. His most enduring and celebrated achievement – the West India Docks – were represented in the background through the framing device of the window, as well as symbolised by the dock plans which rested possessively under his hand. The Lawrence painting became part of the collection of the Port of London Authority and is currently on display at the Museum of London, Docklands.[85]

Book collecting

On 16 March 1829 the sale of part of George Hibbert's book collection commenced. The auction lasted forty-two days and the catalogue comprised 8,794 separate lots, representing around 20,000 volumes with a final value of £21,753 9s. William Younger Fletcher, Assistant Keeper of Printed Books at the British Museum, noted that the collection was rumoured to have cost at least £35,000, meaning the books did not recoup their original investment.[86] The sale was of enough cultural significance for a copy of the catalogue to be held at the British Museum detailing who had purchased each item and the price they paid. In Dibdin's epic *Bibliographical Decameron*, he wrote about George's

Figure 12 *George Hibbert*, Thomas Lawrence, 1811

activities as a bibliophile. Addressing him as 'Honorio',[87] he praised George as 'brave and the bold', adding that:

> I admire his courage and highly approve his taste. No man comes into the field of battle – I should have said the 'field of glory' – with better principles, better taste, or a more resolute determination, than Honorio. Where a work be a 'prime article,' as they designate it, ah, who so courageous, who so vigilant, who so triumphant as Honorio!? And then what follows? Where sleep his treasures? Sleep, did I say? Where are they

opened awake, in broad day, and for the benefit and admiration of his friends?[88]

The text underscored the importance of the discourse of taste as part of the formulation of masculine identity. Depicted as the field of battle and of glory, there was an aggressive virility attached to the competitive bidding of the auction. Despite the combative language, George was presented as generous in his collection, opening it up to his friends rather than hoarding his treasures. This was an aspect of his personality which Markland was also quick to point out. He stated that George 'had none of the ordinary jealousies of a collector, but liberally distributed to others whatever he possessed, which was either new or curious'.[89] Dibdin scoffed at the idea of George's books lying dormant – an important distinction to make if he was going to escape the taint of the ornamental. The trope of the benevolent merchant loomed large in Dibdin's characterisation, he praised George for 'his integrity as a citizen of the world ... his patriotism as senator ... his enlarged and liberal views as a British merchant'.[90] As a transatlantic merchant George could certainly lay claim to being a citizen of the world, although his involvement with slavery raises questions about the limits of his liberality. Dibdin referred to George as 'the De Medici of his day', invoking the figure of the Renaissance merchant prince as a means of historicising mercantile activity in the cultural sphere. Rather than being an upstart interloper, George belonged to a long and illustrious tradition of powerful merchant-collectors.

The sales catalogue for the 1829 auction evidenced George's cultural affinity with the commercial patriciate of the Italian city-states. Two images from George's print collection prefaced the catalogue; the first was Pope Leo X, born Giovanni di Lorenzo de' Medici, and the second was Francesco I Sforza, Duke of Milan. Leo X was the second son of Lorenzo de' Medici, the renowned ruler of the Florentine Republic, a man famed for his lavish financing of the arts. Sforza came from the rural nobility but won the dukedom of Milan following success as a condottieri. Together with several others, these families were credited with fostering the Italian Renaissance through their liberal patronage. That the images were selected from his own personal collection is indicative of the particular meaning they held for him. Like the Hibberts, the Medici and Sforza dynasties were self-made professional people with experience in commerce, banking and the military. In an epilogue to the *Mayor of Garret* penned by George he mused:

Well of my family I'm proud I vow,
We ... are come to high preferment now.
And some of us, the Lord knows how, of late

Be counsellors and Ministers of State.
'Tis a vast height to rise, and much I fear
We do but cut a sneaking figure there.[91]

Both the poem and the prints were knowing nods to the family's mercantile roots. The inclusion of these figures in the sales catalogue gives an impression of the kind of culture which George venerated and a glimpse into the way in which he framed his sense of himself. The Sforza print was acquired by the British Museum in 1861, creating a permanent link between these two self-made men and the cultural worlds they both inhabited.[92]

The preface to the catalogue boasted that George's collection was rivalled only by that of the Duke of Roxburghe.[93] According to R. H. Evans, George had intended that the collection 'should contain at once the Sources of General Information and Amusement, and also choice Specimens, illustrating the Origin, Progress, and Perfection of the Art of Printing'. Evans likened George's library to that of Gian Vincenzo Pinelli, a sixteenth-century Italian bibliophile, botanist and collector. The contents of the collection was summarised for potential buyers:

> It is rich in early-printed Bibles, in the various divisions of Natural History, and is, perhaps, unrivalled in the accumulation of early French Romances, and in its extensive assemblage of the rarest productions of Italian Poetry. In it will also be found many curious and rare Articles of our English poetry.[94]

Many of these volumes had been purchased from the sale of Count Justin de MacCarthy-Reagh's library in 1817. Given George's position as a leading West India merchant, he owned a number of books relating to transatlantic slavery. There were fourteen volumes on the history of Jamaica, including *Account of the island of Jamaica* (2 vols) by William Beckford, a volume on *Slave law in Jamaica* (1828) and Bryan Edwards's *Account of the Maroon war* (1796). There were three books on the history of the West Indies more broadly, notably James McQueen's *West India colonies* (1824). There were several tracts on Caribbean slavery, including Alexander Barclay's *View of the present state of slavery in the West Indies* (2 vols), the anonymous *Tracts on the slave trade* (1792) and James Walker's *Letters on the West Indies* (1818). There were also two books on American slavery – Thomas Jefferson's *Notes on the State of Virginia* (1787) and Jesse Torrey's *On the American slave trade* (1822). Markland outlined the choicest items in the collection, which included 'the first edition of Luther's translation, *his own copy* [italics original]; the Mazarine Bible, of Gutenberg and Fust; and the Polyglott Bible, of Cardinal Ximenes'.[95] Markland considered his uncle's library to be one of the finest in the world, writing that 'With the exception of the libraries of Earl Spencer, Duke of Roxburghe, Mr. Heber, and Mr. Grenville, it may, perhaps, be doubted whether there was ever collected, by a private individual, in this country, an assemblage of books at once so extensive, valuable, and curious.'[96]

The deference shown to these other collectors stemmed from Markland's intimate knowledge of elite bibliophile circles through his membership of the Roxburghe Club. The club was formed at the suggestion of Dibdin, following the death of the great book collector John Ker, third Duke of Roxburghe. On 18 May 1812, the night before the sale of Roxburghe's collection, a group of bibliophiles gathered to commemorate the 'knocking down of that magical article'.[97] The social mixture of the group was varied, 'it was books that levelled the barriers that might otherwise have existed then between them'.[98] The eighteen founders included Earl Spencer, the Dukes of Devonshire, Sutherland and Marlborough, Sir Mark Masterman Sykes Bart., Sir Francis Feeling, Richard Heber, Joseph Haslewood and Markland. George was nominated for membership at the club's anniversary dinner in 1816. Alongside George and his nephew, several other members also had ties to the slave economy, including Robert Lang, George Watson Taylor and John Dent.[99]

The Roxburghe Club was formed around the idea of reprinting rare literature. Members were interested in the classics, chivalric romances, topographical works, antiquarian lore, early travel accounts, natural history and above all black-letter tracts, which were English-language texts that used early printing techniques. The veneration of the printed word was evident in the toast made by the group at their annual dinner. The men raised their glasses to 'The immortal memory of John Duke of Roxburghe, of Christopher Valdarfer, printer of the Boccacio of 1471. Gutenberg, Fust and Schoeffer, the Inventors of the Art of Printing. William Caxton, Father of the British press ... The Prosperity of the Roxburghe Club. The Cause of Bibliomania all over the World'.[100] The toast created a clear line of inheritance from the ancient discipline of philology, to the first Germanic printing techniques, the development of an English printing press and a form of Enlightenment culture embodied by John Ker. The printing press held a central place in the conception of a modern Protestant European culture, having played a vital role in the Reformation, the scientific revolution and the age of Enlightenment. It was this fusion of literary, aesthetic, technological and scientific achievement that the Roxburghe Club celebrated. Possessing the volumes which signified this culture became an act of self-identification with it. The primacy given to the written word also created a hierarchical difference between cultures which were considered literate and those which were based on 'primitive' oral traditions. The book symbolised the cultural difference between Africa, as it was imagined in the minds of men like George, and Europe as it was experienced by the members of the Roxburghe Club.

The practice of members contributing a translation of their own to the Club was a way in which the individual could demonstrate his intellectual accomplishment. George presented a copy of Ovid's *Metamorphoses* in 1819. Prior to finishing it he wrote to Spencer to inform him that 'I am now actually at work upon the "Ovyde" by Caxton for the Roxburghe. The language is curious and the style quaint enough but Caxton does not always render his author faithfully or perhaps he has followed implicitly some French Translator.'[101] In critiquing Caxton and the translator, George contrasted his own superior understanding, increasing his reputation for literary refinement. The British Library holds a copy of George's work, ensuring that his legacy included a remembrance of him in the mode of learned bibliophile and classicist.[102]

Writing in 1866, John Timbs FSA gave a largely unfavourable account of the Roxburghe Club. He mocked the 'follies of the age of paper' and in particular the 'set of book-fanciers, who had more money than wit, [who] formed themselves into a club, and appropriately designated themselves the Bibliomaniacs'.[103] The description also included an account of the Club's famed dinners. The centrality of masculine sociability to club membership can be read in Timbs's assertion that 'It may, however, be questioned whether "the dinners" of the Club were not more important than the literature.'[104] Details of the dining culture were taken from 'The Roxburghe Revels' by Joseph Haslewood, one of the founder members. Defending its depiction of the gluttony of the period, the *Gentleman's Magazine* noted 'the alleged extravagance of the Roxburghe Club Dinners would equally apply, we conceive, to every party patronizing the same expensive houses; and should be regarded as the tax paid for the fancied advantage of being entertained at an aristocratic tavern'.[105] The manuscript described a dinner which took place at on 17 June 1815 at Grillion's Hotel on Albemarle Street. The drinks list consisted of '5 Boutelle de Champagne, 7 Boutelle de harmetage, 1 Boutelle de Hok, 4 Boutelle de Prt, 4 Boutelle de Maderre, 22 Boutelle de Bordeaux, 2 Boutelle de Bourgogne, Bierre e Ail'.[106] For a dinner which took place in 1818 at the Albion in Aldersgate Street the members were treated to a first course of 'turtle cutlets and fins, a fricandeau of turtle, turbot, boiled and roasted chicken, ham, chartreuse, fillets of whitings, sauté of haddock, tendrons of lamb, tongue, cold roast beef, whitebait and John Dory'.[107] The second course consisted of 'two haunches of venison' and the third included 'larded poults, roasted quails, prawns, leveret, goose, peas, artichoke bottoms, Salade Italienne, Crême Italienne, tart, cheesecakes, jelly, cabinet pudding and tourt'. The menu is indicative of a world of luxury – no expense was spared to source food from across the country and even the further reaches of the empire. The atmosphere of the night's entertainment was described by Haslewood:

> Consider, in the bird's eye view of the banquet, the trencher cuts, foh! Nankeen displays; as intersticed with many a brilliant drop to friendly beck and clubbish hail, to moisten viandes, or cool the incipient cayenne. No unfamished liveryman would desire better dishes, or hightasted courtier better wines. With men that meet to commune, that can converse, and each willing to give and receive information, more could not be wanting to promote well-tempered conviviality; a social compound of mirth, wit, and wisdom.[108]

For the club members cultural identity combined private endeavour with public performance. The role of wit and conversation was as important as the collecting and translating of rare texts. Speeches were the order of the day, with Haslewood likening the oratory to that of Demosthenes, Anacreon and Scaliger. The allusion to classical society creates an impression of the sense of continuity felt by the members of the club; here among learned men at the centre of an imperial world, civilisation in its fullest expression could be found.

Botany

The manly pursuit of rational and scientific knowledge was actively cultivated by Clapham's middle-class inhabitants. Both George and his abolitionist rival Robert Thornton were remembered by the Scottish botanist John Claudius Loudon, who wrote: 'George Hibbert, and Thornton of Clapham, opulent commercial men, may be mentioned as great encouragers of gardening and botany. The collection of heaths, Banksias, and other Cape and Botany Bay plants, in Hibbert's garden, was most extensive, and his flower-garden one of the best round the metropolis.'[109] Markland also gave a detailed description of his uncle's botanical activities:

> [T]he collection of plants at his residence in Clapham was commenced about the year 1796. In forming it, he employed agents in almost every part of the globe; and he was the means of introducing into this country many new and beautiful species, and some new genera of plants, some of which are now common in our gardens; others have never blossomed except in his green house. A reference to the botanical works of the day

will sufficiently show the high rank which the Clapham collection held both here and on the Continent.[110]

George was a serious collector and a rivalry grew between him and Sir Joseph Banks, President of the Royal Society and an adviser to the Royal Botanic Gardens at Kew. Markland made a veiled reference to this, stating that George 'had reason to know that orders were given in the highest quarters at home, to impart none of the acquisitions in the Royal Gardens to him'. George spared no expense in pursuing his passion – the building of a hothouse stood testament to his botanical ambitions.[111] He employed a gardener, Joseph Knight, who resided full time on the property, tending to the collection. Knight remained in George's employ until the family removed from Clapham in 1820, at which point he gave Knight his living collection. Knight went on to form the Royal Exotic Nursery on the King's Road, Chelsea.[112]

George's role as a merchant and his involvement with shipping gave him access to networks which enabled him to participate in the global practice of botany. He was interested in projects that combined imperial venture, scientific experiment and commercial concerns. The Hibberts were involved in the expedition to transport breadfruit from the South Pacific to the Caribbean. George's library catalogue included John Ellis's *Description of the mangostan and the breadfruit* (1775).[113] Ellis argued that breadfruit could be used to supply the planters with a cheap source of nourishment for the enslaved. This experiment was championed by Banks, who described the project as one of 'utility and benevolence'.[114] He helped to organise the scheme from London and offered a Royal Society medal for its successful transportation.[115] Captain William Bligh was chosen to lead the expedition; Bligh had connections to the Caribbean through his wife's uncle – Duncan Campbell – an absentee planter and West India merchant who owned the Salt Spring estate in Jamaica.[116] Between 1784 and 1787 Bligh resided at Campbell's great house near Green Island Harbour and acted as his agent.[117] He served on Campbell's ships transporting sugar and rum – Lloyd's register of ships indicated he made ten voyages during that period.[118]

In 1793 Bligh's ship the *Providence* was welcomed into Port Royal. An officer described its appearance as a 'floating forest', noting that it was 'eagerly visited by numbers of every rank and degree'.[119] The local population's interest in the spectacle led another member of the crew to complain that 'the common Civility of going around the Ship with them and explaining the Plants became by its frequency rather troublesome'. On 16 February 1793 the *Royal Gazette* reported that 'The Gentlemen chosen to distribute the ten plants allotted to this parish disposed of them on Wednesday as follows – To Mr. Hibbert one, Dr. Grant one, Mr. Elder one, Mr. Loosely one, and Mr. Paterson one: For the other five there were thirteen other claimants, who drew lots.'[120] The 'Mr. Hibbert' referred to was George's brother Robert junior, who noted the occasion in his diary.[121] To be a named recipient of one of the precious specimens was a mark of esteem; the desire to possess the plant stemmed not only from its potential as a commercially exploitable commodity, but also as a signifier of status. Although initially the enslaved population were resistant to eating the breadfruit, it has now become a staple part of Jamaican cuisine.

This was not the only occasion when the Hibberts were involved in the transfer of botanical specimens, although their contribution seems to have been incidental in these instances. In 1792 the botanist Thomas Dancer recorded '*Amomum Gr. Paradisi* Grains of paradise or Guiney Pepper. Introduced by Mr Hibbert from Africa'.[122] He also noted '*Aka Africana* Another African fruit, introduced by Negroes in some of Mr. Hibbert's ships'. Desperate to take something of Africa to their new lives in the Caribbean, enslaved people carried the seeds with them – a botanical trace of home transplanted into this new alien environment. The common name for the aka in contemporary usage is ackee and the fruit is widely celebrated as one of the national dishes of Jamaica.

In 1798 George tasked the horticulturalist James Niven with travelling to the Cape of Good Hope, where he collected seeds for George's garden.[123] Niven was considered to be one of the most significant experts of his time and was subsequently employed by the Empress Josephine, with whom George exchanged specimens.[124] George sent another of his botanical experts out to collect specimens in Jamaica. James Macfadyen was a Scottish botanist who trained in medicine at Glasgow. He was commissioned by George 'to collect for his private botanical garden in Clapham'.[125] Macfadyen was employed as Island Botanist in Jamaica between 1826 and 1828. He was the founder of the Jamaica Botanic Garden and published *The Flora of Jamaica* (2 vols) in 1837. George's relationship with Macfayden was capitalised upon in 1825, when he was asked by Robert Wilmot-Horton, Under-Secretary of State for War and the Colonies, to look into the possibility of cultivating silk in Jamaica. George replied that:

> I am now sending out a clever young Scotsman, as Curator of the Public Botanic Gardens of the Island – the Legislature will allow him a salary of £400 sterling a year. The Silk Establishment would not probably feed & wash & afford medical aid for all the whites under it & if it did not so I fear that Persons respectable & trust worthy & scientific, could not be had for much less than I am to give my Botanist.[126]

George's cultivation of botanical knowledge and connections conveyed upon him the authority needed to be taken seriously in new scientific ventures directly affecting colonisation and trade.

In 1793 George became a Fellow of the Linnean Society. The Society was founded in 1788 by James Edward Smith after he purchased the collection of Carl Linnaeus. Linnaeus's work formed the basis for modern taxonomy – the hierarchical organisation and classification of the plant and animal world. The practices associated with the taxonomical process – exploration, discovery, naming, categorising – were heavily implicated in the structures of colonialism that privileged European forms of knowledge and representation. In the tenth edition of Linnaeus's *Systema naturae*, he established five categories of the human race; Americanus, Asiaticus, Africanus, Europeanus and Monstrosus. The Africanus was defined as 'being "black, relaxed and negligent" as well as "ruled by caprice" or an all too fickle attention'.[127] Linnaeus's ideas offered a veneer of scientific authority to George's vested interest in the production of knowledge about Africans and their supposed inferior status to Europeans. The Society eventually acquired George's private herbarium.[128] In 1960 the collection was transferred to the Natural History Museum, where it remains today.

In 1811 George became a fellow of the Royal Society. From the mid-eighteenth century through to the immediate aftermath of abolition, twenty-two slave and plantation owners have been identified as Fellows.[129] George's proposers included John Rennie, the engineer for the West India Docks, Richard Sharp, a fellow West India merchant, Joseph Huddart, the hydrographer, Gibbes Walker Jordan, the Agent for Barbados, William Hasledine Pepys of the London Institution and James Edward Smith, the President of the Linnean Society. The importance of networks of masculine association can be read in the cultural and commercial links between these men. The sponsorship document read:

> George Hibbert Esqr MP FLS of Clapham Common, a Gentleman well versed in Natural History & Botany and other Branches of Science, being desirous of becoming a Fellow of the Royal Society, we whose names are hereunto subscribed do on our personal Knowledge, recommend him as deserving of that honor, and likely to become an useful and valuable member.[130]

The Society consisted of both practising scientists and wealthy amateurs, many of whom also functioned as patrons funding the research which was at the heart of the Society's operations.[131] The relationship between applied technological science as a producer of income and as a signifier of polite learning meant it was taken up with great enthusiasm by the aspirant upper-middle-classes.[132] Kenneth Cozens has pointed to the high proportion of merchant men within the Society, suggesting that membership increased the impact of their lobbying activities at governmental level.[133] The men of the Society realised the potential for science and commerce to unite and in doing so harness theoretical knowledge to practical experience in order to think through the problems of imperial trade and colonisation. Richard Drayton has interpreted this expression of Enlightenment culture as the 'rise of an imperialism of improvement' which joined European power 'to the scientific mastery of nature' in the belief that this would 'confer the greatest good on the greatest number'.[134] Enlightenment, enterprise and empire would remake the world, reordering it for the benefit of coloniser and (less convincingly) the colonised.

The combination of an ornamental, productive, imperial and commercial interest in plants created multiple meanings for George's botanical activities. As a man of refined taste it enabled him to establish a famed pleasure garden where friends and family could consume the delights of nature. The effect was captured vividly by Dibdin:

> Must I tell how the Alpine or Chinese roses, how the exotics from America or Japan have given place to the delicious performances – to flowers whose bloom is perennial – from the garden plots of *Spira*, *Jenson*, and *Zarotus* [italics original]? Shall I lead you in imagination to the morroco (not azalia) bowers, and russia (not orange-tree) vistos, of Honorio?[135]

As a merchant and slave owner, his activities held the potential to solve real-world problems. As someone who was keen to establish his public expertise, his collection transformed his home into a place of learning where newly discovered species were introduced. His success with the cultivation of one particular genus resulted in it being named after him. The yellow-flowered *Hibbertia* originated in Australia and was developed at Clapham by James Knight. This horticultural memorial has enshrined a particular kind of identification for George as one of the great amateur botanists of the period. Although George never visited the further reaches of empire, he stocked his garden full of the flora and fauna of the imperial world, creating his own botanical microcosm of the empire in his hothouse in Clapham. For George, his garden became a way in which he was truly at home with the empire.

Conclusion

'A love of letters' was a life-long passion for George, wrote his nephew Markland, who added that 'it was to this passion ... that much of

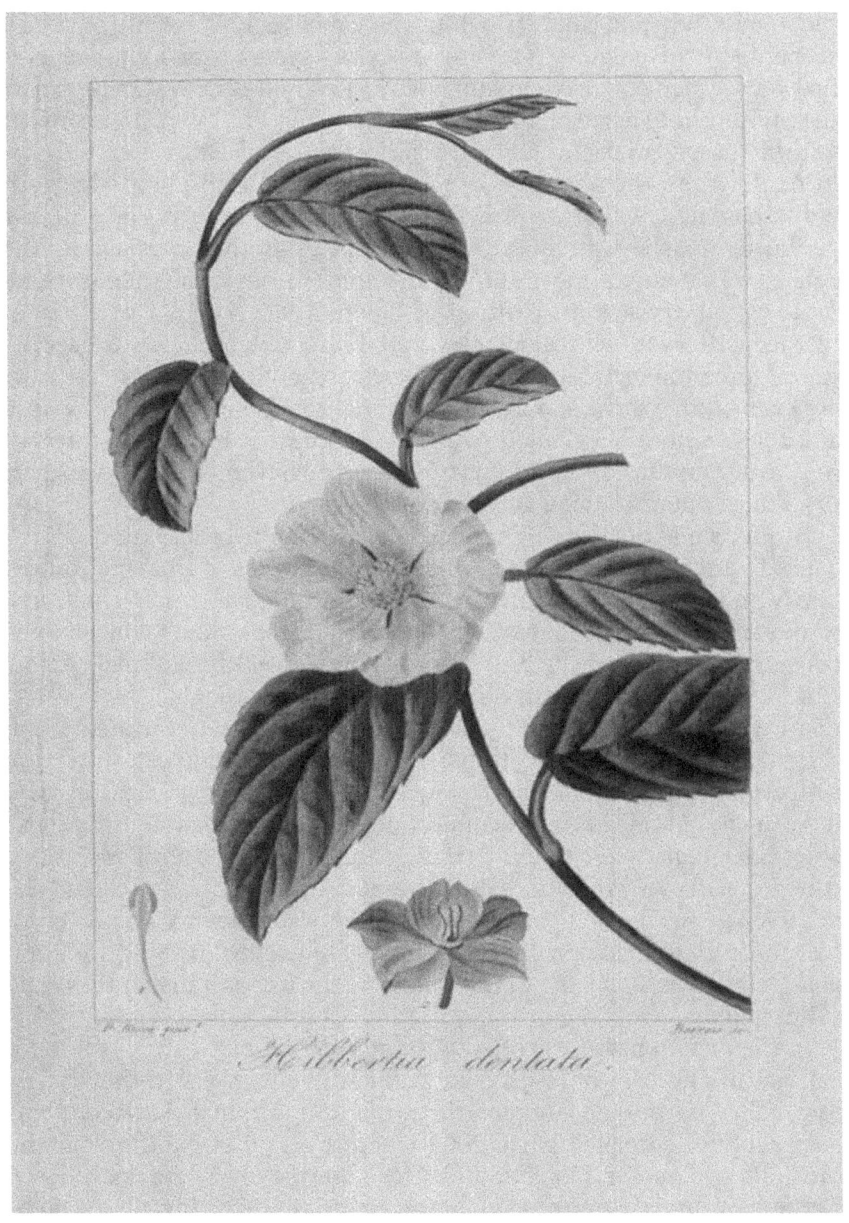

Figure 13 *Hibbertia dentata*

the reputation and success which he enjoyed in after-life is to be attributed'.[136] George's collecting practices secured for him a reputation for learned connoisseurship both in his own time and in the years that followed. This was useful both in terms of embedding himself within the cultural elite and in relation to the debates over slavery. In reference to the absentee Jamaica planter Edward Long, Elizabeth Bohls has argued that he sought to 'project the identity of a highly civilized British gentleman, only to conscript that persona in the defense of Jamaica's most glaring and contentious difference from its mother country: the institution of colonial slavery'.[137] Participation in the polite and genteel practices of Enlightenment culture served to reinforce the racial divisions between the civilised and uncivilised, between those whose superiority ordained them with the right to rule and those whom they ruled over. This argument formed a strand of proslavery discourse which suggested that enslavement itself was part of a process of improving the African.

In more practical terms collecting was a form of speculation that could be monetised to offer both security in times of financial uncertainty and an inheritance that would appreciate over time. The transformation of enslaved labour into the elegant trappings of conspicuous consumption masked the brutal origins of the wealth that made it possible. Evidence of the cultural transference that was enabled by involvement with the slave economy can be found in many of Britain's local, regional and national collections. The extent of the impact on private collections remains largely unknowable. Links to transatlantic slavery in both the exhibition labels and catalogue entries documenting these objects have utilised euphemistic language to describe both sitters and collectors. In many instances these connections are entirely absent. The relative silence around the relationship between slavery and Britain's cultural inheritance continues to propagate exclusionary and incomplete narratives about the development of the nation's institutions and collections.

In the bicentenary year of 2007 some cultural institutions chose to engage in a process of re-examining their connections to the slaving past. The portrait of George Hibbert by Sir Thomas Lawrence has been on public display since 2003 when it was first exhibited at the Museum of London, Docklands in the 'Coming of the Docks' gallery. Georgie Wemyss has noted that originally the painting was accompanied by 'the non ironic caption that although he was a slave owner, he was also a liberal patron of the arts'.[138] In 2007 the portrait was rehung at the centre of the 'London, Sugar, Slavery' exhibition. This time the label focused solely on George's activities as a slave owner, including his role in the defence of the institution with a note on how

Figure 14 *Reconstructed Portrait with Lloyd Gordon as Robert Wedderburn*, Paul Howard, 2007

much compensation his family received. Having listened carefully to the exhibition's advisory board, who cautioned against displaying the portrait in isolation, the work was exhibited next to a specially commissioned partner portrait by Paul Howard of the radical black abolitionist Robert Wedderburn. In a subversion of the original image, the costume and stance mimicked Lawrence's visual language. The sumptuous interior of Lawrence's scene was replaced with the bare boards and barrels of the dock warehouse. The dock designs were substituted for *The Poor Man's Guardian*, a radical newspaper which challenged the political and economic power of the elites. The presence of a Phrygian cap – the symbol of both the French and Haitian Revolutions – reminded the viewer of both the promise and the persistent failings of liberty, fraternity and equality. The docks themselves were reconfigured as Canary Wharf – a towering symbol of financial might and a stark reminder of the ways in which global capitalism continues to shape the relations of class, race and gender. In his own lifetime and in the wake of his death, culture was harnessed as a means of reorientating George's identity and memory. It is only in understanding how that cultivated world was financed and the ways in which it helped to reinforce the racial structures which enabled it that we can begin to unpick the complicated relationship between slavery, race and culture.

Notes

1 For a discussion of this relationship in relation to the East Indies see Maya Jassanoff, *Edge of empire: Lives, culture and conquest in the East, 1750–1850* (New York: Vintage, 2006).
2 J. H. Markland, *A sketch of the life and character of George Hibbert Esq., F.R.S., S.A., and L.S.* (London, 1837), pp. 15–16.
3 Jürgen Habermas, *The structural transformation of the public sphere: An inquiry into a category of bourgeois society* (Cambridge: Polity, 1989).
4 Roy Porter, *Enlightenment: Britain and the creation of the modern world* (London: Penguin Books, 2000), p. 34.
5 Ibid., p. 35.
6 *Authentic copies of the codicils belonging to the last will and testament of Sir Hans Sloane, Bart. deceased, which relate to his collection of books and curiosities* (London: Daniel Browne, 1753), p. 19.
7 James Delbourgo, *Collecting the world: The life and curiosity of Hans Sloane* (London: Allen Lane, 2017), p. 149.
8 Margot Finn, 'Men's things: Masculine possession in the consumer revolution', *Social History*, 25:2 (2000), p. 135.
9 Holger Hoock, ' "Struggling against vulgar prejudice": Patriotism and the collecting of British art at the turn of the nineteenth century', *Journal of British Studies*, 49:3 (2010), p. 570.
10 Sing-Chen Lydia Chiang, *Collecting the self: Body and identity in strange tale collections of late imperial China* (Boston: Brill, 2004), p. 1.
11 Delbourgo, *Collecting the world*, p. xxviii.
12 Simon Gikandi, *Slavery and the culture of taste* (Princeton, NJ: Princeton University Press, 2011), p. 37.
13 Jonathan Richardson, *The works of Mr. Jonathan Richardson: consisting of I. The theory of painting, II. Essay on the art of criticism so far as it relates to painting, III. The science of a connoisseur* (London: T. Davies, 1773), pp. 284–5.
14 David Hume, 'Of national characteristics', in *Essays and treaties on several subjects*, new edn (London: A. Millar, 1758), p. 125.
15 There is a large amount of literature on the relationship between museums and empire including Tim Barringer and Tom Flynn (eds), *Colonialism and the object: Empire, material culture and the museum* (Abingdon: Routledge, 1997); John

M. Mackenzie, *Museums and empire: Natural history, human cultures and colonial identities* (Manchester: Manchester University Press, 2010); Sarah Longair and John McAleer (eds), *Curating empire: Museums and the British imperial experience* (Manchester: Manchester University Press, 2016).
16 The presence of imperial objects within elite homes has been explored in Margot Finn and Kate Smith (eds), *The East India Company at home, 1757–1857* (London: University College London Press, 2018).
17 For an anthology of writings on this subject see Emmanuel Chukwudi Eze (ed.), *Race and Enlightenment: A reader* (Oxford: Blackwell Publishing, 1997). For a critical analysis see Daniel Carey and Lynn Festa (eds), *Postcolonial Enlightenment: Eighteenth-century colonialism and postcolonial theory* (Oxford: Oxford University Press, 2009).
18 Roxann Wheeler, *The complexion of race: Categories of difference in eighteenth-century British culture* (Philadelphia: University of Pennsylvania Press, 2000).
19 Edward Long, *The history of Jamaica; Or, general survey of the antient and modern state of the island, with reflections on its situation, settlements, inhabitants, climate, products, commerce, laws, and government ...*, vol. II (London: T. Lowndes, 1774), p. 364.
20 Julia O'Connell Davidson, *The margins of freedom: Modern slavery* (Basingstoke: Palgrave Macmillan, 2015), pp. 46–51.
21 Robert Hibbert, *Hints to the young Jamaica sugar planter* (London: T. and G. Underwood, 1825), p. 7.
22 Ibid., pp. 5–6.
23 Ibid., p. 6.
24 Charles White, *An account of the regular gradation in man and in different animals and vegetables* (London: C. Dilly, 1799), p. 137.
25 Hibbert, *Hints*, p. 6.
26 Ibid.
27 Ibid., pp. 6–7.
28 Ibid., p. 7. For an analysis of these ideas in relation to archaeological theory and practice see Debbie Challis, *The archaeology of race: The eugenic ideas of Francis Galton and Flinders Petrie* (London: Bloomsbury, 2013).
29 Hibbert, *Hints*, pp. 7–8.
30 www.georgehibbert.com/artcol.html [Accessed 27 February 2018].
31 Markland, *Sketch*, p. 17.
32 *A collection of prints illustrative of English scenery, from the drawings and sketches of Thos. Gainsborough, R.A. in the various collections of the right honourable Baroness Lucas; Viscount Palmerston; George Hibbert, Esq.; Dr. Monro, and several other gentlemen* (London: H. R. Young, 1819), Royal Academy of Arts Collection, 07/3149.
33 Diary of Joseph Farington, quoted in Holger Hoock, 'From beefsteak to turtle: Artists' dinner culture in eighteenth-century London', *Huntington Library Quarterly*, 66:1/2 (2003), p. 41.
34 William Buchanan, *Memoirs of painting, with a chronological history of the importation of pictures by the Great Masters into England since the French Revolution*, vol. I (London: R. Ackermann, 1824), pp. 21–2.
35 Ibid., p. 21.
36 Ibid., p. 46.
37 Ibid., p. 47.
38 Ibid., p. 56.
39 Ibid., p. 57.
40 Ibid., p. 82.
41 Ibid., p. 95.
42 Ibid., p. 107.
43 Ibid., p. 115.
44 Ibid., p. 188.
45 Ibid., p. 252.

46 *Ibid.*, p. 293.
47 *Ibid.*, pp. 293–4.
48 *Ibid.*, p. 294.
49 *Ibid.*, pp. 294–5.
50 Buchanan, *Memoirs of painting*, vol. II, p. 6.
51 'William Young Ottley', Legacies of British Slave-ownership database. www.ucl.ac.uk/lbs/person/view/2146639291 [accessed 20 February 2018].
52 Nicholas Turner, 'Young, William Ottley (1771–1836), writer on art and collector', *Oxford dictionary of national biography* (Oxford: Oxford University Press, 2004), https://doi.org/10.1093/ref:odnb/20941 [accessed 1 March 2018].
53 J. Allan Gere, 'William Young Ottley as a collector of drawings', *British Museum Quarterly*, 18:2 (1953), pp. 44–53
54 Buchanan, *Memoirs of painting*, vol. II, p. 28.
55 HFAC, Diary of Robert Hibbert junior, 22 February 1801.
56 *A catalogue of the well-known and truly valuable collection of drawings, the property of John Woodhouse, Esq. ...: which will be sold by auction by Mr. Christie, at his great room, Pall-Mall, on Friday, the 27th of February, 1801, and following day* (London: H. D. Steel, 1801).
57 'Sir Simon Haughton Clarke', Legacies of British Slave-ownership database. www.ucl.ac.uk/lbs/person/view/1853282328 [accessed 21 February 2018]
58 Buchanan, *Memoirs of painting*, vol. II, pp. 35–6.
59 Darius A. Speith, *Revolutionary Paris and the market for Netherlandish art* (Boston: Brill, 2017), p. 398.
60 Buchanan, *Memoirs of painting*, vol. II, p. 38.
61 *Ibid.*, pp. 38–40.
62 *Ibid.*, p. 51.
63 *Ibid.*, pp. 54–5.
64 *Ibid.*, pp. 56–7.
65 *Ibid.*, pp. 57–8.
66 *Ibid.*, p. 63.
67 'Sale Catalog Br-111, Christie's, 1802 14–15 May 1802', Getty Provenance Index database. http://piprod.getty.edu/starweb/pi/servlet.starweb?path=pi/pi.link5.web&search2=6431# [accessed 21 February 2018].
68 www.georgehibbert.com/artcol.html [accessed 21 February 2018].
69 *Catalogue of a superb assemblage of prints, formed by a gentleman of distinguished taste and judgment ... which will be sold by auction ... 17 April 1809* (London: T. Philipe, 1809).
70 Eleanor Ling, *Prized possessions: Lord Fitzwilliam's album of prints after Adam Elsheimer* (Cambridge: Fitzwilliam Museum, 2010), p. 17.
71 'Adam Elsheimer/Hibbert', Fitzwilliam Museum, Cambridge, Collection Explorer. http://webapps.fitzmuseum.cam.ac.uk/explorer/index.php?qu=Adam%20Elsheimer%20hibbert [accessed 3 February 2019].
72 Description of Sale Catalog Br-3314, Getty Provenance Index database. www.getty.edu/research/tools/provenance/search.html [accessed 7 May 2019].
73 www.georgehibbert.com/artcol.html [accessed 27 February 2018].
74 Dries Lyna, 'Name hunting, visual characteristics, and "New Old Masters": Tracking the taste for paintings at eighteenth-century auctions', *Eighteenth-Century Studies*, 46:1 (2012), pp. 57–84.
75 Tanya J. Tiffany, *Diego Velázquez's early paintings and the culture of seventeenth-century Seville* (University Park, PA: Penn State University Press, 2012), p. 103.
76 Luis Méndez Rodríguez and Jeremy Roe, 'Slavery and the guild in Golden Age painting in Seville', *Art in Translation*, 7:1 (2015), p. 134.
77 Thomas Frognall Dibdin, *Bibliographical Decameron; Or ten days pleasant discourse upon illuminated manuscripts, and subjects connected with early engravings, typography, and bibliography*, vol. III (London: W. Bulmer & Co., 1817), pp. 35–6.
78 http://barber.org.uk/bartolome-esteban-murillo-1617-1682/ [accessed 1 March 2018]

79 Peter Funnell, 'Lawrence among men: Friends, patrons and the male portrait', in A. Cassandra Albinson, Peter Funnell and Lucy Peltz (eds), *Thomas Lawrence: Regency power and brilliance* (London: Yale University Press, 2010), pp. 13–14.
80 A. Cassandra Albinson, Peter Funnell and Lucy Peltz (eds), *Thomas Lawrence: Regency power and brilliance* (London: Yale University Press, 2010), pp. ix, viii.
81 Funnell, 'Lawrence among men', pp. 9–10.
82 www.npg.org.uk/collections/search/portrait/mw193534/Elizabeth-Margaret-Hibbert-ne-Fonnereau?LinkID=mp121639&search=sas&sText=Hibbert&OConly=true&role=sit&rNo=0 [accessed 3 February 2019].
83 www.npg.org.uk/collections/search/portrait/mw193533 [accessed 3 February 2019].
84 John Tosh, 'Gentlemanly politeness and manly simplicity in Victorian England', *Transactions of the Royal Historical Society*, 12:6 (2002), p. 458.
85 https://collections.museumoflondon.org.uk/online/object/726143.html [accessed 3 February 2019].
86 William Younger Fletcher, *English book collectors* (London: Kegan Paul, Trench, Trübner & Co., 1902), p. 301.
87 Dibdin revealed that 'Honorio' was George Hibbert in *Reminiscences of a literary life; With anecdotes of books, and of book collectors*, vol. II (London: John Major, 1836), p. 679.
88 Dibdin, *Bibliographical Decameron*, p. 35.
89 Markland, *Sketch*, p. 16.
90 Dibdin, *Bibliographical Decameron*, p. 35.
91 BL/GHCP, RP5573, 'Epilogue to the Mayor of Garratt', 4 January 1810.
92 Portrait of Francesco I Sforza, Duke of Milan, illustration from George Hibbert's auction catalogue (16 March–6 June 1829), British Museum, London, Collection Online. www.britishmuseum.org/research/collection_online/collection_object_details.aspx?objectId=3652866&partId=1&people=117256&page=2 [accessed 13 February 2019].
93 *A catalogue of the library of George Hibbert Esq., of Portland Place; which will be sold by auction on Monday, March 16, and seventeen following days; and on Monday, May 4, and eleven following days; and on Monday, May 25, and eleven following days, (Sundays excepted) by Mr. Evans, at his house, No.93, Pall Mall* (London: W. Nichols, 1829).
94 *Ibid*.
95 Markland, *Sketch*, p. 17.
96 *Ibid*., p. 18.
97 Nicholas Barker, 'The Roxburghe Club', *London Library Magazine*, 17 (Autumn, 2012), p. 19.
98 www.roxburgheclub.org.uk/history/#membersSub [accessed 22 February 2018].
99 For a summary of members with links to the West Indies see Shayne Husbands, *The early Roxburghe Club 1812–1835: Book club pioneers and the advancement of English Literature* (London: Anthem Press, 2017), pp. 54–7.
100 John Timbs, *Clubs and club life in London with anecdotes of the clubs, coffee-houses and taverns of the metropolis in the seventeenth, eighteenth and nineteenth centuries*, vol. II (London: Richard Bentley, 1866), p. 163.
101 British Library, London, Althorp Papers, Additional MS 76122, Letter from George Hibbert to Lord Spencer, 8 December 1818.
102 British Library, London, General Reference Collection, C.101.a.24, George Hibbert, *Six bookes of Metamorphoseos in whyche ben conteyned the fables of Ovyde. Translated out of Frensshe into Englysshe, by W. Caxton* (1819).
103 Timbs, *Clubs and club life*, p. 164.
104 *Ibid*., p. 159.
105 *The Gentleman's Magazine*, vol. I (London: John Bowyer Nichols, 1834), p. 287.
106 Joseph Haslewood, quoted in Timbs, *Clubs and club life*, p. 160.
107 *Ibid*., p. 161.
108 *Ibid*., p. 162.

109 John Claudius Loudon, *An encyclopaedia of gardening; comprising of the theory and practice of horticulture, floriculture, arboriculture, and landscape gardening; including all the latest improvements, a general history of gardening in all countries; and a statistical view of its present state; with suggestions for its future progress in the British Isles* (London: Longman, Green, Longman, & Roberts, 1860), p. 277.
110 Markland, *Sketch*, p. 16.
111 Surrey History Centre, Woking, G85/2/1/1/134, Sale particulars of residence on north side of Common in Clapham with 6a (George Hibbert Esq) and 5a meadow on the Wandsworth Road.
112 'Trinity Hospice Garden, Lambeth', London Gardens Online. www.londongardensonline.org.uk/gardens-online-record.asp?ID=LAM057a [accessed 26 February 2018].
113 *Catalogue of the library of George Hibbert*, p. 80.
114 Joseph Banks, quoted in Vanessa Smith, 'Give us our daily breadfruit: Bread substitution in the Pacific in the eighteenth century', *Studies in Eighteenth-Century Culture*, 35 (2006), p. 66.
115 Alan Frost, *Sir Joseph Banks and the transfer of plants to and from the South Pacific 1786–1798* (Melbourne: The Colony Press, 1993), p. 38.
116 'Duncan Campbell', Legacies of British Slave-ownership database. www.ucl.ac.uk/lbs/person/view/2146633087 [accessed 26 February 2018].
117 Marguerite Curtin, *The story of Hanover: A Jamaican parish* (Jamaica: Marguerite Curtin, 2007).
118 Caroline Alexander, 'Captain's Bligh's cursed breadfruit', *Smithsonian Magazine* (September 2009). www.smithsonianmag.com/travel/captain-blighs-cursed-breadfruit-41433018/ [accessed 26 February 2018].
119 Ibid.
120 *Royal Gazette*, 16 February 1793.
121 HFAC, Diary of Robert Hibbert junior, 12–13 February 1793.
122 Thomas Dancer, *Catalogue of plants, exotic and indigenous, in the Botanic Garden, Jamaica* (Spanish Town: A. Aikman, 1792), p. 4.
123 Charles Nelson and John P. Rourke, 'James Niven (1776–1827), a Scottish botanical collector at the Cape of Good Hope. His *Hortus siccus* at the National Botanic Gardens, Glasnevin, Dublin (DBN), and the Royal Botanic Gardens, Kew (K)', *Kew Bulletin*, 48:4 (1993), p. 665.
124 Markland, *Sketch*, p. 16.
125 'George Hibbert (1757–1837)', Global Plants database. http://plants.jstor.org/person/bm000044708 [Accessed 26 February 2018].
126 The National Archives, Kew, Colonial Office and Predecessors, CO 137/161/90, Letter from George Hibbert to Robert Wilmot-Horton, 6 June 1825.
127 Natalie M. Phillips, *Distraction: Problems of attention in eighteenth-century literature* (Baltimore, MD: John Hopkins University Press, 2016), p. 19.
128 'George Hibbert (1757–1837)', Global Plants database. http://plants.jstor.org/person/bm000044708 [accessed 26 February 2018].
129 Sir Henry Barkly, John Alleyne Beckles, Henry Browne, Dr James Clarke, Andrew Colvile, George Ellis, George Hibbert, John Grey, Thomas Bayley Howell, Gibbes Walker Jordan, Alexander Macfarlane, James Heywood Markland, Peter McLagan, James Smith, Robert Smith, 1st Baron Carrington, Sir George Leonard Staunton, Clement Tudway Swanston, Sir John Deas Thomson, Benjamin Travers, John Willett Willett, William Philip Perrin and Sir John Mark Frederick Smith, Legacies of British Slave-ownership database. www.ucl.ac.uk/lbs/ [accessed 12 February 2018].
130 The Royal Society, London, EC/1811/09.
131 http://royalsociety.org/about-us/history/ [accessed 26 February 2018]
132 Janet C. Cutler, 'The London Institution, 1805–1933' (PhD thesis, University of Leicester, 1976), p. 5.

133 Ken Cozens, 'George Hibbert, of Clapham – 18th century merchant and "amateur horticulturalist"'. www.academia.edu/12319084/George_Hibbert_of_Clapham_18th_Century_Merchant_and_Amateur_Horticulturalist [accessed 10 January 2010].
134 Richard Drayton, *Nature's government: Science, imperial Britain and the 'improvement' of the world* (London: Yale University Press, 2000), p. xv.
135 Dibdin, *Bibliographical Decameron*, pp. 35–6
136 Markland, *Sketch*, p. 3.
137 Elizabeth A. Bohls, 'The gentleman planter and the metropole: Long's *History of Jamaica* (1774)', in Gerald Maclean, Donna Landry and Joseph P. Ward (eds), *The country and the city revisited: England and the politics of culture, 1550–1850* (Cambridge: Cambridge University Press, 1999), pp. 180–1.
138 Georgie Wemyss, *The invisible empire: White discourse, tolerance and belonging* (Farnham: Ashgate, 2009), p. 42.

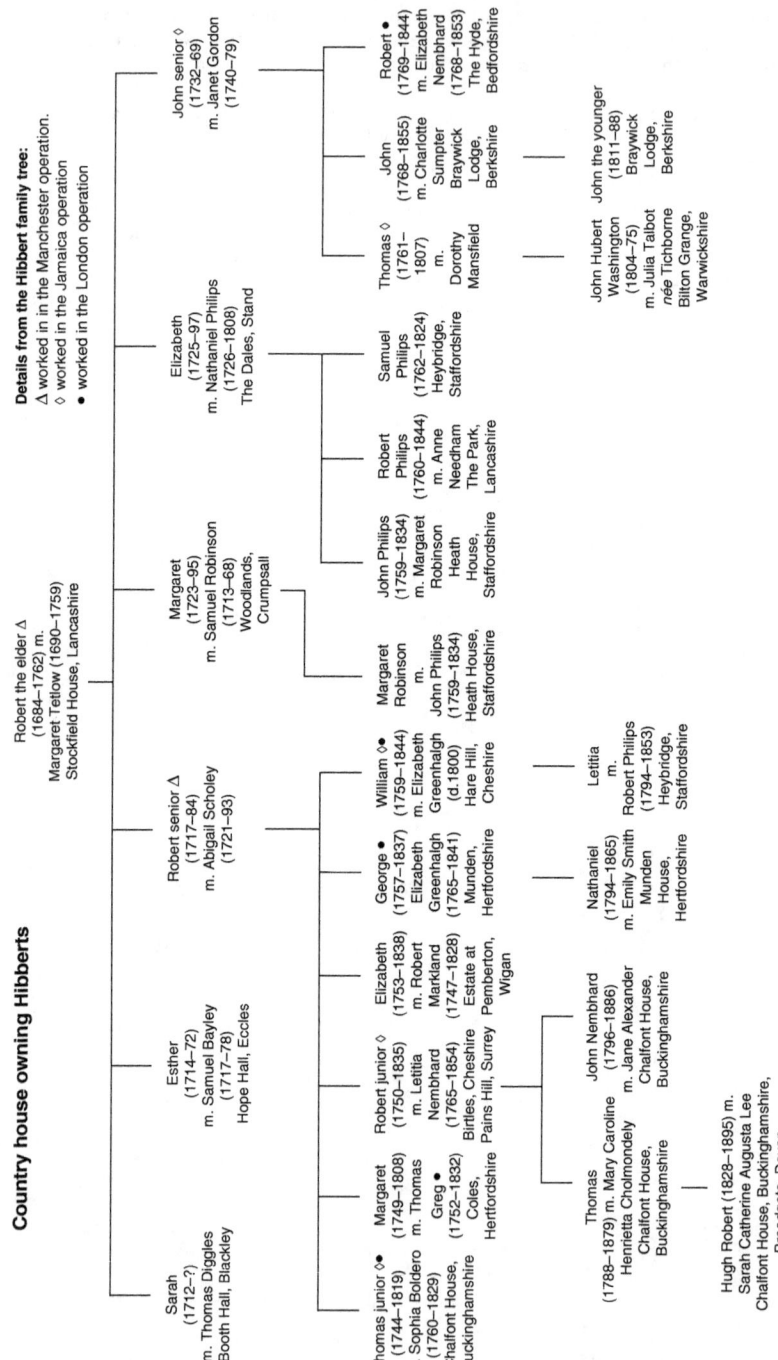

Family tree 7 Country house owning Hibberts

CHAPTER EIGHT

The culture of refinement: country houses and philanthropy

For the first time in my life here I am in England; at the fountain head of pleasure, in the land of beauty, of arts, and elegancies. My happy fate hath given me a good estate, and the conspiring winds have blown me hither to spend it.

Richard Cumberland, *The West Indian*
(Perth: R. Morison Junior, 1790), p. 7

He knew and felt that a heavy responsibility was his; and his highest ambition was to render himself worthy of his stewardship – his greatest reward the consciousness of having endeavoured to fulfil his duty ... Little did he deem that those that then stood foremost in the pride of place and power, would have sunk into comparative oblivion, whilst his unobtrusive and familiar acts would claim an universal sympathy. Little did he deem that while relieving, comforting, and assuaging, he was securing a terrestrial fame; – not decaying, but strengthening with the lapse of Time, – not wasting, – but increasing beneath its silent power.

Thomas Garrard, *Edward Colston, the philanthropist, his life and times; Including a memoir of his father; The result of a laborious investigation into the archives of the city* (Bristol: J. Chilcott, 1852), p. 16

The figure of the West Indian was a recognisable stock character within eighteenth-century society.[1] Caricatured for their excesses, men like William Beckford – the 'fool of Fonthill' – ploughed their fortunes into the purchasing, building and renovation of country estates.[2] Absentee planters were not alone in their attempts to secure a position within the landed elites, wealthy West India merchants also sought to remove themselves from the uncertainty of trade through investment in land. From the relative modesty of Stockfield House, the Hibberts acquired a further eight properties across England using the profits of slavery.

A country estate allowed the family to lay claim to the permanence traditionally associated with the gentry and the aristocracy. Whilst commerce and colonial labour provided the foundations for their new wealth, it was a risky business which was constantly under threat from factors as diverse and uncontrollable as the vagaries of the market, uprisings by the enslaved, the unpredictable tropical climate and in later years the abolitionists. An investment in land in Britain offered both stability and a legacy for the generations to come.

Once installed in their rural mansions the work of gentlemanly improvement could begin. Houses were remodelled using the finest-quality materials and most sought-after architects. Interiors were transformed with the accoutrements of fashion, from Chinese wallpaper to Persian rugs. Landscape gardening and proper husbandry enhanced both the aesthetics and practical usage of the estate. Employing Britain's premier designers, planters and merchants created a lasting imprint on the nation's physical heritage. Until relatively recently this legacy has been largely ignored within the scholarship on, and interpretation of, the country house.[3] In his exploration of changing attitudes to country houses, Peter Mandler has suggested that 'The stately homes of England, it is often now claimed, are that country's greatest contribution to Western civilisation. They are the quintessence of Englishness; they epitomise the English love of domesticity, of the countryside, of hierarchy, continuity and tradition.'[4] This understanding of the country house becomes increasingly difficult to sustain when we consider both the content of the houses and the origins of the wealth that made their ownership possible. The bicentenary of the abolition of the British slave trade offered a period of public reflection on these relationships; however, most of the exhibits within the houses were temporary and have since been removed.[5] Given the centrality of the country house to notions of Englishness, the uncovering of connections to both slavery and empire destabilises an insular construction of national identity. The issue of country house ownership also challenges the port city narrative that has dominated the historical representation of slavery. Rural connections to the slave economy penetrated into Britain's agrarian interior, linking local histories to the imperial world.

Country house ownership brought with it a responsibility for the communities who inhabited the land. Philanthropic gestures aimed at enriching the spiritual, physical and educational well-being of tenants were common. Philanthropy was not simply an exercise in generosity, it was also an expression of power that confirmed the social position of those giving and those receiving charity. An identification with paternal benevolence reinforced an idealised vision of the social relations between the classes. As a writer for *The Philanthropist* stated, 'The different orders in society may be considered as links in a chain, all connected with, and all dependent upon each other: the rich can no more dispense with the services of the poor, than the poor can be made comfortable without the aid of the rich.'[6] Philanthropy was about maintaining the balance of inequality, as opposed to restructuring the system. Charity was not unconditional – entrance into almshouses and schools often came with strict rules regarding the conduct expected from those to whom charity was extended. The making of model tenants enforced codes of respectability which were as much about increasing efficiency and maintaining the reputation of the land owner, as they were about improving life for the local populace. For those Hibberts who were without a landed estate, the practice of benevolence took different forms. These projects reflected the commercial, political and cultural interests of their benefactors. Located in city centres rather than the countryside, these Hibberts participated in a distinctly urban form of philanthropy. Keen to exercise their civic duty, wealthy merchants in places like London, Manchester and Liverpool created a different kind of philanthropic culture. Their activities were characterised as useful, rational and practical – a reflection of the ways in which they chose to distinguish themselves from the aristocracy and gentry.

For those involved in the slave economy the cultivation of benevolence served a political purpose. As a leading spokesman for the West India interest, George was aware of the reputational damage being done by abolitionist representations of the slave owners as cruel tyrants. Attempts to defend the slave trade through the rhetoric of improvement were rebuffed in Parliament by men like Sir John Doyle, who scoffed 'O amiable philanthropist! O benevolent crusaders! Thus to become voluntary missionaries in this perilous pilgrimage, purely to impart happiness to the sable sons of sorrow!'[7] George countered with a series of speeches decrying the treatment of the poor and vulnerable of the metropole. Painting a picture of the degradation of modern industrial society, George accused the abolitionists of turning a blind eye to the suffering of their fellow Britons. Signalling towards his own credentials as a philanthropist, he stated:

> Sir, there are others in this house who can better judge than I can, whether my understanding has been so perverted, and whether, in extending relief to the calamities which in this life, and in this country, one sees, God knows, often enough occurring around us, I am or am not as prompt and zealous as my neighbours.[8]

For the slave owners charity offered both a means of repairing their tarnished reputations and a buttress to the rhetoric of planter paternalism. In the longer term an identification with benevolence created an alternative legacy and memory separate to that of either slave owner or merchant. Philanthropy's 'silent power' offered participants an opportunity to be remade as generous benefactors securing for them 'terrestrial fame' across the generations.[9]

Country houses

As a mercantile family the Hibberts had both business and residential properties in the capital. Up until the 1790s they were listed only in London's commercial handbooks. A change in their status can be read through the inclusion of Thomas junior's address at 38 Weymouth Street in *Boyle's court guide* in 1796. The newly developed Marylebone area, including the Portman Estate, was popular with absentee West Indians, giving Thomas junior an instant network for social and business calling.[10] Over the next thirty years an increasing number of Hibberts were included in this type of publication. By 1830 *The royal blue book. Fashionable directory for 1830; containing the town and country residences of the nobility and the gentry* listed seven family members; George at 38 Portland Place, George junior at 4L Albany, John at 47 Great Ormond Street, Nathaniel at 10 King's Bench Walk, Samuel at 78 Harley Street, Thomas at 16 Berkeley Street and William junior at 36 Upper Harley Street. The possession of a fashionable London address was essential for a family like the Hibberts. Close to the City of London, Parliament and the entertainments of the season, their residences in the capital were an important marker of their social position.

Away from the bustle of urban living the Hibberts purchased and inherited estates, allowing them to adopt the lifestyle of the landed gentry. The estates owned by the family included Stockfield House in Lancashire, Birtles Hall and Hare Hill in Cheshire, Chalfont House in Buckinghamshire, Munden in Hertfordshire, Bilton Grange in Warwickshire, Pains Hill in Surrey, The Hyde in Bedfordshire and Braywick Lodge in Berkshire. Birtles Hall, Chalfont House, Pains Hill, The Hyde and Hare Hill were all purchased during the period of slavery. Munden was inherited by George through his wife Elizabeth. Bilton Grange and Braywick Lodge were purchased shortly after abolition, their owners having been in receipt of inherited slave-based fortunes. Further properties were acquired in the later Victorian period. The family stamped their mark on these spaces through extensive renovation, rebuilding and landscaping. Over the generations most of the family gradually withdrew from commerce and severed their ties with the West Indies. It was this process which finally transformed them from planters and merchants into country gentlemen.

THE CULTURE OF REFINEMENT

Figure 15 View of Portland Place, Anon., c. 1814

The first to purchase a country house was Robert junior. In 1791 he bought Birtles Hall, located to the west of Macclesfield. Having lived for many years in Jamaica, Robert junior spent increasing amounts of time in England owing to his wife's ill health and their children's education. The original house having been demolished, the property was described in 1810 by Daniel and Samuel Lysons as a 'modern mansion'.[11] To place his stamp on the fabric of the building Robert junior had the Hibbert coat of arms carved into the balustraded parapet.[12] He also purchased paintings, china, glass, furniture and plate to fit Birtles Hall out in style. Having held similar positions of civic authority in Jamaica, Robert junior became the High Sheriff of Cheshire in 1798. The post required deep pockets owing to the expenses the High Sheriff was expected to defray. However, it conferred on the post-holder a recognition of their status. As Lord Colborne noted, 'The office of high sheriff was a very arduous task imposed on a very useful class of society – namely, the country gentlemen.'[13] Like the property itself, the title was also enjoyed by both Robert junior's son and grandson.

Birtles Hall was close to Robert junior's heart and he would countenance no risk to it, even for the sake of the family business. When financial problems struck the Hibbert counting house in 1796 he received 'a letter as usual from George inform'g me that matters were drawing to a crisis, and that it w'd be necessary for me to mortgage Birtles which I point blank refuse'.[14] Birtles Hall was not just a status symbol, it formed part of a legacy which would be passed down to his children. On his death in 1835, Robert junior bequeathed Birtles Hall to his eldest son Thomas, who lived there with his wife Mary Caroline Henrietta Cholmondeley. She was the eldest daughter of Charles Cholmondeley of Overleigh, the head of a long-established Cheshire family with a country seat at Vale Royal Abbey. The couple had eight children and the estate was passed on to their eldest surviving son, Hugh Thomas Hibbert. Birtles Hall went out of the Hibberts' ownership around the time of Hugh's death in 1895. After being damaged by fire in 1938 the house was reconstructed by the Arts and Craft architect James Henry Sellers. Historic England has designated Birtles Hall a Grade II listed property, although its interior has now been transformed into six luxury apartments.

In 1794 Thomas junior acquired the estate of Chalfont House in Buckinghamshire. Ten years earlier he had married Sophia Boldero, the daughter of the London banker John Boldero. In 1786, before they settled into country house living, the couple left for a European tour. In the years after their return they 'passed several Summers at Clifton, Tunbridge, Cheltenham, & in travelling in Wales, Scotland'.[15] Thomas junior had been deeply unhappy in Jamaica, and perhaps viewed this new life of pleasure as a consolation for the decades of misery spent under his uncle in the colonies. Chalfont House was built in 1755 for Colonel Charles Churchill and was designed by the architect John Chute. The deeds reveal the extensiveness of the property, which also included a number of farms, dwellings and pasture land. In 1799 Thomas junior added to his estate by buying the Greyhound Inn, along with several other parcels of land and a water corn mill, from Anne Whitchurch.[16] In 1800 he purchased the Swan Inn from John and Nicholas Mercer and in subsequent years acquired numerous cottages and surrounding land.[17] As a significant local landowner, Thomas junior was keen to play his part in county society and in 1796 became High Sheriff of Buckinghamshire.

Despite the relative newness of Chalfont House, Thomas junior wanted to make his own impression on the estate. This led him to hire John Nash to modify the house and Humphrey Repton to landscape the gardens, which had originally been designed by Capability Brown. During this period Thomas junior commissioned both Thomas Girtin and J. M. W. Turner to paint watercolours of the estate. Whilst several of the Girtin and Turner paintings remain in private hands, the Tate has both a watercolour and a sketch by Turner in its collection.[18] Thomas junior also hired several more artists to produce work to adorn the walls of his country house. Two portraits of Thomas junior survive in the collection at Dyrham Park in Gloucestershire, the first an

THE CULTURE OF REFINEMENT

Figure 16 *Chalfont House from the South-West*, J. M. W. Turner, c. 1799

aquatint after John Russell RA and the second a pastel on paper by Hugh Douglas Hamilton RHA. Now a National Trust property, Dyrham's connection to the Hibberts came through the marriage of Thomas junior's great-niece Mary Sarah Hibbert Oates to the Reverend Wynter Thomas Blathwayt, the second son of Dyrham Park's proprietor. Both Thomas junior and his wife were painted by Thomas Gainsborough FRSA. Thomas junior's likeness remained in private family hands, whilst Sophia's portrait has achieved international acclaim as a fine example of the artist's work. *Portrait of Mrs Thomas Hibbert* (1786) was sold to Baron Alphonse de Rothschild of Paris for 10,000 guineas in 1885.[19] It was purchased by the Neue Pinakothek in Munich in 1977 and remains in its collection.[20]

Despite their life of opulence, the union between Thomas junior and Sophia did not last and they separated in 1796. Simon Taylor, who had known Thomas junior during his time in Jamaica, wrote a letter describing the couple's marriage. Always attuned to the financial detail of any given issue, Taylor regarded Sophia in bald monetary terms, noting 'I believe she was very expensive' before adding that her dowry was £700 per annum.[21] In terms of their relationship, he stated that he 'never did conceive that Thos Hibbert and his wife were a fond couple,

Figure 17 *Portrait of Mrs Thomas Hibbert*, Thomas Gainsborough, 1786

but I had no idea that it would come to a separation'. This account contrasted with that of Robert junior's great-grandson, who recalled that after the separation, 'Thomas bought for her [Sophia] a house called Westcott Hill, near Dorking ... There she lived till her death, on excellent terms with her husband: she taking his portrait (by Gainsborough) and he keeping hers at Chalfont.'[22] Taylor thoroughly disapproved of what he described as Thomas junior's 'idle, dissipated and extravagant way of life'.[23] When he had been resident in Jamaica, 'he constantly attended his counting house' but since he had returned to England he had squandered rather than augmented his wealth. Taylor speculated, 'I do not suppose that taking in the interest with it, he can have spent less than £100000 since he has been at home.' If Jamaica was a place of industry in which great fortunes were raised, for the absentees Britain was a land of leisure in which fortunes could be spent.

In the early 1800s, a few years after the request from George to secure a loan against Birtles Hall, the counting house was again under financial threat. In 1803 Thomas junior allowed his brother George to offer Chalfont House as security against a loan from Taylor. Having separated from his wife and with no children to inherit, perhaps Thomas junior was not as attached to the idea of legacy building as Robert junior. Chalfont House, then, was both an ornamental status symbol and a practical capital investment that could be lent upon to support the Hibberts when necessary. With the loan repaid using the compensation money from the West India Docks scheme, Thomas junior lived comfortably at Chalfont House until his death.[24] In his later years George fretted in his diary about his brother's ailing health. In particular he worried that his short-term memory loss was affecting his ability to manage his estate. In 1817 George wrote:

> My brother William and myself a fortnight ago paid a visit to my Brother at Chalfont and as to his general health we think him not declining sensibly, but he moves about very little and that little now with difficulty, we thought that he indulged this growing unfitness for motion and that a little effort on his part might accomplish more. He lives now quite a recluse and is too much under the management of his servants.[25]

To aid his mobility George's wife Elizabeth 'sent him down a garden Chair, in which whenever the weather will admit it he may be pushed about his Garden and grounds'.[26] Six months after he first asked to do so, George was allowed to take over some aspects of his older brother's affairs. It was a relief to George, who commented that 'I saw his inability to look into such matters himself and know that many of those bills had remained long unsettled.'[27] If George had tried to spare his brother's feelings in the past, the necessity for sensitivity had passed, as Thomas junior's 'state of mind and capacity is now such as to take away from us all delicacy on the subject'.[28] The downward turn allowed George and William to discuss openly their fears about 'the manner in which his rents are collected and applied' and 'the state of his Accounts with his respective Tenants'. For a former slave owner who once exerted absolute control over the lives of so many people, the loss of physical and financial autonomy represented a huge shift in power. Finally, after several years of deterioration, on 25 May 1819 Thomas junior 'quietly expired, without any struggle'.[29]

Thomas junior willed Chalfont House and its valuable contents to his brother Robert junior on payment of £25,000.[30] Having left his main residence of Birtles Hall to his eldest son, Robert junior bequeathed Chalfont House to his younger son John Nembhard. John Nembhard lived at Chalfont House with his wife Jane, the daughter of Sir Robert Alexander, a Governor of the Bank of Ireland. In 1836 he hired the architect Anthony Salvin to remodel the house in the newly fashionable Gothic style. After John Nembhard's death in 1886 Chalfont was sold by his executors to Captain Berton.[31] Chalfont House has been designated a Grade II listed building by Historic England and is currently the premises of the British Aluminium Company Limited.[32]

In 1797, six years after Robert junior purchased Birtles Hall, his younger brother William acquired Hare Hill in Cheshire from Sir J. F. Leicester.[33] The two estates bordered each other with a two-mile ride between them. Like his older siblings, William had been sent out to Jamaica in the early 1780s. In 1782 he won £20,000 on the Benefit Lottery and promptly returned to England.[34] On 3 November 1784 he married Elizabeth Greenhalgh, a Lancashire heiress whose sister Mary had married William's brother Samuel junior in 1781. In 1800 William had a 'small hunting lodge' built at Hare Hill.[35] The same year Elizabeth died following the birth of their son Charles. Robert junior wrote to his sister Mary in Leeds, 'ruminating on our poor Brother William's melancholy situation' and 'thinking it is a great pity that your residence should be at such an Inconvenient distance from him'.[36] In 1812 William purchased a property at Crescent Grove in Clapham, putting him a short walk away from both his brother George and his sister-in-law Mary. After William's death in 1844, Hare Hill was sold to the Brocklehurst family. The house is designated a Grade II listed building and remains in private ownership, though the gardens are now part of the National Trust.[37]

In 1798, with Birtles Hall already in his possession, Robert junior established a country seat closer to London. He purchased the 230-acre property Pains Hill in Surrey from the estate of Benjamin Bond Hopkins. The house and gardens were meticulously detailed by Edward Wedlake Brayley, who remarked that the 'demesne of Pains Hill has been long celebrated as one of the earliest and finest examples of the modern style of English landscape gardening'.[38] The Hibberts took advantage of their new home, inviting guests to come and admire the property. In 1798 a party made up of Jamaican absentees, including the Mitchell family and Nathaniel Phillips and his wife, came to 'see the Place'.[39] Despite their enjoyment of the estate, Robert junior decided to sell in 1801. He offered the property 'all included' for £27,000 to his Jamaica-born cousin Thomas, who, like him, had inherited a third share of their uncle Thomas senior's estate.[40] Thomas was extremely hesitant about buying the property, as Robert junior noted:

> Find my Cousin had been at our house extremely anxious abo' Paines Hill ... Next day my Cousin calls and we settle abo' Paines Hill. Tuesday Mrs. B. goes with Mrs. H. to see the poor gentleman. Wednesday morn'g a note from T.H. to tell me that his wife can't sleep. Thursday morn'g another note that he declines the purchase.[41]

In the end Robert junior auctioned the house through Christie's in 1802. The property was sold to William Moffat, a London banker, Member of Parliament and East India Company stockholder.[42] Today part of the grounds have been bought and preserved by the Painshill Park Trust and are open to the public. The park has been listed Grade I by Historic England.[43]

The last to acquire a property during the period in which slavery was still legal was Thomas' younger brother Robert. In 1806 he purchased the estate of The Hyde, East Hyde in Bedfordshire. This led his cousin George to give him the nickname 'East Hyde Bob'. Like his cousins, Robert adopted the mantle of High Sheriff of Bedfordshire in 1815. He also served as a Justice of the Peace between 1814 and 1830. The decision to fulfil his civic duties paid off unexpectedly when his neighbour, the Marquis of Bute, supported his petition to the House of Lords regarding the payment of slavery compensation. Bute gave a lengthy statement extolling Robert's virtues:

> I have known this gentleman for many, many years, and my acquaintance with him, and with his conduct, enables me to state that he is a most valuable and active magistrate in the parish where the greater part of my property lies, in England; and I have the pleasure to assure your Lordships that he stands pre-eminent in that neighbourhood for acts of generosity, charity and universal benevolence.[44]

Robert's commitment to the duties of an English land owner enabled him to cultivate a reputation as a respectable benefactor. In 1833, the same year that slavery was abolished by law, Robert sold The Hyde to Levi Ames, a Bristol merchant and ship owner. Levi's brother George Henry Ames was a partner in the Bristol West India merchant house of Baillie, Ames & Baillie.[45] Before him their father Jeremiah Ames had been involved in another Bristol partnership involved in the slave economy – Pinney, Ames & Co.[46] In this instance the country house can tell the story of not one but two different families, each of whom owed a debt to the profits of slavery.

Unlike his brothers and cousin, George's country house came to him through an inheritance. In 1828 his wife Elizabeth's uncle Rogers Parker died leaving his Munden estate in Hertfordshire to his niece. The position of the property in Hertfordshire consolidated the Hibberts' extended family interest in the area. The Thellussons – into whose family George's sister-in-law Mary Anne had married – were the proprietors of Brodsworth Hall, a 4,320-acre estate in the county.[47] George's sister Margaret and her husband Thomas Greg owned Coles Park, which he had purchased in 1783 for £3,137.[48] He went on to acquire the nearby Knighthills Estate for £5,250 in 1784, as well as spending £8,000 on Tiller's End, a 249-acre property. By 1825 Greg had accumulated 1,481 acres in the parish of Westhill, where Coles Park was located. In 1829 George relinquished his property at 38 Portland Place and 'retired from London' to apply himself to 'improving and ornamenting his newly inherited property'.[49] In contrast to his siblings' desire to be remade as country gentlemen, George retained his identity as a man of commerce. Instead of burying his ties to trade, George had them etched into his memorial inscription on the family vault in Aldenham. The tribute remembered him as 'George Hibbert Esq. of Munden in this county, and of the City of London, merchant'.[50]

The original house was neither fashionable nor elegant, 'at the time of the death of Rogers Parker in 1828 Munden was merely an old fashioned farm-house'.[51] George himself described the property as 'Munden's modest mansion', although the land holdings comprised 1,100 acres.[52] Looking to the future, George realised that with the right balance of capital investment and taste, Munden held the potential to become a respectable family seat. The need for extensive renovation work to be carried out necessitated George selling part of his famous art and book collections. The book sale alone raised £21,753 9s, enabling George to transform the unassuming property into a resplendent Tudor Gothic mansion. On George's death Munden was passed to his wife. Following Elizabeth's death in 1841, the property went to their eldest son Nathaniel, allowing him to claim the status of country gentleman. Today Munden is a Historic England Grade II listed building and remains within the Holland-Hibbert family.[53]

The final two properties were acquired by the family after the ending of Caribbean slavery. Both of the men involved benefited significantly from the slavery business. John Hubert Washington's father Thomas owned the Hibbert family plantation Agualta Vale at the time of his death in 1807, just three years after John Hubert Washington was born. Having turned down the offer to buy Pains Hill, Thomas realised that he would die without having settled an estate in England. Given the dynastic importance of bequeathing a country house, Thomas left instructions for his trustees to 'purchase a freehold mansion and estate for £40,000'.[54] Despite the stipulation in his will, the request was not carried out. Thomas left each of his children £10,000, with a further £10,000 for each son who lived to the age of twenty-five. As well as inheriting the wealth that had been generated through slave trading and plantation ownership, John Hubert Washington was also a recipient of slavery compensation money.[55] Along with his older brother Thomas, John Hubert Washington was awarded £3,817 6s 11d for 194 enslaved people on Agualta Vale Pen and £5,013 2s 1d for 291 enslaved people on an unnamed property in St Mary's parish which was most likely the main plantation Agualta Vale.

In 1839 John Hubert Washington married Julia Talbot *née* Tichborne, the third daughter of Sir Henry Joseph Tichborne. The same year he rented Bilton Grange in Warwickshire, where he resided with his wife, his mother Dorothy and his older brother Thomas. In 1821 Thomas was declared a lunatic following a period of mental instability in his early twenties.[56] In 1846, a year after Thomas's death, John Hubert Washington purchased Bilton Grange from Abraham Hume.[57] He remodelled the house, employing the Gothic architect Augustus W. Pugin to design both the exteriors and interiors. John Hubert Washington's decision to hire Pugin may have been a result of his wife's connection to the Talbot family, into which she had previously married. John Talbot, the sixteenth Earl of Shrewsbury, was one of Pugin's most important patrons. Both Julia and the Talbot family were Catholic and John Hubert Washington converted in 1846. Given the relationship between Pugin, the Gothic and the Catholic revival, it is possible that this impacted on the choice of architect.[58] The work took ten years to complete and has been described as 'one of the other great domestic schemes of Pugin's mature years'.[59] Relations between architect and patron were strained, with 'frequent disputes' breaking out. Details of the renovations carried out at Bilton Grange offer a glimpse into the craftsmanship and design:

> Pugin greatly expanded a small eighteenth-century house, adding a new wing that completely dominated the existing structure, and creating a sequence of new rooms which included a galleried Great Hall with stained-glass windows. There was a dramatic staircase with carved newel posts in the form of heraldic beasts and birds, some fine carved stone fireplaces with heraldic andirons or firedogs, a rich array of carved and painted panelling, elaborate chandeliers, and decorative metalwork including some finely wrought keys, a Pugin speciality. A range of specially designed tiles and wallpapers featured the Hibbert initials and coat of arms. In its diversity, Bilton Grange represented a typically extravagant and completely coordinated Pugin interior, in his modern medieval style.[60]

In 1866 the Hibberts sold Bilton Grange and moved to London. They had transformed the house and surrounding buildings, earning the estate a Grade II listing.[61] In 1887 Bilton Grange became an educational institution and it continues today as an independent preparatory school.

John Hubert Washington's uncle John was the last of the Hibberts to make a purchase with funds that could be easily traced back to the family's involvement with slavery. John was the son of John senior and Janet Gordon. Although he was not involved with the merchant house, on his brother Thomas's death in 1807 he was appointed a trustee and given the use of all of his 'real estate and stock in Jamaica'.[62] He married Charlotte, the daughter of Thomas Sumpter of Histon House. John's country estate Braywick Lodge was described in a local history as 'a handsome mansion in a small but picturesque park adjoining the Maidenhead and Windsor Road. The house, which has of late been greatly improved by its worthy owner, was formerly the residence of Thomas Slack Esq.'[63] John left Braywick Lodge to his son John the younger. A local history website states that 'Braywick Lodge, home of the Hibbert family, no longer stands but its grounds are a public park and Hibbert Road remembers the family'.[64]

Acquiring landed property was part of the mechanism for transforming a mercantile fortune into a more stable and respectable form of wealth. Works of improvement were part of the lexicon of polite culture; a gentleman might converse at his club about new innovations upon his English estate in ways that he could no longer do in relation to his Caribbean holdings. Participating in local politics or involvement in rural traditions like the hunt allowed the relative outsider to embed themselves within the networks of influence that operated away from the capital. Land offered a sense of permanency which trade could not guarantee, although maintaining these vast estates over time could become an untenable financial burden. If managed well, country houses could be passed along the generations. The Hibberts had risen from their involvement in the slavery business, but they were shrewd enough to recognise that investment in land ownership in England offered far greater long-term security. In the wake of the growing controversy over slavery, the acquisition of an estate also gave the Hibberts an opportunity to distance themselves from the roots of their wealth by refashioning themselves as country gentlemen.

Philanthropy

Country house culture modelled the land owner through the concept of *noblesse oblige*. In its most idealised form this meant taking responsibility for the social, moral and spiritual well-being of those who dwelt within their sphere of influence. The Hibberts provided churches, hospitals and schools, as well as support for the poor through contributions to relief funds and the establishment of almshouses. The family saw no incompatibility between their actions as philanthropists and their status as slave owners, indeed it was their activities out in the empire which enabled their largesse at home. George declared to Parliament that 'the rational principle of self-love ... first puts the centre in motion, and then extends itself in progressive circles of beneficence to the extremities'.[65] In this construction charity should begin at home. Nationality and race created a prior claim on the pity and purse of the philanthropic British citizenry. Despite their misery and corruption, the metropolitan poor belonged to the nation and held the potential to be remade as useful and productive workers. For men like George, African people and their descendants would never be Britons. 'Slaves', wrote George, 'are considered as Property, they are not distinguished from ordinary articles of Merchandize.'[66] Their function was to labour, their improvement merely an unwanted by-product of political expediency.

The Hibberts' benevolent activities were also about legacy building. The success of this strategy can be read in a local council brochure published in 2007 that described John the younger of Braywick Lodge as 'a local philanthropist'.[67] Charitable acts endowed the Hibberts with a moral authority that justified their position within society. The family's reputation for good works was enshrined in local memory through the installation of plaques and the naming of buildings, streets and charitable institutions, some of which are still in existence today. These physical remnants of the Hibberts' presence remain dislocated from the history of the family's involvement in slavery. It was this disconnection that allowed a pamphlet to be printed in 2007 – the bicentenary of the abolition of the slave trade –uncritically celebrating John the younger as a philanthropist without gesturing to the origin of his wealth.

The provision of spiritual sustenance was a common expression of philanthropy. It was a lesson that had been learnt through the generations, with successive Hibbert men acting as trustees for the Cross Street Chapel in Manchester. Saint Marie's Catholic Church in Rugby owes its existence to John Hubert Washington of Bilton Grange. Initially the family invited local worshippers to attend a chapel at their home. It soon became clear that the needs of the Catholic community outweighed this provision so John Hubert Washington purchased land on Dunchurch Road and commissioned Augustus W. Pugin to design a church. When the congregation required an extension he raised the funds for Pugin's son Edward Welby Pugin to undertake the work. In recognition of the part the Hibberts played in the founding of the church the old chancel became known as the Hibbert chapel. The Hibbert coat of arms can be seen entwined with that of his wife Julia in tiling in the church. Having built the church, John Hubert Washington requested that the Rosiminians, otherwise known as the Institute of Charity, would run it. His request was granted and two priests and four lay brothers arrived in 1849.[68] In later years John Hubert Washington acquired further land with the intention of setting up a college and novitiate for the order. He also founded Catholic schools for both boys and girls, as well as a convent with four Sisters of Providence. Despite having moved to London in 1866, the family's connections to the church remained strong. In 1872 John Hubert Washington paid for a 200-foot tower and spire designed in the Gothic style by Bernard Wheelan. He also ordered eight bells from the Whitechapel Foundry, which are still rung today. On their deaths, John Hubert Washington and Julia were interred in the family vault beneath the Hibbert chapel. The church has been designated a Grade II listed building by Historic England.[69]

John the younger of Braywick Lodge was responsible for the construction of St Mark's Hospital Church. Opened in 1873, the church served the Cookham Workhouse inmates and the poor of Maidenhead. John the younger was a Chairman of the Board of Guardians and contributed the entire £2,000 cost of erecting the church, purchasing an organ and all the necessary furnishings.[70] In memory of his father, he paid for the chancel window, underneath which was a memorial plaque. The church at Cookham is now a Grade II listed building.[71] Prior to the founding of the church, John the younger had already established himself as a local benefactor. In 1857 he contributed £269 16s 5d to the Bray School in Maidenhead, which meant that 'the schoolroom was enlarged, and a preparatory school added'.[72] He also served on the Committee of Management. He helped to fund three hospitals, Maidenhead Cottage Hospital, Windsor Hospital and Jesus Hospital. The donation for Jesus Hospital became known as Hibbert's Gift and was documented in a history of Bray:

> In 1857, John Hibbert, Esq., of Braywick Lodge, presented to the funds of this hospital the sum of 1000l on condition that the married parishionary almspeople should receive an extra weekly allowance of 2s ... A second donation of 1000l was given by J. Hibbert, Esq., in 1860, for the benefit of 34 parishionary almsmen.[73]

John the younger is remembered in Maidenhead's online 'Heritage Hall of Fame' as 'A great example of Victorian philanthropy ... He was one of the most generous benefactors of Victorian Maidenhead, and whenever a charitable cause needed sponsorship he was always one of the first to offer support.'[74]

Following on from his less than successful attempts to encourage the spread of Christianity through missionary activities on his plantations, Robert of The Hyde founded the Hibbert Trust. Like his forebears in Manchester, Robert was a committed Unitarian. His new institution was designed to promote 'the spread of Christianity in its most simple and intelligible form, and ... the unfettered exercise of the right of private judgment in matters of religion'.[75] In 1847 a deed of trust was executed that conveyed $50,000 in 6 per cent Ohio stock and £8,000 in railway shares to Robert's Manchester relations, Robert and Mark Philips, as trustees for the new organisation. The Trust offered divinity scholarships for candidates that came from institutions 'where degrees were granted without subscription to the articles of religion'.[76] It also published the *Hibbert Journal* between 1902 and 1968. The Trust is still in existence and awards grants in line with its founder's wishes. Its website carries no biographical details about Robert, other than the date of his will and his status as a Unitarian. His association with slavery is dealt with, albeit sympathetically, in two texts – Jerom Murch's *Memoir of Robert Hibbert, founder of the Hibbert Trust* (1874) and Alan Rushton's *The Hibbert Trust: A history* (1984). Rushton's work captured eloquently the power of philanthropy to remake and preserve an individual's memory. He wrote that 'Robert Hibbert would be an almost forgotten man if it were not for his Trust Fund. It has given him a form of immortality with his name being perpetuated in published works that circulate in religious and academic circles the world over.'[77]

Robert also invested in improving conditions for the poor. In 1819 he funded twelve cottages on Castle Street in Luton for twenty-four destitute widows. These cottages were later demolished, but new almshouses replaced them and the street they were built on was named Hibbert Street. Hibbert Street still exists, as does the Robert Hibbert Almshouse Charity, which offers housing for 'elderly persons with preference being given to those living in the ancient borough of Luton'.[78] Robert's memory was honoured by the scholar Claude Goldsmid Montefiore, who wrote that 'His life included very many acts of quiet, thoughtful, unobtrusive and unself-advertising benevolence. Of wide sympathies, kindly, tolerant and gentle, he was also a sturdy liberal in politics and a sturdy Unitarian in religion.'[79] The impression created of Robert is difficult to reconcile with his role as a slave owner and the views on race that he espoused. The duality of this position was captured by Murch, who wrote that 'though he was always an eminently kind master, he had no repugnance for this kind of property on moral grounds'.[80] Recognising the seemingly contradictory notion of the slave-owning philanthropist, Murch added that 'at the close of the last century, and the beginning of the present, the national conscience had not been enlightened and awakened as it afterwards was'.

It was not only the Hibbert men who participated in the practice of charity. Philanthropy provided an acceptable way for middle-class women to enter the public sphere. As a tribute to their father William, sisters Sarah and Mary Anne erected an almshouse for women on the Wandsworth Road in Clapham in 1859. The memorial inscription, which is still visible on the building today, dedicated the endeavour to William's memory. The almshouse was run by the two sisters until Sarah's death in 1869. The building was designed by Edward I'Anson, a leading architect in the City of London. It is now designated a Grade II listed building by Historic England.[81] The rules for entry into the almshouse made it clear that the female 'inmates' were expected to subscribe to a code of respectable behaviour.[82] Rule 18 decreed that 'if at any time it should appear that any inmate of the Alms Houses shall be given to insobriety, immoral or unbecoming conduct, or shall infringe any of these rules' then the Hibbert sisters and their trustees reserved the right to 'forthwith displace such person or persons so misbehaving'. Whilst philanthropy might offer some respite from the harsh conditions of poverty, it was also a method of control which differentiated between the worthy and unworthy poor. The charity is still in operation, providing accommodation for the over-sixties in need in the parish of Clapham.[83]

In 1891 Jane, the wife of John Nembhard of Chalfont, bequeathed £300 for the benefit of two almshouses.[84] In combination with two other local women, she also established the Cottage Hospital in Chalfont through a legacy which was invested in the North British Railway Company. The same legacy also paid towards a school in Chalfont. A pamphlet written by a local action group in 2006 remembered the Hibberts and their philanthropic activities:

> The Estate of Chalfont Park was bought by Thomas Hibbert in 1794 whose descendants were responsible for many charitable bequests in the village. In the mid 19th century John Hibbert bought land on Gold Hill Lane (now Market Place) as allotments for the villages, endowed two almshouses and an infants' school and set up the first Cottage Hospital of six beds on the present site.[85]

As well as omitting any mention of Thomas junior's connection to slavery, the publication completely erased Jane's contribution, wrongly attributing her bequests to her husband.

THE CULTURE OF REFINEMENT

Outside of the customary philanthropic activities associated with country house ownership, several of the Hibberts pursued projects that reflected their own personal interests. Having been embedded for many years within London's elite cultural circles, George decided to focus his attentions on the founding of a new institution which would both ornament and improve the capital. Whilst membership of a learned society conveyed a sense of cultural belonging, founding an institution marked a man out as someone who not just followed but actively shaped the cultural landscape. The affluent commercial men of the City were not simply content to mimic the cultural mores of the aristocracy. They sought to establish institutions which were defined by their own sense of cultural identity.[86] Founded after the Liverpool Athenaeum but before the Royal Manchester Institution, the London Institution was first discussed at a meeting that took place in 1805. An address justifying the need for such an organisation decreed:

> The metropolis of the British Empire is still destitute of a public library, upon any scale at all commensurate to the want of its inhabitants, or to the dignity of its situation as the first city in the world, the seat of the arts, of learning, and of opulence.[87]

The relationship between culture, colonialism and commerce underpinned the foundation of the new institution. Civilisation was what imbued Britain with its right to rule, it was what distinguished the European from the various so-called 'savage' races. In order to fashion a nation fit to govern, the imperial centre needed to produce citizens who reflected its claims to cultural and intellectual superiority. On a practical level, the Institution would 'afford rational amusement or instructive employment to the young or unoccupied'.[88] This would have the improving effect of withdrawing the citizenry 'from vicious or frivolous pursuits' as well as providing them with 'talents adapted to prove beneficial to society'. Thus the Institution would serve the needs of commerce and industry by increasing the knowledge, productivity and efficiency of the urban populace. Subscribers were drawn from the City's mercantile and banking elite. In recognition of his leading role in establishing the Institution, George acted as President or Vice-President throughout the years 1805–30. At different times the management included a number of men with interests in the slave economy: Sir Francis Baring, John Julius Angerstein, Thomas Baring, Beeston Long, William Manning, Job Matthew Raikes, Richard Sharp, Samuel Bosanquet, Samuel Boddington, John Peter Hankey, William Alers Hankey, John Anderdon, Nathaniel Bogle French, Sir Richard Neave, Thomas Hughan and Abraham Wilday Robarts. In another example of the ways in which cultural spaces facilitated

Figure 18 The London Institution, Thomas Hosmer Shepherd, 1827

pro and antislavery interactions, the management also included the abolitionists Zachary Macaulay and Henry and John Thornton.[89]

The London Institution was designed to act as a monument to London's commercial culture. In order for it to be recognised as such it needed a suitably impressive architectural presence. From humble beginnings on Old Jewry, the Institution was eventually moved to a purpose built premises on Finsbury Square. The magnificent building was designed by William Brooks and constructed by Thomas Cubitt. Despite the strain it put on the Institution's finances – an additional library in the attic had to be abandoned – the frontage of the building was rendered in Portland stone. This was thought 'a more conspicuous and ornamented edifice, proportionate to its honourable pretentions and the lofty name by which it is designated'.[90] Lectures took place on the subjects of chemistry, mineralogy, natural philosophy and botany. The Institution enjoyed a well-stocked library and reading rooms. Regular exhibitions took place, designed to showcase the superiority of metropolitan culture through the juxtaposition of objects from the empire, scientific and technical equipment and European high art. On one occasion the exhibits were listed as:

Costume of Madeira in small figures, Improved rotary air pump, Apparatus for heating buildings by hot water, Two cats designed and executed by Caffies, Two Chinese females on glass, Marriage of St. Catherine, Bells cast in 1568, Specimen of sculpture, Chinese umbrella, Drawing by Gainsborough, Model of a frigate in ivory, Bamboo jacket from India.[91]

The marshalling of these objects was designed to signify the power and reach of Britain's commercial empire, with a number of items lent by the East India Company. In a coup for the Institution they secured the Gresham Lectures, which had previously taken place at the Royal Exchange. The Court of Proprietors noted that Gresham lived 'At the period when the Merchants of London were as princes and Monarchs were their Guests, Sir Thomas Gresham was first among their number, and acquired an immortal name rather by munificence than Wealth.'[92] This sentiment harked back to George's admiration of the Medici and Sforza dynasties of the Italian Renaissance and tells us something of the way in which the commercial men of the London Institution saw themselves and their achievements.

On George's retirement as President he was remembered fondly by the Chairman of the Institution, Sir William Blizard, as a 'much-respected and kind President'.[93] On behalf of the Managers, he commended 'a well spent, honourable, and most useful life'. In a line which spoke to the cultural anxieties of the commercial class, Blizard praised George's 'high example, learning, and talents', which had 'ennobled and dignified the character of the British Merchant'. The Institution closed its doors in 1912, whereupon the library was broken up, with parts of the collection going to the British Museum (later the British Library), the Guildhall Library and the University of London. The building itself was afterwards occupied by the School of Oriental Studies before being demolished in 1936.

One of the Hibberts' enduring charitable legacies came about through George's role in financing what would eventually become the Royal National Lifeboat Institute. As West India merchants with their own shipping fleet, the Hibberts were deeply connected to the maritime community. At a more personal level the family were well used to the perils of the sea, with various members regularly making the Atlantic crossing. In 1810 Mary, the widow of George's brother Samuel junior, witnessed a shipwreck during a visit to Thomas Greg's house in Norfolk. She described it in one of her letters:

> We were on the sea coast during the late dreadful storms – & were witness to such scenes of distress amongst the shipping as I hope I shall never see again – A Fine strong Ship was wrecked exactly opposite to Mr

Greg's house and so close to the shore, that we could distinctly see the poor Men who clung to the masts to the last moment, washed off one after another and eighteen poor souls lost their lives close to us without our having the power to give them the least assistance. Never never can I forget this dreadful scene! Tom and Caroline were with us at the time, and it was a long time before we could any of us get the better of it.[94]

The anguish Mary expressed at having watched the terrible events unfold was in pointed contrast with her brother-in-law Robert junior's reaction to the sinking of various slave ships off the coast of Jamaica. Following the wreck of both the *Enterprise* and the *Cator*, Robert junior's only concern was to try and rescue the lost profits through the quick sale of the survivors. For enslaved people the solution to the loss of life at sea was an insurance policy to cover the destruction of property.

The establishment of the National Institution for the Preservation of Life from Shipwreck in 1824 was in large part due to the efforts of Sir William Hillary. Like George, Hillary was involved in the slave economy in Jamaica and owned a part share in the Adelphi plantation. Hillary recruited George to help generate funds from his mercantile connections in the City. The two men had had an uneasy relationship after Hillary absconded in 1808 owing the Hibbert mercantile partnership £19,607 15s 8d. Over the ensuing years they had clearly resolved their differences enough to work together on the project. A preliminary meeting took place on 12 February 1824 at the London Tavern. Attendees included aristocrats, clergy, politicians, bankers, merchants, naval officers and several men with interests in the West India trade, including the Hibberts' partner John Vincent Purrier and the merchant William Vaughan.[95] At a later meeting on 4 March 1824 George, who by then had been appointed as a Vice-President, was joined by the abolitionist William Wilberforce.[96] This was not the first time the two opponents had been brought together by shared philanthropic causes – both men were Vice-Presidents of the Royal Jennerian Society for the Extermination of the Small Pox. On 5 October 1854, the organisation's name was changed to the Royal National Lifeboat Institution, under which name the charity's work continues to the present. The RNLI's website includes a brief history of its founding. George's role is acknowledged, although he is referred to as a 'shipping magnate' and a 'Chairman of the West Indies Merchants' in a somewhat opaque reference to his participation in the slavery business.[97]

In a departure from the respectable philanthropic activities of the rest of the family, Julian Hibbert was described as 'wealthy supporter of radical causes such as free thought'.[98] Along with his brothers John Hubert Washington and Thomas, Julian received £20,000 from his father, whose fortune had been amassed through both slave trading and plantation ownership. Unlike his brothers he did not appear in the slave compensation records, although this was likely owing to his death in 1834, a year before the compensation money was awarded, rather than as a result of any moral objection. Following his education at Eton and Trinity College, Cambridge, Julian wrote and published a number of atheist works using his personal printing press. His circle included the radical activist and Chartist James Watson. When Watson was struck by illness, Julian took him into his house and cared for him. In Watson's own words:

> I was attacked by cholera, which terminated in typhus and brain fever. I owe my life to the late Julian Hibbert. He took me from my lodgings to his own house at Kentish Town, nursed me, and doctored me for eight weeks, and made a man of me again.[99]

In 1831 Julian gave his printing press to James Watson. As George William Erskine Russell noted, 'With the help of Hibbert's legacy, Watson commenced business as a printer and publisher on his own account, and for something like a quarter of a century sent forth a flood of the most advanced literature of the day.'[100] During the early 1830s Julian used his money to support radicals who had been imprisoned for publishing material deemed illegal by the Government. He was the Chairman and Treasurer of the Victim Fund when the *Poor Man's Guardian*, of which he was an editor, came under attack.[101]

Julian shared a close relationship with Richard Carlile, helping him financially when he was imprisoned between 1831 and 1834. Both men were involved in the establishment of the National Union of the Working Classes and the transformation of the Blackfriars Rotunda into a meeting place for London's radicals. Christina Parolin has stated that the formation of the Union in 1831, 'combined the talents of radical artisans William Lovett, Henry Hetherington, James Watson, John Cleave, William Carpenter, John Gast and the veteran ultra William Benbow, with Rotunda financier and radical strategist Julian Hibbert'.[102] In 1830, when Carlile took over the Blackfriars Rotunda, the building was in urgent need of renovation. As Parolin has documented, 'With the assistance of wealthy freethinking allies, William Devonshire Small and Julian Hibbert, as well as anonymous donations to the cause of "rational debate", Carlile undertook refurbishments to fit the building for public use at the considerable sum of £1300.'[103]

Carlile's daughter Theophila Carlile Campbell wrote a history of the struggle for press freedoms in which she dedicated several passages to Julian's role. Describing him as 'so good, so generous, and so noble', her text revealed the tensions between Julian and the Hibbert family.[104] She wrote that his 'ample fortune' had 'enabled him to live in a way that sheltered him from the storms as well as the battles of life', providing the means for him 'to devote his life to study, to writing, and to acts of benevolence'. Yet Julian had 'separated himself from his family at an early age, and never spoke of them or of his birth to anyone, as far we know. His family affairs were a secret to his most intimate friends.' Theophila recorded that 'there was no doubt that he came of some fine family', though she added 'of that or of any other part of his past, or youth, he never spoke'. Julian was so concerned to erase his past that 'At his death he laid the embargo of silence on all his friends as to himself, and begged them as they loved him to burn all his letters and to cease to speak of him.' Was Julian's attitude towards his family a result of their extensive participation in the slavery business? Radicalism's relationship to antislavery was a complicated one and 'radicals frequently disagreed with each other on the West Indies'.[105] Certainly men like George had appropriated a diluted version of the radical discourse of 'white slavery' during the parliamentary debates on the slave trade. Julian, it seems, was uncomfortable enough about his past to attempt to obscure his origins from his radical friends. Despite distancing himself from his family, Julian's fortune traced its roots back to the system of slavery that had supported his father Thomas and his grandfather John senior before him.

Conclusion

Examples of the country houses owned by absentees and merchants are today in the care of local councils, the National Trust and Historic England. Some remain in private hands and still other have fallen into ruin. These estates form part of a very particular kind of heritage experience, which is steeped in a very particular kind of understanding of British history and culture. Visitors to these sites are not usually invited to confront the disturbing history of enslavement that underpinned the privileged existence of their previous inhabitants. In most instances the excellent, if patchy, interpretative work done in 2007 to make the links between the Caribbean slave economy and the British country house has either disappeared or been relegated to the organisation's online offering.[106] In his analysis of Jane Austen's novel *Mansfield Park*, Edward Said urged the adoption of a practice of contrapuntal reading in order to fully understand 'what is involved when an author shows, for instance, that a colonial sugar plantation is seen as important to the process of maintaining a particular style of life in England'.[107] This critical practice, which emerged briefly in the bicentenary year, has been largely abandoned in favour of the 'dead silence' which Fanny Price was met with when she enquired about the origins of Sir Thomas Bertram's Antiguan fortune.[108] The sustainability of this approach in the face of both a multicultural visiting public and institutional efforts towards diversifying heritage remains to be seen. Despite the lack of permanent signage explaining the transatlantic histories of these properties, for those willing to read the cultural archive contrapuntally these houses will continue to function as physical monuments to the extensive accumulation of wealth which was made possible by the brutal practice of slavery.

The relationship between slave-based wealth and philanthropy has created a set of legacies that Britain continues to grapple with in the present. For illustrious slave-owning benefactors their actions not only secured a reputation for them in their own time, but they also created a legacy which has sustained their memory (or a particular version of it) over time. The efficacy of this can be read in the ongoing contestations over the philanthropic giving of men like the slave trader Edward Colston, who served as Deputy-Governor of the Royal African Company. Described as 'the nearest thing Bristol has to a patron Saint', Colston invested heavily in worthy causes in his home town.[109] His generosity has resulted in over twenty different sites in the city being named for him as well as a statue being erected in 1895. As David Olusoga has argued, 'the good burghers of Bristol were happy to use Colston's philanthropy to whitewash his and his city's role in the Atlantic slave trade. It was they who kept the cult of Colston alive, and they who kindled a distorted history that celebrated his charity while utterly erasing slavery.'[110] For many years campaigners have objected to what they see as the celebration of a man who sold others into bondage. Recently Colston Hall has decided to change its name and Colston's Girls School has cut him out of their annual service of commemoration. Against the weight of Colston's public memory these changes mark a small but significant shift.

The existence of these benevolent bequests raise uncomfortable questions for contemporary society regarding the ways in which slavery benefited different local communities, and indeed the nation as a whole, both then and now. They pose a challenge to the idea that only those directly involved with the slavery business were enriched by it. Their presence in the form of statues, buildings and street names is a continued source of tension in part because they serve as a visible reminder of the continuity of privilege, persisting forms of inequality and the limits of community belonging. The question of what to do with the philanthropic afterlife of those associated with the slave economy has been subject to heated discussion. Should the statues come down? Should the buildings be renamed? As debates continue around what to do with these symbols and the history they represent, it is perhaps the public dialogue that is the most meaningful in terms of reinscribing the history of slavery into the history of Britain. In re-establishing the links between these metropolitan gentleman improvers and the violent exploitation of colonial slavery, the sources and limitations of that benevolent largesse are left exposed. From the country house to the almshouse, the sometimes fraught and confrontational conversations that are taking place about the slaving past must surely bring about a greater understanding than the embrace of 'dead silence'.

Notes

1. Nicholas Draper, *The price of emancipation: Slave-ownership, compensation and British society at the end of slavery* (Cambridge: Cambridge University Press, 2010), p. 9.
2. 'William Thomas Beckford', Legacies of British Slave-ownership database. www.ucl.ac.uk/lbs/person/view/22232 [accessed 10 July 2018].
3. Two notable exceptions include Madge Dresser and Andrew Hann (eds), *Slavery and the British country house* (Swindon: English Heritage, 2013); Stephanie Barczewski, *Country houses and the British empire, 1700–1930* (Manchester: Manchester University Press, 2014). In 2018 Arts Council England funded a new five-year project, 'Colonial Countryside', led by Corinne Fowler at the University of Leicester which will examine country house links to slavery and empire in National Trust properties.
4. Peter Mandler, *The fall and rise of the stately home* (New Haven, CT and London: Yale University Press, 2009), p. 1.
5. Some of these exhibitions have been digitised in the 'Remembering 1807' online archive. http://antislavery.ac.uk/solr-search?q=&facet=collection%3A%22Remembering+1807%22 [accessed 4 June 2018].
6. 'On the duty and pleasure of cultivating benevolent dispositions', *The Philanthropist*, vol. I (London: Longman & Co., 1811), p. 7.
7. Sir John Doyle, HC Deb., 23 February 1807, vol. 8, cc. 945–95.
8. George Hibbert, HC Deb., 23 February 1807, vol. 8, cc. 945–95.
9. Thomas Garrard, *Edward Colston, the philanthropist, his life and times; Including a memoir of his father; The result of a laborious investigation into the archives of the city* (Bristol: J. Chilcott, 1852), p. 16.
10. 'Slave owners in Fitzrovia and on the Portman Estate', Legacies of British Slave-ownership database. www.ucl.ac.uk/lbs/project/fitzroviamap [accessed 6 February 2019].
11. Daniel and Samuel Lysons, *Magna Britannia; Being a precise topographical account of the several counties of Great Britain*, vol. II, part II: *Containing the County Palatine of Chester* (London: T. Cadell & W. Davies, 1810), p. 725.
12. https://historicengland.org.uk/listing/the-list/list-entry/1329626 [accessed 24 May 2018].
13. Lord Colborne, HL Deb., 27 June 1839, vol. 48, cc. 921–3.
14. HFAC, Diary of Robert Hibbert junior, 23 March 1796.
15. JFSGRL, 'Annals of T. H.' (originally compiled by Robert junior's wife Letitia Nembhard, two pages were contributed by her brother-in-law Thomas junior). www.jamaicanfamilysearch.com/Members/bcarib28.htm [accessed 17 January 2018].
16. Centre for Buckinghamshire Studies, Aylesbury, Chalfont Park Estate, D107/2, Deeds of the Greyhound Inn and other property in Chalfont St Peter.
17. Centre for Buckinghamshire Studies, Aylesbury, Chalfont Park Estate, D107/3, Deeds of the Swan Inn and other property in Chalfont St Peter.
18. www.tate.org.uk/art/artworks/turner-chalfont-house-from-the-south-west-d02226 [accessed 9 February 2019].
19. Ibid.

20 www.pinakothek.de/en/node/2736 [accessed 17 January 2018].
21 ICS/SHL/TVAP, M965/14 (B)/24, Letter from Simon Taylor to Robert Taylor, 24 July 1797. My thanks to Christer Petley for providing a transcription.
22 'Annals of T. H.'.
23 ICS/SHL/TVAP, M965/14 (B)/24, Letter from Simon Taylor to Robert Taylor, 24 July 1797.
24 ICS/SHL/TVAP, M965/17/47, Letter from George Hibbert to Simon Taylor, 5 September 1803.
25 JFSGRL, Diary of George Hibbert, 9 March 1817. www.jamaicanfamilysearch.com/Members/bcarib28.htm [accessed 17 January 2018].
26 *Ibid.*, 19 April 1818.
27 *Ibid.*, 13 September 1818.
28 *Ibid.*, 12 February 1819.
29 *Ibid.*, 20 June 1819.
30 The National Archives, Kew, PROB 11/1619/404, Will of Thomas Hibbert of Chalfont House.
31 'Parishes: Chalfont St. Peter', in William Page (ed.), *A history of the county of Buckinghamshire*, vol. III (London: Constable, 1925), pp. 193–8. www.british-history.ac.uk/report.aspx?compid=42545 [accessed 1 October 2012].
32 https://historicengland.org.uk/listing/the-list/list-entry/1332523 [accessed 31 January 2018].
33 J. H. Hansall, *The history of the County Palatine of Cheshire* (Cheshire, 1823), p. 519.
34 *Felix Farley's Bristol Journal*, 21 December 1782.
35 www.nationaltrust.org.uk/hare-hill/features/the-story-of-hare-hill [accessed 18 January 2018].
36 GA/BFDP, D1799/C153, Letter from Robert Hibbert junior to Mary Oates, Kingston, 9 November 1800.
37 http://www.britishlistedbuildings.co.uk/101139611-hare-hill-over-alderley#.WmDlX1XLh0s [accessed 18 January 2018].
38 Edward Wedlake Brayley, *A topographical history of Surrey*, vol. II (London: G. Willis, 1850), p. 371.
39 HFAC, Diary of Robert Hibbert junior, 6 May 1798.
40 *Ibid.*, 21 January 1802.
41 *Ibid.*, 8 March 1802.
42 'William Moffat (1737–1822)', History of Parliament. www.historyofparliamentonline.org/volume/1790-1820/member/moffat-william-1737-1822 [accessed 15 January 2018].
43 https://historicengland.org.uk/listing/the-list/list-entry/1000125 [accessed 31 January 2018].
44 Marquis of Bute, 31 May 1833, in *The debates in Parliament on the resolution and Bill for the Abolition of Slavery in the British Colonies. With a copy of the Act of Parliament* (London: Maurice & Co., 1834), pp. 207–8.
45 'George Henry Ames', Legacies of British Slave-ownership database. www.ucl.ac.uk/lbs/person/view/47002 [accessed 18 January 2018].
46 'Jeremiah Ames', Legacies of British Slave-ownership database. www.ucl.ac.uk/lbs/person/view/2146632312 [accessed 18 January 2018].
47 Susanne Seymour and Sherylynne Haggerty, 'Slavery connections of Brodsworth Hall, 1600–1830'. Final report, English Heritage, 2010. https://content.historicengland.org.uk/images-books/publications/slavery-connections-brodsworth-hall/slavery-connections-brodsworth-hall.pdf/ [accessed 18 January 2018].
48 Michael James, *From smuggling to cotton kings: The Greg story* (Cirencester: Memoirs, 2010), pp. 46–7.
49 J. H. Markland, *A sketch of the life and character of George Hibbert Esq., F.R.S., S.A., and L.S.* (London, 1837), p. 21.
50 *Ibid.*, p. 18.
51 'Watford: Manors', in William Page (ed.), *A history of the county of Hertfordshire*, vol. II (London: Constable, 1908), pp. 451–64. www.british-history.ac.uk/report.aspx?compid=43308 [Accessed 16 January 2012].

52 BL/GHCB, RP5573, George Hibbert, 'Farewell to Blackbirds'.
53 https://historicengland.org.uk/listing/the-list/list-entry/1346895 [Accessed 31 January 2018].
54 The National Archives, Kew, PROB 11/1470/175, Will of Thomas Hibbert.
55 'John Hubert Washington Hibbert', Legacies of British Slave-ownership database. www.ucl.ac.uk/lbs/person/view/17795 [accessed 9 February 2019].
56 'Thomas Hibbert', Legacies of British Slave-ownership database. www.ucl.ac.uk/lbs/person/view/43365 [accessed 23 January 2018].
57 https://historicengland.org.uk/listing/the-list/list-entry/1001378 [accessed 23 January 2018].
58 David Meara, 'The Catholic context', in Paul Atterbury (ed.), *A. W. N. Pugin: Master of Gothic revival* (New Haven, CT: Yale University Press, The Bard Centre for Studies in the Decorative Arts, 1996), pp. 45–62.
59 Paul Atterbury, 'Pugin and interior design', in Paul Atterbury (ed.), *A. W. N. Pugin: Master of Gothic revival* (New Haven, CT: Yale University Press, The Bard Centre for Studies in the Decorative Arts, 1996), pp. 193–4.
60 *Ibid.*, p. 194.
61 https://historicengland.org.uk/listing/the-list/list-entry/1001378 [accessed 31 January 2018].
62 The National Archives, Kew, PROB 11/1470/175, Will of Thomas Hibbert.
63 Charles Kerry, *The history and antiquities of the hundred of Bray in the county of Berks* (London: Savill & Edwards, 1861), p. 82.
64 www.berkshirehistory.com/villages/braywick.html [accessed 13 February 2018].
65 George Hibbert, HC Deb., 23 February 1807, vol. 8, cc. 945–95.
66 TNA/COP, CO 137/146/168, Letter from George Hibbert to Earl Bathurst, April 1818.
67 'The Greenway: Walk to a healthy future', Royal Borough of Windsor and Maidenhead (2007), p. 2.
68 www.stmaries.co.uk/history-of-st-maries?showall=&start=5 [accessed 31 January 2018].
69 https://historicengland.org.uk/listing/the-list/list-entry/1365006 [accessed 31 January 2018].
70 https://ukga.org/england/Berkshire/towns/Maidenhead.html [accessed 31 January 2018].
71 https://historicengland.org.uk/listing/the-list/list-entry/1117590 [accessed 31 January 2018].
72 Kerry, *The history and antiquities of the hundred of Bray*, p. 65, p. 67.
73 *Ibid.*, p. 77.
74 http://maidenheadheritage.org.uk/hall-of-fame-2/john-hibbert/ [accessed 31 January 2018].
75 Jerom Murch, *Memoir of Robert Hibbert, founder of the Hibbert Trust: With a sketch of its history* (Bath: William Lewis, 1874), p. 50.
76 *Ibid.*, p. 34.
77 Alan Rushton, *The Hibbert Trust: A history* (London: The Hibbert Trust, 1984), p. 1.
78 http://beta.charitycommission.gov.uk/charity-details/?regid=227358&subid=0 [accessed 31 January 2018].
79 Rushton, *The Hibbert Trust*, p. 2.
80 Murch, *Memoir*, p. 15.
81 https://historicengland.org.uk/listing/the-list/list-entry/1065711 [accessed 1 February 2018]
82 National Trust, Dyrham Park, Gloucestershire, NT 456203, Rules of the Hibbert Almshouse Charity.
83 www.hibbertalms.org.uk/ [accessed 1 February 2018].
84 'Parishes: Chalfont St. Peter'.
85 'Chalfont St. Peter: The Report of the Community Appraisal Steering Group and Action Plan for 2006', p. 3.

86 For a discussion of the class-based rivalries between the Royal Institution and the London Institution see Janet C. Cutler, 'The London Institution, 1805–1933' (PhD thesis, University of Leicester, 1976), pp. 6–10.
87 London Metropolitan Archives, London, Letters, printed notices and papers relating to the founding of the London Institution 1805–1817 (LMA/LI), CLC/009MS03080.
88 *Ibid.*
89 LMA/LI, CLC/009MS03080, Minutes of the Annual and Special General Meetings of the Court of Proprietors. Henry Thornton was elected Manager in April 1810. John Thornton was elected Manager on 29 April 1813 and 29 April 1819. Zachary Macaulay was elected as Manager on 13 November 1812 and 29 April 1819.
90 LMA/LI, CLC/009/MS03075, Minutes of the Annual and Special General Meetings of the Court of Proprietors, Report from the Committee of Enquiry read to the Court of the Proprietors, 14 August 1812.
91 LMA/LI, CLC/009/MS02753, List of books, paintings and objects displayed at the evening parties given at the Institution, with names of contributors.
92 LMA/LI, CLC/009/MS03075, Minutes of the Annual and Special General Meetings of the Court of Proprietors, 15 January 1830.
93 *Ibid.*, 30 April 1835.
94 Lancashire Archives, Preston, Pilkington Family Papers, DDPI 5/6, Letter from Mary Hibbert, 17 October 1810.
95 Sir William Hillary, *An appeal to the British nation on the humanity and policy of forming a national institution for the preservation of lives and property from shipwreck* (London: Geo. B. Whittaker, 1825), p. 43.
96 *Ibid.*, p. 49.
97 https://rnli.org/about-us/our-history/timeline/1824-our-foundation [accessed 1 February 2018].
98 Joel H. Wiener, 'Julian Hibbert', in Joseph O. Baylen and Norbert J. Gossman (eds), *Biographical dictionary of modern British radicals* (Hassocks: Harvester, 1979), p. 221.
99 Roderick Cave, *The private press* (New York: R. R. Bowker Co., 1983).
100 George William Erskine Russell, *Dr. Pusey* (London: A. R. Mowbray & Co., 1907), p. 16.
101 Laurel Brake and Marysa Demoor (eds), *Dictionary of nineteenth-century journalism in Great Britain and Ireland* (Ghent: Academia Press, 2009), p. 501.
102 Christina Parolin, *Radical spaces: Venues of popular politics in London, 1790–1845* (Canberra: Australian National University Press, 2010), p. 231.
103 *Ibid.*, p. 200.
104 Theophila Carlile Campbell, *The battle of the press as told in the story of the life of Richard Carlile by his daughter, Theophila Carlile Campbell* (London: A. & H. B. Bonner, 1899). www.gutenberg.org/files/38370/38370-h/38370-h.htm [accessed 2 February 2018].
105 Michael J. Turner, '"Setting the captive free": Thomas Perronet Thompson, British radicalism and the West Indies, 1820s-1860s', *Slavery & Abolition*, 26:1 (2005), p. 115.
106 Historic England have a web presence for some of the research that was undertaken by them in 2007 exploring slavery connections to their properties, 'Researching Slavery Connections'. https://historicengland.org.uk/research/inclusive-heritage/the-slave-trade-and-abolition/slavery-and-the-british-country-house/ [accessed 15 January 2018].
107 Edward Said, *Culture and imperialism* (London: Random House, 1994), p. 78.
108 Jane Austen, *Mansfield Park* (London: Macmillan & Co., 1902), p. 176.
109 Will Heaven, 'Must Colston fall? Bristol's struggle with the complicated legacy of a slaver', *The Spectator*, 22 July 2017.
110 David Olusoga, 'Bristol: The city that lauds the slave trader', *The Guardian*, 27 April 2017.

Epilogue: Family legacies: after abolition

Robert junior wrote in 1807 that he feared for the fate of the next generation of Hibberts in the aftermath of abolition. On his death in 1835, the year after the enactment of emancipation, he left a £250,000 fortune built up through slave trading, slave ownership and the trade in slave-produced commodities.[1] Having inherited Birtles Hall from his father, Robert junior's eldest son Thomas left the property to his son Hugh in 1879. Hugh entered the British army and in 1850 was commissioned as a lieutenant in the 7th Royal Fusiliers. He went to the Crimea in 1854 and was severely wounded.[2] In 1861 he married Sarah Catherine Augusta Lee, the daughter of the artist Frederick Richard Lee RA. The couple had five daughters and one son. Shifting from the West Indies to the East, Hugh was posted to India in 1858 and in 1863 he was raised to commanding officer after purchasing a commission for £3,500.[3] In 1871 he retired to Broadgate, Barnstaple, Devon, the home of his father-in-law. When he died in 1895 he left £6,189 9d.[4] Birtles Hall was sold shortly afterwards and Broadgate was auctioned by his widow in 1918 to pay their son Hugh Thomas's debts.[5] Robert junior's vast wealth maintained the family for two generations following his death; however, a withdrawal from commerce removed the source of capital accumulation which had enabled him to amass the greatest of the Hibbert fortunes. The social prestige of the country gentleman might have outstripped that of the merchant man, but in pecuniary terms the merchant house proved to be far more productive than the country house.

George's eldest son Nathaniel inherited Munden, where he lived as a 'Landed Proprietor and Fund Holder'.[6] His marriage to Emily Smith brought with it an important social network. Emily's elder sister Saba was the second wife of Sir Henry Holland. Holland had two sons by his first wife, the eldest of whom was Henry Thurston Holland. In 1852 Nathaniel and Emily's daughter Elizabeth married Sir Henry's eldest son. As the heiress to Munden and a close, if not blood relation,

EPILOGUE: FAMILY LEGACIES

her marriage represented a good prospect for amalgamating the family interest. Although she promised property, when her father Nathaniel died his effects were valued at under £9,000, making Munden the bulk of her inheritance.[7] Henry Thurston had an illustrious political career and was made Viscount Knutsford in 1895. In 1855 the couple had twin sons – Arthur and Sydney. Elizabeth died shortly afterwards and Henry Thurston married again, this time to Margaret Trevelyan. She was the daughter of Charles Trevelyan and Hannah More Macaulay. The granddaughters of proslavery George Hibbert and abolitionist Zachary Macaulay were thus linked by marriage, and it was Margaret who raised George's great-grandsons. Arthur entered the Royal Navy as an acting lieutenant but retired upon inheriting Munden. There was a stipulation in his mother's will that required him to take the additional surname of Hibbert, which he assumed by Royal Licence in 1876. Following in the family tradition, Arthur was elected as Chairman of the East and West India Dock Company. He served as a Director of the English, Scottish and Australian Bank, the Underground Electric Railways Company, the City and South London Railway and the London and Scottish Life Assurance Company. In 1914 he succeeded his father as Viscount Knutsford. His twin brother Sydney inherited the vast majority of his great-uncle George junior's mercantile fortune, which was valued at £70,000 in 1877.[8] Sydney pursued a successful legal career and served as Director of the English and Scottish Australian Bank, the Electric Underground Railway Company and the London and Lancashire Life Insurance Company. His philanthropic work earned him the title 'The Prince of Beggars' after he wrote thousands of letters to raise money for the London Hospital.[9] When his twin brother died in 1931 the title passed to Arthur. Munden remains within the Holland-Hibbert family today.

Of the next generation it was William's son, William junior, who accrued the greatest wealth. Unlike his country-house-owning cousins, William junior remained faithful to the Hibberts' commercial roots. Like his cousins George junior and Samuel, he invested in the insurance industry and acted as a Director of the Royal Exchange Assurance Corporation for over twenty years from the 1840s. William junior also sought to exploit the new opportunities offered by a timely expansion into different theatres of empire away from the Caribbean. He was a member of the Canada Company's Provisional Committee established in 1824.[10] The Company was incorporated by an Act of Parliament on 27 July 1825 to facilitate the colonisation of Upper Canada. From 1826 until the 1840s William junior regularly served as one of the Company Directors. The 41,421-acre Hibbert Township in Ontario is named for the family. In the mid-1830s savvy merchants and financiers scrambled to set up a new banking system in the Caribbean in response to the capital injection represented by the large sums of slavery compensation money that were paid out by the British Government. As Kathleen Butler has explained, 'the compensation award represented a potential reservoir of investment to be channelled through colonial and metropolitan financial institutions ... The new metropolitan bank was designed to serve these investments and to remove most of the risk from the remaining private merchant houses that traded with the West Indies.'[11] On 1 June 1836 the Colonial Bank received its Royal Charter and became 'in effect, the investment channel for the compensation that remained in Britain'. William junior paid £2,000 as a subscriber and served as a Director.[12] Offices were opened in Jamaica, Barbados, British Guiana, Trinidad and St Thomas.[13] Having seen off less successful rivals, the Colonial Bank survived into the early twentieth century. In 1881 William junior died at Postford House, Chilworth, Surrey, leaving a personal estate of £165,288 1s 11d.[14]

The Hibberts' story is one of many family stories tangled up in Britain's history of slavery and empire. They represent a particular narrative of colonial success – of rags to riches through buccaneering entrepreneurship in the Torrid Zone. They fulfilled the imperial fantasy of extracting untold wealth from the empire before returning home, remade as gentlemen, to enjoy all the opulence of the metropole. The country houses and the beautiful things that filled them, the works of improvement, the acts of benevolence, the elevated social circles and the access to political power were all enabled by the Hibberts' prolonged and systematic exploitation of enslaved labour. The tangible inheritance of property and wealth, alongside the intangible transference of privilege through social networks and cultural capital, created a legacy for their progeny that sustained them over time, even after the system that had initially propelled their elevation had been brought to an end. Just as multiple generations of the Hibbert family inherited their position in society from their predecessors, so too did the enslaved men, women and children on their plantations. How many generations of enslaved families were destined from birth to remain tied to the land, forced to repeat the same cycle of life, labour and death that their forebears had endured? For them, their family inheritance was a bitter draught to swallow.

Whilst the family enjoyed tremendous personal gain through their individual participation, their story is revealing of the ways in which slave-based wealth enriched metropolitan society at both local and national level. In tracing the impact made by a single family, this book gives an impression of the incredible reach of slavery into the lives not just of the elite planter-merchant families who gained directly from it, but also those whose benefit was incidental. From the building of the West India Docks and the provision of employment, to the purchase of fine art and books which can still be found in the nation's museums and galleries, the profits of slavery filtered through to different arenas, impacting on the social, cultural, economic and political development of Britain. A common response to the public discussion of transatlantic slavery was articulated by one reader in response to an article by Catherine Hall in *The Guardian*. The comment read: 'Fail to see how slavery benefited ordinary people in the UK. They became enslaved to the mine owners and iron ore owners ... Slavery is a blight on the history of the British upper classes not us the working class.'[15] The work of the 'Legacies of British Slave-ownership' project in bringing the 46,000 slavery compensation claims to light has demonstrated that it was not only the elites in Britain who were involved in the practice of slave ownership. Claimants varied from powerful families like the Hibberts, to Dorothy Little of Clifton, Bristol, a widow who drew an annual income of £80 per year from the labour of eight enslaved people resident in Jamaica.[16] The wider slavery business – the attendant industries that grew up around the core activities of the merchants and planters – generated an income for people across a broad spectrum of society. These people did not engage in the violent extraction of labour from the enslaved but were supported by it nonetheless.

Catherine Hall has drawn on Michael Rothberg's theory of the 'implicated subject' to consider how to frame an understanding of the 'large and heterogeneous collection of subjects who enable and benefit from traumatic violence without taking part in it directly'.[17] In understanding trauma Rothberg argues for the need to move beyond simplistic dichotomies which focus solely on the victim and perpetrator, and instead has urged the need to take into account the 'indirect responsibility of subjects situated at temporal or geographic distance from the production of social suffering'.[18] This shift creates a space to think about the ways in which those people who are seemingly disconnected from the events might draw some form of privilege or benefit as a result. It enables a greater understanding of the power structures and ideologies which underpin individual action, particularly within the context of mass events like transatlantic slavery. This construction is useful in relation to a country like Britain, which has consistently chosen either imperial nostalgia or imperial forgetting as a way of disavowing the troubling aspects of its history of empire.[19] A refusal to understand and acknowledge the complicated ways in which transatlantic slavery benefited Britain, both in the past and through the legacies that connect it to the present, is a way of denying the central role played by the system in shaping modern society. The histories we construct for ourselves have a bearing on how we view our responsibilities in the present. As Rothberg has stated, 'the concept of implication asks us to think how we are enmeshed in histories and actualities beyond our apparent and immediate reach, how we help produce history through impersonal participation rather than direct perpetration'.[20] It is not just the act of violence and trauma that raises questions of responsibility, it is the ways in which we chose to historicise and represent such acts that create new implicated subjects. As Gurminder Bhambra has argued, 'If we are interested in questions of inequality in the present, we have to think about how inequalities are constituted by ... historical processes, nationally and internationally.'[21] This requires a fundamental re-evaluation of how we construct the past. Described by Bhambra as 'reparative histories', this process would force a critical engagement with 'questions of violence and the appropriation of resources'. This shift in understanding opens the door to new possibilities for relations between the former colonial powers and the societies that they helped to forge through the practice of colonialism. Bhambra has further argued that 'If we were to recognise that their poverty is generated by the same processes that created our wealth, and that inequality is generated by historical processes like imperialism, extraction and appropriation, from which we continue to benefit, we could think about how to take responsibility for what we enjoy.'

If the metropole gained materially as a nation in the wake of slavery, what then of the Caribbean? In the context of the British narrative, the story of transatlantic slavery almost always ends with the triumphant moment of the passing of the Slavery Abolition Act in 1833. There is very little public knowledge of the system of apprenticeship and indenture which followed, the labour struggles as formerly enslaved peoples fought for their rights, or the process by which the Caribbean nation states emerged in the wake of decolonisation. The ending of slavery did not create, nor was it designed to create, an equal society. Land ownership and political power remained entrenched within the white elites. When the period of apprenticeship finally drew to a close, the Governor of Jamaica, Sir Lionel Smith, made an announcement setting out the terms of freedom. He wrote:

> Where you can agree and continue happy with your own masters, I strongly recommend you to remain on those properties on which you have been born, and where your parents are buried. But you must not mistake in supposing that your present houses, gardens, or provision grounds are your own property. They belong to the proprietors of

the estates, and you will have to pay rent for them in money or labour, according as you and your employers may agree together.[22]

Despite having built their homes and tended to their grounds for multiple generations, formerly enslaved people were not legally entitled to the rights of ownership. Their affective and family ties to the land were strong; in some instances the boundaries of the plantation marked the limits of the known world, intimate family life (however fragile and precarious) had been lived in these spaces, beloved relations had been laid to rest in the grounds of the estates. It was not a home of their choosing, but for some enslaved families its soil was sown with the seeds of trans-generational memory and it was imbued with a sense of ownership, even if the claim was not recognised under the law. Redistribution of the land did not occur as part of the process of making freedom and some planters actively blocked its sale to the formerly enslaved. This inspired initiatives by the abolitionists to acquire land of behalf of the newly emancipated population, leading to the creation of free villages. It also brought about the practice of squatting, in which free people seized illegal land holdings on vacant Crown land or land which was lying unused by the planters. Jean Besson has cited the example of Aberdeen, a former plantation which was squatted by freed workers from 1845 and which was 'later retrieved by the plantocracy and sold for registration and taxation in the official legal system. Descending generations of the ex-slaves who purchased these legal freeholds have transformed them, through customary tenure and transmission, into "family lands".'[23] In 2015 a case went to court over a land dispute involving what had originally been the Golden Vale plantation in Portland. The attorney defending a group of sixty families who work and live on the land claimed the planter had gifted it to his apprenticed labourers in 1838.[24] Unlike the Hibberts, whose property rights were legally recognised, guaranteed and compensated, the existence of a two-tier system of ownership claims has created a legal legacy of precarity and disputed land rights which persists within present-day Jamaican society.

Hoping to control the flow of labour, the plantocracy attempted to curb mobility by passing legislation that bound people to the estates. As Governor Smith made clear, 'Idle people who will not take employment, but go wandering about the country, will be taken up as vagrants and punished in the same manner as they are in England.'[25] Claiming the freedom to redefine one's position within the labour matrix could result in incarceration in the workhouses and forced labour. In order to shore up labour supplies and reduce the bargaining power of the free black labourers, a system of indentured labour was introduced into the Caribbean in the 1840s. Indian and Chinese workers were imported into the former slave colonies to make up the labour deficit. It was the realisation of the system of unfree labour advocated for by George Hibbert in the wake of slave trade abolition. The continuation of exploitative labour practices, alongside the lack of access to land and political rights, culminated in the 1865 Morant Bay Rebellion. Thomas Holt described the events as 'Laying bare the contradictions of British policy and ideology, their revolt summed up the whole unfortunate history of Jamaican emancipation. In its aftermath, problems of labour and politics, ideas about freedom and race, were unravelled and rewoven.'[26] Following a protest led by the black preacher Paul Bogle, in which several hundred people marched on the Morant Bay court house, Governor John Eyre suppressed the rebellion with brutal force, resulting in an official death toll of 439. The savageness of the violence meted out by the Government forces created a controversy in Britain that saw calls for Governor Eyre to be tried for murder.[27] Many luminaries of metropolitan society supported Eyre, including John Hubert Washington Hibbert.[28] In the wake of the rebellion, Jamaica became a Crown colony under direct rule from Westminster. For Holt, the perceived failures of emancipation

> fuelled racist thinking and imperialist ambition. When ex-slaves chose to define the content of their freedom in apparent opposition to market forces, they became *themselves* vulnerable to redefinition ... These wayward children of the human family were fit subjects for a 'beneficent despotism'. Projected to the world stage beneficent despotism became the 'white man's burden', the bittersweet fruit of his imperial adventure into the heart of darkness.[29]

Independence came to Jamaica in 1962, almost a century after the Morant Bay Rebellion. The failures of emancipation did not simply resolve themselves with decolonisation, and the island's economic and political sovereignty continues to be shaped by external influences. Even outside of the particularly pernicious mechanisms of control exercised through enslavement, the practice and processes of freedom require 'a constant struggle'.[30]

The history of slavery not only shaped Britons' ideas about race and empire, it also had a direct impact on the development of the nation and the ways in which national identity was, and is, constructed. The relative position of slavery within the narrative of British history has real ramifications for understanding how and why the nation emerged as a global power in the eighteenth and nineteenth centuries, and as a multicultural society in the twentieth. The sub-dividing of 'British history' and 'imperial history' is a synthetic imposition which masks the interconnectedness and interdependency of the metropole and colony. Britain, as Bhambra has argued, 'has not been an independent country, but part of broader political entities; most significantly empire, then the Commonwealth and, from 1973, the European Union. There has been no independent Britain, no "Island nation".'[31] In an interview carried out during the elections in Sleaford in 2016, journalist John Harris asked a pro-Brexit voter why she had made that decision. Her reply was that 'I think it's better to come out ... we've stood on our own in the past, and I think we can do it again.'[32] The ability to perceive Britain's history as one of splendid isolation and ethnic homogeneity requires the forgetting or active suppression of the memory of empire. However, as Jamaica-born cultural theorist Stuart Hall argued:

> People like me who came to England in the 1950s have been there for centuries; symbolically, we have been there for centuries. I was coming home. I am the sugar at the bottom of the English cup of tea. I am the sweet tooth, the sugar plantations that rotted generations of English children's teeth ... That is the outside history that is inside the history of the English. There is no English history without that other history.[33]

An established and long-standing presence in the historical narrative matters absolutely for claims to citizenship, rights and belonging. The history of empire is fundamental to understanding the patterns of colonial and post-independence waves of migration into Britain. During the 2018 'Windrush scandal', which saw British subjects deported to the Caribbean because they could not produce the requisite bureaucratic proof of their right to citizenship, the issue of historical memory was raised in relation to slavery and the ties that bind both families and nations. David Lammy, Member of Parliament for Tottenham, addressed the Commons with a speech which made reference to his own family history. He stated:

> I am here, because you were there. We are here, because you were there. My ancestors were British subjects. But they were not British subjects because they came to Britain. They were British subjects because Britain came to them, took them across the Atlantic, colonised them, sold them into slavery, profited from their labour and made them British subjects. That is why I am here. That is why the Windrush generation are here.[34]

Slavery and colonialism created a new sense of Britishness, one which was constructed through both the forced and voluntary experience of imperialism. The Hibberts saw the empire as an intrinsic part of the nation and national identity. Their vision of imperial subjecthood did not include the enslaved and for many years the racialisation of national identity has continued to perpetuate the historic exclusions that find their roots in the relationship between the colonised and the coloniser. It is an issue which persists today. As Lammy pointed out, '[S]ome 230 years after those in the abolitionist movement wore their medallions around their necks, I stand here as a Caribbean, black, British citizen and I ask the Minister, on behalf of those Windrush citizens, am I not a man and a brother?'

The bonds of family and history, of nation and empire, of privilege and inequality, continue to tie Britain, the Caribbean and Africa together. Time and distance have not weakened a web of interconnections that were centuries in the making. The remembrance and disavowal of slavery continues to draw such emotive responses because we continue to live with its unresolved legacies. Slavery transformed the lives of families in the past and it shapes the lives of families in the present. The grand narrative of British history – the nation's family story – is complex, contradictory and at times disturbing. In her book exploring changing attitudes to family secrets, Deborah Cohen has argued that 'Contrary to the old saying', you can 'at least to some degree, choose your family, at least the extended and mythical version of it.'[35] For the Hibberts this meant the erasure of Jane Harry from the family Bible, although in more recent times she has been reclaimed. For the nation this dynamic explains to some degree why the name of Wilberforce remains familiar, whilst those of his opponents have sunk into obscurity. Shame and pain characterise the keeping of family secrets, but it is a 'desire to know and for many, a need to tell' that unlocks the knowledge of the past.[36] The acknowledgement and acceptance of the brutal system of transatlantic slavery as a core part of national history is part of a process of deconstructing the mythologisation of British isolationism and benign imperial rule. The knowledge of it refutes the idea that British history can be framed through the golden thread of liberty because, just like most family histories, there are ghosts, and skeletons, and shattered fragments of past lives that sever the claim to an unbroken narrative of freedom. Telling different stories is about repairing the tears and disjunctures of historical power. As Fred D'Aguiar has written, the past is 'where death has begun but remains unfinished because it recurs ... The ghosts feed on the story of themselves. The past is laid to rest when it is told.'[37] Redressing the historical narrative will not in and of itself restore what has been lost or provide a solution to the structural inequalities which find their roots in the history of slavery and empire. It does, however, represent the opening of a necessary dialogue in which the unpalatable parts of the past are silenced no longer.

EPILOGUE: FAMILY LEGACIES

Notes

1 The National Archives, Kew, PROB 11/1842/325, Will of Robert Hibbert junior.
2 Cheshire Archives and Local Studies, Chester, Telegram, DHB/76, 12 September 1855.
3 www.britishempire.co.uk/forces/armyunits/britishinfantry/fusiliershughhibbert.htm [accessed 18 January 2018].
4 The National Archives, Kew, National Probate Calendar (Index of Wills and Administrations), 1895.
5 www.henrywilliamson.co.uk/bibliography/a-lifes-work/the-village-book [accessed 9 February 2019].
6 The National Archives, Kew, Census of England, Wales, Scotland, Channel Islands and Isle of Man, 1861.
7 The National Archives, Kew, National Probate Calendar (Index of Wills and Administrations), 1866, p. 241.
8 *Illustrated London News*, 81:2254 (15 July 1882), p. 74.
9 Keir Waddington, *Charity and the London hospitals, 1850–1898* (Woodbridge: Boydell Press, 2000), p. 13.
10 Robert C. Lee, *The Canada Company and the Huron Tract, 1826–1853: Personalities, profits and politics* (Ontario: Natural Heritage, 2004), Appendix C, 'Huron Tract township names and their origins'.
11 Kathleen Mary Butler, *The economics of emancipation: Jamaica and Barbados, 1823–1843* (Chapel Hill: University of North Carolina Press, 1995), p. 137.
12 G. Aubrey Goodman and C. P. Clarke, *Laws of Barbados: Revised and consolidated* (London: Advocate Printing Works, 1912), p. 14.
13 Butler, *The economics of emancipation*, p. 134.
14 The National Archives, Kew, National Probate Calendar (Index of Wills and Administrations), 1881.
15 Catherine Hall, 'Britain's massive debt to slavery', *The Guardian*, 27 February 2013.
16 Hannah Young, 'Women, slavery compensation and gender relations in the 1830s' (MA thesis, University College London, 2013), p. 14.
17 Catherine Hall, keynote address, 'Bluecoats 300: Charity, philanthropy and the Black Atlantic', International Slavery Museum, Liverpool, 24 November 2017.
18 Michael Rothberg, 'Trauma theory, implicated subjects, and the question of Israel/Palestine', May 2014. www. profession.mla.org/trauma-theory-implicated-subjects-and-the-question-of-israel-palestine/ [accessed 14 June 2018].
19 Catherine Hall and Daniel Pick, 'Thinking about denial', *History Workshop Journal*, 84:1 (2017), pp. 1–23.
20 Rothberg, 'Trauma theory'.
21 Charlotte L. Riley and Gurminder K. Bhambra, 'How a history of conquest shapes the present', *New Humanist*, 3 July 2017. https://newhumanist.org.uk/articles/5204/how-a-history-of-conquest-shapes-the-present [accessed 18 June 2018].
22 Sir Lionel Smith, quoted in Frances Wright D'Arusmont, *Political letters; Or observations on religion and civilization*, vol. II (Dundee: Myles, 1844), pp. 39–40.
23 Jean Besson, 'Folk law and legal pluralism in Jamaica: A view from the plantation-peasant interface', *Journal of Legal Pluralism and Unofficial Law*, 31:43 (2013), p. 32.
24 Barbara Gayle, 'Battle rages over slave-owner's land', *Jamaica Gleaner*, 11 January 2015.
25 Sir Lionel Smith, quoted in D'Arusmont, *Political letters*, p. 40.
26 Thomas C. Holt, *The problem of freedom: Race, labour, and politics in Jamaica and Britain, 1832–1938* (Baltimore, MD: John Hopkins University Press, 1992), p. 264.
27 For a detailed study see Gad Heuman, *Killing time: Morant Bay Rebellion Jamaica* (Knoxville: University of Tennessee Press, 1995).
28 Nicholas Draper, *The price of emancipation: Slave-ownership, compensation and the British society at the end of slavery* (Cambridge: Cambridge University Press, 2010), p. 337.
29 Holt, *The problem of freedom*, p. 309.
30 *Ibid.*, p. 402.

31 Gurminder Bhambra, 'Brexit, class and British "national" identity', *Discover Society*, 5 July 2016. https://discoversociety.org/2016/07/05/viewpoint-brexit-class-and-british-national-identity/ [accessed 18 June 2018].
32 John Harris, 'Sleaford's Brexit byelection: A people united by fear for the future', video, *The Guardian*, 30 November 2016, 07:27–07:32. www.theguardian.com/commentisfree/video/2016/nov/30/sleaford-lincolnshire-brexit-byelection-young-video [accessed 19 June 2018].
33 Stuart Hall, 'Old and new identities, old and new ethnicities', in Anthony D. King (ed.), *Culture, globalization, and the world-system: Contemporary conditions for the representation of identity* (Minneapolis: University of Minnesota Press, 1997), pp. 48–9.
34 David Lammy MP, 'Speech on the Windrush crisis in Parliament', 30 April 2018. www.davidlammy.co.uk/single-post/2018/05/29/Speeches-on-the-Windrush-crisis-in-Parliament [accessed 20 June 2018].
35 Deborah Cohen, *Family secrets: Shame and privacy in modern Britain* (Oxford: Oxford University Press, 2013), p. 262.
36 *Ibid.*, p. 260.
37 Fred D'Aguiar, *Feeding the ghosts* (London: Vintage, 1998), p. 230.

SELECT BIBLIOGRAPHY

Archives

Bodleian Library, Oxford
Papers of Cardinal Henry Edward Manning

British Library, London
Althorp Papers
Correspondence and papers of the 2nd Earl of Liverpool
Correspondence of Admiral of the Fleet Sir Thomas Byam Martin
George Hibbert's Commonplace Book

Cambridgeshire Archives, Ely
Tharp Family of Chippenham Records

Derbyshire Record Office, Matlock
Wilmot-Horton of Osmaston and Catton Papers

Devon County Record Office, Exeter
Addington Family Papers

Gloucestershire Archives, Gloucester
Blathwayt Family of Dyrham Papers

Hibbert Family Private Archive and Collection, Melbourne, Australia
Jamaica Diaries of Robert Hibbert junior

SELECT BIBLIOGRAPHY

Institute of Commonwealth Studies, Senate House Library, London
Taylor and Vaneck-Arcedekne Papers
West India Committee Papers

Jamaica Archives and Record Department, Kingston, Jamaica
Crop Accounts
Journals of the House of Assembly

Lancashire Archives, Preston
Pilkington Family Papers

London Metropolitan Archive, London
Letters, printed notices and papers relating to the founding of the London Institution
Records of Holy Trinity, Clapham Common

Merseyside Maritime Museum, Maritime Archives and Library, Liverpool
Earle Collection

The National Archives, Kew
Colonial Office and Predecessors: Jamaica, Original Correspondence
Office of Registry of Colonial Slavery and Slave Compensation Commission Records

National Library of Wales, Aberystwyth
Slebech Papers and Documents

Historical Society of Pennsylvania, Philadelphia, Library Company of Philadelphia Collection
Powell Family Papers

Sir John Soane's Museum and Collection, London
West India Dock Compensation Committee Papers

Wilberforce Institute for the Study of Slavery and Emancipation, Hull
Letters of William Smith

SELECT BIBLIOGRAPHY

Newspapers and periodicals

Anti-Slavery Monthly Reporter
Christian Observer
Curtis's Botanical Magazine
Jamaica Gazette
John Bull
Gentleman's Magazine
Guardian
London Gazette
Morning Chronicle
The Times

Printed sources

An abstract of the evidence delivered before a Select Committee of the House of Commons in the years 1790, and 1791; on the part of the petitioners for the abolition of the slave-trade (London: James Phillips, 1791)

At a very numerous and respectable meeting at the London Tavern, May 23, 1805: The following resolutions were unanimously adopted ... [Account of the founding of the London Institution] (London: Phillips & Fardon, 1805)

A catalogue of Italian, Spanish, French, Flemish, and Dutch pictures the property of George Hibbert: which will be sold by auction, by Mr. Christie on June the 13th 1829 (London: Christie, Manson & Woods Ltd, 1829)

A catalogue of the library of George Hibbert, Esq. of Portland Place; which will be sold by auction on Monday, March 16, and seventeen following days; on Monday, May 4, and eleven following days; and on Monday, May 25, and eleven following days, (Sundays excepted) by Mr. Evans, at his house, No. 93, Pall Mall (London: W. Nichol, 1829)

A collection of prints illustrative of English scenery, from the drawings and sketches of Thos. Gainsborough, R.A. in the various collections of the right honourable Baroness Lucas; Viscount Palmerston; George Hibbert, Esq.; Dr. Monro, and several other gentlemen (London: H. R. Young, 1819)

An historical account of the London Institution: Including bibliographical notices and a synoptical view of the library; With a sketch of the scientific history of the establishment, and of the various courses of lectures which have been delivered in the theatre (London: Charles Skipper & East, 1835)

A letter to the most honourable the Marquis of Chandos (London: T. Brettell, 1830)

Marly; Or, a planter's life in Jamaica (London: R. Griffin, 1828; repr. Oxford: Macmillan Education, 2005, ed. Karina Williamson)

Parliamentary register, or history of the proceedings and debates of the House of Commons, 45 vols (London, 1780–96)

Report from the Select Committee appointed to consider of the means of improving and maintaining the foreign trade of this country, the West India Docks (London: House of Commons, 1823)

SELECT BIBLIOGRAPHY

Report of the Incorporated Society for the Conversion and Religious Instruction and Education of the Negroe Slaves in the British West India islands (London: R. Gilbert, 1824)

Baker, Sir Thomas, *Memorials of a dissenting chapel, its foundation and worthies; Being a sketch of the rise of non-conformity in Manchester and the erection of the chapel in Cross Street, with notices of its ministers and trustees* (Manchester: Johnson and Rawson, 1884)

Bellamy, Thomas, *The benevolent planter* (London: J. Debrett, 1789)

Bickell, Richard, *The West Indies as they are; Or a real picture of slavery: But more particularly as it exists in the island of Jamaica* (London: J. Hatchard and Son, 1824)

Bissett, Robert, *The history of the negro slave trade, in its connection with the commerce and prosperity of the West Indies, and the wealth and power of the British empire*, 2 vols (London: W. McDowall, 1805)

Buchanan, William, *Memoirs of painting, with a chronological history of the importation of pictures by the Great Masters into England since the French Revolution*, 2 vols (London: R. Ackermann, 1824)

Burke, John, *A genealogical and heraldic history of the commoners of Great Britain & Ireland enjoying territorial possessions of high official rank but uninvested with heritable honours*, 2 vols (London: Henry Colburn, 1835)

Clarkson, Thomas, *History of the rise, progress and accomplishment of the abolition of the African slave trade by the British Parliament* (London: Longman, Hurst, Rees & Orme, 1808)

Cobbett, William, *Parliamentary history of England. From the Norman conquest, in 1066, to the year 1803*, 36 vols (London: T. C. Hansard, 1806–20)

Cooper, Thomas, *Correspondence between George Hibbert, Esq., and the Rev. T. Cooper: Relative to the condition of the negro slaves in Jamaica, extracted from the Morning Chronicle, also a libel on the character of Mr. and Mrs. Cooper, pub. in 1823 in several of the Jamaica journals, with notes and remarks* (London: J. Hatchard & Son, 1824)

Cooper, Thomas, *A letter to Robert Hibbert, Jun. Esq., in reply to his pamphlet, entitled, 'Facts verified upon oath, in contradiction of the report of the Rev. Thomas Cooper, concerning the general condition of the slaves in Jamaica,' &c. &c: to which are added, a letter from Mrs. Cooper to R. Hibbert, jun. esq., and an appendix containing an exposure of the falsehoods and calumnies of that gentleman's affidavit-men* (London: J. Hatchard & son, 1824)

Cumberland, Richard, *The West Indian: A comedy* (Perth: R. Morison Junior, 1790)

Dibdin, Thomas Frognall, *Bibliographical Decameron; Or ten days pleasant discourse upon illuminated manuscripts, and subjects connected with early engravings, typography, and bibliography*, 3 vols (London: W. Bulmer & Co., 1817)

Dibdin, Thomas Frognall, *Reminiscences of a literary life; With anecdotes of books, and of book collectors*, 2 vols (London: John Major, 1836)

Edwards, Bryan, *The history, civil and commercial, of the British colonies in the West Indies* (London: B. Crosby, 1793–1801)

SELECT BIBLIOGRAPHY

Equiano, Olaudah, *The interesting narrative of the life of Olaudah Equiano or Gustavus Vasssa, the African* (London: printed by the author, 1794)

Francklyn, Gilbert, *Observations occasioned by the attempts made in England to effect the abolition of the slave trade* (London: Logographic Press, 1789)

Hakewill, James, *A picturesque tour of the island of Jamaica from drawings made in the years 1820 and 1821* (London: Hurst & Robinson, 1825)

Harvey, Thomas and Joseph Sturge, *The West Indies in 1837* (London: Hamilton, Adams & Co., 1837)

Hibbert, George, *Substance of three speeches in Parliament on the Bill for the Abolition of the Slave Trade and the petition respecting the state of the West India trade in February and March 1807* (London: Lane, Darling & Co., 1807)

Hibbert, George, 'Remarks on the Slave Registry Bill and upon a special report of the African Institution, recommending that measure', *The Pamphleteer*, 7:14 (March 1816), pp. 545–74

Hibbert, Robert, *Facts verified on oath in contradiction of the report of Rev. Thomas Cooper, concerning the general condition of slaves in Jamaica; and more especially relative to the management and treatment of the slave upon Georgia estate, in the parish of Hanover, in that island* (London: John Murray, 1824)

Hibbert, Robert, *Hints to the young Jamaica Sugar planter* (London: T. & G. Underwood, 1825)

Innes, William, *The slave trade indispensible: In answer to the speech of William Wilberforce, Esq. on the 13th May, 1789. By a Merchant.* (London: Debrett, 1789)

Long, Edward, *The history of Jamaica: Or, general survey of the ancient and modern state of that island, with reflections on its situation, settlements, inhabitants, climate, products, commerce, laws, and government in three volumes. Illustrated with copper plates* (London: T. Lowndes, 1774)

Macaulay, Zachary, *Negro slavery; Or a view of some of the more prominent features of that state of society, as it exists in the United States of America and in the colonies of the West Indies, especially in Jamaica* (London: Richard Taylor, 1823)

Markland, J. H., *A sketch of the life and character of George Hibbert Esq., F.R.S., S.A., and L.S.* (London, 1837)

Murch, Jerom, *Memoir of Robert Hibbert, founder of the Hibbert Trust: With a sketch of its history* (Bath: William Lewis, 1874)

Oliver, Vere Langford, *Caribbeana: Being miscellaneous papers relating to the history, genealogy, topography, and antiquities of the British West Indies*, 4 vols (London: Mitchell Hughes and Clarke, 1919)

Philipe, T., *Catalogue of a superb assemblage of prints, formed by a gentleman of distinguished taste and judgment* (London: T. Philipe, 1809)

Smith, Adam, *An inquiry into the nature and causes of the wealth of nations* (New York: Modern Library, 1937)

Timbs, John, *Clubs and club life in London with anecdotes of the clubs, coffee-houses and taverns of the metropolis in the seventeenth, eighteenth and nineteenth centuries*, 2 vols (London: Richard Bentley, 1866)

SELECT BIBLIOGRAPHY

Venables, Thomas, *The reviewer reviewed; Or some cursory observation upon an article in the Christian Observer for January 1816, respecting the Slave Registry Bill in a letter to a Member of Parliament* (London: J. M. Richardson, 1816)

Wakefield, Gilbert, *Memoirs of the life of Gilbert Wakefield, B.A. late Fellow of Jesus College, Cambridge* (London: J. Deighton,1792)

Watkins, John, Frederic Shoberl and William Upcott, *A biographical dictionary of the living authors of Great Britain and Ireland* (London: Henry Colburn, 1816)

Wilberforce, Robert and Samuel Wilberforce, *The life of William Wilberforce*, 5 vols (London: John Murray, 1838)

Wilberforce, William, *A practical view of the prevailing religious system of professed Christians in the higher and middle classes of this country, contrasted with real Christianity* (New York: Leavitt, Lord & Co.,1835)

Wilmot-Horton, Robert, *The West India question practically considered* (London: John Murray, 1826)

Winn, T. S., *A speedy end to slavery in our West India colonies by safe, effectual and equitable means for the benefit of all parties concerned* (London: J. Hatchard & Son, 1825)

Younger Fletcher, William, *English book collectors* (London: Kegan Paul, Trench, Trübner & Co., 1902)

Secondary sources

Altink, Henrice, 'Forbidden fruit: Pro-slavery attitudes towards enslaved women's sexuality and interracial sex', *Journal of Caribbean History*, 39:2 (2005), pp. 201–35

Andrew, D. T., 'Alderman and the big bourgeoisie of London reconsidered', *Social History*, 6:3 (1981), pp. 359–64

Andrew, D. T., *Philanthropy and police: London charity in the eighteenth century* (Oxford: Princeton University Press, 1989)

Appadurai, Arjun (ed.), *The social life of things: Commodities in cultural perspective* (Cambridge: University of Cambridge Press, 1986)

Bannet, Eve Tavor, *Empire of letters: Letter manuals and transatlantic correspondence, 1680–1820* (Cambridge: Cambridge University Press, 2006)

Barczewski, Stephanie, *Country houses and the British empire, 1700–1930* (Manchester: Manchester University Press, 2014)

Barker Benfield, G. J., *The culture of sensibility: Sex and society in eighteenth-century Britain* (Chicago: University of Chicago Press, 1992)

Barrett, Ian John, 'Cultures of pro-slavery: The political defence of the slave trade in Britain c.1787–1807' (PhD thesis, King's College London, 2009)

Barringer, Tim and Tom Flynn (eds), *Colonialism and the object: Empire, material culture and the museum* (London: Routledge, 1997)

Beck Ryden, David, *West Indian slavery and British abolition, 1783–1807* (Cambridge: Cambridge University Press, 2009)

SELECT BIBLIOGRAPHY

Beckert, Sven, *Empire of cotton: A new history of global capitalism* (London: Allen Lane, 2014)

Beckles, Hilary, *Britain's black debt: Reparations for Caribbean slavery and native genocide* (Kingston: University of the West Indies Press, 2013)

Bermingham, Ann and John Brewer (eds), *The consumption of culture, 1600–1800: Image, object, text* (London: Routledge, 1995)

Bindman, David, *Ape to Apollo: Aesthetics and race in the eighteenth century* (London: Reaktion, 2002)

Bourdieu, Pierre, *Distinction: A social critique of the judgement of taste* (London: Routledge, 2010)

Braithwaite, Edward, *The development of Creole society in Jamaica, 1770–1820* (Oxford: Clarendon Press, 1972)

Brewer, John and Susan Staves (eds), *Early modern conceptions of property* (London: Routledge, 1996), pp. 497–529

Brown, Christopher Leslie, *Moral capital: Foundations of British abolitionism* (Chapel Hill: University of North Carolina Press, 2006)

Brown, Vincent, *The reaper's garden: Death and power in the world of Atlantic slavery* (London: Harvard University Press, 2008)

Burnard, Trevor, *Mastery, tyranny and desire: Thomas Thistlewood and his slaves in the Anglo-Jamaican World* (Chapel Hill: University of North Carolina Press, 2004)

Burnard, Trevor and Kenneth O. Morgan, 'The dynamics of the slave markets and slave purchasing patterns in Jamaica, 1655–1788', *William and Mary Quarterly*, 58:1 (2001), pp. 205–28

Butler, Kathleen, *The economics of emancipation in Jamaica and Barbados, 1823–1843* (Chapel Hill: University of North Carolina Press, 1995)

Cain, P. J. and A. G. Hopkins, 'Gentlemanly capitalism and the British expansion overseas I: The old colonial system, 1688–1850', *Economic History Review*, 39:4 (1986), pp. 201–25

Cardinal, Roger and John Elsner (eds), *The cultures of collecting* (London: Reaktion, 1994)

Checkland, S. G., *The Gladstones: A family biography 1764–1851* (Cambridge: Cambridge University Press, 1971)

Christopher, Emma, *Slave ship sailors and their captive cargoes, 1730–1807* (Cambridge: Cambridge University Press, 2006)

Chukwudi Eze, Emmanuel, *Race and the Enlightenment* (Oxford: Blackwell Publishing, 1997)

Cleall, Esme, Laura Ishiguro and Emily Manktelow (eds), 'Imperial relations: Histories of family in the British Empire', *Journal of Colonialism and Colonial History*, Special Issue, 14:1 (Spring 2013)

Cohen, Michèle and Tim Hitchcock (eds), *English masculinities 1660–1800* (London: Longman, 1999)

Colley, Linda, *Britons: Forging the Nation 1707–1837* (London: Pimlico, 1994)

Cooper, Frederick and Ann Laura Stoler (eds), *Tensions of empire: Colonial cultures in a bourgeois world* (Berkley: University of California Press, 1997)

SELECT BIBLIOGRAPHY

Curtin, Marguerite, 'Mr. Hibbert of Stanton Street', unpublished manuscript, Jamaica National Heritage Trust (1983)

Cutler, Janet C., 'The London Institution, 1805–1933' (PhD thesis, University of Leicester, 1976)

Davidoff, Leonore, *Thicker than water: Siblings and their relations, 1780–1920* (Oxford: Oxford University Press, 2012)

Davidoff, Leonore and Catherine Hall, *Family fortunes: Men and women of the English middle class 1780–1850* (London: Routledge, 2002)

Delbourgo, James, *Collecting the world: The life and curiosity of Hans Sloane* (London: Allen Lane, 2017)

Devine, T. M. (ed.), *Recovering Scotland's slavery past: The Caribbean connection* (Edinburgh: Edinburgh University Press, 2016)

Ditz, Toby, 'Shipwrecked; or, masculinity imperilled: Mercantile representations of failure and the gendered self in eighteenth century Philadelphia', *Journal of American History*, 81:1 (1994), pp. 51–80

Donington, Katie, Ryan Hanley and Jessica Moody (eds), *Britain's history and memory of slavery: Local nuances of a 'national sin'* (Liverpool: Liverpool University Press, 2016)

Draper, Nicholas, 'The City of London and slavery: Evidence from the first dock companies, 1795–1800', *Economic History Review*, 61:2 (2008), pp. 432–66

Draper, Nicholas, *The price of emancipation: Slave-ownership, compensation and British society at the end of slavery* (Cambridge: Cambridge University Press, 2009)

Drayton, Richard, *Nature's government: Science, imperial Britain and the 'improvement' of the world* (London: Yale University Press, 2000)

Drescher, Seymour, *Econocide: British slavery in the era of abolition* (Pittsburgh: University of Pittsburgh Press, 1977)

Dresser, Madge, *Slavery obscured: The social history of slavery in an English provincial port c.1698–c.1833* (Oxford: Radcliffe Press, 2007)

Dresser, Madge and Andrew Hann (eds), *Slavery and the British country house* (London: English Heritage, 2013)

Dumas, Paula, *Proslavery Britain: Fighting for slavery in an era of abolition* (London: Palgrave Macmillan, 2016)

Dwyer Amussen, Susan, *Caribbean exchanges: Slavery and the transformation of English society, 1640–1700* (Chapel Hill: University of North Carolina Press, 2007)

Dyer, Richard, *White: Essays on race and culture* (London: Routledge, 1997)

Earle, Rebecca (ed.), *Epistolary selves: Letters and letter writers, 1600–1945* (Aldershot: Ashgate, 1999)

Ellis, Markman, *The coffee house: A cultural history* (London: Orion, 2005)

Farrell, Stephen, Melanie Unwin and James Walvin (eds), *The British slave trade: Abolition, Parliament and the people* (Edinburgh: Edinburgh University Press, 2007)

Finn, Margot, 'Men's things: Masculine possession in the consumer revolution', *Social History*, 25:2 (2000), pp. 133–55

SELECT BIBLIOGRAPHY

Finn, Margot, *The character of credit: Personal debt in English culture, 1740–1914* (Cambridge: Cambridge University Press, 2003)

Foucault, Michel, *The order of things: An archaeology of the human sciences* (London: Routledge, 1989)

Franklin, Alexander, 'Enterprise and advantage: The West India interest in Britain 1774–1849' (PhD thesis, University of Pennsylvania, 1992)

Freyer, Peter, *Staying power: The history of black people in Britain* (London: Pluto Press, 1984)

Furness, A. E., 'George Hibbert and the defense of slavery in the West Indies', *Jamaican Historical Review*, 5:1 (1965), pp. 56–71

Gauci, Perry, *Emporium of the world: The merchants of London, 1660–1800* (London: Continuum, 2007)

Gauci, Perry, *William Beckford: First Prime Minister of the London empire* (New Haven, CT: Yale University Press, 2013)

Gerzina, Gretchen, *Black England: Life before emancipation* (London: John Murray, 1995)

Gikandi, Simon, *Slavery and the culture of taste* (Oxford: Princeton University Press, 2011)

Gilroy, Paul, *After empire: Melancholia or convivial culture?* (London: Routledge, 2004)

Glymph, Thavolia, *Out of the house of bondage: The transformation of the plantation household* (New York: Cambridge University Press, 2012)

Goodman, Danielle, Sophia Seebom and Chloë Stewart, 'Headquarters House, Kingston, Jamaica, 1755–1990' (unpublished manuscript, Jamaica National Heritage Trust, 1989)

Green, Joseph, J., 'Jenny Harry, later Thresher (c. 1756–1784)', *Friends Quarterly Examiner* (1913), pp. 559–82

Green, Joseph J., 'Jenny Harry, later Thresher (c. 1756–1784) (concluded)', *Friends Quarterly Examiner* (1914), pp. 43–64

Green, William A., *British slave emancipation: The sugar colonies and the Great Experiment, 1830–1865* (Oxford: Oxford University Press, 1991)

Haakonssen, Knud (ed.), *Enlightenment and religion: Rational dissent in eighteenth-century Britain* (Cambridge: Cambridge University Press, 2006)

Habermas, Jürgen, *The structural transformation of the public sphere: An inquiry into a category of bourgeois society* (Cambridge: Polity, 1989)

Haggerty, Sherylynne, *'Merely for money': Business culture in the British Atlantic, 1750–1815* (Liverpool: Liverpool University Press, 2012)

Hall, Catherine, *Civilising subjects: Metropole and colony in the English imagination 1830–1867* (Cambridge: Polity, 2002)

Hall, Catherine, 'Gendering property, racing capital', *History Workshop Journal*, 78:1 (2014), pp. 22–38

Hall, Catherine, Nicholas Draper, Keith McClelland, Katie Donington and Rachel Lang, *Legacies of British slave-ownership: Colonial slavery and the formation of Victorian Britain* (Cambridge: Cambridge University Press, 2014)

SELECT BIBLIOGRAPHY

Hall, Catherine and Sonya O. Rose (eds), *At home with the empire: Metropolitan culture and the imperial world* (Cambridge: Cambridge University Press, 2006)

Hall, Douglas, *A brief history of the West India Committee* (London: Ginn, 1971)

Hall, Douglas, 'Absentee proprietorship in the British West Indies, to about 1850', *Journal of Caribbean History*, 35:1 (2001), pp. 97–121

Hamilton, Douglas, *Scotland, the Caribbean and the Atlantic World, 1750–1820* (Manchester: Manchester University Press, 2005)

Hamilton, Douglas, Kate Hodgson and Joel Quirke (eds), *Slavery, memory and identity: National representations and global legacies* (London: Pickering & Chatto, 2012)

Hancock, David, *Citizens of the world: London merchants and the integration of the British Atlantic community, 1735–1785* (Cambridge: Cambridge University Press, 1995)

Higman, Barry, 'The West India "interest" in Parliament, 1807–1833', *Historical Studies*, 13:49 (1967), pp. 1–19

Higman, Barry, *Plantation Jamaica, 1750–1850: Capital control in a colonial society* (Kingston: University of the West Indies Press, 2005)

Hitchcock, Tim and Michèle Cohen, *English masculinities, 1660–1800* (London: Longman, 1999)

Holt, Thomas C., *The problem of freedom: Race, labour and politics in Jamaica and Britain, 1832–1938* (Baltimore, MD: Johns Hopkins University Press, 1992)

Hoock, Holger, 'From beefsteaks to turtles: Artists' dinner culture in eighteenth century London', *Huntington Library Quarterly*, 66:1/2 (2003), pp. 27–54

Hoock, Holger, '"Struggling against vulgar prejudice": Patriotism and the collecting of British art at the turn of the nineteenth century', *Journal of British Studies*, 49:3 (2010), pp. 566–91

Hoppit, Julian, 'Compulsion, compensation and property rights in Britain, 1688–1833', *Past & Present*, 210:1 (2011), pp. 93–128

Hunt, Margaret R., *The middling sort: Commerce, gender, and the family in England, 1680–1780* (London: University of California Press, 1996)

Huzzey, Richard, *Freedom burning: Anti-slavery and empire in Victorian Britain* (Ithaca, NY: Cornell University Press, 2012)

Inikori, Joseph, *Africans and the Industrial Revolution in England* (Cambridge: Cambridge University Press, 2002)

James, C. L. R., *The Black Jacobins* (London: Penguin Books, 2001)

Jennings, Judith, *The business of abolishing the slave trade, 1783–1807* (London: Frank Cass, 1997)

Jennings, Judith, 'A trio of talented women: Abolition, gender, and political participation', *Slavery & Abolition*, 26:1 (2005), pp. 55–70

Jennings, Judith, *Gender, religion, and radicalism in the long eighteenth century: An 'ingenious Quaker' and her connections* (Aldershot: Ashgate, 2006)

Jones, Cecily, *Engendering whiteness: White women and colonialism in Barbados and North Carolina* (Manchester: Manchester University Press, 2007)

SELECT BIBLIOGRAPHY

Jones, Geoffrey and Mary B. Rose, 'Family capitalism', *Business History*, 35:4 (1993), pp. 1–16

Kirby, M. W. and M. B. Rose, *Business enterprise in modern Britain from the eighteenth to the twentieth century* (London: Routledge, 1994)

Knapman, David, *Conversation Sharp: The biography of a London gentleman. Richard Sharp (1759–1835) in letters, prose and verse* (Dorchester: The Dorset Press, 2003)

Kriz, Kay Dian, *Slavery, sugar and refinement: Picturing the British West Indies, 1700–1840* (London: Yale University Press, 2008)

Lambert, David, *White Creole culture, politics and identity during the age of abolition* (Cambridge: Cambridge University Press, 2005)

Lambert, David and Alan Lester (eds), *Colonial lives across the British empire: Imperial careering in the long nineteenth century* (Cambridge: Cambridge University Press, 2006)

Lewis, Matthew, *Journal of a West India proprietor kept during a residence in the island of Jamaica* (Oxford: Oxford Paperbacks, 2008)

Linebaugh, Peter, *The London hanged: Crime and civil society in the eighteenth century* (London: Penguin Books, 1991)

Linebaugh, Peter and Marcus Rediker, *The many-headed Hydra: Sailors, slaves, commoners, and the hidden history of the revolutionary Atlantic* (London: Verso, 2000)

Livesay, Daniel, *Children of uncertain fortune: Mixed-race Jamaicans in Britain and the Atlantic family, 1733–1833* (Chapel Hill: University of North Carolina Press, 2018)

Matthews, Gelien, *Caribbean slave revolts and the British abolitionist movement* (Baton Rouge: Louisiana State University Press, 2012)

Midgley, Clare, *Women against slavery: The British campaigns, 1780–1870* (London: Routledge, 1992)

Mintz, Sidney, *Sweetness and power: The place of sugar in modern history* (London: Penguin Books, 1985)

Molineux, Catherine, *Faces of perfect ebony: Encountering Atlantic slavery in imperial Britain* (London: Harvard University Press, 2012)

Monteith, Kathleen E. A. and Glen Richards (eds), *Jamaica in slavery and freedom: History, heritage and culture* (Kingston: University of the West Indies Press, 2001)

Morgan, Kenneth O., *Slavery, Atlantic trade and the British economy, 1600–1800* (Cambridge: Cambridge University Press, 2000)

Morgan, Kenneth O., 'Remittance procedures in the eighteenth-century British slave trade', *Business History Review*, 79:4 (2005), pp. 715–49

Morrison, Toni, *Playing in the dark: Whiteness and the literary imagination* (London: Harvard University Press, 1992)

Mullen, Stephen, 'The Glasgow West India interest: Integration, collaboration and exploitation in the British Atlantic world, 1776–1846' (PhD thesis, University of Glasgow, 2015)

Oldfield, John, *Popular politics and British anti-slavery: The mobilisation of public opinion against the slave trade, 1787–1807* (Manchester: Manchester University Press, 1995)

SELECT BIBLIOGRAPHY

Oldfield, John, *'Chords of freedom': Commemoration, ritual and British transatlantic slavery* (Manchester: Manchester University Press, 2007)

O'Shaughnessy, Andrew J., 'The formation of a commercial lobby: The West India interest, British colonial policy and the American Revolution', *Historical Journal*, 40:1 (1997), pp. 71–95

Page, Anthony, '"A species of slavery": Richard Price's rational dissent and antislavery', *Slavery & Abolition*, 32:1 (2011), pp. 53–73

Page, Anthony, 'Rational dissent, Enlightenment and abolition of the British slave trade', *Historical Journal*, 54:3 (2011), pp. 741–72

Palmer, Jennifer L., *Intimate bonds: Family and slavery in the French Atlantic* (Philadelphia: University of Pennsylvania Press, 2016)

Pares, Richard, *A West India fortune* (London: Longman, 1950)

Pares, Richard, *Merchants and planters* (Cambridge: Cambridge University Press, 1960)

Parker, Matthew, *The sugar barons: Family, corruption, empire and war* (London: Hutchinson, 2011)

Partington, Anthony, 'A memorial to the Hibberts', *Mariner's Mirror*, 93:4 (2009), pp. 441–58

Patterson, Orlando, *The sociology of slavery: An analysis of the origins, development and structure of negro slave society in Jamaica* (London: Cox and Wyman, 1967)

Pearce, Susan A., *On collecting: An investigation into collecting in the European tradition* (London: Routledge, 1999)

Pearsall, Sarah, *Atlantic families: Lives and letters in the later eighteenth century* (Oxford: Oxford University Press, 2010)

Penson, Lillian, 'The London West India interest in the eighteenth century', *English Historical Review*, 36:143 (1921), pp. 373–92

Penson, Lillian, *The colonial agents of the British West Indies: A study in colonial administration, mainly in the eighteenth century* (London: University of London Press, 1924)

Perry, Adele, *Colonial relations: The Douglas-Connolly family and the nineteenth-century imperial world* (Cambridge: Cambridge University Press, 2015)

Petley, Christer, *Slaveholders in Jamaica: Colonial society and culture during the era of abolition* (London: Pickering & Chatto, 2009)

Petley, Christer, '"Devoted Islands" and "That Madman Wilberforce": British proslavery patriotism during the age of abolition', *Journal of Imperial and Commonwealth History*, 38:3 (2011), pp. 393–415

Petley, Christer, and Stephen Lenik (eds), 'Material cultures of slavery and abolition in the British Caribbean', *Slavery & Abolition*, Special Issue, 35:3 (2014)

Pickering, Paul A. and Alex Tyrell (eds), *Contested sites: Commemoration, memorial and popular politics in nineteenth-century Britain* (Farnham: Ashgate, 2004)

Pointon, Marcia (ed.), *Art apart: Art institutions and ideology across Britain and North America* (Manchester: Manchester University Press, 1994)

SELECT BIBLIOGRAPHY

Porter, Roy, *Enlightenment: Britain and the creation of the modern world* (London: Penguin Books, 2000)

Powers, Anne (ed.), *A parcel of ribbons: The letters of an eighteenth-century family in London and Jamaica* (Anne Powers, 2012)

Rabuzzi, D. A., 'Eighteenth-century commercial mentalities as reflected and projected in business handbooks', *Eighteenth-Century Studies*, 29:2 (1995/96), pp. 169–89

Radburn, Nicholas, 'Guinea factors, slave sales, and the profits of the transatlantic slave trade in late eighteenth-century Jamaica: The case of John Tailyour', *William and Mary Quarterly*, 72:2 (2015), pp. 243–86

Ragatz, Lowell J., *The decline of the planter class in the British Caribbean, 1763–1833* (New York: Octagon, 1977)

Raven, James A., *Judging new wealth: Popular publishing and responses to commerce in England, 1750–1800* (Oxford: Clarendon Press, 1992)

Rawley, James A., *London: Metropolis of the slave trade* (London: University of Missouri Press, 2003)

Rediker, Marcus, *The slave ship: A human history* (London: John Murray, 2008)

Rice, Alan, *Creating memorials, building identities: The politics of memory in the Black Atlantic* (Liverpool: Liverpool University Press, 2012)

Richardson, David, Anthony Tibbles and Suzanne Schwartz (eds), *Liverpool and transatlantic slavery* (Liverpool: Liverpool University Press, 2007)

Rogers, Nicholas, 'Money, land and lineage: The big bourgeoisie of Hanoverian London', *Social History*, 4:3 (1979), pp. 437–54

Roper, Michael and John Tosh (eds), *Manful assertions: Masculinities in Britain since 1800* (London: Routledge, 1991)

Rothschild, Emma, *Inner lives of empire: An eighteenth-century history* (Princeton, NJ: Princeton University Press, 2011)

Rupprecht, Anita, 'Excessive memories: Slavery, insurance and resistance', *History Workshop Journal*, 64:1 (2007), pp. 6–28

Said, Edward, *Culture and imperialism* (London: Vintage, 1994)

Seed, John, 'Gentlemen dissenters: The social and political meaning of rational dissent in the 1770s and 1780s', *Historical Journal*, 28:3 (1985) pp. 229–325

Seed, John and Janet Wolff (eds), *The culture of capital: Art, power and the nineteenth-century middle class* (Manchester: Manchester University Press, 1990)

Shepherd, Verene (ed.), *Working slavery, pricing freedom: Perspectives from the Caribbean, Africa and the African diaspora* (Kingston: Ian Randle, 2002)

Sheridan, Richard, 'The commercial and financial organisation of the British slave trade, 1750–1807', *Economic History Review*, 11:2 (1958), pp. 249–63

Sheridan, Richard B., 'Simon Taylor, sugar tycoon of Jamaica', *Agricultural History*, 45:4 (1971), pp. 285–96

Sherwood, Marika, *After abolition: Britain and the slave trade since 1807* (London: I. B. Tauris, 2007)

Sinha, Mrinalini, *Colonial masculinity: The manly Englishman and the effeminate Bengali* (Manchester: Manchester University Press, 1995)

SELECT BIBLIOGRAPHY

Smith, Laurajane, Geoffrey Cubitt, Ross Wilson and Kalliopi Fouseki (eds), *Representing enslavement and abolition in museums: Ambiguous engagements* (Abingdon: Routledge, 2011)

Smith, Simon D., *Slavery, family, and gentry capitalism in the British Atlantic* (Cambridge: Cambridge University Press, 2006)

Stern, Walter M., 'The first London dock boom and the growth of the West India Docks', *Economica*, 19:73 (1952), pp. 59–77

Stoler, Ann Laura, *Along the archival grain: Epistemic anxieties and colonial common sense* (Oxford: Princeton University Press, 2009)

Stott, Anne, *Wilberforce: Family and friends* (Oxford: Oxford University Press, 2012)

Stuart, Andrea, *Sugar in the blood: A family's story of slavery and empire* (London: Portobello Books, 2012)

Swaminathan, Srividhya, 'Developing the proslavery position after the Somerset decision,' *Slavery & Abolition*, 24:3 (2003), pp. 40–60

Swaminathan, Srividhya, *Debating the slave trade: Rhetoric of British national identity, 1759–1815* (Farnham: Ashgate, 2009)

Tadmor, Naomi, 'The concept of the household-family in eighteenth-century England', *Past & Present*, 151 (1996), pp. 111–40

Taylor, Clare, 'The journal of an absentee proprietor, Nathaniel Phillips of Slebech', *Journal of Caribbean History*, 18 (1984), pp. 67–82

Thorne, R. G., *The History of Parliament: The House of Commons, 1790–1820* (London: Secker and Warburg, 1986)

Tosh, John, 'Gentlemanly politeness and manly simplicity in Victorian England', *Transactions of the Royal Historical Society*, 12:6 (2002), pp. 455–72

Tosh, John, *Manliness and masculinities in nineteenth-century England: Essays on gender, family and empire* (London: Longman, 2004)

Tosh, John, *A man's place: Masculinity and the middle-class home in Victorian England* (London: Yale University Press, 2007)

Trouillot, Michel-Rolph, *Silencing the past: Power and the production of history* (Boston: Beacon Press, 1995)

Turley, David, *The culture of English antislavery, 1780–1860* (London: Routledge, 1991)

Turner, Mary, *Slaves and missionaries: The disintegration of Jamaican slave society, 1784–1834* (Kingston: University of the West Indies Press, 1982)

Vickery, Amanda, *Behind closed doors: At home with the Georgians* (London: Yale University Press, 2010)

Wadsworth, Alfred P. and Julia De Lacy Mann, *The cotton trade and industrial Lancashire, 1600–1780* (Manchester: Manchester University Press, 1965)

Wahrman, Dror, *Imagining the middle class: The representation of class in Britain, c.1780–1840* (Cambridge: Cambridge University Press, 1995)

Walker, Timothy, *Twixt the Commons: The development of a south London suburb* (Timothy Walker, 2010)

Walvin, James, *The trader, the owner, the slave: Parallel lives in the age of slavery* (London: Vintage, 2008)

SELECT BIBLIOGRAPHY

Wemyss, Georgie, *The invisible empire: White discourse, tolerance and belonging* (Farnham: Ashgate, 2009)

Wheeler, Roxann, *The complexion of race: Categories of difference in eighteenth-century British culture* (Philadelphia: University of Pennsylvania Press, 2000)

White, Jerry, *London in the nineteenth century: A human awful wonder of God* (London: Vintage, 2008)

Whitehead, Maurice, *The academies of the Reverend Bartholomew Booth in Georgian England and revolutionary America: Enlightening the curriculum*, Mellen Studies in Education (Lewiston, NY: Edwin Mellen Press, 1996)

Williams, Eric, *Capitalism and slavery* (London: Andre Deutsch, 1964)

Wilson, Kathleen, *The island race: Englishness, empire and identity in the eighteenth century* (London: Routledge, 2003)

Wilson, Kathleen (ed.), *A new imperial history: Culture, identity, and modernity in Britain and the Empire, 1660–1840* (Cambridge: Cambridge University Press, 2004)

Wood, Betty and Martin Lynn (eds), *Trade, travel and power in the Atlantic, 1765–1884*, Camden Miscellany 35 (Cambridge: Cambridge University Press, 2002)

Wood, Marcus, *Blind memory: Visual representations of slavery in England and America, 1780–1865* (Manchester: Manchester University Press, 2000)

Wright, Phillip (ed.), *Lady Nugent's Journal* (Kingston: University of the West Indies Press, 2002)

Websites

www.antislavery.ac.uk/aboutremembering1807
www.archive.org
www.british-history.ac.uk/survey-london/vols43-4/pp248-268
www.british-history.ac.uk/vch/lancs/vol4/pp174-187
www.bromfield.us/archives/Tharp_Papers_3.html
www.colonialcountryside.wordpress.com
https://convictrecords.com.au
www.georgehibbert.com
www.getty.edu/research/tools/provenance/search.html
www.globalcottonconnections.wordpress.com
www.hansard-archive.parliament.uk
www.hibbertfamily.com/genealogy/ancestors-corner/solomon-augustus-hibbert/introduction
www.historicengland.org.uk/listing/the-list
www.historicengland.org.uk/research/inclusive-heritage/the-slave-trade-and-abolition/sites-of-memory
www.historyofparliamentonline.org
www.jamaicanfamilysearch.com
www.leighday.co.uk/News/2014/March-2014/CARICOM-nations-unanimously-approve-10-point-plan

SELECT BIBLIOGRAPHY

www.measuringworth.com/ppoweruk
www.nationaltrust.org.uk
www.nationaltrustcollections.org.uk
www.nottingham.ac.uk/isos/research/rural-legacies.aspx
www.oxforddnb.com
www.qmulreligionandliterature.co.uk/research/the-dissenting-academies-project/dissenting-academies-online
www.revealinghistories.org.uk/home.html
www.slavevoyages.org
www.ucl.ac.uk/lbs
www.westindiacommittee.org/about-us/wic-history

INDEX

abolition
  free villages 287
  gradual 112, 139
  iconography 55
  ideas about Africa 12
  imperial reform 107–8
  interactions with proslavers 14, 32–3, 44, 185, 196, 200–4, 272, 274
  memorialisation 43–4, 208
  popular mobilisation 111
  pro-natalist policy 117
  representations of slave owners 12, 14, 120, 134–5, 142, 185, 207–8, 255
  targeting of the Hibberts 18, 134
ackee 240
absentees 13, 69, 109, 200, 208, 244, 253, 256, 261
Admiralty 112–14, 200
Africa
  children 196
  culture, denigration of 221, 237
  plants 240
  proslavery, representations of 116–18, 125, 222
African Institution 136
Agent for Jamaica 18, 83, 87, 91, 114, 121, 129, 133–4, 141, 148, 161, 191
  see also George Hibbert
Agualta Vale plantation 8, 17, 64–6, 70, 72, 90, 163, 167, 170, 264–5
Albion plantation 66–7, 92, 147–8
Allardyce & Watt 55
Allardyce, Alexander 55, 61, 114
almshouses 255, 267, 269–70
  see also philanthropy

amelioration 18, 65, 69, 117, 134, 139, 141, 143–4
  proslavery co-opting of 68, 125, 137–8, 140
  see also Canning's Resolutions
America 10, 28, 38, 42, 45n.7, 107, 122, 138
  American Civil War 43
  American Revolution 108, 136, 138, 169, 200
  War of 1812 198
Angerstein, John Julius 223–4, 229, 271
anti-abolition 13, 108–9, 112–13, 118, 120
antislavery
  concepts of Brtitishness 11–13
  non-conformity and 33
  radicalism and 276
  visual culture 135
apprenticeship 68, 150, 286–7
Arcedekne, Chaloner 61
archives
  absence 71
  family 10
  power 16–17, 181
art 5, 13, 44, 83–4, 166, 204–5, 207, 217–32 *passim*, 244, 258–9, 264, 272, 285
  see also collecting
attorney 35, 41, 67–71 *passim*, 85, 87, 90, 145, 171–3 *passim*
auction 155n.82, 219, 222, 224–8, 232, 234, 263, 282
Aviva 82

Bance Island 83
Bank of England Directors 82, 186, 187
banking 87, 271, 284
Banks, Sir Joseph 239

INDEX

Baptist War (1831–32) 67, 150
Barbados 41, 51, 139, 142
Barber Institute of Fine Art,
 University of Birmingham 228
Baring, Sir Francis 83, 224, 229, 271
Bathurst, 3rd Earl Bathurst, Henry
 139, 148, 161
Bayley, Samuel 36–7
Beckert, Sven 27, 43
bibliophile 41, 198, 204, 232–7 *passim*
bicentenary of the abolition of the
 slave trade (2007) 11, 44, 208,
 244, 254, 267, 276, 281n.106
Bickell, Reverend Richard 66–7, 147
Bilton Grange, Warwickshire
 256, 265–6
Birmingham 39, 167
Birtles Hall, Cheshire 176–7, 256–8,
 261, 282
Biscoe, Vincent 85–6
Blackfriars Rotunda 275
Blackwood, William 41
Blathwayt family 259
Bligh, Captain William 239–40
Boddington, Samuel 5, 37, 128, 202,
 223, 271
Bogle, Paul 71, 288
Booth, Reverend Bartholomew 39
Boswell, James 167
botany 238–43
Braywick Lodge, Maidenhead 195,
 256, 266–8
breadfruit 239–40
Brexit 12, 289
British Museum 218–19, 226, 232,
 235, 273
 see also Sir Hans Sloane
British national identity 11–13, 108,
 124, 254, 288–90
Brookes slave ship 55–6, 111
Brown, Gordon 11
Bussa's Rebellion (1816) 139
Buxton, Thomas Fowell 139–41
 see also antislavery

Cambridge University 143, 196, 275
 see also education

Camden, Calvert & King 187
Cameron, David 11, 72
Canada Company 82, 283
Canary Wharf 97, 246
Canning's Resolutions 139–41
Caribbean Community and Common
 Market (CARICOM) 12, 72
 see also reparations
Carlile, Richard 275
Catholic emancipation 202
Catholic Revival 265
Chalfont House 5, 88, 256–62
 passim, 270
charity 13, 254–5, 263, 267, 270,
 274, 277
 see also philanthropy
Christianity 146
 justifications for slavery 124, 228
 marriage 184, 190
 promotion to enslaved 134, 138, 269
 see also individual denominations;
 religion
Christie's 155n.82, 226–7, 263
City of London 78–9, 95–6, 102n.91,
 107, 122, 184, 187–8, 218, 224,
 264, 271, 274
civic power 2, 32, 34–5, 61, 255,
 257, 263
 see also High Sheriff
civilising 11, 66, 79, 84, 98, 126
 civilising mission 108, 122, 134,
 138, 141–2, 196
Clapham 14, 183–4, 196, 199–207
 passim, 223, 238–9, 242, 262, 270
 Clapham Saints 115, 185, 203, 208
 Holy Trinity Church, Clapham 14,
 193, 202–4
Clarence, Duke of (William IV)
 112–13, 198
Clarke, Sir Simon Haughton 223,
 226
classical civilisation 39, 51, 59, 124,
 204, 206, 228, 237–8
cloth trade 1, 27–8, 30–1, 34, 44, 186
 see also cotton
Clothworkers' Company 122
Cobbett, William 114–16, 125, 137

[310]

INDEX

Codrington plantation 41
Coles estate 43, 264
collecting 13, 40, 219, 244
   art 223–32
   books 232–8
   botany 238–43
colonial agents 133
Colonial Bank of the West Indies 82, 284
Colonial Office 133
colonial rights and liberties 60, 124, 134, 136
Commercial Road Company 96
commonplace book 16, 188–9, 192, 195
Company of Merchants Trading to Africa 34, 37
compensation
   slavery 3, 6, 15, 20, 41, 57–8, 70, 89, 93–4, 116, 118–9, 123, 128, 135, 139, 148–52, 172–3, 226, 244–5, 263, 265, 275, 284–5
   West India Dock 88, 95, 261
connoisseurship 2, 13, 217, 220, 223, 244
conspicuous consumption 84, 118, 220, 229, 244
convict ship 91
Cooper, Reverend Thomas 68–9, 143–7, 160, 171
cotton 17, 27–31, 36–7, 41, 43–4
   see also cloth trade
country house ownership 5, 15, 36, 40, 176–7, 183, 253–66 *passim*, 276, 282
   see also land ownership; property
Coventry plantation 67, 70
credit 1, 4, 52, 57, 61, 79–81, 84, 89, 92–4, 115, 118, 135, 150, 224, 226
Creole
   difference 38, 161, 178–9
   women 19, 161, 178–9
Cross Street Chapel, Manchester 28, 32–3, 35–7, 42, 163, 267

   see also dissenters; Unitarianism
Cruikshank, Isaac Robert 125
Cuba 50, 54
Cumberland, Richard
   The West Indian 178, 253
Curates Act (1817) 142, 144

death 5, 7–8, 14, 58, 64, 80, 85, 162, 166, 169, 174–5, 187, 189, 199, 246, 276, 284, 290
debt 81, 84, 87–8, 135, 144, 282
   colonial debt 4, 52, 57–8, 66, 89, 92–4, 118–9
   see also mortgage
Demerara 142
Dibdin, Reverend Thomas Frognall 204, 228, 232, 234, 236, 242
Dickens, Charles 125
Diggles, Thomas 32, 37
disease 19, 51–2, 117, 162, 170, 190, 199
dissenters 27–8, 32–7, 42, 166, 193, 202
   see also Cross Street Chapel, Manchester; Unitarianism
dissenting academy 39, 196
domesticity 184–6, 188, 208, 232, 254
   see also gender; marriage
Dominica 42, 200
Dundas, 1st Viscount Melville, Henry 112
Dundee plantation 68

East and West India Dock Company 96, 283
East India Company 108, 187, 197, 247n.16, 263, 273
East Indians 88, 109, 197
education 35–40 *passim*, 144–5, 164, 173, 196, 257, 266, 275
   see also individual institutions
Ellis, Baron Seaford, Charles Rose 141–2
Ellis, William Beckford 64

[311]

INDEX

emancipation 136, 140–1, 145, 148–50, 282, 288
empire 3, 7, 11, 15–16, 20, 27, 43, 51, 78–9, 98, 108–9, 119, 124, 196, 199, 218, 221, 232, 242, 254, 271–3, 283–90 *passim*
enlightened 40, 135, 142, 184, 188, 270
enlightenment 207, 218, 221, 236, 242, 244
Equiano, Olaudah 51
Eton 196, 275
   see also education
Evangelicals 184, 203
Eyre, Governor John Edward 71, 288
   see also Morant Bay

family
   business 3–5, 37, 64, 80, 82, 177, 197, 257
   children 4–6, 16, 29, 31, 33–4, 37, 41, 69, 117, 119, 125, 145, 159–72, 175–80, 185, 190–4, 199, 202–3, 207–8, 222, 258, 261, 284
   dispute 168
   empire and 7, 21n.19
   history 7–10, 17, 31, 289
   letters 15–16, 161, 194
   networks 3–4, 15, 17, 28–9, 32, 43–4, 70, 161, 181, 186, 199, 282, 284
   see also merchant networks
   separation 162, 176, 180, 184, 260
   structure 4–5, 7, 80, 176
   transatlanticism 176–7
   see also illegitimacy; inheritance; marriage; mixed heritage; slave families
Fitzwilliam Museum 227
Fonnereau family 186, 206
Fonthill Abbey 253
France 91, 95, 124, 138, 186
free people of colour 50, 145, 164, 287
free trade 31
French Revolution 120, 124, 173, 223–4

Frend, William 143
Furh, Edward 81, 84, 94, 177

Gainsborough, Thomas 223, 259–60, 273
gender 3, 7, 15–16, 117, 160, 167, 180, 184–5, 189–90, 196, 220, 246
   femininity 188–9, 192, 204, 206, 229
   masculinity 18, 29, 59, 63, 86, 159, 185, 187–9, 196, 199, 203–4, 213n.8, 219, 232, 234, 237, 241
   patriarch 54, 63, 168, 207
   separate spheres 184, 204
Georgia plantation 68, 70, 143–7, 171
Gordon family 172–3
Grant, Dr David 172–3
Great Valley plantation 67–8, 70, 150, 171
   see also Baptist War
Greg family 41–44, 206
Greg, Robert Hyde 42–3
Greg, Samuel 42–3
   see also Quarry Bank Mill
Greg, Thomas 41–3, 81–2, 92, 95, 110, 264, 273–4

Haiti 246
   see also Saint Domingue
Hakewill, James 60, 65–6, 69
Hall, Catherine 4, 20, 31, 60, 134, 164, 184–5, 285
Hall, Stuart 289
Hancock, David 84–6, 97
Hare Hill, Cheshire 256, 262
Harry, Charity (?-1793) 7, 63, 159–71 *passim*, 174
Harry, Jane (1756–1784) 7, 9, 159, 162–9, 173, 176, 180–1, 201, 209n.11, 290
Heywood, Sir Benjamin 32, 35
Hibbert, Abigail (née Scholey) 34, 37, 41, 173, 184, 190–1, 194
   Creole difference 161, 177–80
   letter writing 15–16, 161

INDEX

Hibbert, Arthur Holland
  (1855–1935) 283
Hibbert, Eliza (née Nembhard) 177
Hibbert, Elizabeth (née Fonnereau)
  110, 183, 185–200 *passim*, 206,
  229, 231, 256, 261, 264
Hibbert, George (1757–1837) 2–3
  Agent for Jamaica 87, 91, 129,
    133–5, 141, 148, 161, 191
  Alderman of the City of London
    95, 122, 188
  art collecting 5, 223–32
  book collecting 232–38, 264
  botany 238–43
  business 37, 58, 70, 80–94
    passim, 98
  children 71, 80, 82, 189–99, 282–3
  compensation 123, 128,
    135, 148–52
  country house 43, 186, 197–8, 256,
    264, 282–3
  cultural identity 217–18, 220,
    234–5, 273
  education 39–40
  evidence to Parliament 2, 89, 91,
    109, 115, 118–20, 144–5
  family life 183–199, 207
  home 43, 204–7
  inheritance 186–7, 256, 264
  marriage 186–90
  Member of Parliament for Seaford
    91, 122–9
  memorialisation 97–8, 208
  memory 220, 242–4, 246
  pamphlets 134, 136–9
  philanthropy 14, 107, 124–5,
    203–4, 255, 267, 271–4
  proslavery strategy
    108–115 *passim*, 151
  slavery reform 120–2, 141–2, 144
  West India Docks 83, 94–7
  see also Clapham; domesticity;
    gender; Reverend Thomas
    Cooper; Society of West India
    Planters and Merchants;
    Thomas Venables

Hibbert, George junior (1796–1882) 82,
  96–7, 110, 196, 198, 256, 283
Hibbert, Henry Robarts (1806–25) 71,
  196–7, 199
Hibbert House, Kingston, Jamaica
  59–60, 71
  see also town house
Hibbert, Janet (née Gordon)
  172–3, 266
Hibbert, John (1768–1855) 266
Hibbert, John Hubert Washington
  (1804–75) 71, 264–8,
  274–5, 288
Hibbert, John junior (1748–1770) 7–8,
  37, 39, 54, 173, 197
Hibbert, John senior (1732–69) 8, 54,
  63, 69, 91, 161, 170–3, 197,
  266, 276
Hibbert, Julian (1800–34) 274–6
Hibbert, Letitia (née Nembhard) 30,
  118, 170, 174–80
Hibbert, Margaret (née Tetlow)
  31–2, 163
Hibbert, Nathaniel (1794–1865) 110,
  196–8, 256, 264, 282–3
Hibbert, Robert (1769–1849) 172–3
  business 81, 173
  country house 263
  education 143, 173
  Hibbert Trust 269
  ideas about race 221–3
  marriage 177
  plantation purchase 68–9
  see also Revered Thomas
    Cooper
Hibbert, Robert junior (1750–1835)
  2–3, 7, 37, 110, 240
  attitude to slavery 16, 58, 274
  attitude to white working
    class 116
  Baptist War 67, 150
  business 41, 53–8, 80–1, 92
  children 175–7, 180, 196
  civic positions 61, 257
  country house 5, 257–8, 262–3
  diaries 16, 54–5

[313]

INDEX

Hibbert, Robert junior (1750–1835) (*cont.*)
  drunkenness 63
  evidence to Parliament 18, 109, 115–18, 179
  homesickness 8, 172
  ideas about race 116–18
  illegitimate children 70, 163, 170–1
  inheritance 66, 168
  marriage 118, 173–5
  plantation purchase 64, 66–7
  political ambitions 123
  relationship with Thomas senior 63–4
  sex 170, 175
  transatlantic figure 8, 176–7, 207
  wealth at death 282
  West India Dock 95
Hibbert, Robert senior (1717–1784) 5, 34–5, 37, 41, 54, 187
Hibbert, Robert the elder (1684–1762) 30–6 *passim*
Hibbert, Robert the eldest (1654–1709) 30
Hibbert, Thomas (1761–1807) 54, 63–4, 66, 80, 90, 168, 171, 263–6, 276
Hibbert, Thomas junior (1744–1819) 1–2, 4, 34
  apprenticeship 37–9, 53
  attitude towards abolition 108
  attitude towards slavery 58, 126
  business 54, 57, 66, 78–81, 87–8, 95
  correspondence with Jane Harry 168
  civic positions 61, 258
  death 261–2
  homesickness 8
  illegitimate children 69, 170–1
  inheritance 66, 168, 191, 262
  marriage 87, 173–4, 258–61
  West India Dock 95
  see also Chalfont House

Hibbert, Thomas senior (1710–1780) 1–2, 31, 50, 71–2
  Agualta Vale 64–66, 72
  Attic Club debate 58–9
  business 52–59, 78, 86, 91
  Creole identity 8, 162
  death 64, 80, 162, 167, 180
  mixed-heritage children 19, 69, 159–70, 176, 180
  relationship with Charity Harry 7, 63, 159–70
  relationship with nephews 63–4
  politics 59–61
  wealth 58
  see also Charity Harry; Jane Harry
Hibbert, Samuel (1783–1867) 14, 82, 96, 110, 193, 256, 283
Hibbert, Samuel junior (1752–86) 37, 39, 178, 262, 273
Hibbert Samuel senior (1719–81) 34
Hibbert, Sophia (née Boldero) 87, 258–60
Hibbert Street
  Clapham 208
  Jamaica 71
  Luton 269
Hibbert, Sydney Holland (1855–1931) 96, 283
Hibbert, William (1759–1844) 14, 31, 36–7, 39, 43, 81, 110, 190, 196, 200, 203, 261–2, 270, 283
Hibbert, William junior (1792–1881) 82, 110, 256, 283–4
Hibbert Trust 269
  see also philanthropy; Robert Hibbert
High Sheriff 257–8, 263
  see also civic power
Hillary, Sir William 71, 93–4, 274
  see also Royal National Lifeboat Institution for the Preservation of Life from Shipwreck (RNLI)
Historic England 258, 262–4, 268, 270, 276, 281n.106
horse-breeding 64

INDEX

Horton, Thomas 78, 81, 110
housekeeper 6–7, 159–60, 162, 209n.11
House of Commons 109, 112, 114–15, 122–4, 128, 139, 141, 202, 289
House of Lords 68, 109, 112–13, 123, 263
Howard RA, Henry 206, 223, 227
Huguenot 186–7
humanitarianism 11, 13, 108, 119–20, 128
Hyde family 42

illegitimacy 6–7, 69, 117, 159, 162–3, 165–6, 170–1, 175, 181, 186, 207
see also family
'implicated subjects' 285–6
Indemnity Marine Assurance Co. 82
indentured labour 128, 287
industrial capitalism 44
industrialisation 29, 43
Industrial Revolution 36, 44, 45n.7
inheritance 5–7, 42, 66, 82, 119, 152, 162, 167–8, 198, 244, 256, 264–5, 282–4
insurance 1, 5, 42, 79–80, 82, 89, 91–2, 107, 118, 187, 224, 274, 283
see also Lloyds of London
International Slavery Museum, Liverpool 9
Ireland 42, 147, 262
Isle of Dogs 95–6
see also West India Docks

J. and N. Philips & Company 35
Jackson, Samuel 53, 173
Jamaica 1, 20, 50–2, 58, 71–2, 79, 85, 98, 235, 286–9
 Botanic Garden 240
 House of Assembly 6, 60–1, 87–9, 133–4, 136–7, 141, 162–3, 172
 amelioration 137, 141–2, 161
 mixed-heritage people and 16, 162–3

Jamaica National Heritage Trust 71
Kingston 2, 38, 50–3, 58–66 *passim*, 71, 80, 91, 113, 160, 162–73 *passim*, 181, 197
 national cuisine 240
 place of industry 261
 society 160–4
Jamaica Coffee House, London 83
Jefferson, Thomas 222, 235
John Bull 125, 145
Johnson, Samuel 9, 136, 167, 188

kinship 4, 29, 44, 193
Knowles, Mary Morris 166–7, 169, 180

Lancashire 27–8, 35, 43, 178, 256, 262, 283
 Cotton Famine (1861–65) 43–44, 48n.83
 see also American Civil War
land ownership 5, 64, 266, 286
 see also country house ownership; property
Laurens, Henry 38
Lawrence PRA, Sir Thomas 228–9, 232–3, 244–5
Leeds 29, 35, 41, 69, 187, 262
Legacies of British Slave-ownership Project 10, 285
Lightbody, Hannah 44
Lincoln, Abraham 43–4
Linnean Society 126, 241
 see also enlightenment
Liverpool 1, 9–10, 28, 34, 37–40, 43, 53, 55, 79, 110, 255, 271
Lloyd family of Birmingham 167
Lloyds of London 42, 82–3, 92, 239
 see also insurance
lobbying 3, 13–15, 79, 88, 90, 107–12 *passim*, 133, 142, 144, 151–2, 242
London 2, 13, 15, 37, 42, 78–9, 80, 83, 89, 97–9, 109, 166–7, 218–19, 255–6
London County Council 208
London Dock Company 95
 see also West India Docks

INDEX

London (cont.)
  London Institution 14, 83, 241, 250n.132, 271–3
    see also philanthropy
  London Missionary Society 142
    see also civilising mission
  'London, Sugar, Slavery' 98, 244
    see also Museum of London, Docklands
  Port of London 79, 91–2, 232
Long, Edward 56, 244
  Creole women 178–9
  History of Jamaica 221
  ideas about race 164, 221

Macaulay, Zachary 14, 136, 143, 145, 185, 196, 202, 208, 272, 283
Malthus, Thomas 126–7
Manchester Abolition Society 33
Manchester Literary and Philosophical Society 44
Manning, William 83, 120, 122, 128, 142, 271
manufacturing 17, 27–8, 30–7 *passim*, 41–4 *passim*, 78, 107, 217
Markland & Wright, 41
Markland, Cookson & Fawcett 41
Markland, James Heywood 40–1, 110–1, 185, 188–9, 204–5, 217–18, 223, 234–9 *passim*, 242–4
Markland, Robert 41
Markland, Robert junior 17, 41, 90
marriage 4, 6, 16, 140
  Christianity and 190
  commercial networks and 29, 33–7, 87, 110, 186
  companionate marriage 184, 187–90, 229
  cousin marriage 29, 36
  daughters and 41–3, 166, 168, 185, 190–3, 206
  dissenting networks and 17, 186
  dowry 225, 259
  gender and 187–90
  plantocracy and 161, 164, 172, 174–77

property and 186–7, 264, 283
social networks and 282
  see also family; spinsterhood
memorial 8, 66, 72, 80, 97, 181, 197, 242, 264, 268, 270
memory 10, 19, 72, 162, 167, 180–1, 208, 220, 246, 256, 267–70, 277, 287, 289
merchant
  apprenticeship 4, 9, 29, 37–9, 53
  class anxiety 217–18, 273
  collectors 40, 219, 224, 234
  correspondents 15, 30, 38, 57, 80, 84–9, 92, 109, 127
  counting house 34, 79, 83–5
  culture 4, 13–14, 32, 98, 217–19, 223–4, 232, 234, 242, 255, 271–3
  education 37–40
  letters 58, 85–6, 90
  marriage 29, 31, 33–7 *passim*
  networks 3–4, 28–9, 32, 43, 57, 70, 79–80, 85, 93, 98, 112, 114, 150, 186, 199, 239, 241
  partnerships 1, 5, 34, 37, 41–2, 52–4, 78, 80–94 *passim*, 173, 226, 274
    G., W., S. Hibbert & Co 82
    Geo., Rob., Wm. & Sam. Hibbert 82
    Hibbert & Co. 82, 172
    Hibbert & Jackson 53
    Hibbert & Sprigg 53
    Hibbert & Taylor 54
    Hibbert, Fuhr & Hibbert 81
    Hibbert, Hall & Fuhr 53–4
    Hibbert, Purrier & Horton 80–1, 83, 85–7
    Hibbert, Purrier & Fuhr 70, 87, 88, 112
    Hibbert, Taylor & Markland 93
    Robert & Thomas Hibbert 53
    Robert Hibbert & Co. 54
  personnel 4, 18, 29, 41, 80

INDEX

planters and 60–1
prince 218, 234, 273
Middle Passage 55, 162
Miles, Philip John 88–9
Milligan, Robert 95, 98
Mincing Lane 81, 83–4, 87, 183
missionary 68, 142–4, 146, 255, 269
  see also civilising mission; Reverend Thomas Cooper
mixed-heritage 6, 63, 159, 163, 165–6, 168, 171, 180, 201
Modern Slavery Act (2015) 11
monopoly 31, 37, 82, 96, 119
monument 65, 72, 222, 272, 277
Morant Bay 71, 288
  see also Governor Eyre
mortgage 58, 70, 93, 102n.75, 115, 150, 171–2, 257
motherhood 4, 175, 179
  breast feeding 117, 179
  childbirth 16, 190, 194, 262
  enslaved 117–18, 163, 171, 145
  miscarriage 16, 118, 145, 175
  pregnancy 175–6, 190
  see also reproductive labour
Munden House, Hertfordshire 43, 186, 197–8, 256, 264, 282–3
Murillo, Bartolemé Esteban 204, 226–9
Museum of London, Docklands 98, 232, 244
  see also 'London, Sugar, Slavery'; West India Docks

Nash, John 258
National Portrait Gallery 232
National Trust 259, 262, 276, 278n.3
National Union of the Working Classes 275
Natural History Museum 241
Nelson, Admiral Lord Horatio 63, 113, 198, 228
Newington Green 37
  see also education
Niven, James 240
Nugent, Lady Maria 160, 178–80

Oates, George Hibbert 35, 38, 69–71
  Cooper, Reverend Thomas 145–7, 160
  illegitimate children 170–2
Oates, George William 35
Oates, Mary (née Hibbert) 35, 69, 194
Orléans, Louis Philippe, Duc de 224–7
  see also collecting
Ottley, William Young 223, 225–6

Pains Hill, Surrey 256, 262–4
pamphlet 18, 69, 134, 145–6, 151, 173, 221
Park, Mungo 126
patriotism 12, 112, 114, 118, 124, 198–9, 224, 234
patronage 13, 19, 86–7, 122, 198–9, 205, 218, 223, 228–9, 234, 241, 244, 265, 277
philanthropy 2, 13, 44, 94, 283
  abolitionism and 107, 120, 124, 135, 255
  almshouses 255, 267, 269–70, 278
  churches 203–4, 267–8
  class and 125, 254–5, 270
  hospitals 267–8, 270, 283
  legacies 256, 267, 277–8
  proslavery and 120–2, 125, 253, 267, 269–70
  schools 255, 268, 270, 277
  telescopic 125
  women and 270
Philips, Mark 36, 44, 269
Philips, Nathaniel 35–6, 42–3
Philips, Theresa Constantia 59
Phillips, Nathaniel 56–8, 78, 81, 85–7, 112, 170, 190–1, 262
Pitt, William 107, 111, 122
plantation 4, 64–71*passim*, 85, 93, 116–18, 134, 141–7 *passim*, 160, 171, 185, 200, 276, 284, 287
  see also individual plantation names
planter paternalism 69, 144, 255–6
planter picturesque 66

[317]

politeness 14, 39–40, 59, 84, 97–8, 137, 165, 185, 199, 207–8, 219, 229, 232, 241, 244, 266
Poor Man's Guardian 246
portrait 71, 192, 223, 228–32, 244–5, 258–60
Price, Richard 37
property 3, 5–7, 9, 36, 60, 65, 74n.59, 108, 119, 126, 128, 135, 140, 148–51 *passim*, 162–3, 186, 221, 266–7, 270, 274, 284, 286–7
  see also compensation; country house ownership; land ownership; individual plantation names
proslavery 3, 12, 41, 142, 145, 151–2
  culture 13–14
  metropolitan and colonial difference 88
  propaganda 41, 66
  rhetoric 18, 79, 111, 117–18, 124, 244
  support of the royal family 113
  see also Society of West India Planters and Merchants
public history 8, 10–11, 44, 244–6, 254, 277
  see also individual museums
Pugin, Augustus 265, 267–8
Purrier family 70, 84, 110
Purrier, John senior 78, 81, 84
Purrier, John Vincent 82, 94–5, 188, 274

Quaker 150, 166–81 *passim*, 201
  see also Society of Friends
Quarry Bank Mill 43
  see also Samuel Greg

race 1, 7, 145, 246
  abolitionists and 12
  Britain and 165
  categories 241
  class and 44, 64, 117, 246
  climate 116, 221
  culture and 13, 138, 220–3, 271
  gender and 117, 160, 180

justification for slavery 116
  monogenesis 221
  national identity and 267, 288–90
  polygenesis 221–2
  stadial theory 221
radical politics 33, 37, 44, 108, 114, 143, 245–6, 274–6
railways 97, 269–70, 283
Reform Act (1832) 36
religion 3, 13, 33, 68, 144, 166–7, 180, 207, 269
  see also Christianity, individual denominations
reparations 12, 72
  see also Caribbean Community and Common Market (CARICOM)
reparative history 286
reproductive labour 4
  see also motherhood
Repton, Humphrey 258
reputation 4, 14, 29, 38, 43, 53, 57, 80, 82–7 *passim*, 115, 121, 134–6, 142, 145–6, 191, 194, 205, 207–8, 220, 224, 237, 244, 255, 263, 267, 277
respectability 2, 12, 14, 19, 27–8, 32, 59, 79, 83–4, 119, 147, 150, 160, 163–5, 184–6, 189, 191, 196, 202–3, 207–8, 229, 255, 263, 266
Revealing Histories 44
Reynolds, Sir Joshua 166
risk 4–5, 42, 52, 91, 177, 254, 284
Rodney, Admiral Lord George Brydges 63, 113–14
rotten borough 123, 186
Roxburghe Club 198, 236–8
Royal Academy of Arts 223
Royal African Company 127, 277
Royal National Lifeboat Institution for the Preservation of Life from Shipwreck (RNLI) 94, 273–4
  see also philanthropy; Sir William Hillary
Royal Navy 3, 112–13, 188–9, 196, 198–9, 283

INDEX

Royal Society 239, 241–2
Rumbold, Thomas 38–9, 53

Saint Domingue 16, 120, 124, 139, 179
　see also Haiti
Scots in Jamaica 114, 172, 211n.68, 240–1
Select Committee on the Extinction of Slavery 67
Select Committee on the Slave Trade 58, 89, 114–15, 120, 148
Sharp, Richard 'Conversation' 128, 202, 241, 271
shipping 1, 42, 79, 89–91, 107, 118, 239, 273–4
shipwreck 55–6, 273–4
Shrewsbury, Reverend William 142–3, 146
Sierra Leone 196
Sierra Leone Company 120–1
slave
　factor 2, 38, 51–3, 55, 57, 59, 78, 90
　families 144, 176, 181, 185, 284, 287
　nurse 176, 179
　pen 51, 53
　punishments 65, 67–9, 140, 144–5
　sale 16, 38–9, 52–8 passim, 63, 80, 90, 274
　seasoning 51, 55
　ship 53, 55–6, 89, 111, 274
　see also women
Slave Registry Bill (1816) 135–9
Slavery Abolition Act (1833) 3, 11, 148, 286
Slave Trade Act (1807) 109, 128
Sloane, Sir Hans 218–19
　see also British Museum
Smith, Adam 85, 126
Smith, Reverend John 142
Smith, Reverend Sydney 197–8
Smith, William 202
Soane, Sir John 95
Society for Effecting the Abolition of the Slave Trade (SEAST) 107–8, 111, 115, 169
　see also antislavery

Society for the Conversion and Religious Instruction and Education of the Negro Slaves in the British West India Islands 142
Society for the Mitigation and Gradual Abolition of Slavery throughout the British Dominions 139
Society for the Propagation of the Gospel in Foreign Parts 41
Society of Friends 148–50
　see also Quakers
Society of West India Merchants 2, 90, 111, 148
Society of West India Planters and Merchants (SWIPM) 15, 41, 88, 90, 95, 109–15 passim, 120, 128, 136, 139–42, 151
　see also proslavery
Spencer, Lord John Charles 198–9, 236–7
spinsterhood 194–5
　see also marriage
Sprigg, Nathaniel 52–3, 86, 165–6, 173
Steele, Nicholas Hibbert 10, 14, 54, 63, 170, 181, 227
Stephen, James 136–7, 208
Sturge, Joseph 67–8
suburban villa 183, 204–5
sugar 5, 57, 64, 79, 85, 87–8, 90, 92, 94, 97–8, 109, 128, 239, 276, 289

taste 19, 59, 84, 185, 204–5, 218–20, 228–9, 233–4, 242, 264
Tate Britain 258
Taylor & Renny 87
Taylor, Simon
　abolition 112–15 passim, 122–3, 127
　Hibbert business and 81, 85, 87–8, 90, 93–4
　Jamaica politics 61
　mixed-heritage children 160, 164
　slave trading 41, 54, 56–7, 90

[319]

Taylor, Simon (*cont.*)
   Thomas Hibbert junior's marriage 259–60
   trustee 88–9
Tharp, John 56, 85, 88–9, 93, 95
The Hyde, Bedfordshire 256, 263
Thellusson family 110, 186–7, 197, 206, 264
Touchet, John 37
town house
   Kingston 59–64, 71, 113
   London 256
trust 4–5, 28, 31, 57, 70, 80, 85, 108, 161, 193
trustee 6, 14, 32–3, 35, 41, 88, 150, 187, 203, 265–6, 269
Turner, James Mallord William 227–8, 258–9

Unitarian 17, 32–3, 37, 68, 143, 166, 202, 269
   see also Cross Street Chapel; dissenters

Vaughan, Benjamin, 202
Vaughan family 37
Vaughan, Samuel 147
Vaughan, William 274
Venables, Thomas 136, 142
   see also George Hibbert
vouching 4, 38, 81

Wakefield, Gilbert 173
war of representation 134–5, 141
Warrington Academy 35, 173
   see also education
Watt, Richard 55

Wedderburn family 200
Wedderburn, Robert 245–6
West India Dock Company 83, 96–7, 200, 232, 261, 283
West India Docks 80, 92, 94–9, 232, 241, 246, 261, 285
   see also compensation; London Docks; Museum of London, Docklands
White, Charles 222
Whitehall plantation 56, 174–5
Wiggins Quay 83, 92, 95
Wilberforce, William 11, 112–14, 115, 124, 127, 136, 139, 142, 183–4, 200, 202, 204, 208, 229, 274, 290
Williams, Eric 28–9
Wilmot-Horton, Robert 139–40, 142, 148, 240
Winchester 196
   see also education
'Windrush scandal' 289–90
Winn, T. S. 133–4, 144, 151
women
   enslaved 4, 7, 19, 53, 63, 67–8, 117–18, 144, 160–1, 163, 170–2, 175, 179
   heiress 34, 186–7, 226, 262, 282
   slave ownership 6, 56–7, 119–20, 169, 285
   see also Creole women; gender; marriage; motherhood; spinsterhood
working class 44, 114, 285
Woolton Hall 40
   see also education

EU authorised representative for GPSR:
Easy Access System Europe, Mustamäe tee 50,
10621 Tallinn, Estonia
gpsr.requests@easproject.com

www.ingramcontent.com/pod-product-compliance
Lightning Source LLC
Chambersburg PA
CBHW071400300426
44114CB00016B/2130